Trade, Doha, and Development
A Window into the Issues

Richard Newfarmer
Editor

THE WORLD BANK
Trade Department
Poverty Reduction and Economic Management Vice-Presidency
Washington D.C.

ISBN-10: 0-8213-6437-5   ISBN-13: 978-0-8213-6437-6
eISBN: 0-8213-6438-3   DOI: 10.1596/978-0-8213-6437-6

Cover photo by Chris Stowers.

Library of Congress Cataloging-in-Publication Data has been requested.

Table of Contents

Foreword

A s 2005 comes to an end, debate over the Doha Development Agenda is becoming heated. The international community faces a relatively simple choice in Hong Kong in December: will nations overcome powerful, if narrow, interest groups at home to promote more rapid economic growth in the future, or will they be unable to reach a meaningful agreement, leading to an uncertain future for the Doha Round and the world trading system?

The choice nations collectively make at the upcoming ministerial meeting of the World Trade Organization (WTO) is important to development. For decades the global trading system has been stacked against growth in developing countries. The products that the poor produce—mainly agricultural products and labor-intensive manufactures—face disproportionately high barriers to trade. And their chief asset, their own labor, faces greater restrictions to global mobility than any other asset. This situation has arisen because previous rounds of multilateral trade negotiations reduced protection on manufacturing products, the primary interest of the early members of the negotiating club representing the dominant countries. Now the membership of the WTO has grown to include most developing countries. It is for this reason that the Doha Round is important: It has given all countries of the world the opportunity to work collectively on barriers of interest to developing countries and to the world's poor.

Although the choice is simple, it is not easy. The underlying details of the issues are notoriously complex. Observers have a difficult time penetrating the veil of legal and economic opacity that envelops the negotiations. The details are sufficiently technical and multifarious that experts in one area are often unaware of technical details in another.

And details make the difference between opening markets and merely appearing to do so through a vacuous agreement that looks good on the surface but does little or nothing to widen opportunities for poor traders in the global market place. This book provides succinct analyses of the most critical issues facing negotiators, highlighting the choices that most affect development. It is a window into the issues.

The WTO negotiations are not the only ones shaping the world trading system. Regional trade agreements in growing numbers are introducing preferential trade arrangements between subsets of the international community. Some extend trade and support development through "open regionalism." But others distort trade, retard development, and undermine the multilateral system with a web of discrimination. For that reason, we have included a section on these arrangements.

A third subject of international policy discussions—"aid for trade"—affects developing countries' opportunities to participate in the global market. Without such aid, many countries will not have the infrastructures and institutions necessary to take advantage of new market opportunities, whether from Doha or regional arrangements. The debate over aid for trade poses hard questions: How much aid is warranted in view of competing needs, say in health or education? And how can new aid be channeled to be most effective?

Gathered here are trade notes written by World Bank staff and distinguished academics for a series inaugurated in 2003, as well as new essays prepared especially for this volume. All of the material pertains directly to the issues at stake in the WTO ministerial meetings in Hong Kong in December. We hope that it will contribute to a better world trading system, one that is more equitable and more supportive of development.

Uri B. Dadush
Director, Trade Department
World Bank

Acknowledgments

This book was prepared by staff in the World Bank's Trade Department, including experts from the Poverty Reduction and Economic Management Trade Unit, the Development Economics Department (Trade Research team and Prospects Group), and the World Bank Institute as well as the Latin America and Africa regions. We also benefited from the contributions of leading academics from around the world. All of the contributors gave generously of their time to prepare these papers, often deferring other urgent work to produce a much needed chapter. This compilation would not have been possible without their willingness to share their considerable expertise and their devotion to the ideas of this book.

Dorota Nowak managed the project with deftness and dedication from conception to publication. Her farsighted planning, systematic attention to detail, and unflappable tenacity made the book a reality. Carlos A. Primo Braga, William J. Martin, and Bernard Hoekman provided unfailingly generous comments, suggestions, and help. John Panzer, manager of the PREM Trade Unit, provided constant encouragement and willingly pitched in whenever necessary. The book was produced under the general direction of Uri Dadush, director of the Trade Department, and under the guidance of Danny Leipziger, vice-president of the Poverty Reduction and Economic Management Network.

And finally, I would like to thank the production team who worked under Dorota Nowak's direction—Maria Amparo Gamboa who typeset the book and was truly a mainstay of this project through too many weekends; Michael Paul for proofreading and assisting in other matters; Awatif Abuzeid for assistance with the front matter; Mombert Hoppe, Martha Denisse Pierola, and Katherine Rollins for their work on the figures and tables; Araceli J. Jimeno who assisted with revisions; and Abdennour Azeddine for his invaluable technical support. Steven Kennedy, with his careful editorial pen, managed to improve even the most turgid of our prose. Stuart Tucker of the World Bank's Office of the Publisher coordinated the printing process.

Richard Newfarmer
Trade Department
World Bank

Acronyms and Abbreviations

ACP	Africa, Caribbean and Pacific Group of States
AD/CVD	Antidumping/Countervailing Duty
AGOA	African Growth Opportunity Act
AMS	Aggregate Measure of Support
APEC	Asia-Pacific Economic Cooperation
ARV	Antiretroviral
ASEAN	Association of Southeast Asian Nations
ATC	Agreement on Textiles and Clothing
CAFTA	Central American Free Trade Agreement
CARICOM	Caribbean Community
CEPII	Centre d'Etudes Prospectives et d'Informations Internationales
CETs	Common External Tariffs
CFF	Compensatory Financing Facility
CGE	Computable General Equilibrium
COMESA	Common Market of Eastern and Southern Africa
COMTRADE	U.S. Commodity Trade Statistics
DAC	Development Assistance Committee
DDA	Doha Development Agenda
DSB	Dispute Settlement Body
DTIS	Diagnostic Trade Integration Study
EBA	Everything But Arms
EBRD	European Bank for Reconstruction and Development
EC	European Communities
ECCAS	Economic Community of Central African States
EDF	European Development Fund
EPAs	Economic Partnership Arrangements
EPZs	Export Processing Zones
EU	European Union
FAO	Food and Agriculture Organization
FAPRI	Food Agricultural Policy Research Institute
FDA	Food and Drug Administration
FDI	Foreign Direct Investment
FTAs	Federal Trade Agreements
GATS	General Agreement on Trade in Services

GATT	General Agreement on Tariffs and Trade
GDP	Gross Domestic Product
GI	Geographical Indications
GSP	Generalized System of Preferences
GTAP	Global Trade Analysis Project
HACCP	Hazard Analysis and Critical Control Point
HIV/AIDS	Human immunodeficiency virus/acquired immune deficiency syndrome
ICAC	International Cotton Advisory Committee
IDB	Inter-American Development Bank
IF	Integrated Framework
IMF	International Monetary Fund
IPR	Intellectual Property Rights
ITO	International Trade Organization
LDCs	Least Developed Countries
MFN	Most Favored Nation
MPS	Market Price Support
NAFTA	North America Free Trade Agreement
NAMA	Non-agricultural Market Access
NFIDCs	Net-Food-Importing Developing Countries
OECD	Overseas Economic Cooperation Development
OIE	Office International des Epizooties
OTDS	Overall Trade-Distorting Support
PROCAMPO	Programa para el Campo
PRS	Poverty Reduction Strategy
PSE	Producer Support Estimate
R&D	Research and Development
RII	Review of International Investors
RLCA	Revenue Loss Compensation Arrangement
RTAs	Regional Trade Agreements
SACU	Southern African Customs Union
SAM	Social Accounting Matrix
SCM	Subsidies and Countervailing Measures
SDT	Special and Differential Treatment
SPS	Sanitary and Phytosanitary
STEs	State Trading Enterprises
TFNG	Trade Facilitation Negotiating Group
TIM	Trade Integrated Mechanism
TRAINS	Trade Analysis Information System
TRIPS	Trade-Related Intellectual Property Rights
TRQ	Tariff Rate Quota

UEMOA	Union Economique et Monétaire Ouest Africaine
UNCTAD	United Nations Commission for Trade and Development
UR	Uruguay Round negotiations
URAA	Uruguay Round Agreement on Agriculture
USTR	United States Trade Representative
VAT	Value-Added Tax
WAEMU	West African Economic and Monetary Union
WCO	World Customs Organization
WITS	World Integrated Trade Solutions
WTO	World Trade Organization

Through the Window: Beacons for a Pro-Poor World Trading System

Richard Newfarmer

While enormously beneficial for most people in developing countries, globalization has bypassed many of the poorest countries and poorest people.[1] Domestic policies and obstacles matter, but inequities in the world trading system also put developing countries at a disadvantage. Three forces have the potential to open global markets to more people: the current round of multilateral trade negotiations, regional trade negotiations, and the prospect of new "aid for trade" to help the poorest countries invest in infrastructure and institutions necessary to participate more effectively in the global marketplace.

The Doha Round hangs precariously in the balance. Even if there is an agreement in Hong Kong (China), a pro-poor outcome is not automatic. Results depend critically on the details of any trade agreement. This book peers through the mass of complexity—in agriculture, nonagricultural market access, services, and trade facilitation—to see what really matters for poor people.

Even as multilateral negotiations continue, many developing countries are engaged on a second front of negotiations, regional trade agreements. Some 75 countries are negotiating so-called Economic Partnership Agreements (plurilateral free trade agreements) with the European Union. The United States, having just completed a free trade agreement with Central America and the Dominican Republic as its seventh FTA, has a half-dozen new agreements in train. Many developing countries are following a similar path; consider Chile's recent free trade agreement with China.

Regional trade agreements can widen markets, deepen integration, and promote economies of scale in regulation and investment. However, they also are inherently discriminatory. Often the weakest countries are excluded; in effect, they pay for the preferences received by others. So how can these new arrangements minimize the disadvantages of preferential agreements and maximize advantages? A section of this book sets out guideposts for evaluating the development effects of upcoming regional negotiations.

Even with greater access to markets, many of the poorest countries may be unable to seize the opportunities that come with more open markets, either because of inadequate infrastructure, poorly performing trade-related institutions (such as customs), or domestic policies that create disincentives or impediments to trade. Still other developing countries may need additional help in adjusting domestic, regional, or global policy reforms to take advantage of new trade opportunities. For these reasons, the G-8 summit in Gleneagles in July 2005 supported calls for additional "aid for trade." A final section of this book discusses aid for trade related to standards, trade facilitation, and managing any adjustment costs from the erosion of preferences or from higher food prices that developing countries may experience as a consequence of a trade deal.

This introduction, drawing on the chapters of this volume, highlights the key decisions that will mean the difference between the success and failure of current efforts to open markets for products of the poor. In that sense, it provides "policy beacons" to assess outcomes in the three broad areas: multilateral negotiations, regional negotiations, and aid for trade.

Realizing the development promise of the Doha Agenda

A Doha Round agreement that slashed trade barriers would stimulate trade and raise incomes around the world, leading to a substantial reduction in global poverty. Although any agreement is not likely to be ambitious enough to generate the $290–460 billion in annual income that full liberalization might bring to the global economy, it could realize part of this potential and lift incomes of poor countries—and poor people—over the long term. The opening chapters by Anderson, Martin, and van der Mensbrugghe use quantitative methods[2] to assess where the main pay-offs are to be found in merchandise trade liberalization, with the conclusion that agriculture is the key to the Doha Round.

Agriculture is the locomotive of the development round

Agriculture is central to the development promise of this trade round. First, some 70 percent of the world's poor live in rural areas. Second, most of the world's trade protection is applied to agricultural products. Agriculture alone would produce roughly two-thirds of the gains that could be anticipated from full liberalization of merchandise trade. Progress can be made in increasing access to markets, reducing trade-distorting domestic support, and export subsidies.

Market access

Protection facing developing-country exporters in agriculture is four to seven times higher than in manufactures in the Organisation for Economic Co-operation (OECD) countries, and two to three times higher in developing countries. *Tariff peaks* against products from poor countries are particularly high in rich countries. *Tariff escalation* that discourages development of further processing is more pronounced in agriculture than in manufactures in both rich and poor countries. And hefty *specific duties* are common in rich countries. Because they automatically increase protection when commodity prices fall, specific duties throw the burden of adjustment onto global prices and poor countries. Forty-six percent of agricultural tariff lines in Europe contain such duties.

Tariff- and budget-based support to agriculture in OECD countries amounted to $350 billion in 2004—of which some $280 billion went directly to producers (roughly one-third from the budget and two-thirds from border measures).[3] Nontariff measures—including antidumping and other forms of contingent protection, sanitary standards, and technical barriers to trade—augment formal barriers. In fact, such measures may restrict trade more than border barriers (World Bank 2005). The combined effect of all of these forms of support is to stimulate overproduction in high-cost rich countries and shut out potentially more competitive products from poor countries. As Mitchell's chapter shows, the European Union went from being a net importer of sugar in the early 1980s to being a net exporter today.

The chapters by Anderson, Martin, and van der Mensbrugghe and by de Gorter set out important benchmarks of success in overcoming the problems posed by restrictive trade policies in agriculture. Increasing market access is by far the most important element of success. Their chief findings are as follows:

- *Tariff cuts must be deep to have effect.* This is true because WTO-agreed ceilings (bound tariffs) are well above today's applied rates, so negotiators will have to agree on cuts of 70 percent or more to ensure that applied rates decline (or at least do not rise).
- *Exclusions for sensitive products have to be extremely limited.* Exempting even 2 percent of tariff lines is enough to render virtually meaningless any deal that is likely to emerge from Doha. Why? Because most countries rely on tariff peaks in just a few product lines, but those lines account for a significant share of trade.
- *Capping all tariffs at 100 percent would help.* In many countries, very high tariffs, often in combination with tariff rate quotas, keep out products. Establishing binding caps can prevent or limit this effect. Steps should be taken to limit the application of specific duties, reduce tariff escalation, and curb nontariff barriers.
- *All countries have to contribute.* While agricultural protection is highest in rich countries, many developing countries also have high protection.[4] It is in the interest of all countries—and of great interest to the world's poor—to reduce protection everywhere.

Domestic support

Domestic support, while less damaging to developing countries than border barriers, greatly distorts trade in particular commodities and for particular countries.

Sugar is illustrative. In the European Union, Japan, and the United States a combination of quotas, tariffs, and subsidies allows domestic sugar producers to receive more than double the world market price. OECD governments support sugar producers at the rate of $6.4 billion annually—an amount nearly equal to all developing-country exports of sugar.[5] Prices are so high that it has become economic to grow sugar beets in cold climates and to convert corn to high-fructose corn syrup. Sugar imports in the OECD have shrunk to next to nothing.

Similarly, U.S. subsidies to cotton growers totaled $3.1 billion in 2003, about 1.5 times higher than U.S. foreign aid to Africa (see chapter by Baffes). These subsidies depress world cotton prices by 10–20 percent, reducing the income of thousands of poor farmers in West Africa, Central and South Asia, and other poor countries. In West Africa alone, where cotton is a critical cash crop for many small-scale and near-subsistence farmers, annual income losses for cotton growers surpass $150 million annually.

More than 70 percent of subsidies in rich countries are directed to large (often corporate) farmers. These farmers have incomes that are higher—often substantially so—than average incomes in Europe, Japan, and, to a lesser extent, the United States. Subsidies make the rich richer and the poor poorer. What should be done about domestic support in agriculture?

- *Deep cuts in bound levels of support are required to discipline actual levels.* As with tariffs, the bindings in the Uruguay Round were exceedingly generous, and applied levels of support have usually fluctuated well below the ceilings. Therefore, cuts in excess of 70 percent are required to have positive effects—and to protect against the temptation to raise applied levels of support. At the same time, loopholes that allow relaxation of disciplines on trade-distorting subsidies have to be closed.

Export subsidies

Although export subsidies distort world trade less than border barriers and domestic support, they are not trivial. Of the $280 billion in support to farmers, some $10–12 billion takes the form of export subsidies. The WTO's July 2004 Framework on agriculture contained a commitment to phase them out upon successful conclusion of the round. At issue is the timetable.

- *Phasing out of export subsidies by 2010, mentioned by some G-8 leaders at the Gleneagles summit in July 2005, would promote development.*

Nonfarm trade is important to growth in poor countries

Having grown at nearly twice the rate of agricultural exports, exports of manufactures now constitute nearly 80 percent of all developing-country exports. Tariffs on manufacturing in high-income countries are on average lower than in developing countries. But the tariffs that rich countries charge developing countries are about twice those they charge other industrial countries, in the aggregate. Exporters of manufactures from industrial countries face, on average, a tariff of 1 percent on their sales to other industrial countries; exporters in developing countries, by contrast, pay anywhere from 1.2 percent (if they are from Latin America, where NAFTA weighs heavily) to 5.4 percent (if they are from South Asia). However, the problem is not solely a North–South issue. Latin American exporters of manufactures, for example, face tariffs in South Asia that are thirteen times higher than in industrial countries. Similarly, Sub-Saharan African exporters face tariffs in South Asia that are nearly six times higher than the tariffs they face when exporting to industrial countries. Tariffs that East Asian exporters pay to Latin America are three times higher than those they face in high income countries.

Protection takes forms other than tariffs—among them quotas, specific duties, and contingent protection measures such as antidumping duties. As with tariffs, both rich and poor countries tend to use these measures more frequently against labor-intensive products from developing countries, particularly textiles and clothing. Average antidumping duties are seven to ten times higher than tariffs in industrial countries, and around five times higher in developing countries (World Bank 2005).

Textiles and clothing are particularly important for developing countries. The good news is that the quotas under the Agreement on Textiles and Clothing (ATC) ended on January 1, 2005; the bad news is that behind those quotas remains a wall of high tariffs. As Brenton and Hoppe point out in their chapter, the feared takeover by China of textile and clothing exports with expiration of the ATC quotas has been overblown. With increasing trade volumes in general, many developing countries, including least developed countries (LDCs) such as Bangladesh, have expanded their market share in the European Union and United States in the half-year since the end of quotas. At the same time, exports especially of some relatively high-wage exporting regions, such as Hong Kong (China), Taiwan (China), and Republic of Korea have declined. Some adjustment is sure to be required, and the international community should be ready to help those countries that experience difficulties—a challenge taken up in the aid-for-trade discussions.

Martin and Ivanic point to guideposts for reform of nonfarm trade:

- *The tariff ceilings chosen and the formula for cutting the highest tariffs will determine how much new access to markets Doha will provide.* As with agriculture, exempting a large number of tariff lines from cuts could easily eviscerate the gains from any cutting formula adopted.

Services liberalization could raise productivity

Services are the fastest-growing component of the global economy. Even in developing countries, services exports grew more rapidly than manufactures in the 1990s (World Bank 2001: chapter 3). More efficient backbone services—in finance, telecommunication, domestic transportation, retail and wholesale distribution, and professional and business services—improve the performance of the whole economy through broad linkage effects. Estimates suggest that, after controlling for other determinants of growth, countries that fully liberalized trade and investment in finance and telecommunications grew on average 1.5 percentage points faster than other countries over the past decade (Mattoo and others 2001).

So far, however, the Doha Round has fallen far short of its potential to unlock access to foreign markets for services exports. While many countries have made ambitious requests, the responding offers are said to be disappointing. This is despite the fact that many developing and industrial countries have an interest both in liberalizing their own services markets and obtaining improved access to the markets of their trading partners.

Mattoo, in reviewing the lack of progress to date, suggests a set of negotiating goals with which both the business and the development community could identify: locking in the current openness of cross-border trade for a wide range of services; eliminating barriers to foreign investment, either immediately or in a phased manner if regulatory inadequacies need to be remedied; and allowing greater freedom of international movement at least for intra-corporate transferees and for service providers engaged to fulfill specific services contracts.

Three types of actions might pave the way to these goals.

- *First, self-selected groups of WTO members could articulate their broad liberalization goals in model commitments and regulatory principles for specific modes or sectors*—along the lines of the Understanding on Financial Services and the Telecommunications Reference Paper. Once a critical mass of members sign up, they could extend the benefits to all WTO members on a most-favored-nation (MFN) basis; others could join later when they felt it in their interest to do so. An individual member's incentive to participate in a particular sector or mode would, of course, depend on the willingness of its trading partners to make commitments in modes and sectors (within and outside services) in which the member had an export interest.

- *Second, the international community should establish a mechanism to provide policy advice and regulatory assistance for developing countries at their request,* helping them to identify services that they can comfortably liberalize without fear of dislocation or macroeconomic turbulence and others that may require improvements in regulation and supervision prior to liberalization.

- *Third, to spur progress on labor mobility, governments in countries that supply labor could assume responsibility for screening and selecting workers, facilitating and verifying their return, and for combating illegal migration.* Immigration authorities in member countries would be requested to define a set of obligations that source countries would have to fulfill to be eligible for an allocation of temporary-presence visas; these could be limited, at least at the outset of the program, to just a few categories of individuals, such as intra-corporate transferees and service providers engaged to fulfill specific services contracts.

The larger services framework advanced by Mattoo would allow members, on the basis of greater confidence in their regulatory frameworks and the scope for regulatory cooperation, to respond more meaningfully to the requests for liberalization made by their fellow WTO members.

Regional trade agreements and unilateral preferential regimes

Regional trading agreements constitute a second front of trade negotiations for many developing countries. With the expiration of the European Union's Cotonou Agreement with the African, Caribbean, and Pacific countries (ACP), some 75 developing countries are undertaking complex negotiations with the European Union to establish new Economic Partnership Agreements. The United States, meanwhile has opened discussions of free trade with the Andean countries, the Southern African Customs Union, and others. Developing countries, too, are engaged in a quickening pace of negotiations: China with the ASEAN countries, India, and Brazil; and Chile with Republic of Korea, to name a few examples. All in all, regional trade agreements (RTAs) are proliferating rapidly, now covering more than 40 percent of world trade.

As many as half of all RTAs are counterproductive: they divert trade and end up depriving countries of income. RTAs are most likely to increase national incomes over time if they pursue a strategy of "open regionalism" (World Bank 2004). For that reason, regional negotiators should follow a few basic rules.

- *Negotiators in North–South plurilateral arrangements should work with partners to ensure that intraregional obstacles to trade are phased out and that a competitive external MFN regime is in place before trade preferences for the northern trade partners are introduced*, a suggestion elaborated in the chapter by Hinkle, Hoppe, and Newfarmer.
- *Liberal rules of origin can make the difference between genuine market openings and illusory ones.* The Blair Commission recommended a 10 percent value-added rule or a change in tariff heading for transformed goods. Rules would be less burdensome if they were uniform across agreements (see Brenton's chapter).
- *Rules and regulations governing investment and intellectual property rights must be appropriate to the development context in which they are promulgated*, as Fink and Hoekman argue in their respective chapters.
- *Openings in services should be introduced with adequate regulation, permit entry on an MFN basis and, where possible, encourage competition.*

Even RTAs based on open regionalism grant preferences to some while discriminating against others. The best way to minimize those effects is to bring down the high tariffs that create the discriminatory benefits offered to preferred countries. That can be done only through multilateral agreement.

Unilateral and voluntary preferential regimes—such as the U.S. African Growth and Opportunity Act and the European Union's Everything But Arms program—are a prominent feature of some countries' trade regimes. Each has different rules and exemptions that have the effect of limiting market access. As Brenton shows in his chapter, the actual value of trade preferences is remarkably low for all but a few developing countries. One reason is that rich countries grant preferences voluntarily rather than as part of a binding multilateral negotiation; those preferences often come laden with restrictions, product exclusions, and administrative rules that prevent beneficiaries from taking full advantage of them. For example, only 39 percent of potentially preferred imports into the Quad countries—Canada, the European Union, Japan, and the United States—under the Generalized System of Preferences (GSP) actually took advantage of preferential access, and usage rates are declining.

To make preferences more effective, especially for LDCs:

* *Programs in the Quad countries should be expanded to cover all exports of LDCs, with an indefinite time period.*
* *Restrictive rules of origin that raise the cost of taking advantage of preferences should be replaced with a simple rule that facilitates access and use of globally sourced competitive inputs.* A nonrestrictive rule of origin, as with RTAs generally, would require no more than 10 percent value added or a change of tariff heading (see Brenton's chapter).

Aid for trade

Market access is not the whole development story. Even if developing countries succeed in obtaining access to new markets, they will have to adopt complementary policies—removing obstacles to private investment, improving public investment in infrastructure, and providing education—to ensure that domestic firms respond to the new opportunities and that benefits are transmitted to the poor. Said differently, liberal trade policies must be embedded in a coherent development strategy—they are not a substitute for it. Aid for trade, as Nielson shows in her chapter, can play an important role in helping countries design complementary trade policies.

The cost of moving goods across international borders is often as important as formal trade barriers in determining the landed cost of goods—and ultimately market share. Every day spent in transit because of poor roads or delays in customs adds nearly one percent to the cost of goods on average (Hummels 2001). In developing countries, moreover, transit costs are routinely two to four times higher than in rich countries.

Additional aid for trade through investments in roads, ports, logistics, and through policy advice on reforms of trade-related institutions such as customs can play an important role. Eliminating delays in developing countries would lower trading costs very significantly, particularly if accompanied by liberalization of transport and telecommunications and streamlined regulations to promote domestic competition. As Jaffee's chapter makes clear, adapting to standards set in the high-income countries can be costly and prevent access to markets, although the effort to adapt usually brings rewards. Multilateral efforts are under way outside the WTO to promote—and in some cases finance—institutional changes to facilitate trade and meet rising food-safety standards. Key players include the bilateral donors, the World Customs Organization, the regional development banks, and the World Bank. Newfarmer and Nowak in their chapter describe how the World Bank is increasing its aid-for-trade efforts and how those efforts have moved away from the policy conditionality of the 1980s. Even with these increased efforts, however, resources are likely to fall short of demand.

- *Greater development assistance for much-needed trade infrastructure, help with standards and compliance, and support for policy reforms could help overcome impediments to exports.* Abundant examples come from the 20 or so trade diagnostic studies undertaken as part of the Integrated Framework, as described in the chapter by Newfarmer and Nowak.

The inclusion of trade facilitation in the WTO General Council's decisions of July 2004 is appearing increasingly felicitous. Many countries now share the view that reforms to lower the costs of trading make good development sense. McLinden's chapter reviews progress to date in negotiations on trade facilitation, noting that discussions on binding disciplines have taken a back seat to the dissemination of best practice in institutional reforms. McLinden offers recommendations on how to make the most of the opportunity presented by the launch of negotiations:

- *High-income countries should make disciplines flexible enough to accommodate countries that have low capacity to implement accords, and developing countries should view the WTO negotiations as an opportunity to advance their domestic reform agenda* and accelerate the implementation of best practices. On the basis of close consultations between negotiators in Geneva and specialists at home, governments should secure agreement on practical measures that will enable their traders to compete better in regional and international markets.

Aid for trade can also help in managing adjustment to a new world of incentives. A Doha Round agreement may precipitate a terms-of-trade loss for *a few* developing countries, as Hoekman, Martin, and A. Primo Braga show in their chapter. Likewise, Mitchell and Hoppe show that if Doha succeeds in reducing rich-country subsidies to food production, *a few* countries may experience terms-of-trade losses. Such losses are likely to be limited for several reasons. The value of preferences for most countries is actually quite small (see Brenton), and these are eroding under pressure from regional trade agreements and domestic adjustment in the US and EU. Similarly, only a few food importers are likely to suffer income losses from terms of trade. First, any upward price movement is estimated to be less than half the average adjustments these economies experience *annually* as a result of normal cyclical fluctuations in prices (see the Mitchell and Hoppe chapter). Second, many food importers also export other agricultural products that will benefit from liberalization;

moreover, some food importers will gain access to new markets in nonagricultural products and be able to export. Third, countries that now impose tariffs on food imports can lower those tariffs to offset any increase in global prices on poor domestic consumers. Fourth, since prices will change relatively slowly, some food importers will increase domestic production in response to higher prices and become self-sufficient or even net exporters. All these caveats notwithstanding, some countries nonetheless may require help and need additional resources, and that should be forthcoming.

- *Donor countries and development institutions should make additional resources available to support internal and external adjustment in countries that clearly stand to suffer from a Doha agreement.* To be effective, these have to be supportive of a coherent program of domestic reform to promote growth rather simply dedicated to maintaining unsustainable consumption without resource reallocation.

The world's trading system at the crossroads?

A. Primo Braga and Grainger-Jones in their chapter consider differing views on the evolution of the WTO negotiations, including the possibility that the world trading system is entering a systemic crisis. Ultimately they discount that notion, in part because all countries have an interest in maintaining and strengthening the system. The expansion of global trade at nearly twice the rate of world GDP growth has fueled an unprecedented prosperity, for which the multilateral system, by lowering trade barriers and preventing endemic trade wars, can claim much of the credit. At the same time, Primo Braga and Grainger-Jones also caution against complacency.

Complacency and unwillingness to tackle domestic forces of protection could well spell the demise of the Doha Round. However, positive action is the antidote, and now would be a good time to act in all three of the policy arenas discussed here: doing a pro-poor Doha deal, designing trade-creating regional agreements, and augmenting aid for trade. High-income countries could take the lead by, among other things, moving forward with assertive new steps to open agricultural markets, offering less restrictive rules of origin in regional accords, and providing additional aid for trade. Middle-income countries, with their now established interest in the global system, could contribute through assertive new proposals in manufactures and services. Low-income countries, which have a new interest in and responsibility for the emerging global system, could contribute by accepting core disciplines consistent with their development interests, crafting proposals in regional negotiations that link domestic reforms to trade reforms, and working with donors to use aid for trade effectively. In the event the Doha agenda were to founder, the regional trade agenda and aid for trade effort will assume an ever greater importance for developing countries. Here too both rich and poor countries have a responsibility to design these agreements so they create trade and reinforce domestic reforms rather than preempt them. The challenges are daunting. But the rewards are substantial.

Notes

1. The author is Economic Adviser, International Trade Department, World Bank. He gratefully acknowledges comments from Carlos A. Primo Braga, Bernard Hoekman, Aaditya Mattoo, and Julia Nielson.

2. These models are necessarily limited because, as described in the chapter, they do not take into account services liberalization; they assume all preferences are utilized; they do not account for increasing returns to scale, and they cannot account for the effect that new market opportunities have in spurring new products and diversification; all of these tend to underestimate the effect of trade liberalization on income. On other hand, it is assumed that all countries will be able to respond to shifts in relative prices and demand, an assumption that will not hold in some countries because of inadequate infrastructure and/or other supply side constraints.

3. The difference goes to spending on research and development, food programs for low-income consumers, and other programs that indirectly benefit agriculture.

4. The WTO has a wide definition of "developing countries" that includes some members of the OECD, such as Republic of Korea.

5. This figure includes transfers from consumers associated with border barriers.

References

Finger, Michael J., and Julio Nogues. 2006. *Fighting Fire with Fire: Safeguards and Anti-dumping in Latin American Trade Liberalization.* New York: Palgrave Macmillan and the World Bank.

Hummels, David. 2001. "Time as a Trade Barrier". Mimeo. Department of Economics, Purdue University, Lafayette, Indiana.

Mattoo, A., R. Rathindran, and A. Subramanian. 2001. "Measuring Services Trade Liberalization and its Impact on Economic Growth: An Illustration." World Bank Policy Research Paper No. 2655. World Bank, Washington, D.C.

World Bank. 2001. "Trade in Services: Using Openness to Grow." In *Global Economic Prospects 2002: Making Trade Work for the World's Poor.* Washington, D.C.

_____. 2004. *Global Economic Prospects 2005: Trade, Regionalism and Development.* Washington, D.C.

_____. 2005. *Global Monitoring Report.* Washington, DC.

Further reading

Anderson, K., and W. Martin, eds. 2006. *Agricultural Trade Reform and the Doha Development Agenda.* New York: Palgrave Macmillan .

Evenett, Simon, and Bernard Hoekman, eds. 2006. *Economic Development and Multilateral Trade Cooperation.* New York: Palgrave Macmillan.

Hertel, Thomas, and L. Alan Winters, eds. 2006. *Poverty and the WTO: Impacts of the Doha Development Agenda.* New York: Palgrave Macmillan.

The Multilateral Trading System: Mid-Flight Turbulence or Systems Failure?

Carlos A. Primo Braga and Elwyn Grainger-Jones

The current round of multilateral trade negotiations, the first since the founding of the World Trade Organization (WTO), was launched in November 2001 in Doha, Qatar. Organized around the so-called Doha Development Agenda (DDA), it is intended to enhance the development relevance of the WTO. Expectations for its successful conclusion remain mixed. The failure of the WTO Ministerial in Cancun, Mexico, in September 2003 underscored the difficulties faced by negotiators. The August 1, 2004, WTO General Council decisions, by contrast, were hailed by many as an important achievement that helped put the DDA back on track after the "detour" in Cancun. The agreed negotiation frameworks—particularly on agriculture—were an important step in the right direction. As the limited progress achieved since then suggests, however, negotiators still face major challenges in bringing this round to a successful conclusion.[1]

This cyclical pattern of good and bad news on the multilateral trade system (as exemplified by the "downs" in Seattle (1999) and Cancun (2003) and the "ups" in Doha (2001) and Geneva (2004)) has motivated an ongoing debate about its health.[2] 2005 will be a critical year for the DDA. Many expect the Hong Kong Ministerial (December 13–18, 2005) to be a harbinger of the fate of the "development" round. Moreover, the outcome of the Doha Development Agenda—a first for the WTO— is considered an important factor in shaping the future of the institution.

Are the WTO and the multilateral rules-based system facing a serious crisis, or are the problems experienced so far in the DDA the usual turbulence that characterizes complex trade negotiations? More specifically, can the multilateral trading system deliver a "development round"? In summarizing the debate surrounding these questions, this note presents three stylized perspectives on the health of the multilateral trade system. The first sets out the business-as-usual view, according to which current difficulties are nothing new and, as in previous rounds, will be resolved when the time for a deal is right. The second focuses on the lack of progress in the negotiations and argues that current circumstances conspire against the capacity of the system to deliver an ambitious outcome. The third paints a bleaker picture of "systemic crisis."

The note starts with a brief historical review of the system. It goes then into an analysis of the evolution of the DDA and the main obstacles to a successful conclusion of the round. It concludes with an evaluation of the dangers of failure in the negotiations. This discussion led us to conclude that claims of a systemic crisis may well be exaggerated, but that complacency about the health of the multilateral trade system is not warranted.

A bit of history

The modern multilateral trade system, with its emphasis on nondiscrimination, was born in 1948, when the General Agreement on Tariffs and Trade (GATT) entered into force. The GATT era witnessed eight rounds of multilateral trade negotiations. The last, the Uruguay Round (1986–94), culminated in the establishment of the World Trade Organization on January 1, 1995. The Uruguay Round led to the most comprehensive set of multilateral trade agreements to date. It not only extended multilateral rules to services and trade-related aspects of intellectual property rights but also brought agricultural trade back under GATT disciplines. Not surprisingly, there was unfinished business. Some 30 items in the Uruguay Round included a "built-in agenda" for further negotiations. There also was a large unfinished agenda in agriculture, as evidenced by the desire of some WTO members (particularly the European Communities, EC) to extend the scope of WTO disciplines to new themes such as competition, investment, transparency in government procurement, and trade facilitation, themes that became known as the Singapore issues. The unfinished agenda led to calls for a new round of negotiations in the late 1990s.[3]

The DDA was launched in Doha, Qatar, at the Fourth WTO Ministerial (November 2001) amid much optimism about the ability of the multilateral system to transcend national differences. The tragic events of September 11, 2001, weighing heavily on national capitals in the run-up to that meeting, encouraged major trading nations to build bridges in multilateral forums. Optimism was fueled by a sense that the major players would not allow a repeat of the failed Seattle Ministerial. Many developing countries, particularly Asian and African countries, agreed to launch negotiations on the understanding that the new round would be a "development" round. The DDA would cover most of the core elements of the WTO—agriculture, services, and nonagricultural market access. The decision on the Singapore issues was left to the Fifth WTO Ministerial (Cancun) with the proviso that it would require explicit consensus.

The early momentum was soon lost. The Doha mandate established a series of interim deadlines on a variety of subjects with a view to concluding the round by the end of 2004. All major deadlines were missed and extended, fueling cynicism about the ability of the WTO process to deliver negotiations within the original timetable. WTO members failed, for example, to meet the self-imposed deadline of March 31, 2003, to agree on general terms for a deal on agriculture—an issue seen by most as the deal breaker for the round. Members also failed to meet a similar deadline for negotiations on manufacturing tariffs. Deadlines were extended twice in discussions on special and differential treatment (SDT), but members still failed to reach agreement before the Cancun Ministerial. The end-December 2002 deadline for a compulsory-licensing solution to problems faced by countries with no pharmaceutical manufacturing capacities was also missed, although a solution was subsequently found prior to Cancun.

The Cancun WTO Ministerial meeting in September 2003 was mandated from Doha as a "mid-term review" to provide guidance on moving negotiations forward and to make decisions in several areas—most importantly how to proceed with respect to the Singapore issues. Missed deadlines meant that what was envisaged as a mid-term review was bound to become a forum for divisive confrontations. Ministers failed to agree on the text prepared in advance of the meeting, thus relegating negotiations to further months of drift.

There were three key trigger points that, at least on the surface, precipitated the collapse of negotiations at Cancun: agriculture, cotton, and the Singapore issues.

- On agriculture, developing countries—in particular, the coalition known as the G-20—refused to accept the limited ambitions on subsidy cuts, market access, and elimination of export subsidies by northern countries.[4]
- Cotton was chosen by nongovernmental organizations as the poster child of the unfairness of the multilateral trade system, with subsidies in industrialized countries tilting the playing field against developing countries. In mid-2003, Benin, Burkina Faso, Chad, and Mali proposed the elimination of cotton subsidies worldwide and the establishment of a compensation fund to reimburse the least developed countries (LDCs) for revenues lost because of subsidies in industrialized countries. There was no agreement in Cancun on this request.
- On the Singapore issues, the European Union offered to unbundle the four issues at the eleventh hour and to begin negotiating on one or two (starting with trade facilitation). However, the countries that objected to negotiations on these topics saw too few concessions on agriculture to agree to proceed, with most advocating that all four subjects should be dropped entirely or relegated for further clarification by WTO working groups.

Cancun was followed by a period of mutual recrimination in which the reasons for the failure of the meeting were extensively analyzed.[5] By March 2004, however, negotiations restarted in earnest. There was broad recognition that the political calendar in some of the main trading nations was not particularly conducive to bold commitments in the near future. At the same time, it was also recognized that if agreement on the negotiating frameworks could not be reached by mid-2004, the round would be in serious trouble.

In the early hours of August 1, 2004, the WTO General Council reached decisions on frameworks to continue with multilateral negotiations on agriculture and industrial products, on a series of recommendations concerning services and development-related issues, and on a text on modalities for negotiations on trade facilitation, which included a decision to drop the other three Singapore issues from the DDA. These decisions became known as the "July package".[6]

The framework for agriculture laid the foundations for reform of global agricultural trade.[7] It called for the parallel elimination of all forms of *export subsidies*, as well as all export measures with equivalent effect (export credits, export credit guarantees and insurance programs, trade-distorting practices of exporting state trading enterprises, and food aid). The end date for the elimination of all forms of export subsidies and the time profile for the implementation, however, remained to be negotiated.

The framework also committed member countries to substantial reductions of *trade-distorting domestic support*, encompassing the so-called Amber and Blue boxes, as well as *de minimis* subsidies. In the first year of implementation of the agreement, countries are expected to cut at least 20 percent of the overall level of trade-distorting support. The framework calls for substantial improvements in *market access* for all products. Tariff reductions are expected to be made from bound rates and expected to foster greater harmonization of tariff regimes, with deeper cuts in higher tariffs. In the case of sensitive products, "substantial improvement" is to be achieved through a combination of tariff-quota expansion and tariff cuts. The framework, however, leaves to the next stage of the negotiations the details of the tiered formula to be applied (for example, number of bands and type of tariff reduction in each band) and the criteria for selection of sensitive products. Market access remains the most controversial pillar of the agricultural negotiations. Finally, there was agreement that *cotton* would be dealt as a priority, but in the context of the overall agricultural negotiations rather than as a stand-alone issue.

The framework on nonagricultural market access set the stage for the pursuit of tariff cuts according to a nonlinear formula and the reduction or elimination of nontariff barriers. Many issues, however, remained open to debate, and some developing-country members (particularly African countries) have been vocal in criticizing what they perceive as the limited flexibility afforded to them. In the area of *services*, WTO members agreed to intensify their efforts with a view to ensuring a substantive outcome with respect to market access. A new date (May 2005) was established for presenting new and revised offers.[8] Concrete recommendations on how best to make *SDT* provisions more operational were also postponed to July 2005.[9]

The July 2004 package reinvigorated the Doha Round. Negotiations over the next 12 months, however, proceeded slowly. Limited progress was achieved in addressing some technical questions—such as the methodology for calculating *ad valorem* equivalents for specific duties in agriculture—but, overall, the negotiating targets often referred to as benchmarks for evaluating progress by July 2005 were missed, [10] reigniting doubts about the ability of WTO members to reach a timely conclusion of the DDA. In what follows, we review different perspectives on the prospects of the current negotiations.

Just mid-flight turbulence?

Some analysts point out that current difficulties in the negotiations resemble the turbulence experienced in past negotiations. Moreover, they argue that with appropriate corrective actions, the DDA could still deliver a substantive outcome.[11] There are five main planks to their argument.[12]

First, failures and delays in trade negotiations are nothing new.[13] Multilateral trade rounds have always taken a long time and often have lasted longer than originally intended, with "failed" ministerial meetings preceding an agreement. Indeed, the predecessor to the WTO—the GATT—was a "provisional" agreement that lasted until 1994 because of the failure of the United States to agree on the establishment of the International Trade Organization (ITO) proposed in an ambitious draft charter in the late 1940s. A ministerial meeting in Geneva, intended to launch a new round, failed in 1982. Two years into the Uruguay Round, begun in 1986, negotiations on a mid-term review in Montreal ended in deadlock. A ministerial meeting in Brussels in 1990, in turn, was not able to bring the negotiations to a closure, with treatment of agriculture as the main sticking point. In the WTO era, the failed ministerial meeting at Seattle in 1999 was followed by a successful launch of negotiations at the next ministerial in Doha. In this light, some argue that highly publicized failures such as Seattle may be necessary to shock the system into action.

In the same vein, the fact that the original deadline for the conclusion of the round (December 2004) was missed does not constitute in itself a major indictment of the system. That deadline was always more of a target to keep the pressure on negotiations than a plausible end point. This short leash allowed the WTO to push for progress in what would otherwise have been a dormant period.

Second, the growing complexity and breadth of the negotiations means that, inevitably, negotiations will take longer than before. The duration of negotiations gradually extended from one year for the first four rounds up to eight years for the Uruguay Round (table 1). In parallel, the number of negotiating partners swelled from 23 in 1947 to 148 in the current negotiations. Further, the breadth of the negotiating agenda has expanded significantly. The first five rounds essentially covered market access (focusing on tariffs). The Kennedy Round added some nontariff measures and antidumping measures; the Tokyo Round added "plurilateral agreements"[14]; and the Uruguay Round covered all existing areas, plus rules, services, intellectual property, and dispute settlement, while strengthening multilateral disciplines for trade liberalization with respect to textiles and clothing and agriculture. The DDA covers most of the above plus so-called development issues (in particular, SDT), and, at least initially, a discussion of whether to launch full negotiations on the Singapore issues. These themes, in turn, are influenced by the continuous debate on the so-called implementation issues, reflecting concerns raised by some developing countries about difficulties in implementing Uruguay Round agreements.

Third, negotiations have already achieved some results. WTO members reached a deal on the compulsory licensing issue in TRIPS and health shortly before Cancun. At the technical level, WTO members have built up their understanding of each others' positions on all the main issues, as illustrated by the July package and, more recently, by the agreement on how to calculate *ad valorem* equivalents with respect to specific duties in agriculture. Moreover, one of the controversial Singapore issues (trade facilitation) became one of the most dynamic areas in the negotiations, with a large number of proposals on the table, including joint proposals by developed and developing countries. Less tangible but equally important is a change in negotiating dynamics: the WTO is becoming a truly *world* trading organization. Developing countries are increasingly assertive, leading many to argue that the silver lining of the failure of Cancun was that developing countries found their voice in the negotiations.

Fourth, there is a well-established tradition for trade negotiators to "talk up" and exaggerate their differences until the very last minute. Negotiators often engage in a game of "chicken" in which each tries to demonstrate its strength to the other by standing firm on its position.[15] These tactics can exaggerate the perceived gulf between country positions. There are numerous examples of apparently intractable differences falling away as trade negotiators are replaced by government ministers in the endgame of negotiations. For example, a deal on the Singapore issues seemed unlikely going into the Doha Ministerial, but, in the interest of securing the launch of the round, the European Union at the last minute moderated its proposals. For the same reason, the United States changed its position to agree to launch negotiations on antidumping in the DDA.

Finally, some analysts argue that even though the negotiations are facing a series of difficulties, the political environment since September 11 is such that failure is not an option. According to this perspective, the "war on terror" will engender strong political support from the top to achieve a prodevelopment outcome when the time is ripe for the completion of the negotiations.[16]

According to those that embrace the "business as usual" perspective, the problems identified above can be surmounted as long as key trading nations keep their commitment to a liberal rules-based trade regime. There may be a need for some adjustment with respect to the governance structure of the WTO, and countries may need to show restraint in engaging in preferential trade agreements, but the multilateral trade system and the DDA, while confronting many challenges, are experiencing in-flight turbulence, not systemic crisis.[17]

The DDA: a mismatch between expectations and reality?

Many commentators argue that the experience of the first four years of the Doha Round suggests little cause for optimism for significant trade liberalization. Doubts from developing countries about the benefits of multilateral liberalization, unrealistic expectations about the capacity of the system to deliver development outcomes, and lack of enthusiasm from traditional *demandeurs* are often mentioned in this context.[18] These concerns are well captured by Curtis and Ciuriak (2005) who point out that to launch "the Doha Round in late 2001, before completing and digesting the Uruguay Round results and China's accession to the WTO and integration into the global trading system, might well have been a great mistake." The following arguments support that perspective:

First, the Doha Round was an unwanted child for some members of the WTO. The European Union was its main champion, proposing an ambitious agenda that would extend the WTO's mandate further into domestic regulation. Many developing countries initially resisted the launch of a new round. Their main objections were that (i) they were still struggling to implement Uruguay Round agreements; (ii) they were not ready for more trade liberalization; (iii) they did not have the capacity to negotiate a new round at that point in time; and (iv) they were not convinced that developed countries would be prepared to offer enough in the way of subsidy and tariffs cuts in sensitive areas to justify the costs of new negotiations. It is also worth noting that many developing countries feared that MFN liberalization would worsen their competitive position by eroding preferences.[19]

Second, expectations were too high at the launch of negotiations. The current negotiations are often referred to as the "Development Round"—a term that was already being used in the late 1990s.[20] The communiqué of the Doha Ministerial framed the negotiating agenda in terms of its potential benefits for developing countries. The text was full of references to development, increasing technical assistance, cutting agricultural subsidies in the North, addressing developing-country concerns on SDT and implementation, lowering tariff barriers on products of interest to developing countries, providing duty- and quota-free access to products from LDCs, and addressing concerns about the impact of TRIPS on the capacity of developing countries to deal with health crises.

Third, some seemingly intractable issues were papered over at the Doha Ministerial only to resurface at a later date. This is not unusual in international negotiations. The DDA contained a number of early deadlines on issues of importance to those resisting new negotiations—among them an ambitious agenda to review Uruguay Round commitments on SDT. Those deadlines occupied a great deal of negotiators' time following the launch of the round, with limited results.

Overly high expectations and a difficult agenda were not a good start for the round. There was also little early progress on the core issue of agriculture, with the European Union and United States seen to favor a limited reform agenda.[21] In the absence of many early deliverables, the European Union's attempts to launch negotiations on the Singapore issues failed to garner support from most developing countries.

Fourth, there was no consensus on what a "Development Round" meant in terms of new concessions granted to, or offered by, developing countries. Widely varying views on the role of trade policy in the development process added to the complexity of the negotiations. To take one example, SDT proposals related to GATT Article 28 call for greater freedom to restrict trade to protect infant industries. This was seen as a development deliverable by some developing-country members. In stark contrast, many developed (and some developing) countries argued that greater exemptions to WTO disciplines would harm developing countries.

Underlying most SDT-related disagreements in the WTO is the concept of policy space, which has become synonymous with development for some commentators and some WTO negotiators.[22] To some extent it also has been an organizing theme for those challenging what they perceive as the established trade orthodoxy. Many developing-country negotiators argue that the more advanced countries used infant-industry protection to industrialize, hence WTO rules should allow developing countries to do the same. Further, many argue that the North should open their markets to products from the South and cut subsidies without asking for reciprocal market opening. In contrast, developed countries have sought to explain the benefits of "policy lock-in" through the WTO, questioning the ability of interventionist trade policies to promote growth and emphasizing the costs of not engaging in reciprocal bargaining in the WTO.[23]

Fifth, some observers have claimed that there is no clear leadership in negotiations from the major power blocs. Frequent comparisons are made to the Uruguay Round, where the United States was a driving force in negotiations. There is a perception that the United States is only half-engaged in current negotiations, devoting at least equal energy to the pursuit of new regional and bilateral trade agreements and often adopting unilateral decisions (on steel and agriculture, for example) that called into question its commitment to the multilateral process. The European Union, in turn, although also publicly committed to multilateralism, has been unable to come to terms with its own agricultural problems.[24] And major developing countries (notably Brazil), while effectively pursuing an offensive tactic in agriculture, have adopted a wait-and-see approach with respect to other themes such as services and nonagricultural market access.

Sixth, the private sector in industrialized countries seems lukewarm about the current round. This contrasts with the high level of engagement of business leaders and business organizations during the Uruguay Round. One possible reason for this lukewarm attitude is that the concept of the Development Round may have led business to question the benefits to be gained from the negotiations. Moreover, with the acceleration of the business cycle and increased shareholder concerns with results, business has become more focused on the short term. In this context, it is not surprising that protracted multilateral negotiations have a lower priority in the allocation of resources for lobbying national governments.

All these considerations have been cited in predictions that the initial ambitions of the DDA will not be realized. There is growing concern that the Hong Kong Ministerial in December 2005 may not be able to deliver full-fledged modalities for negotiations in agriculture and nonagricultural market access. If the results of the upcoming ministerial are not significant, it is unlikely that the round will be completed within the lifetime of the current U.S. Trade Promotion Authority. As a consequence, the negotiations could linger on for several additional years.[25]

A systemic crisis?

The previous section outlined a series of arguments that put in doubt the ability of the DDA to deliver an ambitious liberalization outcome. It also underscored the lack of consensus on the meaning of a Development Round. Could these problems, however, reflect a deeper and more profound failure of the multilateral trading system associated with the WTO? There are those who believe that current problems in negotiations are a symptom of multilateralism in crisis.[26]

First, the "global commons" of ideas has swung from seeing trade opening as generally a good thing to something to be feared. In particular, skeptics question the ability of developing countries to compete in their own markets with competition from developed countries and to take advantage of new market opportunities because of weak supply capacity. At the same time, support from the traditional advocates of liberal trade, such as the United States, is being undermined by growing anxieties about the capacity of industrialized economies to compete in agriculture (the Brazilian threat), manufacturing (the Chinese threat), and even in services (the Indian threat).[27]

Second, the "mercantilist motor" of the multilateral trading system may have run out of fuel. The original logic of multilateral trade negotiations was that negotiators would trade tariff reductions. Even though theory tells us that unilateral liberalization is generally a good thing for small economies, the political economy of the process is such that reciprocity becomes a useful lever. Trade liberalization is then presented as the price to be paid for new access to other markets. This model, which served the multilateral trading system well in the past, is coming under pressure for the following reasons: (i) "mercantilist" calculations are much more complex when regulatory issues are involved; (ii) much of the low-hanging fruit was picked in previous rounds, and what protection remains is in sensitive areas where political risks of confronting concentrated vested interests are high (for example, would European governments be able to claim that new market access in the South is adequate compensation for the feared impact on the rural economy arising from liberalization?) and (iii) many developing countries have become increasingly risk-averse in agreeing to new concessions, reflecting the perception that they got a bad deal in the Uruguay Round. In short, the incentives to "free-ride" on the public good of the multilateral rules-based system have increased, weakening the appeal of engaging in reciprocal concessions.

Third, the rapid proliferation of regional and bilateral trade agreements is undermining the core principle (nondiscrimination) of the multilateral trade system, raising several concerns. Regional trade agreements—RTAs—are absorbing scarce time and energy from negotiators. Many of the poorest WTO members are part of several regional and bilateral trade negotiations, distracting them from multilateralism. RTAs may also lock in competing and sometimes incompatible regulatory practices, making it harder to harmonize standards in the multilateral system at a later date. For example, some observers have expressed concerns that the imposition of TRIPs-plus rules on intellectual property rights will further erode flexibilities in the WTO TRIPS agreement—in particular in the area of compulsory licensing.[28] A related concern is that a new generation of RTAs contains dispute-settlement provisions that have the potential to conflict with WTO dispute settlement.

Fourth, slow progress in the DDA is increasing concern about whether the WTO is an effective place to do business. The economically advanced countries may conclude that WTO does not meet their constantly evolving business needs because of difficulties in negotiating and agreeing upon rigorous new standards in the multilateral context, thus hastening the trend toward regionalism. As the negotiating agenda extends into areas beyond tariffs, it has become more difficult to develop rules that reconcile the needs of the advanced trading nations with those of the less advanced countries. The WTO Customs Valuation agreement is a good example. An approach that suited the more advanced countries appears to be expensive and difficult for less advanced countries to implement.[29] Further differentiation in the application of WTO rules based on different implementation capacities appears to be difficult to reconcile in the face of an increasingly legalistic approach to rulemaking.

Moreover, some members came away from Cancun with serious doubts about the ability to reach agreement by consensus among such a heterogeneous and large number of countries, although no clear alternative has been presented.[30] There are therefore real challenges in making the mechanics of a truly representative trade negotiation work effectively.

Finally, there are those that point to a legitimacy crisis of the global governance regime associated with WTO agreements. Although the trade focus of the WTO is perceived by many analysts as a plus, critics emphasize that unless the multilateral trade regime is able to address other important goals—such as poverty and the environment—while promoting a fair distribution of outcomes in a transparent manner, its political legitimacy will be increasingly contested in the streets and in parliaments around the world.[31]

Concluding remarks

These three perspectives are, of course, stylized summaries of the evolving debate on the future of the multilateral trading system. As already mentioned, we believe that claims of a "systemic crisis" may well be exaggerated, but this is not an invitation to complacency. After all, concerns about the DDA outcome become increasingly pertinent as time passes without substantive progress in the negotiations.

Action needs to be taken to avoid the erosion of the multilateral trading system. Renewed progress to meet the ambitious objectives of the DDA would provide a huge confidence boost to the multilateral trading system and make a significant contribution to the world economy.[32] On the other hand, a timid set of reforms and limited multilateral liberalization will generate not only small benefits, but it could also feed skepticism about the capacity of the multilateral trading system to contribute to economic development.

Even worse, a failed DDA would damage the WTO by eroding its relevance. This is not in the long-term interests of developing countries, which have a real stake in a strong rules-based multilateral trading system, irrespective of new market-access gains from the DDA. WTO rules lock in existing access on a nondiscriminatory basis, an increasingly valuable asset in a time of growing protectionist pressures, political tensions, and the potential reemergence of trade blocs. They also promote transparency and good governance. Moreover, the WTO dispute-settlement system provides for a rules-based mechanism that allows developing countries to defend their interests against larger and better-resourced trading partners, as the recent sugar and cotton cases attest.

As the number of WTO stakeholders grows and reciprocity increasingly requires complex trade-offs between greater market access in sensitive areas (such as agriculture) and rules (intellectual property rights), the capacity of the WTO to promote nondiscriminatory trade liberalization is under stress. This puts an additional premium on leadership dedicated to promote the global public good derived from credible multilateral rules.[33] Independently of the direct impact of the DDA on developing economies, the continued use of the WTO as a forum for negotiations is essential to the preservation of the multilateral trade system, which remains an important objective both for developed and developing countries alike. In sum, the answer to the original question posed in this paper—can the multilateral trade system deliver a Development Round?—is a qualified yes, but time is running out.

Table 1. Overview of GATT and WTO negotiating rounds

Round	Year	Number of contracting parties/members [a]		Negotiated items
		Total [b]	Developing country share (percent) [c]	
Geneva	1947	23	48	Tariffs
Annecy	1949	23	48	Tariffs
Torquay	1950–1951	33	46	Tariffs
Geneva	1955–1956	35	46	Tariffs
Dillon	1960–1962	42	50	Tariffs
Kennedy	1964–1967	75	68	Tariffs, some nontariff barriers, antidumping measures
Tokyo	1973–1979	85	71	Tariffs, nontariff barriers, plurilateral agreements
Uruguay	1986–1994	128	77	Tariffs, nontariff barriers, rules, services, intellectual property rights, agriculture, textiles and clothing, institutional issues
Doha	2001–	148	76	Agriculture, nonagricultural market access, services, intellectual property rights, rules, further work on UR items and implementation-related issues, development, and trade facilitation.

Notes: a. Included in the list of contracting parties/members are those countries that were signatories to the GATT by the end of each trade round or became signatories in its immediate aftermath.

b. The European Communities, though an official WTO member in its own right, have been excluded for purposes of statistical continuity in the ratio of developed to developing countries.

c. Developing-country classifications are based on GATT/WTO practices and on Kasteng, Karlsson, and Lindberg (2004).

Source: Compiled by the authors based on WTO/GATT documents.

Notes

1. Elwyn Grainger-Jones is Principal Economist, European Bank for Reconstruction and Development (EBRD). This note was prepared while he was a consultant with the World Bank. Carlos A. Primo Braga is Senior Adviser, International Trade Department, World Bank. Comments and assistance from R. Newfarmer, B. Hoekman, K. Brokhaug, W. Martin, R. Sally, A. Mattoo, H. Corbet, J.P. Chauffour, and P. Reichenmiller are gratefully acknowledged. This note reflects solely the views of the authors. It does not necessarily reflect the views of the World Bank Group, the EBRD, or the Executive Directors of either institution.

2. See, for example, the series on "What's Holding Up Doha?" *Finance and Development* (March 2005).

3. These topics were first introduced in the debate at the Singapore WTO Ministerial of 1996. Accordingly, they became known as the "Singapore issues." Sir Leon Brittan, former EC competition and trade commissioner, was an early champion of the idea of a new trade round.

4. The G-20 came to life on August 20, 2003, as a reaction to a joint U.S.-EU paper on agriculture. It has since become an influential voice in the agricultural negotiations, under the leadership of Brazil. The coalition encompasses both Cairns Group countries (which favor an ambitious liberalization agenda) and G-33 countries, which have defensive interests in agriculture (focusing on food security and rural development). The G-20 has positioned itself as the "pragmatic voice" of the South, aiming for elimination of export subsidies, substantial reductions of trade-distorting support, market access liberalization, and special and differential treatment for developing countries. In March 2005, the group included Argentina, Bolivia, Brazil, Chile, China, Cuba, Egypt, Guatemala, India, Indonesia, Mexico, Nigeria, Pakistan, Paraguay, Philippines, South Africa, Thailand, Tanzania, Uruguay, Venezuela, and Zimbabwe.

5. See, for example, Hoekman and Newfarmer (2003).

6. See WTO (2004).

7. For details see Primo Braga (2004).

8. That deadline was missed. By May 31, there were 62 initial offers (covering 86 members) and 9 revised offers.

9. This deadline was also missed and the Chairman of the Special Session reported to the WTO General Council in July 2005 that recommendations for a decision should be presented by the Hong Kong Ministerial Conference.

10. Speaking at the OECD Ministerial on May 4, 2005, Dr. Supachai Panitchpakti (then WTO Director General) identified the following items as required components for a "substantial breakthrough" at the ministerial: concrete modalities for agriculture and nonagricultural market access, a critical mass of market-opening services offers, significant progress in areas such as rules and trade facilitation, and a proper reflection of the development dimension. He also pointed out that time was running out for the negotiators to achieve these goals. His report, as chairman of the Trade Negotiations Committee to the General Council, further elaborated on these targets and stated that "progress made [since 2004] had been insufficient" (WTO 2005). See also http://www.wto.org/english/news_e/news05_e/dg_oecd_4may05_e.htm.

11. It is worth noting that full merchandise liberalization (ignoring potential dynamic gains associated with productivity increases) could add roughly $300 billion per year to the global economy by 2015. Even though agriculture and food processing account for less than 10 percent of world trade, trade liberalization of agriculture and food would account for 63 percent of gains (with textiles and clothing accounting for 27 percent and other manufactures 10 percent). An ambitious Doha outcome, featuring the elimination of export subsidies and significant cuts in domestic support and tariffs in developed and developing countries, could deliver roughly one-third ($96.1 billion) of the full-merchandise-liberalization scenario, with agricultural liberalization delivering roughly two-thirds of the gains. Services liberalization, particularly for the movement of people, could significantly expand those welfare results. See Anderson, Martin, and van der Mensbrughe

(2005) for detailed calculations of the welfare implications of different DDA scenarios.

12. See, for example, Srinivasan (2003), Cline (2005), and Messerlin (2005).

13. It is worth noting that the negotiations on the Free Trade Area of the Americas, for example, have been going on for more than 10 years and that the completion of the EU-Mercosur negotiations also missed its original target (2004).

14 The Tokyo Round "codes": subsidies and countervailing measures—interpreting Articles 6, 16 and 23 of GATT; technical barriers to trade—sometimes called the standards code; import licensing procedures; government procurement; customs valuation—interpreting Article 7; antidumping—interpreting Article 6, replacing the Kennedy Round code; bovine meat arrangement; international dairy arrangement; trade in civil aircraft.

15. The traditional description of the "chicken game" presents a situation in which two players drive their cars at each other on a narrow road. Each has the choice of swerving to avoid a collision or not swerving. The first to swerve loses face among his peers. If neither swerves, both die.

16. This point is made in Cline (2005).

17. See Sutherland and others (2004) for a detailed discussion on how best to address WTO's institutional challenges in the current economic environment.

18. See, for example, Mattoo and Subramanian (2005) and Curtis and Ciuriak (2005).

19. Mattoo and Subramanian (2004) review challenges faced by poor countries in engaging in WTO negotiations.

20. See, for example, Short (1999), a speech delivered at UNCTAD by the former British secretary of state for international development, the Rt. Hon. Clare Short (see http://www.gene.ch/gentech/1999/Mar–Apr/msg00068.html).

21. See Primo Braga (2004) for a description of the evolution of the agricultural negotiations and the role of different coalitions.

22. See Corrales-Leal, Sugathan, and Primack (2003).

23. These polar positions on the costs and benefits of SDT are well captured in Bhagwati (2004) and Oyejide (2004).

24. Critics cite the Franco-German deal on the mid-term review of the Common Agricultural Policy.

25. For a discussion of U.S. interests in the DDA and the U.S. legislative agenda affecting its trade policies see Schott (2005).

26. See Sally (2004) for a detailed presentation of this perspective.

27. The negotiations take place against a backdrop of significant debate on the benefits of globalization by governments and the public. The debate on the costs and benefits of international economic integration is well captured in Wolf (2004).

28. See Fink and Reichenmiller (2005).

29. See Finger and Schuler (2000).

30. See the discussion on "variable geometry" and plurilateral agreements in Sutherland and others (2004).

31. See, for example, Esty (2002) and Trotman (2004).

32. In October 2005, the U.S. made an important move by presenting a more ambitious proposal for agricultural liberalization. This was followed by a flurry of additional proposals and reactions from other WTO members and coalitions. At the time of writing, however, no consensus had yet emerged on market access with a wide gulf separating the more ambitious proposals from the U.S. and the G-20, for example, vis-à-vis the EU proposal.

33. This leadership is also required to advance the "aid for trade" agenda as discussed in IMF and World Bank (2005).

References

Anderson, K., W. Martin, and D. dan der Mensbrugghe. 2005. "Market and Welfare Implications of Doha Reform Scenarios." Unpublished paper. Development Research Group, World Bank, Washington, DC.

Bhagwati, Jagdish. 2004. "Trading for Development: How to Assist Poor Countries." In *Doha and Beyond: The Future of the Multilateral Trading System*, ed. M. Moore (Cambridge: Cambridge University Press).

Cline, William R. 2005. "Doha Can Achieve Much More than Skeptics Expect." *Finance and Development* (March): 22–23.

Corrales-Leal, Werner, Mahesh Sugathan, and David Primack. 2003. "Spaces for Development Policy: Revisiting Special and Differential Treatment." Paper prepared for the Joint ICTSD–GP International Dialogue: Making Special and Differential Treatment More Effective and Responsive to Development Needs, May 6–7, 2003, Chavannes-de-Bogis, Switzerland.

Curtis, John M., and Dan Ciuriak. 2005. "Scoping the End-Game in the Doha Round: A Roundtable Discussion." Report on a meeting organized by the Centre for International Governance Innovation at the University of Waterloo, IDRC, and the Department of Foreign Affairs and International Trade, Canada, on February 17–18, 2005.

Esty, Daniel C. "The World Trade Organization's Legitimacy Crisis." *World Trade Review* (1): 7–22.

Finger, J. M., and P. Schuler. 2000. "Implementation of Uruguay Round Commitments: The Development Challenge" *World Economy* (23): 511–26.

Fink, Carsten, and Patrick Reichenmiller. 2005. "Tightening TRIPS: The Intellectual Property Provisions of Recent U.S. Free Trade Agreements." Trade Note 20. Development Research Group, World Bank, Washington, DC.

Hoekman, Bernard, and Richard S. Newfarmer. 2003. "After Cancun: Continuation or Collapse." Trade Note 13. Development Research Group, World Bank, Washington, DC.

International Monetary Fund and the World Bank. 2005. "Doha Development Agenda and Aid for Trade." Paper presented to the Development Committee, September 25, Washington, DC.

Kasteng, Jonas, Arne Karlsson, and Carina Lindberg. 2004. "Differentiation between Developing Countries in the WTO." Report 2004:14E, Swedish Board of Agriculture, Stockholm.

Mattoo, Aaditya, and Arvind Subramanian. 2004. "The WTO and the Poorest Countries: The Stark Reality." IMF Working Paper WP/04/81. International Monetary Fund, Washington, DC.

Mattoo, Aaditya, and Arvind Subramanian. 2005. "Why Prospects for Trade Talks Are Not Bright." *Finance and Development* (March): 19–21.

Messerlin, Patrick A. 2005. "Success Requires a 'Grand Vision.'" *Finance and Development* (March): 24–25.

Oyejide, T. Ademola. 2004. "Development Dimensions in Multilateral Trade Negotiations." In *Doha and Beyond: The Future of the Multilateral Trading System*, ed. M. Moore. Cambridge: Cambridge University Press.

Primo Braga, Carlos A. 2004. "Agricultural Negotiations: Recent Developments in the Doha Round." Trade Note 19. Development Research Group, World Bank, Washington, DC.

Sally, Razeen. 2004. "The End of the Road for the WTO? A Snapshot of International Trade Policy after Cancun." *World Economics* 5 (January–March): 1–14.

Schott, Jeffrey J. 2005. "Confronting Current Challenges to U.S. Trade Policy." In *The United States and the World Economy: Foreign Economic Policy for the Next Decade*, ed. C. Fred Bergsten. Washington, DC: Institute for International Economics.

Short, Clare. 1999. "Future Multilateral Trade Negotiations: A 'Development Round'?" Speech to UN Conference on Trade and Development, March 2.

Srinivasan, T. N. 2003. "The Future of the Global Trading System: Doha Round, Cancun Ministerial and Beyond." Unpublished paper, at www.econ.yale.edu/~srinivas/ Yale University

Sutherland, Peter, Jagdish Bhagwati, Kwesi Botchwey, Niall FitzGerald, Koichi Hamada, John H. Jackson, Celso Lafer, and Thierry de Montbrial. 2004. *The Future of the WTO: Addressing Institutional Challenges in the New Millennium.* Geneva: World Trade Organization.

Trotman, LeRoy. 2004. "The WTO: The Institutional Contradictions." In *Doha and Beyond: The Future of the Multilateral Trading System*, ed. M. Moore. Cambridge: Cambridge University Press.

Wolf, Martin. 2004. *Why Globalization Works.* New Haven, CT: Yale University Press.

Doha Policies: Where are the Pay-offs?

*Kym Anderson, Will Martin,
and Dominique van der Mensbrughhe*

The Doha Round could promote development.[1] But it will fall significantly short if it does not liberalize agriculture and include some effort by developing countries as well as high-income countries. The potential gains from full multilateral trade liberalization range from $290 to $460 billion (Anderson, Martin and van der Mensbrugghe 2006a). According to the simulations reported here, a Doha agreement that makes significant cuts in WTO-agreed ceilings (bound rates) for tariffs could bring those gains within reach.

The need for deep cuts in bound rates is especially acute in agriculture, where protection is far higher than in manufacturing and where bound rates exceed applied rates by especially large margins. Two measures are important for capturing potential benefits: (i) capping maximum tariffs and (ii) resisting the temptation to exclude a large number of products from cuts. Exempting even 2 percent of tariff lines could eviscerate the round.

But cuts in bound rates must be more than broad and deep; they must apply to developing as well as developed countries. The benefits to developing countries of an ambitious Doha agreement will come as much from reform in the South as from reform by high-income countries. For that reason, developing countries must participate fully in the round by offering larger tariff cuts and making real reforms rather than seeking shelter under the banner of special and differential treatment (SDT).

This note presents results from modeling five scenarios to assess the effect of different magnitudes and types of cuts in agriculture and nonagricultural products. Before presenting details of these scenarios, we survey the potential gains in both a dynamic and static sense, to provide an idea of what is possible from the right agreement and to lay down a benchmark against which to evaluate possible outcomes of the Doha Round. We then analyze the five scenarios to illuminate some of the major issues that will determine the success of the Doha Round.

The range of the possible: What could full multilateral liberalization deliver?

Full removal of protection—both domestic and at the border—on trade in goods would raise global real income by an estimated $287 billion in 2015, relative to a baseline scenario and assuming that trade reform has no impact on underlying productivity.[2] The gains would be higher for high-income countries in dollar terms, but as a percentage of initial income they would be larger for developing countries (table 1).[3]

The gains in various parts of the world can be decomposed by source (table 2). At the global level, nearly two-thirds of the gains would be derived from the complete removal of protection on agriculture and food, with 14 percent generated by removal of remaining protection on textiles and apparel and only 23 percent by removing protection in all other manufacturing sectors. Agricultural protection is equally important for the gains to developing and high-income countries, accounting respectively for 63 and 64 percent of the regional gains. About 50 percent of the gains to developing countries come from removal of barriers on trade among developing countries. This is also true for agricultural reform. Developing countries gain just about as much whether high-income countries liberalize agriculture and food or developing countries do so.

These estimates of gain assume that trade opening has no impact on productivity and that the only dynamic effect of the gains comes from relatively small changes in investment volumes and structural shifts. In an alternative specification, the change in trade openness—as measured by the export-to-output ratio at the individual sector level—is linked to a change in productivity. The alternative scenario assumes that if trade openness leads to larger export volumes as a share of total output, sectoral productivity will increase. The linkage between exporting and productivity can be motivated by a combination of effects—among them matching international standards, overcoming threshold effects, reaping scale economies, taking advantage of network effects, and learning by doing.[4] The effects of this linkage between trade and productivity can be seen in the columns of table 1 labeled "Full-reform, dynamic." The global gains from this scenario would rise to 1.1 percent relative to the baseline, compared with a rise of 0.7 percent without the productivity boost. However, the gains for developing countries more than double—from $86 billion to $200 billion—as the impacts of reform lead to a higher relative shift to exports compared to the high-income countries.

These simulation results cover only a narrow, if important, set of issues in the context of international trade negotiations. For example, services—which account for between 50 and 80 percent of national output and have high entry barriers—are not covered, nor is trade facilitation. Other factors can influence the size of the gains in merchandise trade reform. For example, the results may be understated because of the assumption of full utilization of preferences, and the pernicious effects of high tariffs may be dampened through product and country aggregation. On the other hand, the gains to low-income countries may be overstated if anticipated supply responses do not materialize—hence the importance of the "aid for trade" agenda being developed to encourage supply responses.

Table 1. Change in real income in alternative Doha scenarios, 2015

a. Dollar change (in billions of 2001 dollars) compared to baseline scenario

Country group	Full reform, static (1)	Full reform, dynamic (2)	Scenario 1 Ag only (3)	Scenario 2 Ag-SSP (4)	Scenario 3 Ag-SSP+cap (5)	Scenario 4 Ag+nonag (SDT) (6)	Scenario 4 + Productivity (7)	Scenario 5 Ag+nonag (all) (8)
High-income	201.6	261.1	65.6	18.1	43.2	79.9	95.8	96.4
Developing	85.7	200.1	9.0	-0.4	1.1	16.1	29.9	22.9
Middle-income	69.5	145.1	8.0	-0.5	1.0	12.5	22.3	17.1
Low-income	16.2	55.0	1.0	0.1	0.0	3.6	7.6	5.9
World	287.3	461.2	74.5	17.7	44.3	96.1	125.7	119.3

b. Percentage change compared with baseline

Country group	Full reform, static (1)	Full reform, dynamic (2)	Scenario 1 Ag only (3)	Scenario 2 Ag-SSP (4)	Scenario 3 Ag-SSP+cap (5)	Scenario 4 Ag+nonag (SDT) (6)	Scenario 4 + productivity (7)	Scenario 5 Ag+nonag (all) (8)
High-income	0.62	0.81	0.20	0.06	0.13	0.25	0.30	0.30
Developing	0.84	1.97	0.09	0.00	0.01	0.16	0.29	0.22
Middle-income	0.85	1.77	0.10	-0.01	0.01	0.15	0.27	0.21
Low-income	0.82	2.79	0.05	0.01	0.00	0.18	0.38	0.30
World	0.67	1.08	0.18	0.04	0.10	0.23	0.30	0.28

Source: Authors' simulations using World Bank Linkage model.

Table 2. Regional and sectoral source of gains from full liberalization of global merchandise trade, developing and high-income countries, 2015

Change in real income in 2015 relative to the baseline scenario

	Gains by region (US$ billions)		
	Developing	High-income	World
Developing countries liberalize:			
Agriculture and food	28	19	47
Textile and wearing apparel	9	14	23
Other merchandise	6	52	58
All sectors	43	85	128
High-income countries liberalize:			
Agriculture and food	26	109	135
Textile and wearing apparel	13	2	15
Other merchandise	4	5	9
All sectors	43	116	159
All countries liberalize:			
Agriculture and food	54	128	182
Textile and wearing apparel	22	16	38
Other merchandise	10	57	67
All sectors	86	201	287
	Share of global gain (percent)		
	Developing	High-income	World
Developing countries liberalize:			
Agriculture and food	33	9	17
Textile and wearing apparel	10	7	8
Other merchandise	7	26	20
All sectors	50	42	45
High-income countries liberalize:			
Agriculture and food	30	54	47
Textile and wearing apparel	15	1	5
Other merchandise	3	2	3
All sectors	50	57	55
All countries liberalize:			
Agriculture and food	63	64	63
Textile and wearing apparel	25	8	14
Other merchandise	12	28	23
All sectors	100	100	100

Note: Small interaction effects are distributed proportionately and numbers are rounded to sum to 100 percent.
Source: Authors' simulation using World Bank's Linkage model.

Modeling possible Doha scenarios

The Doha Round was launched at the WTO's meeting of trade ministers at Doha in late 2001. The following ministerial meeting, in Cancún in September 2003, ended in acrimony and without an agreement on how to proceed. At Cancún, developing countries made it abundantly clear that further progress would not be possible without a commitment by developed countries to significantly lower their agricultural subsidies (notably for cotton). An intense period of consultations in July 2004 ended in the early hours of August 1 with a decision on how the Doha work program should proceed (WTO 2004). The so-called July Framework Agreement hints at how a Doha agreement might be structured. What emerged with respect to the three major agricultural issues, or pillars, is especially important.[5]

To illustrate the different issues involved in a possible Doha outcome, we look at five reform scenarios. The first three deal with different aspects of agricultural reform, which, as noted above, is particularly important as a source of potential gains. The alternative agricultural scenarios show the impacts of allowing for exemptions for so-called special or sensitive products, and allowing for a cap on the highest tariffs. The final two scenarios add manufacturing (also known as NAMA, for nonagricultural market access) to the mix, with the final scenario showing the relative importance of special and differential treatment (SDT).

Underlying these scenarios are the levels of protection actually imposed. One of the key features of protection is the difference between the so-called bound level of protection and the applied level of protection. A country may have an actual tariff of 20 percent on an item, whereas the bound tariff is 100 percent. This allows the country to raise tariffs to 100 percent under current WTO rules. The difference between the bound tariff and the actual tariff is called the "binding overhang." Because the negotiations focus on the bound tariffs, which are substantially higher than applied tariffs in most cases, the proposed reductions will have to be high if any measurable liberalization is to occur. In the case of the example above, even an 80 percent cut in the bound tariff would lead to no liberalization. A cut of 90 percent in the bound tariff would lead to a 50 percent cut in actual protection.

The scenarios envisaged reflect the following assumptions:

- In terms of domestic agricultural support, where there is a huge gap between bindings and actual support, we assume cuts relative to actual support of 28 percent in the United States, 16 percent in the European Union, 10 percent in Australia, and 18 percent in Norway, corresponding to a cut of 75 percent of the bound rates for countries with AMS notifications[6] above 20 percent of the value of production and cuts of 60 percent for all other countries. These assumptions affect only the four economies mentioned.
- Export subsidies are eliminated as inconsistent with WTO rules.
- A Harbinson-type formula (WTO 2003b) is used for agricultural tariffs—that is

top–down progressivity, but on a line-by-line basis rather than an average-cut basis; with greater cuts than in the original Harbinson formula to achieve more impact with respect to market access; and on a marginal-cut basis (as in a progressive income tax) to avoid discontinuities. The simulations are based on a 45 percent, 70 percent, and 75 percent bound-rate cutting rule for developed countries; a 35 percent, 40 percent, 50 percent, and 60 percent cutting rule for developing countries; and no cuts for least developed countries.

- Negotiations on *nonagricultural market access* have lagged behind those on farm products, so in the absence of any clear guidance we assumed a 50 percent cut in bound tariffs by developed countries and 33 percent by developing countries other than least developed (from which no cuts are being demanded).

How high are the tariffs from which these cuts will be made? We draw on the dataset compiled by the Centre d'Etudes Prospectives et d'Informations Internationales (CEPII) for 2001 and use the World Bank's LINKAGE model to project the world economy first to 2005, taking into account the complete implementation of the Uruguay Round, the accession to the WTO by China, and the eastward expansion of the European Union to 25 members. The tariffs so generated are assumed to remain unchanged to 2015 in our baseline scenario (table 3, column 1). The tariffs for farm products are more than three times the average for all goods and so promise to be a major source of gains from reform.

The core agricultural reform scenario (Scenario 1) would reduce tariffs on farm goods by one-third globally but by very little in developing countries because of SDT and a large degree of binding overhang (table 3.a). If "sensitive" and "special" farm products are subjected to smaller cuts, as in Scenario 2, the drop in farm tariffs would be far less. Even when a cap of 200 percent is applied, as in Scenario 3, only some of that effect is restored. When nonagricultural tariffs are also cut, as in Scenario 4, the global average tariff on all goods—4.7 percent in the baseline— falls to 3.5 percent (table 3.b). It would fall even further if developing countries fully engaged in Doha reform, as in Scenario 5; indeed their average tariff would fall nearly as much again in that scenario as by moving from Scenario 1 to Scenario 4.

Estimates of welfare and trade impacts of prospective Doha reforms

Scenario 1 focuses first on agricultural reform alone. Column 3 of table 1 suggests that agricultural liberalization using the harmonizing tiered formula (Scenario 1) would generate a global gain of $75 billion even without the inclusion of nonagricultural tariff reform (column 6)—translating into 80 percent of the gains when NAMA is included. But almost all of those benefits accrue to the reforming high-income countries, such that developing countries would gain only $9 billion

Table 3. Average applied tariffs under different Doha scenarios, 2015

a. Percent tariff rates
Agriculture and food

Country group	Baseline	Scenario 1 Ag only	Scenario 2 Ag-SSP	Scenario 3 Ag-SSP+cap	Scenario 4 Ag+nonag (SDT)	Scenario 5 Ag+nonag (all)
High-income	15.9	8.4	13.5	11.5	8.2	7.5
Developing	14.2	12.5	13.4	13.3	12.4	10.6
Middle-income	12.1	10.4	11.4	11.2	10.3	8.9
Low-income	22.0	20.7	21.5	21.5	20.7	17.5
World	15.2	10.0	13.5	12.2	9.9	8.8

b. All merchandise

Country group	Baseline	Scenario 1 Ag only	Scenario 2 Ag-SSP	Scenario 3 Ag-SSP+cap	Scenario 4 Ag+nonag (SDT)	Scenario 5 Ag+nonag (all)
High-income	2.9	2.3	2.7	2.5	1.6	1.6
Developing	8.4	8.2	8.3	8.3	7.5	6.8
Middle-income	7.2	7	7.1	7.1	6.3	5.6
Low-income	15.5	15.3	15.5	15.4	14.6	13.4
World	4.7	4.2	4.5	4.4	3.5	3.2

Note: Baseline uses tariffs in 2005. Scenario 1 assumes cuts in agriculture only using a modified Harbinson tiered formula with higher percent reductions for higher tariffs. Scenario 2 is the same as Scenario 1, but with exemptions for special or sensitive products. Scenario 3 is the same as Scenario 2, but with a 200 percent cap on the highest tariffs. Scenario 4 is the same as Scenario 1, but includes reductions in manufactured tariffs. Scenario 5 is the same as Scenario 4, but drops special and differential treatment for developing countries.
Source: Authors' simulations using World Bank Linkage model.

because their tariff binding overhang is so great as to lead to almost no cuts in applied tariffs.[7]

In Scenario 2, we consider the effects of allowing countries to exempt up to 2 percent of tariff lines as sensitive products (and another 2 percent in developing countries for "special" farm products). Under this scenario the global gains from a Doha Round would shrink to just $18 billion (column 4 of table 1), and developing countries as a group would be worse off because of deteriorating terms of trade, with little offsetting expansion of export volumes in other areas.

If such exceptions are to be made, it would be important to exploit the opportunity—provided for in the July 2004 Framework—to cap bound tariffs. Scenario 3 shows that even a cap as high as 200 percent on exempted products would restore at least half of the welfare gain foregone by allowing exceptional treatment (column 5 of table 1).

The final two scenarios add nonagricultural tariff cuts to the agricultural reforms in the preceding scenarios. In Scenario 4, the gain to developing countries doubles by adding nonfarm reforms, relative to Scenario 1 where only agriculture is cut, contributing one-third of the extra boost to global welfare ($7.1 billion out of the $21.6 billion difference between the global gains from Scenarios 1 and 4).

Scenario 4 also assumes a productivity boost from trade openness, as in the global reform scenario. In this case, the global gains would increase to $126 billion, an increase of 31 percent over the static gains, but a near doubling of the gains for developing countries (column 7 of table 1).

In Scenario 5, the developing countries (including the least developed) fully engage in the reform process, forgoing the lesser cuts provided for in Scenarios 1 to 4. That boosts their welfare and global welfare substantially, because their cuts in bound tariffs lead to considerably larger cuts in applied tariffs. In percentage terms, the gains for the low-income countries are higher than for the middle-income countries. The deeper cuts from Scenario 5 allow developing countries to reap greater efficiency gains, overcoming potential losses from negative terms-of-trade effects on food-importing countries and losses from preference erosion.[8]

What effect would the reforms discussed here have on agricultural net income (value added by the farming sector)? Agricultural value added would fall in those regions with the highest agricultural protection (Western Europe, Northeast Asia, and, to a lesser extent, the United States). However, in the Doha reform scenario (Scenario 4)[9] none of the developing countries or regions, except for the richer countries of Eastern Europe and Central Asia, would suffer a decline in agricultural net income, despite the lowering of their own agricultural tariffs (table 4). The reason their farmers would fare better than protected rich-country farmers—even though the average agricultural tariff in developing countries is nearly as high as that in high-income countries (14.2 percent compared with 15.9 percent in the baseline)—is that a much larger proportion of developing-country agriculture is internationally competitive and so need not be protected from imports. This result has clear implications for poverty alleviation, given that perhaps as many as 70 percent of the world's poor live in farm households in developing countries.

The trade consequences of Scenario 4 are summarized in table 5. The first column shows that by 2015, annual developing-country exports would be greater by $41 billion for agricultural products, $25 billion for textiles and clothing, and $12 billion for other manufactures. The total increase of $78 billion is smaller than that for high-income countries ($135 billion), but that difference is less when expressed in percentage terms (a 2.6 percent increase for developing countries, compared with 3.1 percent for high-income countries). This scenario thus takes global merchandise trade one-fifth of the way to where it would be with completely free trade in merchandise by causing average real export prices of numerous farm products to rise at least part way toward where they would be in international markets under free trade (figure 1). For other products where export supplies expand more easily, it is the volume of global exports that would rise, rather than their price. This is true particularly for the most-protected farm products—rice, sugar and beef (figure 2a). The percentage increases in developing-country exports of

Table 4. Impact of reform scenarios on agricultural value added, 2015

Changes in value added relative to baseline

| | US$ billions, 2001 | |
	Full global liberalization	Scenario 4 Ag+nonag (SDT)
High-income	−74.6	−34.2
Developing	35.6	24.8
Middle-income	45.3	20.9
Low-income	−9.7	3.9
East Asia and Pacific	5.5	3.9
South Asia	−18.1	1.2
Europe and Central Asia	−4.5	−0.3
Middle East and North Africa	0.3	1.0
Sub-Saharan Africa	4.3	1.1
Latin America and the Caribbean	45.0	16.7
World	−39.0	−9.5
	Percent change	
	Full global liberalization	Scenario 4 Ag+nonag (SDT)
High-income	−19.4	−8.9
Developing	2.9	2.0
Middle-income	5.3	2.4
Low-income	−2.5	1.0
East Asia and Pacific	1.1	0.8
South Asia	−6.8	0.5
Europe and Central Asia	−4.0	−0.3
Middle East and North Africa	0.3	0.9
Sub-Saharan Africa	6.7	1.8
Latin America and the Caribbean	27.4	10.2
World	−2.4	−0.6

Source: Authors' simulations using World Bank Linkage model.

those products would be even larger. Cotton export volume would rise more than 16 percent (figure 2b).

Of particular interest to trade negotiators are changes in *bilateral* trade. Negotiators want to see the extent to which an exchange of market access will be "balanced." Under Scenario 4, developing countries expand their exports of agricultural and textile products to high-income countries more than they expand their imports of such products from high-income countries. But the opposite is true of other manufactures, so that for merchandise trade in total the difference is not great. In f.o.b. terms developing countries would sell $62 billion more to high-income countries in 2015, and would buy $55 billion in return, under Scenario 4 (table 4, columns 2 and 3). This small gap might be tolerated by high-income countries

Table 5. Gains in bilateral trade flows from Doha Scenario 4, 2015

Difference in bilateral trade flows at FOB prices compared to baseline
(US$ billions)

Exporter	Importer		
	World	High-income countries	Developing countries
Agricultural products			
World	56	46	9
High-income	15	15	0
Developing	41	31	10
Textiles and clothing			
World	41	28	12
High-income	16	5	11
Developing	25	23	2
Other manufactures			
World	117	68	49
High-income	105	60	44
Developing	12	8	5
Total			
World	213	142	71
High-income	135	80	55
Developing	78	62	16

Note: Aggregations exclude intra-EU trade.
Source: Authors' simulations using World Bank Linkage model.

as a concession to development, but if necessary it could be narrowed through greater developing-country reform in goods or by having developing countries give more than they get in the opening of trade in services.

Implications for developing countries: What's important?

Among the many policy implications of our analysis, several are worth highlighting. First, with so much to be gained from implementing the July 2004 Framework Agreement (global gains of $95–120 billion per year, or more if dynamic gains are taken into account), the political will must be found to bring the Doha Round to a successful conclusion, and the sooner the better. Multilateral cuts in tariff bindings are helpful because they lock in previous unilateral trade liberalizations that otherwise would remain unbound and hence vulnerable to reversals to higher protection; they also can be used as an opportunity to multilateralize previously agreed preferential trade agreements, thereby reducing the risk of trade diversion caused by those agreements.

Second, agricultural reforms need to be significant if the Doha agreement is to be pro-development and pro-poor. Outlawing agricultural export subsidies is the obvious first step. Doing so will bring agriculture into line with the basic GATT rule against such measures and, in the process, limit the extent to which governments

Figure 1. Effects of Doha Scenario 4 compared with full trade liberalization on world product prices, 2015

(percentage change in the average price)

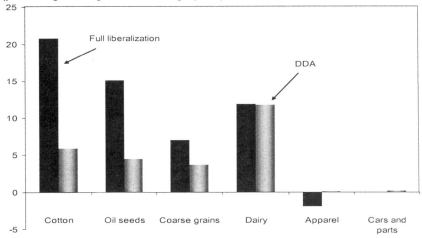

Source: Authors' simulations using World Bank LINKAGE model.

Figure 2a. Effects of Doha Scenario 4 compared with full trade liberalization on global export volumes, 2015

(percentage changes)

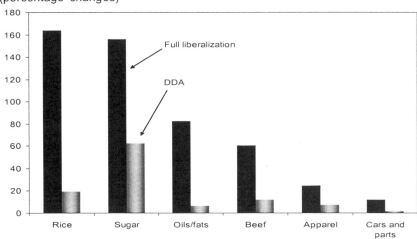

Figure 2b. Effects of Doha Scenario 4 compared with full trade liberalization on export volumes for developing countries, 2015

(percentage changes)

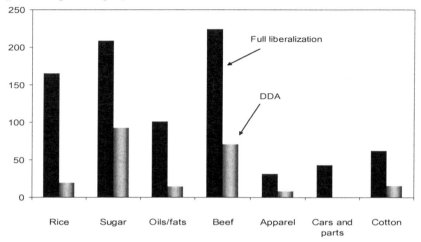

Source: Authors' simulations using World Bank LINKAGE model.

encourage agricultural production by other means (since it would remove one option for, and hence raise the cost of, surplus disposal). Concurrently, domestic support commitments must be cut very substantially to reduce binding overhang. In so doing, the countries with the highest subsidies need to reduce their support, not just for the sake of their own economies, but also to encourage developing countries to reciprocate by opening their markets as a *quid pro quo*. Even more important, agricultural tariff bindings must be cut drastically—so that some genuine market opening can occur. Allowing lesser cuts for even just a few "sensitive" and "special" farm products would greatly reduce the gains from reform, given the tariff peaks currently in place. If it turns out to be politically impossible *not* to designate some products as "sensitive" and "special," it will be imperative to impose a cap, so that bound tariffs in excess of the cap, regardless of the product involved, would have to be reduced.

Third, expanding nonagricultural market access at the same time as reforming agriculture is essential for a balanced exchange of "concessions"—and more than textiles and clothing must be involved. The additional benefits of including other merchandise and services in a liberalization deal are that the resulting trade expansion would be many times greater for both rich and poor countries and the welfare gains substantially larger for developing countries.

Fourth, South–South "concessions" also are needed, because half of the potential benefits to developing countries are to be gained from trade within the developing world. That means reconsidering the extent to which developing countries liberalize. They are trading much more with each other now than in the 1980s and now stand to benefit most from reforms in their own regions. Even least developed countries should consider reducing their binding overhang. Doing so in the context of the Doha Round allows them to demand more concessions (compensation for erosion of preferences or other damage to their terms of trade), something they will not get if they hang on to the opportunity, provided in the July Framework, not to engage in reform.

What emerges from our analysis is that developing countries would not have to reform very much under the most likely Doha deals, because of the large gaps between their tariff bindings and applied rates. But to realize more of their potential gains from trade, they would need to commit to additional trade (and complementary domestic) reforms. High-income countries could encourage them to commit to greater reform not only by being willing to widen access to their own markets but also by providing more targeted aid. To that end, a new proposal has been put forward to reward developing-country commitments to greater trade reform with an expansion of trade-facilitating aid. The new aid would be provided by a major expansion of the current Integrated Framework, operated by a consortium of international agencies for least developed countries (Hoekman and Prowse 2005). This proposal may provide an attractive path for developing countries seeking to trade their way out of poverty. It also is potentially a far more efficient way for developed countries to assist low-income countries than the current systems of tariff preferences.[10]

Notes

1. The authors are grateful for the collaboration of numerous colleagues, especially Tom Hertel, and for research funding from the UK Department for International Development. The views expressed here are the authors' alone. More detailed analysis is can be found in Anderson, Martin, and van der Mensbrugghe (2006a), available at www.worldbank.org/trade/wto.

2. The baseline scenario is a projection of the global economy between 2001 and 2015 that includes some major policy changes—among them the European Union's recent expansion to 25 members, China's WTO accession commitments, the elimination of the quotas on trade in textile and apparel, and final implementation of the other Uruguay Round commitments. These policy changes are phased in between 2001 and 2005. All other policies are fixed at their initial levels.

3. Van der Mensbrugghe (2005) compares the global gain of $287 billion with past World Bank estimates and with other widely cited simulation results.

4. Other potential channels link trade openness and productivity. See Anderson, Martin, and van der Mensbrugghe (2006b) for an overview.

5. More detail on the July 2004 Framework and the importance of the three pillars is available in Anderson, Martin, and Valenzuela (2005).

6. The aggregate measure of support (AMS) is a summary indicator of the level of support accorded a sector and notified by member countries to the WTO.

7. We use World Bank definitions of developing countries. Thus the high-income countries include protective Republic of Korea and Taiwan (China) as well as Hong Kong (China) and Singapore.

8. For more details of our results for Sub-Saharan Africa, see Anderson, Martin, and van der Mensbrugghe (2005c).

9. The remainder of the discussion focuses on Scenario 4. This scenario reflects perhaps the most positive reading of the July 2004 Framework—though other positions have been set forth that reflect even greater reforms—and without the potential eviscerating effects of sensitive and special product exemptions.

10. See also Nielson (2005) in this volume for more on the aid-for-trade agenda.

References
Hoekman, B., and S. Prowse. 2005. "Policy Responses to Preference Erosion: From Trade as Aid to Aid for Trade." Paper presented at the World Bank Conference on Preference Erosion: Impacts and Potential Policy Responses, Geneva, June 13–14.

Nielson, J. 2005. "Aid for Trade." In *Trade, Doha and Development: A Window into the Issues*, ed. R. Newfarmer. Washington, DC: World Bank.

WTO. 2003b. "Negotiations on Agriculture: First Draft of Modalities for the Further Commitments" (Harbinson Draft). TN/AG/W/1/Rev.1. Geneva. March.

_____. 2004. "Decision Adopted by the General Council on 1 August 2004" (July Framework Agreement). WT/L/579. Geneva. August.

Further reading
Anderson, K., and W. Martin. 2006a. "Agricultural Trade Reform and the Doha Development Agenda." Policy Research Working Paper 3607. World Bank, Washington, DC. *World Economy* 28(9):1301-27. September.

———. 2006b. "Agricultural Market Access: The Key to Doha Success." Trade Note 23, World Bank, Washington, DC. July.

Anderson, K., W. Martin, and E. Valenzuela. 2005. "On the Relative (Un-)Importance of Agricultural Subsidies versus Market Access in the WTO's Doha Round." Processed, Washington, DC: World Bank.

Anderson, K., W. Martin, and D. van der Mensbrugghe. 2006a. "Market and Welfare Implications of the Doha Reform Scenarios." In *Agricultural Trade Reform and the Doha Development Agenda*, ed. K. Anderson and W. Martin (chapter 12). New York: Palgrave Macmillan.

———. 2006b. "Global Impacts of the Doha Scenarios on Poverty." In *Putting Development Back into the Doha Agenda: Poverty Impacts of a WTO Agreement*, ed. T. Hertel and L. A. Winters (chapter 17). New York: Palgrave Macmillan.

———. 2006c. "Would Multilateral Trade Reform Benefit Sub-Saharan Africa?" Policy Research Working Paper 3616, World Bank, Washington, DC, June. Forthcoming in the *Journal of African Economies*.

Hoekman, B., and S. Prowse. 2005. "Policy Responses to Preference Erosion: From Trade as Aid to Aid for Trade." Paper presented at the World Bank Conference on Preference Erosion: Impacts and Potential Policy Responses, Geneva, June 13–14.

Nielson, J. 2005. "Aid for Trade." In *Trade, Doha and Development: A Window into the Issues*, ed. R. Newfarmer. Washington, DC: World Bank.

van der Mensbrugghe, D. 2005. "Estimating the Benefits of Trade Reform: Why Numbers Change." In *Trade, Doha and Development: A Window into the Issues*, ed. R. Newfarmer. Washington, DC: World Bank.

WTO (World Trade Organization). 2003a. "Negotiating Group on Market Access: Report by the Chairman" (Girard Text). TN/MA/12. Geneva. September.

———. 2003b. "Negotiations on Agriculture: First Draft of Modalities for the Further Commitments" (Harbinson Draft). TN/AG/W/1/Rev.1. Geneva. March.

———. 2004. "Decision Adopted by the General Council on 1 August 2004" (July Framework Agreement). WT/L/579. Geneva. August.

Estimating the Benefits of Trade Reform: Why Numbers Change

Dominique van der Mensbrugghe

Much attention has been paid to the World Bank's analyses of multilateral trade reform. According to our latest estimates, full liberalization of world merchandise trade would increase global income in 2015 relative to the baseline by $290 to $460 billion, with higher percentage gains for developing countries (0.8 to 2.0 percent) than for high-income countries (Anderson and others 2005). These numbers are significantly lower than earlier World Bank estimates (World Bank 2001, 2003), which put the global gains of full merchandise trade reform at some $400 billion per year in 2015. This note examines why the numbers of have changed and, more generally, why estimates of gains from reform can vary widely.

The answer lies in a mixture of factors: new data on tariffs, incorporation of recent major reforms in trade policy (notably in China), inclusion of preferential trade arrangements, and new poverty elasticities with respect to growth. Beyond these methodological issues, it is important to distinguish the scenario under analysis—whether it is full liberalization (the basis of all calculations and the benchmarks of this note) or partial reforms; whether the analysis is static or dynamic (and includes a productivity response); and whether the scenario includes services (which are usually omitted).

Underlying most estimates are many assumptions that can result in gross over- or underestimates of the effects of merchandise trade reform. As factors contributing to overestimation in the World Bank estimates (and common to many other studies) one might cite the optimistic supply response, the optimism embodied in the baseline,[1] the failure to take into account baseline policy changes and the loss of quota rents, the degree of protection,[2] overstatement of the relation between income growth and poverty reduction, and closure effects.[3] The assumptions that might lead to underestimation include low Armington elasticities and market shares,[4] the failure to consider market structure (procompetition effects) and scale economies, neglect of positive productivity effects, and product aggregation. As well, the baseline may bias the estimate downward, as it probably understates the increase in trade openness—even with constant trade policies—as the global economy pushes forward. Most multilateral trade analyses have also largely ignored reform of services trade, which is generally believed to be highly distorted but is difficult to deal with empirically.

This note introduces the new numbers generated by the World Bank's global trade model, known as LINKAGE.[5] The basic model has not undergone any major change, but changes in the underlying database and the baseline scenario have altered key numbers from earlier estimates, though by and large the main findings still hold. The next section will describe the key changes to the database and baseline. This will be followed by a section on the impact of global merchandise trade reform. A final section will describe how these results line up with some other prominent exercises.

Changes to the database and baseline
GTAP release 6.0

Since the early 1990s, global general equilibrium trade models have increasingly relied on a single database developed, maintained, and updated by the Global Trade Analysis Project (GTAP) located at Purdue University.[6] The GTAP database is a multisectoral and multiregional global social accounting matrix (SAM). It integrates national input–output tables, bilateral trade flows from COMTRADE, and different sources of data on trade protection and domestic support into a single, consistent global SAM. GTAP has just issued its latest release, 6.0, that divides economic activity into 57 sectors and 87 countries and composite regions—70 of which are individual countries.[7] There are two major changes in GTAP6 compared with the previous release. First, it has a new base year—2001 rather than 1997. This represents a change in the relative structure of the global economy, with some countries/sectors growing more rapidly than others, and also greater trade, since growth in trade generally outpaces output.[8]

The second change is the source of GTAP's protection data. Whereas in the past protection data generally came from TRAINS/IDB and, for agricultural protection, the Agricultural Market Access Database, the new data comes mostly from MAcMap—a joint product of the Centre d'Etudes Prospectives et d'Informations Internationales in Paris (CEPII) and the International Trade Centre (ITC) in Geneva.[9] MAcMap is the result of a huge effort to provide a more comprehensive picture of trade protection. The database is collated at the Harmonized Tariff System 6-digit level and incorporates preferential arrangements—both reciprocal and nonreciprocal. It also provides the ad valorem equivalent of specific tariffs and an estimate of the tariff equivalent of TRQs. Finally, it contains effective tariff rates, MFN tariffs, and bound rates. It is thus possible to measure the relative importance of preferential access and the "binding overhang" between bound and applied rates.

In summary, the new database provides a more recent snapshot of the global economy with a 2001 base year instead of 1997 and a more comprehensive picture of trade protection, particularly through the incorporation of preferences.

The tariff rates on goods under GTAP5 and GTAP6 are summarized in table A-1. The two data sets are not compatible since they come from different sources and reflect the use of different methodology. Thus, even though tariffs in 2001 appear to be lower in general than the 1997 assessment, the effect cannot be confidently attributed to a lowering of tariff barriers during the four-year interval. Clearly, the incorporation of preferences into the dataset will have made a significant difference. One example is the Middle East and North Africa, where tariffs on agriculture and food are now evaluated at 14 percent compared with 61 percent in the previous release.

The largest modifications have been made to tariffs on agriculture and food. At the global level they are down nearly 10 percentage points from GTAP5 to GTAP6, and this holds across both developed and developing regions. The changes in the manufacturing sectors are much less pronounced, with a drop of some 2.5 percentage points in textile and clothing and about 1.5 percentage points for all other goods.

These apparent tariff changes suggest that assessments of the gains from global reform should be reduced from those devised on the basis of the GTAP5 database. The expected gains from agricultural reform—as a contributor to the overall gains—also should be reduced. Two factors, however, could influence the results in the other direction, toward greater gains. First, the size and structure of the global economy, different in 2001, could raise the overall gains from trade reform. In particular, the most heavily protected economies have been growing more rapidly than the less protected, while trade has advanced more rapidly than output. Second, the average tariffs may conceal higher peak tariffs the replacement of which could produce larger gains than might appear in estimates prepared on the basis of average tariffs.

Baseline reforms

The current analysis, like past analyses, is predicated on a baseline scenario that takes the global economy from the base year, now 2001, though a future year, typically 2015. The baseline scenario relies on a number of assumptions—most related to supply-side variables such as labor supply, savings behavior (and hence capital stocks), and productivity. The baseline can also incorporate changes to policies, which, in past exercises, were fixed at their base-year levels, with no change in tax or subsidy rates.[10] The new baseline incorporates some policy changes that reflect some (but not necessarily all) existing commitments. The major commitments include the implementation of the final phases of the Uruguay Round, including the elimination of the textile and clothing quotas,[11] the expansion of the European Union to include the 10 new member countries, and the commitments made by China in its WTO accession agreement. Of these elements, the most significant are China's commitments and the removal of the textile and clothing quotas. Their impact will be described below. China's tariffs on agriculture and food are estimated to be reduced by nearly three-quarters (38 percent to 10 percent) and in manufacturing by 50 percent (19 percent to 10 percent in textiles and clothing and 11 percent to 5 percent in other sectors).

Global trade reform
Global welfare

The new estimate of the global welfare impact from full merchandise trade reform—including the elimination of domestic support and export subsidies—is $287 billion, about 30 percent lower than the previous estimate of $413 billion, which was based on GTAP5 (figure 1). Under the new scenario, developing countries garner only 30 percent of the global gains in dollar terms, but continue to gain more in percentage terms (relative to their baseline income) than rich countries.

It is possible to decompose the change into three distinct components—the change in the database, the impact of preferences, and the impact of the baseline policy changes. The GTAP database is available with two different tariff structures. The standard database reflects applied tariffs including all preferences—reciprocal and nonreciprocal. The alternative database assumes that the preferential rates are not used and that imports enter under the applied MFN rate. This latter database, which assumes zero utilization of preferences, is closer than the new standard to the last release of the GTAP5 database.

Figure 1. Global gains from full merchandise trade reform under various scenarios

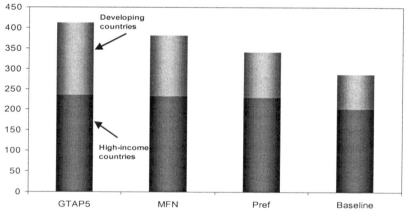

Note: The three right columns are all based on the GTAP6 data base. MFN assumes application of MFN tariff rates. Pref assumes application of preferential tariff rates. Baseline includes preferential tariffs and existing policy commitments, such as China's WTO accession and elimination of the textile and clothing quotas. The "Baseline" column represents the World Bank's current baseline estimate of the gains from full merchandise trade reform.
Source: World Bank simulations.

In dollar terms, assuming the MFN tariff rates obtain, global gains decline from $413 billion in 2015 to $382 billion. While it would be easy to justify the decline by declaring that it reflects reforms undertaken between 1997 and 2001, it is not possible to make this statement simply by comparing tariff schedules between GTAP5 and GTAP6, because the tariff data have been processed using different methodologies. There are two ways to assess the level of reform between 1997 and 2001. The most convincing would be tariff line by tariff line—though the problem of aggregation cannot be ignored if some lines show an increase and others a decrease. The second would be to reproduce a tariff database using the same methodology as was used in the construction of GTAP5. With this caveat in mind, had there been no tariff reform one would expect the global gains to *increase* between 1997 and 2001, for two reasons. The first is inflation—though the change in exchange-rate valuations makes this explanation less than straightforward. The second is the increase in trade openness in most regions, as trade growth typically outpaces income growth. This would tend to increase the distortion induced by a given tariff rate.

On a percentage basis, the global gain, comparing the MFN-based GTAP6 with GTAP5, declines by 0.2 percentage points—from 1.1 percent of baseline income to 0.9 percent (in 2015). The gains to developing countries drop by somewhat more than for high-income countries—from 1.7 to 1.5 percent in the case of the former, and from 0.8 to 0.7 percent in the case of the latter—possibly indicating greater trade reform in developing countries.

A subsequent scenario—using the standard preference-inclusive GTAP6 database—shows the impact of assuming full utilization of available preferences. In this case, the dollar gains from full liberalization drop to $341 billion (from $382 billion). For developing countries, this implies a gain of 1.1 percent from full merchandise trade reform—a rather substantial drop from the gains that appear when using the MFN-based tariffs (1.5 percent) and from GTAP5 (1.7 percent)—which basically assumed MFN tariffs. For the rich countries, there is relatively no impact from assuming application of the preference-based tariffs.

Finally, our new standard baseline also includes quantifiable policy-reform commitments—final implementation of the Uruguay Round, including elimination of apparel and textile quotas, expansion of the European Union to 25 countries, and China's WTO accession commitments. This brings the estimate of the global gains from merchandise trade reform to $287 billion in 2015—equivalent to a gain in global income of 0.7 percent. It also further reduces the gains for developing countries—with the overall gains now at only 0.8 percent of their baseline income—or nearly one-half of the estimate obtained using GTAP5. The most significant drop is for China, which sees its gain fall from 0.6 percent to only 0.2 percent, because the substantial gains from WTO accession are already reflected in the baseline.

One must not conclude from the downward revision of the gain that merchandise trade reform is less important today than it was a year or two ago. First, the lower projected gains reflect gains already secured between 1997 and 2001, as well as those anticipated from existing commitments. Second, the counterfactual scenario against which the new full-reform scenario is being compared is one of consolidated gains. However, a failure to complete the Doha negotiations or a rise in trade tensions could lead to backsliding in trade policy commitments. In agriculture, the rich countries have hardly curtailed domestic support even as they have carried out their commitments to the letter. And though the apparel and textile quotas are now history, there is strong pressure to prevent the structural changes most analysts had predicted would occur from the phaseout. Finally, there is currently no strong domestic constituency for reform in the key stakeholder states that have moved multilateral liberalization forward in the past.

Regional impacts

The impacts of the various baseline assumptions vary across regions (figure 2). Moving from the MFN tariff rates to the preferential rates has significant impacts for Bangladesh, the Middle East and North Africa, and Sub-Saharan Africa, among others. In Africa, the selected Sub-Saharan countries (SSS) regional grouping that includes an eight-country aggregation of small countries sees its global gains drop by 55 percent when the preferential tariff data base is used rather than the MFN-based data base. Bangladesh would actually suffer a loss from global merchandise trade reform against a baseline scenario that incorporated preferential tariffs, because it derives such significant benefits from existing preferences.

The World Bank's final baseline scenario—using the preferential tariffs and incorporating commitments—has different implications in different regions. For China, and the East Asia and Pacific region in aggregate, the incorporation of policy commitments lowers significantly the gains from global reform since a sizeable portion of the reform gains will be reflected in the baseline scenario. South Asia is also affected by the baseline policy changes—but in different ways. India gains less from global reform when the policy commitments are incorporated in the baseline, i.e. it derives positive gains from the baseline policy changes. Bangladesh on the other hand sees more gains from global trade reform when the policy commitments are included. This signifies that it loses from the policy reforms in the baseline, perhaps a consequence of its loss of quota rents from the elimination of the quotas on apparel.

Decomposition

At the global and subregional level, nearly two-thirds of the gains against the new standard baseline are generated by free trade in agriculture and food (table 1). This percentage is somewhat higher than with the former baseline; it also reflects a

Figure 2. Regional impact of alternative scenarios using GTAP6 database

Percent change in real income in 2015 from global merchandise trade reform

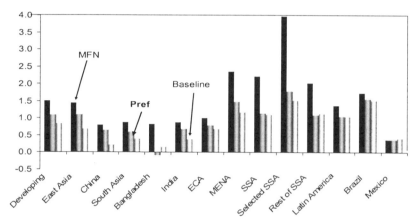

Note: The three columns are all based on the GTAP6 data base. MFN assumes application of MFN tariff rates. Pref assumes application of preferential tariff rates. Baseline includes preferential tariffs and existing policy commitments, such as China's WTO accession and elimination of the textile and clothing quotas. The "Baseline" column represents the World Bank's current baseline estimate of the gains from full merchandise trade reform.
Source: World Bank simulations.

relative rotation between the subregions. Under GTAP5, only about 58 percent of the global gains came from agriculture. But for developing countries, agriculture represented 72 percent of their total gains—of which 53 percent came from their own liberalization of agriculture. Another way to say this is that of the $177 billion in gain garnered by developing countries in the previous global reform scenario, $94 billion came from their own agricultural reform. With the new baseline—which incorporates significant reforms already made—the developing countries' own agricultural reform generates only $27 billion in (additional) gain—or only about one-third of their total gain. The rotation also implies that developing countries have about the same amount at stake from rich country reform in agriculture as from their own reform.

Dynamic vs. static effects

Although the standard LINKAGE model is dynamic, the dynamic effects of trade reform are relatively limited. They come mainly through two channels. First, higher growth and incomes raise saving rates and therefore investment and the stock of capital. Second, the price of capital goods declines as tariff rates are set to zero.

Table 1. Decomposition of gains from full merchandise trade reform by sector and region

Change in real income in 2015

	To developing	To developed	Global	To developing	To developed	Global
			Allocation of gains			
			GTAP6 standard baseline			
	Billions of dollars			*Percent of regional gain from total*		
Reform by developing countries						
Agriculture and food	28	19	47	33	9	17
Manufacturing	15	66	81	17	33	28
All	43	85	128	50	42	45
Reform by developed countries						
Agriculture and food	26	109	135	30	54	47
Manufacturing	17	7	24	18	3	8
All	43	116	159	50	57	55
All countries liberalize:						
Agriculture and food	54	128	182	63	64	63
Manufacturing	32	73	105	37	36	37
All	86	201	287	100	100	100
			GTAP5 standard baseline			
	Billions of dollars			*Percent of regional gain from total*		
Reform by developing countries						
Agriculture and food	94	41	135	53	17	33
Manufacturing	6	135	141	4	57	34
All	100	176	276	57	75	67
Reform by developed countries						
Agriculture and food	34	68	102	19	29	25
Manufacturing	43	–8	35	24	–3	8
All	77	60	137	43	25	33
All countries liberalize:						
Agriculture and food	128	109	237	72	46	57
Manufacturing	49	127	176	28	54	43
All	177	236	413	100	100	100

Source: World Bank simulation.

Therefore countries obtain more from the same nominal level of investment. If the average tariff on capital goods is 10 percent and all capital goods are imported, then the investment rate climbs by 10 percent with tariff reform (assuming no change in nominal savings)—a "static" dynamic gain.[12] The final section of this note compares static dynamic gains with the comparative static version of the model. It shows that static dynamic gains raise the global gain from merchandise trade reform by roughly 23 percent with respect to the pure comparative static gains.

In an alternative scenario, we allow productivity to be influenced by changes in trade. In a true endogenous growth model, changes in productivity would be influenced by changes in research and development and by the technology embodied in imports, either better intermediate inputs (such as agricultural chemicals and seeds) or better equipment. Other channels also have been identified in the literature as possibly affecting productivity. Among these are the procompetitive effects of imports (for example, through rationalization and scale economies), and the procompetitive effects of exporting (learning by doing, matching international standards, overcoming threshold effects, and so on). We have chosen to illustrate dynamic effects through the latter channel (procompetitive effects of exporting) by assuming that a share of productivity can be explained by a trade openness measure defined by the sectoral ratio of exports to output. This is calibrated in the baseline simulation. In the corresponding shock simulation, productivity will increase with the export-to-output ratio.[13] For manufacturing, the elasticity is set at 1; for agriculture, one-half.[14]

The productivity assumption leads to a sizeable increase in the gains from trade reform, particularly for developing countries (table 2). At the global level, the gains from trade increase from $287 billion to $461 billion—a rise of 1.1 percent in global income compared to 0.7 percent with static gains alone. But for developing

Table 2. Full liberalization of global merchandise trade, without and with productivity growth, 2015

Change in real income in 2015 relative to baseline				
	Fixed productivity		Flexible productivity	
	US$ billions	Percent	US$ billions	Percent
High-income countries	202.0	0.6	261.0	0.8
Developing countries	86.0	0.8	200.0	2.0
Middle-income countries	70.0	0.8	145.0	1.8
Low-income countries	16.0	0.8	55.0	2.8
World total	287.0	0.7	461.0	1.1

Source: World Bank Simulations.

countries, the gains rise from 0.8 percent to 2.0 percent and from $86 billion to $200 billion. The main reason the dynamic gains are so much higher for developing countries is that their tariffs are considerably higher, thus the changes in trade structure will be greater. And even if agricultural distortions are high in rich countries, agriculture as a share of GDP is much lower; therefore the increase in productivity in agriculture has less impact, economy-wide, than in developing countries. Low-income countries gain the most on a percentage basis, because on average they have the highest tariff levels.

The dynamic gains are lower in relative terms compared to previous World Bank estimates (2001, 2003). Developing countries' gains are 2.3 times higher in the new estimates, compared with 3.2 times higher in previous estimates (World Bank 2001). There are two main reasons. The first is consistent with what has already been developed: The combination of lower base-year tariffs and incorporation of preferences and policy changes has lowered trade barriers from the levels estimated previously. One therefore anticipates fewer policy-driven changes in the export-to-output ratio and in the resulting changes in productivity. This is particularly true in agriculture, especially in China, from which a significant portion of the dynamic gains were coming. Those productivity gains are now captured in the baseline simulation. The second reason is because we have lowered from 0.75 to 0.5 the elasticity of productivity and trade openness in agriculture from the previous level.

Poverty impacts

The linkages between trade and poverty are complex. The theoretical aspects of those linkages are developed in detail in McCulloch and others (2001). Hertel and Winters (2005) contains an impressive number of country case studies. The simplest way to abstract the relationship is to derive the trade-induced change in GDP and then apply the so-called poverty elasticity to determine the change in the headcount index and then the number of poor. That operation assumes no change in the distribution of income. In previous World Bank estimates (2001, 2003), and in this note, we use a modified version of this simple approach. We equate the rise in the income of the poor to the food wage of unskilled workers—departing from the assumption of distribution neutrality. (Given the comparative advantage of developing countries in unskilled goods, unskilled wages usually will rise more than other factor prices.) We also take the price of food and clothing as the relevant price index for most households, because food and clothing are their main consumption items.

Under these assumptions, and given a baseline poverty forecast and income poverty elasticity, the number of poor living on $1 a day or less would drop by 32 million with global merchandise trade reform, compared to the baseline forecast of 622 million, or a global reduction of roughly 5 percent (table 3). For the $2 a day poverty line, the drop in the number of poor would be 66 million people, compared

Table 3. Poverty impacts under various scenarios

	GTAP6 baseline	Full reform	World Bank (2003) poverty baseline	With World Bank (2003) poverty baseline	Plus with World Bank (2003) change in real wage	Plus with World Bank (2003) poverty elasticity
Poverty headcount in 2015	(1)	(2)	(3)	(4)	(5)	(6)
			$1 a day measure			
Percent						
East Asia and Pacific	0.9	0.8	2.3	2	1.5	1.8
Europe and Central Asia	0.4	0.3	1.3	1.1	1.1	1.2
Latin America and the Caribbean	6.9	6.6	7.6	7.2	7.4	7.2
Middle East and North Africa	0.9	0.7	1.2	1	0.5	0.7
South Asia	12.8	12.5	16.4	15.9	15.6	15.3
Sub-Saharan Africa	38.4	36	42.3	39.7	38.8	34.5
Developing country total	10.2	9.7	12.5	11.8	11.4	10.8
Millions of people	Level	Change	Level	Change		
East Asia and Pacific	18.6	2.2	44.1	4.8	15.0	9.7
Europe and Central Asia	1.7	0.2	5.9	0.7	0.9	0.5
Latin America and the Caribbean	42.9	2.1	45.9	2.2	1.4	2.4
Middle East and North Africa	3.5	0.7	4.3	0.8	2.7	1.9
South Asia	215.9	5.6	267.8	7.0	12.7	17.3
Sub-Saharan Africa	339.5	21.1	365.7	22.7	30.1	67.7
Developing-country total	622.0	31.9	733.8	38.2	62.7	99.4
Poverty headcount in 2015			$2 a day measure			
Percent						
East Asia and Pacific	11.3	10.1	18.2	16.3	12.2	14.2
Europe and Central Asia	5.2	4.8	10.3	9.5	9.4	9.4
Latin America and the Caribbean	19.6	19.0	20.5	19.8	20.1	19.4
Middle East and North Africa	11.9	10.4	10.2	8.9	5.8	5.8
South Asia	54.2	53.6	59.2	58.6	58.1	55.4
Sub-Saharan Africa	69.2	66.9	70.7	68.3	67.6	57.6
Developing-country total	32.0	30.9	36.4	35.0	33.3	31.6
Millions of people	Level	Change	Level	Change		
East Asia and Pacific	229.8	23.6	354.2	36.4	115.2	77.7
Europe and Central Asia	24.7	1.8	47.6	3.5	4.1	4.0
Latin America and the Caribbean	121.8	4.1	124.0	4.2	2.6	6.4
Middle East and North Africa	45.7	6.0	37.7	4.9	16.2	16.3
South Asia	912.2	9.6	968.3	10.2	18.6	62.5
Sub-Saharan Africa	612.2	20.4	611.8	20.4	27.1	113.3
Developing-country total	1946.3	65.6	2143.6	79.7	183.7	280.2

Note: Column (1) represents the most recent poverty baseline for 2015. Column (2) represents the impact of global reform on poverty—in levels for the headcount index, and as a change in the number of poor in millions. For example, the total headcount index falls from 10.2% in the baseline to 9.7% after the reform. This translates into 32 million fewer persons living under the $1 a day poverty line. Column (3) represents an earlier baseline forecast (World Bank 2003). Columns (4) through (6) show the changes in poverty from global reform under various assumptions: (4) using the previous poverty forecast; (5) using the previous poverty forecast and the previous change in the real wage; and (6) using the previous poverty forecast and the previous change in the real wage and a uniform poverty elasticity of 2.

Source: World Bank Simulations.

to a baseline forecast of nearly 2 billion people, a decline of 3.4 percent.

These estimates are significantly below similar estimates generated two years ago (World Bank 2003). Table 3 attempts to reconcile the new estimates with the old.

A first key difference is the change in the baseline poverty forecast. This can be seen by comparing column (3)—the old forecast—with column (1), the current forecast. The $1 a day poverty forecast for 2015 is down by more than 100 million persons, largely because of a revision to the forecasted headcount index, with relatively sharp declines across all regions.[15] Global trade reform applied to the poverty forecast contained in World Bank (2003) would accentuate, modestly, the decline in the number of poor (column 4)—for example to 38 million instead of 32 million for the $1 a day indicator, with the largest absolute change in the East Asia and Pacific region.

The second key difference comes from the impact of the shock on the food wage. Given the change in the dataset—notably the incorporation of preferences and policy commitments—the change in the food wage under the new dataset and baseline is smaller than with the previous results.[16] Using the change in the food wage from the previous reports, the change in the $1 a day number of poor from full reform would be 63 million, not 38 million; and 184 million versus 80 million for the $2 /day indicator.

In the new estimate, we use a revised and region-specific set of income-poverty elasticities. In previous reports, we used a uniform world average[17]—initially for lack of better information. The regional $1/day poverty elasticities are more varied, ranging from around 0.9 for Sub-Saharan Africa to over 3 for East Asia. For $2/day, the global elasticity is less than 2, and the range is from 0.5 in Sub-Saharan Africa to 2.0 in East Asia. Column (6) shows the impact of using a uniform elasticity of 2 rather than the region-specific elasticities. For the $1/day poverty line, the number of poor lifted out of poverty by global trade reform would rise to nearly 100 million.

Of the three changes in the new poverty-impact estimate, the single most important—at the global level—is the change to region-specific elasticities, followed by the change to the impact on the food wage, with the change in the poverty forecast playing only a modest role. The change to region-specific elasticities is particularly important in the context of a dynamic scenario. Given that poverty will be reduced significantly in East Asia, where the income-poverty elasticity is also highest, the average poverty elasticity—weighted by the number of poor—is declining over time as the number of poor becomes more concentrated in low-elasticity regions.

This also raises the important relevance of the time dimension in modeling trade reform. The poverty impacts will depend crucially on assumptions about the baseline level of poverty. If, for example, a comparative static model is used, and the changes to poverty are calculated relative to the base-year level of poverty—say 2001—then the number of poor lifted out of poverty will be much higher than in a realistic forward-looking scenario, where the number of poor in many regions will be much lower in the baseline. In the case of China, using the base year poverty level would imply a reduction of the number of poor of 14.4 million, versus only 1.2 million in our standard forward-looking forecast.

Comparison with GTAP-based models

One of the most widely used models for trade policy analysis is the one developed and supported by GTAP and known as the GTAP model.[18] In many respects it is quite similar to the Bank's LINKAGE model. Most studies using the GTAP model implement the model in comparative static mode, in which there is no time dimension and typically all factor stocks are maintained at their base-year levels. A policy shock involves perturbing one or more policy instruments, re-solving for the new equilibrium, and then comparing the results of the policy simulation with the baseline data. (The baseline data may include a so-called presimulation shock, such as China's WTO accession commitments.)

Model parameters are typically chosen to reflect some medium- or long-term horizon. For example, capital mobility may be fairly restricted for a medium-term horizon, but fairly free if the analyst has a longer-term horizon in mind, that is, one where adjustments have time to work themselves out.

In order to compare LINKAGE and GTAP model results, we must simulate LINKAGE as a comparative static model. This has two effects. First, the dollar-based results will be smaller because they will reflect the economy of 2001 and not that of a projected 2015. Second, the results will tend to be smaller because dynamic effects are ignored. The comparative static simulation is run with different sets of parameters to show the influence of those parameters and to converge toward a behavioral model that is close to the GTAP model.

The model runs test the influence of two key sets of parameters. The first are the Armington parameters, which measure the degree of substitution between domestic goods and imports. The second set reflects the degree of mobility of land. The standard LINKAGE model uses its own set of Armington trade elasticities that have evolved over time based on previous studies, but that have been more or less constant over the last few years (and in recent World Bank estimates). Those elasticities are in the mid-to-high range of those used in global models—between 4 and 6. GTAP has revised its Armington elasticities upward—they had been in the 2–4 range. The new estimates are based on more recent econometric evidence and are closer to the LINKAGE elasticities.[19] The LINKAGE elasticities are still higher—an average of 35 percent overall. All else equal, this will raise the gains from global reform relative to the GTAP model.

On land mobility, GTAP assumes a relatively low degree of land transformation.[20] GTAP has a transformation elasticity of 1, whereas the default assumption in LINKAGE is perfect mobility. LINKAGE moreover allows the overall land supply to fluctuate with land prices—with low supply elasticities for countries with land constraints.

We first scale back the dynamic gains to the 2001 base year to make comparisons easier. The so-called static gain of $287 billion in 2015—from the standard dynamic scenario—is equivalent to $156 billion relative to the 2001 economy.[21] The regional impacts will not add up to the global because the regions are growing at different rates in the baseline. The second column of table 4 shows the impact of global merchandise trade reform in a pure comparative static framework, but using the standard LINKAGE elasticities. A comparison of columns 1 and 2 provides an assessment of the static dynamic gains. Essentially, these come from two sources. The first is the increase in savings and investment generated by higher growth and a reduction in the price of capital goods (from the elimination of tariffs), which combine to raise the capital stock and therefore contribute to the dynamic gains. The second effect comes from the nature of the dynamic baseline itself. The baseline has countries growing at different rates, assumes an increase in the trade-to-GDP ratio, and incorporates other structural changes that would tend to increase the gains from trade reform over time, particularly for developing countries, where the comparative static gains are considerably lower than the static dynamic gains.

The impact of using the GTAP trade elasticities is shown in the third column of table 4. Given that these are lower than the standard LINKAGE elasticities, one would anticipate a decline in the gains from global trade reform. The global gains are about 30 percent lower, but the gains to developing countries are lower by 55 percent. Lowering land mobility, in addition to the lower Armington elasticities in column 4, eviscerates the gains to developing countries, with three of the six regional aggregates

Table 4. Global merchandise trade reform in a comparative static framework

	Scaled dynamics (1)	Comparative static (2)	GTAP trade elasticities (3)	+GTAP land elasticity (4)
High-income countries	109.8	103.7	77.9	75.8
Developing countries	43.9	23.7	10.6	2.0
East Asia and Pacific	9.4	6.9	3.7	0.6
South Asia	2.2	−1.2	−2.1	−1.5
Europe and Central Asia	3.5	3.9	2.3	1.9
Middle East and North Africa	8.1	3.8	2.2	1.6
Sub-Saharan Africa	2.8	0.7	0.2	−0.1
Latin America and the Caribbean	17.9	8.1	4.0	−0.5
World	156.4	127.4	88.5	77.8

Source: World Bank simulations.

showing losses. Reducing land flexibility lowers the ability of some of the developing regions to respond to new agricultural market opportunities—particularly Sub-Saharan Africa and Latin America.

Conclusions

This note describes some of the key changes to the World Bank's assessment of global merchandise trade reform over the last year and compares those changes with earlier assessments. Our assessment of the gains from global merchandise trade reform—global and regionally—are lower now for two main reasons:

1) Adoption of a new base year incorporating reforms between 1997 and 2001.
2) The baseline scenario now accounts for the use of trade preferences and for significant policy reforms—notably, elimination of the apparel and textile quotas and China's WTO accession commitments.

These two factors have different effects across developing countries. The incorporation of preferences lowers the estimate of overall gains from global reform for countries in Sub-Saharan Africa and other low-income countries, whereas incorporation of policy reforms in the baseline largely reduces estimated gains to China.

Perhaps inevitably, the focal point of trade analysis has been the so-called welfare gain (or gain in real income). But therein lies a frustration, since so many other factors are changing—most of which have more policy relevance than the overall gains. For example, identifying who wins and who loses will drive the political dynamics of trade

Table A1. Average tariffs—GTAP5 versus GTAP6

Percent

	Agriculture and food		Textile and clothing		Other industry		Total merchandise trade	
	GTAP5	GTAP6	GTAP5	GTAP6	GTAP5	GTAP6	GTAP5	GTAP6
World average	**27.2**	**16.7**	**12.8**	**10.2**	**5.5**	**4.2**	**7.5**	**5.2**
High-income	26.6	16.0	10.1	7.5	2.9	1.9	4.8	2.9
Australia, Canada, New Zealand	15.9	7.4	13.1	10.7	2.2	1.9	3.0	2.3
United States	10.8	2.4	11.2	9.8	2.4	1.8	2.9	1.8
European Union	22.4	13.9	10.4	5.2	4.2	2.2	6.0	3.2
Japan	50.3	29.4	11.6	9.7	1.6	1.4	9.2	5.2
Korea and Taiwan	49.4	55.0	7.6	9.2	5.7	4.1	8.8	7.6
Developing countries	28.1	17.7	18.5	17.0	10.6	9.0	12.5	9.9
East Asia and Pacific	27.8	26.3	22.7	17.8	10.9	9.3	12.2	10.5
China	38.8	37.6	24.1	19.4	13.8	12.1	15.6	13.6
South Asia	24.4	33.9	29.5	20.1	24.9	22.0	24.8	23.5
India	25.9	50.3	29.2	26.6	21.7	25.6	22.0	28.1
Europe and Central Asia	18.5	14.8	12.7	10.7	7.4	4.8	8.8	6.0
Middle East & North Africa	61.0	14.1	20.2	27.1	10.9	9.1	18.2	9.8
Sub-Saharan Africa	27.5	18.2	23.7	23.7	13.1	11.6	14.7	12.6
Latin America and Caribbean	16.2	10.3	14.5	11.3	9.7	7.5	10.3	7.7

Note: Averages are weighted using import shares. EU average excludes intra-EU trade.

reform more than the overall income gain.[22] Digging deep into the model results to elucidate the key mechanisms behind the gains and losses, undertaking sensitivity analysis to test the robustness of the conclusions to key assumptions, and comparing results across models will increase our appreciation of the importance of trade reform and improve the credibility of these modeling exercises. Notwithstanding their limitations, this class of models has become an important part of the analysis of global policy issues, with trade policy foremost among them.

Notes

1. For example, the changing net trade position of Sub-Saharan Africa.

2. By ignoring preferences, for example.

3. Lump-sum taxation to replace lost tariff revenues is considered to be distortion-free, but it is not a realistic option in most countries. There will be additional costs to alternative fiscal measures.

4. Prohibitive tariffs typically mean that initial trade shares are zero. Most models cannot create market shares if the shares are zero initially.

5. The model's specification is provided in van der Mensbrugghe (2005).

6. See www.gtap.org.

7. Input–output tables do not exist for the composite regions. They are assigned proto-typical economic structures scaled to the published national accounts. The trade data accurately reflects the information from COMTRADE.

8. There are also valuation changes, because all national data is converted to a single currency, the U.S. dollar.

9. See Bouët and others (2004) for more information.

10. The only change was the household direct tax rate, which evolved to maintain a fixed fiscal deficit. Public expenditures are assumed to grow at the same rate as GDP in the baseline.

11. The textile and clothing quotas are implemented using export-tax equivalents. These introduce a price wedge between the producer price in the source country and the consumer price in the destination country. However, unlike an import tariff, the revenue accrues to the exporting country. The wedges have been calibrated to existing information on the price of auctioned quotas.

12. A brief note on terminology: comparative static gains are the gains from global reform based on the static base-year structure of the economy, i.e. 2001 in the case of GTAP6. The 'static' dynamic gains are based on a dynamic baseline, in the present case through 2015, which incorporates changes in the structure of the global economy over a 14-year period. Among other things, the global economy will be much larger (50 percent if it grows on average by 3 percent per annum). We call these 'static' dynamic gains because there is no influence of the reforms on productivity. Finally, the 'dynamic' gains arise from allowing for a linkage between the reforms and productivity

13. For example, if productivity in a given sector is 2 percent in the baseline and the export-to-output ratio increases by 10 percent in that sector, then sectoral productivity will increase to 2.08, an elasticity of 0.4, because only 40 percent of sectoral productivity is linked to openness.

14. The agricultural elasticity is lower than in previous studies. Because the existing empirical evidence relates to manufacturing, we have made a modest assumption in agriculture by halving the elasticity.

15. The poverty forecast relies on two main elements. The first is the long-term economic forecast. This has not changed appreciably over the last few years, although better-than-

expected performance between 2001 and 2005 has led to some upward revision. The second is the estimate of the income poverty elasticity. This is constantly evolving as new household surveys become available and the methodology is improved.

16. Both the unweighted and population-weighted average change is about 50 percent.

17. The standard estimate at the world level is an elasticity of 2; that is, for each percentage-point increase in developing-country income, the headcount index declines by 2 percent.

18. See Hertel (1997) for more details.

19. We considered moving to the new GTAP elasticities but decided against doing so for two reasons. First, the new GTAP elasticities were close enough to the standard LINKAGE elasticities. Therefore, the advantage of comparability of results over time and across LINKAGE model simulations outweighed the advantages of using a new set of econometrically estimated parameters. Second, the ranking of some of the new GTAP elasticities were puzzling and raised questions about the robustness of the estimates. For example, sugar and oil seeds have a lower substitution elasticity than other crops or clothing.

20. Both models use a constant-elasticity-of-transformation function to allocate aggregate land across sectors based on relative returns to land.

21. I.e. apply the percentage gain in 2015 to the level of global GDP in 2001.

22. See for example Anderson and others (2005).

References

Anderson, Kym, Will Martin, and Dominique van der Mensbrugghe. 2005. "Market and Welfare Implications of Doha Reform Scenarios." In *Agricultural Trade Reform and the Doha Development Agenda*, ed. Kym Anderson and Will Martin. New York and Washington, DC: Palgrave Macmillan and World Bank.

Bouët, Antoine, Yvan Decreux, Lionel Fontagné, Sébastien Jean, and David Laborde. 2004. "A Consistent, *Ad Valorem* Equivalent Measure of Applied Protection across the World: The MAcMap–HS6 database." *CEPII Working Paper* 2004-22, Centre d'Etudes Prospectives et d'Informations Internationales, Paris. December.

Hertel, Thomas W. (ed.). 1997. *Global Trade Analysis: Modeling and Applications.* Cambridge: Cambridge University Press.

Hertel, Thomas W., and L. Alan Winters (eds.). 2005. *Putting Development Back into the Doha Agenda: Poverty Impacts of a WTO Agreement.* Washington, DC: World Bank.

McCulloch, Neil, L. Alan Winters, and Xavier Cirera. 2001. *Trade Liberalization and Poverty: A Handbook.* Centre for Economic Policy Research, London, UK.

van der Mensbrugghe, Dominique. 2005. "LINKAGE Technical Reference Document: Version 6.0." Unpublished paper. Development Prospects Group, World Bank, Washington, DC.

World Bank. 2002. *Global Economic Prospects and the Developing Countries 2002: Making Trade Work for the Poor.* Washington, DC: World Bank.

_____. 2004. *Global Economic Prospects: Realizing the Development Promise of the Doha Agenda.* Washington, DC: World Bank.

_____. 2005. *Global Economic Prospects: Trade, Regionalism, and Development*, World Bank, Washington, DC.

Agriculture: The Key to Success of the Doha Round

Kym Anderson and Will Martin

Agriculture accounts for almost two-thirds of the economic gains that could be obtained by dismantling the present global system of merchandise trade barriers and farm subsidies. This truth holds for the world as a whole and for developing countries as a group. Developing countries are therefore right to focus on agriculture in the Doha Round negotiations.[1]

To date, the agricultural policies of developed countries have captured most of the attention. That is understandable, as many developing countries believe that they were shortchanged in the Uruguay Round and are determined to obtain greater concessions from developed countries before liberalizing their own markets. However, our modeling suggests that over half of the gains to developing countries from global agricultural reforms would come from liberalization by developing countries themselves (table 1). This is true for two reasons: first, because agricultural tariffs are slightly higher in developing than developed countries (18 percent compared with 16 percent on average in 2001) and, second, because a growing share of developing country trade is now with other developing countries.

The three pillars

Developing countries—among them the G-20—are emphasizing the need for cuts to agricultural subsidies in the developed world, partly because they think that is the main distortion[2] but also because they do not want to lower their own food import restrictions. But the focus on subsidies alone is misplaced. Our modeling results indicate that 93 percent of the welfare gains from removing global distortions to agricultural incentives would come from reducing import tariffs. Just 2 percent of distortion is due to export subsidies and 5 percent to domestic support measures (table 2). It is certainly important to discipline domestic subsidies and to phase out export subsidies, both to prevent redirection of assistance from tariffs toward domestic subsidies and to bring agriculture into line with non-farm trade in not using export subsidies. But to ignore market access in the Doha Round would be to forgo most of the potential gains from trade reform.

The current Doha Round has the advantage of beginning from the framework of rules and disciplines agreed in the Uruguay Round Agreement on Agriculture, in particular, the three clearly identified "pillars" of market access, export subsidies, and domestic support. True, negotiators took more than three years to agree on a framework for the current talks, reached at the end of July 2004, but that agreement now is likely to guide the negotiations for some time. It therefore provides a strong

Table 1. Effects on developing country economic welfare of full trade liberalization by groups of countries and products, 2015 (percent)

	From full liberalization of:			
	Agriculture and food	Textiles and clothing	Other manufactures	All goods
Percentage due to:				
Developed country policies	30	17	3	50
Developing countries' policies	33	10	7	50
All countries' policies	63	27	10	100

Note: Developed countries include the transition economies that joined the European Union in April 2004. The definition of developing countries used here is that adopted by the WTO. Thus it includes the four East Asian tigers: Hong Kong (China), Korea, Rep., Singapore, and Taiwan (China).
Source: Anderson and Martin (2005, Table 4).

basis for undertaking *ex ante* analysis of various options potentially available to WTO members during the Doha negotiations.

Pondering what might be achievable under a Doha partial reform package, it is clear that the devil will be in the details. For example, commitments on domestic support for farmers are currently so much higher than actual support levels that the 20 percent cut in the total bound aggregate measure of support (AMS), promised in the July 2004 Framework Agreement will require no actual reductions in support by any World Trade Organization (WTO) member. A cut of 75 percent in bound AMS levels would be needed to get some action from those countries that provide the most domestic support; and even such a cut would produce reductions in 2001 levels of domestic support by only four WTO actors: the United States (28 percent), European Union (18 percent), Norway (16 percent), and Australia (10 percent). Because the European Union and Australia have already introduced reforms, they might not need to make further reductions even with a 75 percent cut in bound levels.

Large cuts in bound rates also are needed to erase substantial binding overhang in agricultural tariffs. The average bound rate in developed countries is almost twice as high as the average applied rate, and in developing countries the ratio is even greater (table 3). Thus large reductions in bound rates are needed before it is possible to bring about *any* improvements in market access. To bring down the average actual agricultural tariff by one-third, bound rates would have to be reduced for developed countries by at least 45 percent, and by up to 75 percent for the highest tariffs, under a tiered formula.

Even large cuts in bound tariffs do little if "sensitive products" are exempted. If members succumb to the political temptation to put limits on tariff cuts for the most sensitive farm products, much of the prospective gain from Doha could evaporate. Even if only 2 percent of agricultural tariff lines (in the 6-digit harmonized classification, HS6, with around 800 lines for agriculture and food) in developed countries are classified as sensitive (and 4 percent in developing countries, to incorporate their "special products" demand), and are thereby subject to just a 15 percent tariff cut (as a substitute for the tariff rate quota (TRQ) expansion mentioned in the Framework Agreement), the welfare gains from global agricultural reform would shrink by three-quarters. If at the same time bound tariffs in excess of 200 percent had to be reduced to that cap rate of 200 percent, welfare gains would shrink by one-third.

Given the high binding overhang of developing countries, relatively few countries would have to cut their actual tariffs and subsidies at all, even if tiered formulae were used to make the greatest cuts in the highest bindings. That is even more true if "special products" are subjected to smaller cuts. Politically binding overhang makes it easier for developing and least developed countries to offer big cuts on bound rates.

Combining agricultural and nonagricultural market access

Expanding nonagricultural market access would add substantially to the gains from agricultural reform .Adding a 50 percent cut to nonagricultural tariffs by developed countries (and 33 percent by developing countries and zero by least developed countries (LDCs)) to the tiered formula cut in agricultural tariffs would double the gains from Doha for developing countries. That would bring the global gains to $96 billion from Doha merchandise liberalization, roughly one-third of the potential welfare gains from full liberalization ($287 billion).

These absolute numbers undoubtedly underestimate the actual magnitudes of prospective benefits. First, merchandise trade liberalization opens domestic markets to new competition and improved technology. This, together with scale effects

Table 2. Distribution of global welfare effects of removing all agricultural tariffs and subsidies, 2001 (percent)

Agricultural liberalization component	Beneficiary region		
	High-income[a] countries	Developing countries	World
Import market access	66	27	93
Export subsidies	5	−3	2
Domestic support	4	1	5
All measures	75	25	100

[a] High-income countries include the newly industrialized East Asian economies of Hong Kong (China), Korea, Rep., Singapore, and Taiwan (China) as well as the transition economies that joined the European Union in April 2004.
Source: Anderson and Martin (2005, Table 5); Anderson, Martin and Valenzuela (2005).

Table 3. Agricultural weighted average import tariffs, by region, 2001 (percent, ad valorem equivalent, weights based on imports)

	Bound tariff	Applied tariff[a]
Developed countries[b]	27	14
Developing countries	48	21
of which: LDCs	78	13
World	37	17

a. Includes preferences and in-quota Trade Rate Quota (TRQ) rates where relevant, as well as the ad valorem equivalent of specific tariffs.
b. Developed countries include the transition economies that joined the European Union in May 2004. The definition of developing countries used here is that adopted by the WTO. Thus it includes the four East Asian tigers: Hong Kong (China), Korea, Rep., Singapore, and Taiwan (China).
Source: Anderson and Martin (2005, Table 2).

from specialization, tends to increase productivity. These dynamic productivity effects can multiply the gains several times. Second, our calculations assume that preferences in regional and other preferential trading arrangements are fully utilized, and that developing countries have access at the listed rates. Detailed analysis shows that this is rarely the case. Brenton (2003), for example, found that much eligible trade does not take advantage of preferential access, probably because of onerous rules of origin obligations or quantitative limits built into the schemes. Because our modeling cannot take this underutilization into account, it overstates the degree of liberalization in the base year and thus understates the effects of further most-favored-nation (MFN) liberalization. Third, the analysis here considers only merchandise trade effects and does not incorporate effects of distortions in services trade. With services negotiations proceeding fitfully, the amount of new liberalization may prove to be minimal. Nonetheless, services liberalization has a powerful growth effect (Mattoo and others 2001), which is not included in our calculations. Working in the opposite direction is the fact that benefits are not as automatic as the models assume because real-world constraints on supply response may impede exporters in developing countries from taking advantage of new opportunities. Nonetheless, the weight of the foregoing considerations, taken together, suggests that the absolute benefit of Doha merchandise liberalization is likely to be larger than the $96 billion in our calculations.

Tracing the gains

Within the developing world, most of the gains from the comprehensive Doha scenario go to large countries, notably Argentina, Brazil, others in Latin America, India, Thailand, South Africa, and others in southern Africa. The rest of Sub-Saharan Africa gains when nonagricultural market access is expanded—especially when developing countries participate as full partners in the negotiations and offer substantial reductions in their own rates of protection. An important part of this result stems from increases in market access—on a nondiscriminatory basis—by other developing countries.

Some least developed countries in Sub-Saharan Africa and elsewhere may be slight losers in our static Doha simulations when developed countries cut their tariffs and those LDCs choose not to reform. Their losses result from deterioration in their terms of trade because of erosion of tariff preferences affecting their exports or, if they are net food importers, because they would face higher prices on imports of temperate foods. Our simulations overstate the benefits of tariff preferences for LDCs, however, since they ignore the trade-dampening effect of complex rules of origin and the grabbing of much of the rents from preferences by developed country importers. But even if they continued to be losers after correcting for those realities, it remains true that preference-receiving countries could be compensated for preference erosion through increased aid at relatively small cost to current preference providers. In the process, other developing countries currently hurt by LDC preferences would enjoy greater access to the markets of reforming developed countries.

What is to be done?

Several clear implications for the Doha Round follow from this analysis. First, in addition to outlawing agricultural export subsidies, domestic support bindings must be cut very substantially to reduce binding overhang. In so doing, the countries with the highest subsidies, namely the European Union and the United States, need to reduce their support, not just for the sake of their own economies but also to encourage developing countries to reciprocate by opening their markets as a *quid pro quo*. An initial cut of 20 percent would be nothing more than a start in eliminating the overhang.

Second, agricultural tariff bindings must be cut very deeply to allow some genuine market opening to occur. Getting rid of the tariff binding overhang that resulted from the "dirty tariffication" of the Uruguay Round should be the first priority, but more than that is needed if market access is to expand. Exempting even just a few "sensitive" and "special" products is undesirable, as it would greatly reduce the gains from reform and tend to divert resources into, instead of away from, enterprises in which countries have their least comparative advantage. If it turns out to be politically impossible not to designate some products as sensitive or special, it would be crucial to impose a cap such that for any product with a bound tariff in excess of, say, 100 percent, that tariff would have to be reduced to the cap rate.

Third, it is essential to expand nonagricultural market access while reforming agriculture. A balanced exchange of concessions is impossible without adding other sectors. With other merchandise included, moreover, trade expansion would be four times greater for both rich and poor countries—and poverty in low-income countries would be reduced considerably.

And fourth, *developing countries have to contribute to the round*, particularly through South–South "concessions." Since developing countries are trading so much more with each other now, they are the major beneficiaries of reforms within their own regions. Upper-middle-income countries might consider giving least developed countries duty-free access to their markets (mirroring the recent initiatives of developed countries) or, even better, making MFN tariff reductions. Even least developed countries should consider reducing their tariff binding overhang, since doing so gives them more scope to demand "concessions" (or compensation for preference erosion and other factors affecting their terms of trade) from richer countries, without requiring them to cut their own applied tariffs very much.

Conclusion

The good news is that there is a great deal to be gained from liberalizing merchandise trade—especially agricultural trade—under Doha, with a disproportionately high share of that potential gain (relative to their share of the global economy) available to developing countries. To realize that gain, significant reform in agriculture is required. However, the political sensitivity of farm support programs, coupled with the complexities of the measures introduced in the Uruguay Round Agreement on Agriculture and of the modalities set out in the Doha Framework Agreement of July 2004, ensure that the details of the final Doha agreement will be important and hotly contested. To realize more of their potential gains from trade, developing and least developed countries will need to participate fully in trade reforms, as well as adopt complementary domestic reforms and invest more in trade facilitation. High-income countries could encourage them to take the necessary steps by opening up their own markets to developing country exports and by providing more targeted aid.

To that end, The World Bank and IMF have advanced a new proposal to reward developing country commitments to trade reform by expanding trade-facilitating aid through the Integrated Framework, now operated by a consortium of international agencies for least developed countries (see chapter on Aid for Trade in this volume). This proposal, which was endorsed at the IMF and World Bank Annual Meeting in late September 2005 may provide an attractive path for developing countries seeking to trade their way out of poverty, not least because it would dampen the tendency of expanded aid to provoke a rise in the real exchange rate. It also offers a far more efficient way for developed countries to assist low-income countries than the current systems of tariff preferences.

Notes

1. This note is based on the authors' article in the September 2005 issue of *The World Economy* and on *Agricultural Trade and the Doha Development Agenda*, edited by the authors, published by Palgrave Macmillan and the World Bank in November 2005. It was prepared by Lead Economists, Kym Anderson and Will Martin in the Development Research Group of the World Bank. The authors are grateful for the collaboration of numerous colleagues, especially Dominique van .der Mensbrugghe and Tom Hertel, and for research funding from the UK Department for International Development.
2. For an explanation of why there is so much confusion over the importance of subsidies versus barriers to imports, see Anderson, Martin and Valenzuela (2005).

References

Anderson, K., and W. Martin. 2005. "Agricultural Trade Reform and the Doha Development Agenda." Policy Research Working Paper 3607, World Bank, Washington, DC. May. And in *The World Economy* 28:9:1301-27 (September 2005).

Anderson, K., W. Martin and E. Valenzuela. 2005. "On the Relative (Un-) Importance of Agricultural Subsidies versus Market Access in WTO's Doha Round. Mimeo. World Bank, Washington, DC.

Brenton, P. 2003. "Rules of Origin in Free Trade Agreements." Trade Note 4, Development ' Economics Department, World Bank, Washington, DC. http://www.worldbank.org/trade/

Hoekman, B., and S. Prowse. 2005. "Development and the WTO: Beyond Business as Usual." *Bridges* no. 2–3 (February–March), International Centre for Trade and Sustainable Development, Geneva.

Mattoo, A., R. Rahindran, and A. Subramanian. 2001. "Measuring Services Trade Liberalization and Its Impact on Economic Growth: An Illustration." Policy Research Working Paper 2655, World Bank, Washington, DC.

Further Reading

Anderson, K., W. Martin, and D. van der Mensbrugghe. 2005. "Would Multilateral Trade Reform Benefit Sub-Saharan Africa?" Policy Research Working Paper 3616, World Bank, Washington, DC. July. And in the Journal of African Economies 15 (forthcoming 2006).

Market Access Barriers in Agriculture and Options for Reform

Kym Anderson, Harry de Gorter and Will Martin

Agricultural protection and subsidies account for about two-thirds of the trade distortion caused by government policies. And most of the distortion traceable to agricultural policies is generated by import barriers. For that reason, negotiating wider market access in agriculture is critical to the success of the Doha Round.[1]

The World Trade Organization (WTO) Agriculture Framework Agreement of July 2004 calls for significant tariff cuts using a tiered formula that imposes larger percentage cuts in higher tariffs. (See table 1 for a summary of all of the provisions.) This proposed approach is a vast improvement over the average-cut formula applied in the Uruguay Round Agreement on Agriculture, which allows countries to meet their commitments through large proportional reductions in tariffs that were already low and small reductions in high tariffs.

The new formula still will require substantial cuts in tariffs before meaningful trade liberalization is realized. This is because of the prevalence in agriculture of tariff peaks (a small number of tariff lines protect the bulk of domestic production), binding "overhang" (bound tariffs are above applied tariffs), "water" in the tariff (tariff reductions initially have no impact), and tariff escalation (higher tariffs on processed raw materials). Furthermore, the Framework Agreement contains a Sensitive Product designation that would allow some commodities to escape the full extent of tariff cuts in exchange for an expansion of tariff rate quotas (TRQs).

A fundamental requirement for success in any trade negotiation is balance between flexibility and discipline. There must be enough flexibility to accommodate the unique needs of each member, and enough discipline to yield the gains in export market opportunities that are the *raison d'être* of trade negotiations. The tiered formula appears to strike a balance between discipline and flexibility by creating bands that allow for progressive tariff cuts. But Sensitive Products may introduce flexibility at the cost of the discipline needed to widen market access. The level of trade liberalization realized, therefore, will depend critically on *key details*, such as the level of tariff cuts in each tier, the maximum tariff level to be negotiated, reductions in tariff escalation, and the requirement for an overall cut in average tariffs.

This note analyzes these issues and lays out some options for meaningful trade liberalization, consistent with the language and provisions outlined in the Framework Agreement.

Table 1. Summary of the market access provisions of the WTO Framework Agreement on Agriculture

Tariff cuts	•Substantial improvement in market access through tariff reductions from bound rates. •Single approach for all countries: tiered formula to ensure progressivity. Types of commitments within bands and number of bands to be negotiated. •Role of a tariff cap to be evaluated. •Designation of an "appropriate number" of sensitive products, which would be subject to a mix of tariff cuts and TRQ expansion.
Tariff rate quotas	•Reduce in-quota tariffs and improve administration (as part of balance of concessions). •Some TRQ expansion for all sensitive products.
Safeguards	•Future of special agricultural safeguard (SSG) under negotiation. •Establish new special safeguard mechanism (SSM) for developing countries.
Special and differential treatment for developing countries	•Proportionately less tariff reductions for developing countries, with longer implementation period. •Developing countries may designate special products on criteria of "food and livelihood security," which would be subject to more flexible treatment. •Fullest possible liberalization of trade in tropical products and alternatives to illicit narcotic crops by developed countries.
Other	•Tariff escalation reduced by formula to be agreed upon. •Erosion of preferences to be addressed using Harbinson paragraph 16 as reference.

Source: Josling (2005).

Background

Although developing countries have almost doubled their share of world trade in manufactures over the last two decades, their share in agricultural trade has remained about 30 percent. During the 1990s, the growth of developing-country agricultural exports to industrial countries slowed as exports to other developing countries accelerated. Today's middle-income countries have managed to increase their global market share, principally by entering other developing countries' markets and by aggressively diversifying into nontraditional exports, such as seafood products, fruits, vegetables, cut flowers, and processed foods. Growth of these nontraditional exports, which generally have low protection, has outpaced growth of traditional commodities by three to one (figure 1). Meanwhile, many low-income countries have had less success; their share of world agricultural trade has declined.

These trade patterns reflect the structure of global protection. Although the conversion of nontariff barriers to tariffs during the Uruguay Round was an important step forward, import protection in agriculture remains high, nontransparent, and antidevelopment. Average agricultural tariffs remain much higher than manufacturing tariffs, which average less than 4 percent and are about 10 percent of what they were 60 years ago. The average agricultural tariff is 62 percent, by contrast, with high variation among countries and commodities. In addition, about 50 percent of domestic production in countries belonging to the Organization for Economic

Cooperation and Development (OECD) is protected by TRQs. Studies show that preferences to developing countries barely begin to compensate for these high levels of protection (Brenton and Ikezuki 2005).

Widespread use of specific tariffs in developed countries (which make up two-thirds of their agricultural tariffs) obscure actual levels of protection, because specific duties are generally higher than the simpler and more transparent *ad valorem* tariffs that are generally used in developing countries (figure 2). The use of specific tariffs causes a bias against developing countries because it results in higher tariffs on lower-priced imports. Even more important are the cyclical implications of such tariff structures: as world price go down, specific tariffs go up when expressed in percentage terms. While conversion of specific tariffs into *ad valorem* form would be desirable in principle, it would raise many of the dangers that emerged in the conversion of nontariff barriers into tariffs during the Uruguay Round. To avoid another round of "dirty tariffication" through large, covert increases in protection, it will be important during the conversion of specific tariffs to include in the modalities governing the negotiations a provision to ensure that a transparent approach is followed (similar to paragraph 9 of the Harbinson Draft).[2]

Figure 1. Developing country exports have surged in nontraditional products with low protection

Composition of developing countries exports, percent

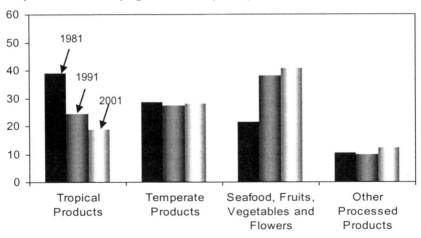

Note: Tropical products: coffee, cocoa, tea, nuts, spices, textile fibers, sugar and confectionery. Temperate products: meats, milk, dairy, grains, animal feed, edible oil, and oil seeds. Other processed products include: tobacco and cigarettes, alcoholic and nonalcoholic beverages, and other processed food.
Source: World Bank 2003.

Figure 2. Specific duties hide high protection

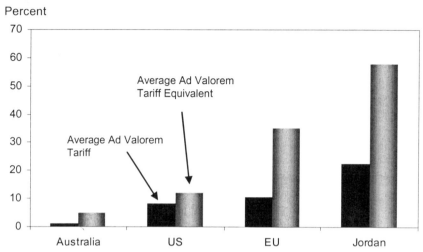

Source: World Bank 2003.

Tariffs are typically higher for processed raw materials (figure 3). By discouraging diversification into value-added and processed products—areas in which trade is expanding rapidly—such escalation punishes investors in developing countries who seek to add value to production for export. It also helps account for developing countries' generally poor penetration of developed-country markets in processed foods.

Two other key features of agricultural tariffs are the large difference between bound and applied rates and their extremely high peaks. The first feature, known as "binding overhang" (figure 4), means that a larger reduction in bound rates must be made before applied rates change. High peaks result in large differences between average rates and maximum tariff rates (called "tariff dispersion") in developed countries (table 2), compared with developing countries, which are characterized by low tariff dispersion. Developing countries have higher average agricultural tariffs than industrial countries, but the level of protection in developed countries is higher than average tariffs (figure 5) because of the prevalence of tariff peaks: just a few tariff lines protect most of domestic production in high-income countries. One consequence of those peaks is that most of the economic welfare cost of global agricultural distortions is accounted for by a small number of commodities. Rice and beef alone are responsible for the bulk of that cost, with sugar, oilseeds and other livestock products accounting for another quarter (table 3).

Figure 3. Tariffs escalate for final products

Average tariffs, percent

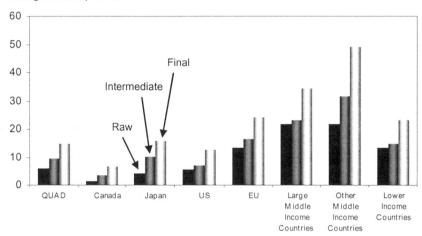

Source: World Bank 2003.

Table 2. Tarfiff Peaks and Variance in Selected Countries (percent)

Country or Group	Average Tariff	Maximum Tariff	Standard Deviation
Canada	4.1	238.0	13.5
Japan	10.9	50.0	10.1
United States	9.9	350.0	26.5
European Union	19.0	506.3	27.3
Republic of Korea	39.9	917.0	107.9
Brazil	13.2	55.0	5.6
Costa Rica	14.2	154.0	18.0
Morocco	67.4	376.5	70.6
Indonesia	8.9	170.0	25.6
Malawi	16.5	25.0	8.5
Togo	15.6	20.0	6.1
Uganda	13.6	15.0	3.2

Source: Aksoy 2005.

Tariff rate quotas

Tariff rate quotas (TRQs) on imports, implemented in the Uruguay Round Agreement on Agriculture for sectors in which nontariff barriers were converted into tariffs, are a complicating factor. Countries agreed to allocate quotas for imports up to 5 percent of domestic consumption ("minimum access" quotas) and to safeguard current levels of access if imports exceeded 5 percent of consumption ("current access" quotas). Countries were to permit imports under the quota at lower tariffs (called the "in-quota" tariff), whereas imports over the quota would face the higher MFN tariff. In-quota tariffs, unlike over-quota tariffs, were neither bound nor reduced in the Agreement on Agriculture. The average over-quota bound tariff of 115 percent is substantially higher than both the average in-quota tariff and the average tariff for all of agriculture, both of which are 59 percent.

But TRQs are the source of a host of potential problems. First, because they protect about 50 percent of OECD agricultural production, it would be unwise to allow all the products they protect to be deemed Sensitive Products, as was suggested in some proposals before the July 2004 Framework Agreement. Second, many quotas are not filled, suggesting that reductions in over-quota tariffs may have less impact than might otherwise be expected. Actual problems with TRQs are evident, as well. The first-come, first-served approach to their administration (used by many countries), for example, sometimes causes imports to be rushed and domestic prices to fall. Import licenses allocated on demand allow high-cost firms to operate, while licenses allocated on the basis of historical shares fail to ensure competition. Some state trading enterprises have been known to import low-quality products for animal feed to fulfill their obligations yet continue to protect their domestic farmers. More problems abound from a plethora of additional regulations. For example, seasonal licenses, time limits, limits per firm, and a domestic purchase requirement all impose extra costs on importing firms. These and several other regulations were found (de Gorter and Klianga 2005) to affect over $30 billion in trade. For these reasons, it is doubtful that the path to wider market access in agriculture lies through TRQs.

Designing the tariff reduction formula

Large cuts in high tariffs are the key to unlocking the development potential of market access in agriculture. The July 2004 Framework Agreement advanced the agricultural market access negotiations in several ways. By moving from the flawed average-cut methodology imbedded in the Uruguay Round Agreement on Agriculture, it provides scope to increase market access by making the greatest reductions in the highest and most distorting tariffs. But the thresholds and number of bands have yet to be negotiated.

The tiered approach of the Framework Agreement ensures some degree of harmonization of national systems of agricultural tariffs (although much less than could be achieved using a Swiss formula that not only reduces higher tariffs more than lower tariffs but also has a common maximum tariff for all countries). But the tiered formula poses some critical design issues—among them the placement of the bands, the depth of cuts, and the presence or absence of a tariff cap. Recognizing these issues, the G-20 proposal of July 8, 2005, proposes a tariff cap of 100 percent for developed countries and 150 percent for developing countries. Scenarios analyzed by the World Bank (Jean, Laborde and Martin 2005) show that only formulas that bring about very deep cuts in bound rates will have a substantial impact on average applied tariffs and hence on market access, particularly when allowance is made for some degree of slippage from designations of Sensitive and Special Products. A progressive tariff reduction formula that imposed cuts of 45, 70, and 75 percent in bound tariffs in developed countries would reduce the average tariffs facing developing countries from 15 percent to 10 percent—an important gain in market access, but only one-third of the way to complete liberalization.

The need to limit the number of tariff lines for Sensitive Products is also recognized in the G-20 proposal. The scenario analysis of the World Bank found extraordinary sensitivity of the results to self-selected Sensitive and Special Products. For example, if 2 percent of tariff lines are excluded from reductions as Sensitive Products and a further 2 percent as Special Products in developing

Table 3. Commodity contributions to global welfare cost of food and agricultural subsidies and tariffs

	Share of total welfare cost of protection (percent)
Rice	35
Beef and sheepmeat	18
Sugar	8
Oilseeds	7
Pork and poultry	6
Dairy products	5
Coarse grains	5
Wheat	4
Other processed food	12
Total	100

Source: Unpublished GTAP model results by K. Anderson and E. Valenzuela, World Bank (September, 2005).

Figure 4. Bound tariffs exceed applied rates

Bound and applied tariffs on agriculture, percent

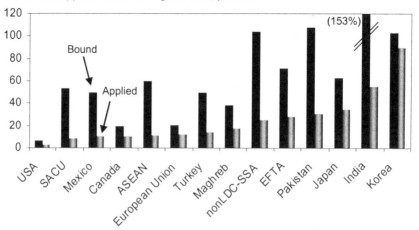

Source: Jean, Laborde and Martin 2006.

Figure 5. Border protection and average tariffs for selected countries

Border protection and average tariffs for selected countries, percent

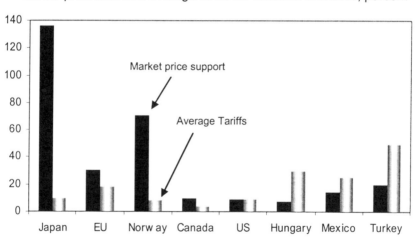

Note: MPS measures the tariff equivalent of all tariff and nontariff barriers to imports using OECD data but excludes protection afforded by taxpayer-funded production subsidies and the like.
Source: World Bank 2003.

Figure 6. Bands and Cuts for Developed Countries: Proposals

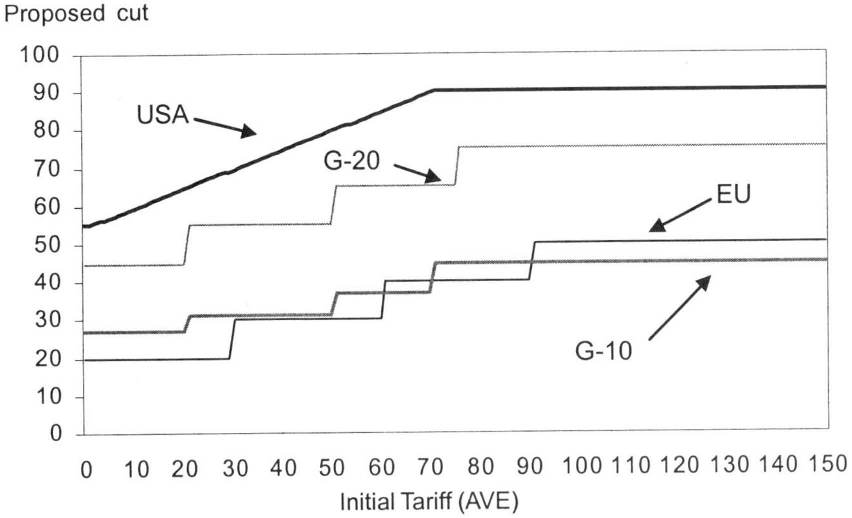

Proposed cut

Initial Tariff (AVE)

Source: Marcos Jank, Institute for International Trade Negotiations (ICONE), 2005.

Figure 7. Bands and Cuts for Developing Countries: Proposals

Proposed cut

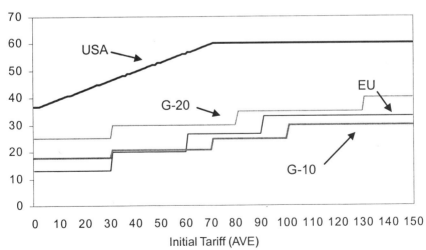

Initial Tariff (AVE)

Source: Marcos Jank, Institute for International Trade Negotiations (ICONE), 2005.

countries, the liberalization of applied duties is reduced by two-thirds overall and much more in Canada, Japan, and Republic of Korea. The cut in applied tariffs falls even more—by 80 percent. A tariff cap would help reduce the losses to liberalization resulting from designations of Sensitive and Special Products, particularly by bringing about substantial reductions on cereals. Clearly, if the Doha Round is to be successful in increasing market access, it will be important to ensure (a) that only a small share of products is accorded special treatment, (b) that substantial reductions in protection are made even on these products, or (c) that the number of products is restricted in a more meaningful way than by restricting the number of tariff lines.

Another design issue related to the simple tiered formula is the discontinuities between bands that can result from a system of higher cuts for tariffs in bands with higher tariff rates. Assume, for example, a tariff threshold of 90 percent. If there were a 10 percentage point difference between the rates of cut, tariffs just over that threshold would end up nearly 10 percentage points below tariffs at the threshold. One possible solution to this problem is to implement a tiered formula similar to that of a progressive income tax, whereby higher marginal rates of reduction are made on tariffs in higher tariff bands. Another possibility is a rate of cut that increases with the height of the tariff.

Recent reform proposals by the U.S. (2005), the G-20 (2005), the EU (2005) and the G-10 (2005) have elaborated considerably on the Framework. These proposals specify tiered formulas for tariff reduction with maximum reduction rates in industrial countries of 90 percent, 75 percent, 60 percent and 45 percent respectively. In developing countries, the cuts are smaller, and increases in cuts take place from higher tariff levels. The relationship between the proposed cuts is shown in figures 6 and 7. The proposals also differ crucially in the number of "sensitive" products allowed; the U.S. proposed 1 percent of tariff lines, the EU has proposed 8 percent and the G-10 has proposed 10 or 15 percent. Jean, Laborde and Martin (2005) show that even 2 percent of sensitive products can almost eliminate the market access gains resulting form a tiered formula.

Policy options

If governments wish to promote development through increased market access, they have several options:

- Limit the number of tariff lines in the Sensitive and Special Product categories. Research shows that placing just 2 percent of tariff lines in those categories can eviscerate the benefits of trade liberalization.
- Impose a tariff cap at the 100 percent level suggested by the G-20 to overcome the effects of tariff peaks, binding overhang, and gaps between applied tariffs and the protection actually provided.
- Impose an overall reduction in average tariffs to ensure that the tiered approach is effective and as a further guard against the adverse effects of the Sensitive

and Special Product categories.

- Build progressivity into every tariff band to ensure reduction in tariff escalation and avoid discontinuities or overlap between tariffs in the bands.
- Convert all specific tariffs into *ad valorem* equivalents using a transparent methodology that will not allow a clandestine increase in protection.
- Encourage full participation by developing countries, especially as Special Products designations could reduce their liberalization substantially.
- Require reductions in in-quota tariffs, or eliminate them altogether. In-quota tariffs can put a significant brake on the trade liberalizing effects of quota expansion.
- Increase minimum access quotas from 5 percent to 10 percent of domestic consumption in the base year.
- Expand current access quotas, which account for 58 percent of trade under TRQs. Because minimum access quotas frequently go unfilled, an expansion in current access quotas may be more effective.
- Do not leave to importing countries the choice of whether to reduce over-quota tariffs *or* expand quotas. Research shows that the minimum trade expansion under each scenario is far less than either the tariff reduction or quota expansion scenario alone, so governments wishing to protect farmers can do so more easily if given the choice.
- Switch all TRQs to applied tariffs with no limits on imports, or require the licenses to be auctioned. Quota underfill frequently indicates potential problems with administration methods.
- Phase out TRQ regulations such as time limits, past trading performance, limits per firm, seasonal quotas, and domestic purchase requirements because they impose costs on importing firms and may contribute to high rates of underfilled quotas.

Notes

1. This note draws on findings from a research project funded by the United Kingdom's Department for International Development and the World Bank-Netherlands Partnership program. It was written by Kym Anderson and William J. Martin, both Lead Economists in the World Bank Development Research Group (DECRG)) and the International Trade Department and by Harry de Gorter, Associate Professor of Agricultural Economics at Cornell University in Ithaca, New York.

2. The former negotiations' chairperson, Stuart Harbinson, drafted a "modalities" paper in 2003 in search for a compromise to lead to a final agreement (WTO 2003). The "modalities" are targets (including numerical targets) for achieving the objectives of the negotiations, as well as issues related to rules.

References

Aksoy, M.A. 2005. "Global Agricultural Trade Polices." *In Global Agricultural Trade and Developing Countries* (chapter 3), ed. A. Aksoy and J. Beghin. Washington, DC: World Bank.

Brenton, P. and T. Ikesuki. 2005. "The Impact of Agricultural Trade Preferences, with Particular Attention to the Least Developed Countries." *In Global Agricultural Trade and Developing Countries* (chapter 4). ed. A. Aksoy and J. Beghin. Washington, DC: World Bank.

de Gorter, H., and E. Kliauga. 2005. "Reducing Tariffs versus Expanding Tariff Rate Quotas." In *Agricultural Trade Reform and the Doha Development Agenda* (chapter 5), ed. K. Anderson and W. Martin. New York: Palgrave Macmillan.

EU. 2005. "Making Hong Kong a Success: Europe's Contribution." European Commission, Brussels, October 28, 2005.

G-10. 2005. G-10 Agriculture Proposal. October 10, 2005. www.insidetrade.com.

G-20. 2005. G-20 Proposal on Market Access. October 12, 2005. www.insidetrade.com.

Jean, S., D. Laborde, and W. Martin. 2005. "Consequences of Alternative Formulas for Agricultural Tariff Cuts." In *Agricultural Trade Reform and the Doha Development Agenda* (chapter 4), ed. K. Anderson and W. Martin. New York: Palgrave Macmillan.

Josling, T. 2005. "The WTO Agricultural Negotiations: Progress and Prospects." Choices 20 (2)

Martin, W. 2004. "Market Access in Agriculture: Beyond the Blender." Trade Note 17. Development Research Group, World Bank, Washington, DC. July.
http://web.worldbank.org/WEBSITE/EXTERNAL/TOPICS/TRADE/
0,contentMDK:20115046~pagePK:148956~piPK:216618~theSitePK:239071,00.html.

U.S. 2005. U.S. Proposal for Bold Reform in Global Agricultural Trade. October 10, 2005. www.ustr.gov.

World Bank. 2003. "Agricultural Policies and Trade." In *Global Economic Prospects 2004: Realizing the Development Promise of the Doha Agenda* (chapter 3). Washington, DC: World Bank.

WTO. 2003. "Negotiations on Agriculture: First Draft of Modalities for Future Commitments." WTO Document TN/AG/W/1/Rev.1 Geneva.

Domestic Support in Agriculture: The Struggle for Meaningful Disciplines

Harry de Gorter and J. Daniel Cook

The current basis for multilateral negotiations of global agricultural trade is the July 2004 Agriculture Framework of the World Trade Organization (WTO). Negotiators had hoped to reach an agreement on how, by how much, and when cuts in agricultural support should be made by the end of July 2005, but that hope was not realized because of major disagreements on the level and method of reductions. The focus now is how to move from the 2004 Agriculture Framework to a more specific agreement in time for approval at the WTO's Hong Kong Ministerial in December 2005, so that agreed modalities can be translated into draft schedules of subsidy reductions.

This note examines the provisions of the July 2004 Framework concerning disciplines specific to domestic support, discusses the main issues under negotiation and their prospects for success, and makes specific recommendations for more effective disciplines.[1]

Domestic support disciplines in the WTO Agreement on Agriculture and in the July 2004 Framework

Domestic support—support provided through subsidies paid by government to producers or through administered prices—is classified under the WTO 1995 Agreement on Agriculture as falling into three "boxes." *Amber Box policies* are those deemed to be the most trade-distorting and hence are subject to disciplines. The extent of subsidies is gauged by the "aggregate measurement of support" (AMS) that they provide. Exempted from discipline is so-called *de minimis* support—defined as subsidies up to a fixed proportion (presently 5 percent) of the current value of production in each category of product-specific and non-product-specific support. *Blue Box policies* are potentially trade-distorting, but because they include supply restrictions they are currently exempted from reductions. *Green Box payments* are not related to current output and therefore are considered minimally trade-distorting. Like Blue Box policies, they are exempt from reductions.

The Agreement on Agriculture called on developed countries to reduce Amber Box support (or total AMS) by 20 percent by 2000. Developing countries were to reduce AMS by 13 percent by 2004. For developing countries, a wider list of policies was exempt from reductions. The least developed countries were wholly exempt from subsidy-reduction commitments.

The July 2004 Framework retains many of the concepts of the 1995 Agreement on Agriculture but adds new ideas of great significance. In addition to disciplining the AMS, the framework calls for a minimum 20 percent cut in "overall trade-distorting support" (OTDS), defined as the sum of the AMS bound ceiling and the allowed maxima of Blue Box payments and *de minimis* support (table 1). In addition, it also caps each component of overall support—specifically AMS, *de minimis* support, and Blue Box subsidies. Reductions in support for each component are to count toward the country's commitment to reduce overall support. The overall commitment to reduce trade-distorting support may become binding when the ceilings are below actual overall support. Similarly, one or more of the individual component reduction commitments may require reduction in actual support to be under the ceiling. Reduction commitments for individual categories are required even if together they exceed the required reduction in overall support. In addition, the framework calls for deeper cuts in OTDS and its individual components by countries that provide higher levels of support. This tiered approach to progressively reduce domestic support is designed to help harmonize support levels among countries. The specific details of the tiered formula are not specified in the framework.

The framework calls for an expansion of the Blue Box criteria to include payments on fixed areas and yields that are not linked to production constraints. Total Blue Box subsidies would be limited to 5 percent of an historical average value of production. The framework includes an exception for countries currently above the cap to gradually make reductions to the 5 percent cap during the implementation period. Green Box definitions are to be reviewed and clarified, but the framework does not call for a numerical cap on this form of support. However, tighter scrutiny, along with implementation of the outcome of the WTO Cotton Panel, could yet cause some significant adjustments in Green Box criteria and policies.

An empirical assessment of the 2004 framework for a sample of countries

The likely effects of the framework on current support ceilings for a select group of countries are illustrated in table 2. Product-specific and non-product-specific *de minimis* and Blue Box ceilings are each 5 percent of the value of production, except for EU Blue Box payments, where actual levels exceed the 5 percent limit by $8.74 billion.

The actual level of OTDS is much lower than the ceilings for all countries. For example, the current level of OTDS in the European Union is $62.7 billion, well under the ceiling of $93.5 billion. This begs the essential question of whether commitments to reduce support will affect current policies at all. As for the individual components of OTDS, current support is also below the ceiling except for Blue Box payments in the European Union. Also notable are several cases where the current level of support is close to the ceilings: AMS and non-product-specific support in the United States, AMS in Korea, and non-product-specific support in Canada.

Because of the wide gap between the permitted level of support and the actual level of support, a gap often known as "water," a reduction in ceilings and permitted

Table 1. Summary of the domestic support provisions of the WTO Framework Agreement on Agriculture, July 2004

Overall trade-distorting support	Move to harmonize maximum allowed levels of or ceilings in overall trade-distorting support - OTDS - defined as the total Aggregate Measurement of Support (AMS) plus *de minimis* plus Blue Box. A tiered formula is to be used: greater efforts to reduce support by countries with higher OTDS ceilings.
	Reduce overall trade-distorting support substantially: downpayment (20%) in first year.
Amber Box	Reduce the total AMS substantially by use of a tiered formula: greater efforts to reduce support by countries with higher Amber Box support.
	Cap product-specific AMS levels at historical averages.
	Reductions in total AMS should lead to product-specific reductions.
Blue Box	Redefine to include payments with production limiting requirement and those with no production required: include payments based on fixed areas and yields and headage as well as payments based on less than 85% of base production.
	Cap payments to 5% of agricultural production from start of implementation period.
Green Box	Review Green Box criteria and improve surveillance and monitoring.
***De minimis* level**	Negotiate the reduction of the level of *de minimis* support.
Special and differential treatment for developing countries	Developing countries: • have longer implementation periods. • have lower reduction coefficients and higher *de minimis* levels. • retain the use of Article 6.2, allowing extra scope for domestic programs.

Source: Josling (2005).

Table 2. Analysis of the 2004 Framework Agreement proposals on domestic support, selected countries (in millions of U.S. dollars)

	EU [a]	U.S.	Japan	Korea	Mexico	Canada
Current ceilings						
Overall trade-distorting support (OTDS)	93,503	44,118	43,622	7,261	15,476	5,412
AMS	59,538	19,103	34,031	1,321	8,718	2,771
Product-specific *de minimis* [b]	1,428	5,773	1,497	2,132	2,703	692
Non-product-specific *de minimis*	11,900	9,621	4,047	2,539	2,703	974
Blue Box	*20,637*	9,621	4,047	1,269	1,352	974
Current levels						
OTDS	62,679	23,299	7,096	1,814	876	1,391
AMS	41,505	16,026	6,017	1,325	876	577
Product-specific *de minimis*	103	102	131	121	0	137
Non-product-specific *de minimis*	434	7,171	175	368	0	677
Blue Box	*20,637*	0	772	0	0	0
Potential "water" in the AMS due to price gap [c]	29,058	5,862	3,725	1,317	777	287

Note: The data in the table correspond to the average of the last three years of notified support for each region or country: European Union and United States = 1999–2001; Japan = 2000–02; Korea and Canada = 1998–2000; Mexico = 1996–98.

a. The EU blue box ceiling here is the historical average of actual support, higher than the permitted 5 percent of value of production of $11.9 billion.

b. Product-specific *de minimis* ceiling is less than 5 percent of the total value of production because support for some products are over five percent of the value of production and so is included in the AMS. The proportion varies by country, with the European Union having the highest share of *de minimis* in the AMS, whereas Mexico has none.

c. Assumes all countries eliminate official support prices without actually changing support, so the price-gap portion of the AMS simply evaporates.

Source: WTO notifications and authors' calculations.

levels is likely to have much less impact on actual policy—for several reasons. First, proposed reductions affect the AMS ceilings and the newly created maximum permitted levels for *de minimis* and Blue Box support—*not the actual levels of support*. This alone greatly dilutes the disciplines. The permitted level of *de minimis* support (10 percent of the value of production—5 percent each for product- and non-product-specific) is a large number by itself. The maximum allowed *de minimis* would average one-third of the producer support estimate (PSE) for OECD countries in 2001 and 87 percent of the domestic-support component of the PSE (defined as total support less border support). Current use of *de minimis* support is already quite significant for some countries. Current levels in Canada, for example, exceed notified total AMS support by more than 40 percent (see the last column in table 2). U.S. *de minimis* support is almost 50 percent of total notified AMS.

But additional water has accumulated because of an inflated baseline, shifting between boxes, and double counting of border support. Policy shifts occurring after the base period of the Agreement on Agriculture (1986–88) but before the implementation period (starting in 1995) are exemplified by the European Union's conversion of approximately $20 billion of Amber Box support to the Blue Box in 1992, which lowered reported AMS relative to the baseline that included these payments. Another factor was the shift of payments from the Blue Box to the Green Box during the implementation period. Crop deficiency payments in the United States, for example, were in the Blue Box before the 1996 Farm Bill. But with decoupling in the 1996 Farm Bill, this program was shifted into the Green Box. The change in policy was a positive step, but the baseline remained high and allowed water to accumulate in the Blue Box, as shown in the U.S. column in table 2.

Another source of water in domestic support ceilings is the peculiar manner in which the AMS is calculated. In addition to trade-distorting, taxpayer-funded domestic subsidies, the AMS includes "market price support," defined as eligible production multiplied by the difference between the administered price and a fixed world reference price. The product of that operation does not depict "domestic support" per se. Instead, it is a faulty measure of support provided at the border through tariffs, import quotas or export subsidies (box 1) since and administered price cannot be sustained without supporting border measures. Reducing or even eliminating an official support price without altering border protection need not have any market impact. Japan is a case in point. There the official support price for rice was eliminated in 1997, and Japan's total AMS, as notified to the WTO, dropped by $20 billion. However, because the country made no changes in import controls, effective support remained the same. So a substantial portion of the water in Japan's total AMS of approximately $34 billion (table 2) can be attributed to an adjustment made to an administered price in order to "achieve" reduction commitments without actually reducing support. As discussed below, the redundancy of this "price-gap" component of the AMS must be recognized when assessing the impact of any given cuts.

Because of the ambiguity of the legal text of the Agreement on Agriculture and the discretion given to governments in how they declare specific support programs, there is evidence that support has been moved from box to box to meet domestic support disciplines. This is possible because there are no product-specific limits for the Amber Box—it is an aggregate sectorwide limit for all agricultural products and policies. This enables countries that reform policies in one sector to increase support in other sectors or introduce new support for the reformed sector.

Support can be shifted between, as well as within, boxes. Lax criteria have allowed countries to move support toward either undisciplined or less constrained categories. For example, the United States declared the new emergency crop subsidies of 1998–2001 as non-product-specific *de minimis* support even though they were based on specific product prices. This move allowed the United States to circumvent the ceiling on total AMS. In anticipation of ceilings becoming a constraint, the 2004 framework now proposes to expand the definition of the Blue Box and its

Box 1. How part of the AMS can evaporate without changing actual support

The Agreement on Agriculture included a measure of border protection in the AMS called "market price support" (MPS), which is measured by production multiplied by the difference between the current administered "official" domestic price support and a fixed world reference price in 1986–1988:

$$MPS = Q*(P_d^{off} - P_w^{ref})$$

where Q is current production, P_d^{off} is the official domestic price support and P_w^{ref} is the fixed world reference price. Actual world prices fluctuate above and below the world reference price, while domestic market prices do likewise relative to the domestic administered price. Measuring MPS in this way can cause a major discrepancy between actual MPS levels and the level notified to WTO. So the MPS component of the AMS is a poor measure of border protection for a subset of commodities that have official domestic support prices. This problem in measuring the AMS is highlighted by the fact that it sometimes is notified to the WTO as a negative number (when the support price is below the fixed world reference price) and thus may offset taxpayer-financed, trade-distorting subsidies. At the other extreme, support prices have sometimes been so far above world reference prices that the AMS has exceeded the OECD's total PSE for some countries in the past, even though the AMS is supposed to measure trade-distorting domestic support, which is just one component of the PSE. But most importantly, the MPS component of the AMS is very arbitrary because a country can simply reduce or eliminate the official price support without changing actual support.

Source: Baffes, Cook, and de Gorter (2005).

ceiling to 5 percent of an historical value of production for all of agriculture. With little change in the levels of emergency payments (except in name: they are now called countercyclical payments), the United States will be able to dramatically reduce its non-product-specific *de minimis* support by shifting it to the Blue Box. The United States and other countries will be able to do so simply because of a proposed change in the definition of what is "less trade distorting."

Current Formula Proposals

Since October 10, the United States, EU and G-20 have advanced specific proposals based on the July 2004 Framework Agreement. These all involve tiered reductions with larger cuts in those economies with the largest absolute amount of domestic support.[2] The U.S. proposal calls for a 75 percent reduction in Overall Trade Distorting Support (OTDS) for countries with over $60 bil., a 53 percent reduction for OTDS between $10 and $60 bil., and a 31 percent reduction for lower levels of OTDS. The corresponding reductions in the Aggregate Measurement of Support (AMS) are 83-60-37 percent.[3]

The EU calls for 70-60-50 percent cuts in each of OTDS and AMS. The EU places itself in the highest band, the United States in the middle and all others except Japan in the lowest. The proposal calls for the Japan to be in the middle band for OTDS, but either in the highest for AMS or otherwise in the middle with "additional contributions".[4] The G-20 is the most ambitious of all, with 80-75-70 percent cuts in OTDS ceiling and 80-70-60 percent cuts in AMS ceilings

The United States calls for a 50 percent reduction in allowed *de minimis* (to 2.5 percent of the value of production) for each of product and non-product specific support. The EU calls for an 80 percent reduction in allowed *de minimis* to one percent of the value of production while G-20 argues for reductions in *de minimis* as needed to meet overall OTDS reductions.

All three proposals agree with the expanded definition of the Blue Box as put forth in the July Framework to encompass payments with production-limiting requirements and payments that do not require production. However, the United States calls for the cap to be set at 2.5 percent of the value of production, instead of five percent as proposed in the July Framework.

Both the United States and the EU propose product specific caps in the Amber box but with differing base periods: the United States recommends a base period of 1999-2001 while the EU argues that product-specific caps should be based on the entire implementation period.

An empirical assessment of the October proposals

The effects of these proposals on AMS and OTDS levels are shown in Figures 1 and 2. The height of the bars in each figure shows the ceilings, while the percentage above the bar shows the share of that support that could be eliminated without reducing actual support[5]. Therefore, the white area is equivalent to actual support levels and the grey area represents overhang (i.e., "water") in the ceiling. The three lines across the bars show the level of the ceilings after the reductions implied by each proposal.

These figures highlight the very large gaps between committed and actual support in recent years, and the consequent need for large reductions in ceilings before any real policy changes will be required.

In Figure 1, the EU would be required to reduce OTDS relative to the historical benchmark under all three proposals. This is politically feasible as the EU will be converting most of its trade distorting payments into green box payments after the 2003 CAP reforms.[6]

The ceiling for U.S. OTDS in Figure 1 shows that no reduction in support relative to the historical benchmark would be required under its own proposal, while a slight reduction would be required under the EU proposal and a significant reduction under the G-20 proposal. Of the other countries considered only the EU would be required to reduce its AMS support relative to 1999-2001 levels, and only by 1 percentage point under the G-20 proposal.

In regards to the AMS ceilings for each of the three proposals shown in Figure 2, only the United States would be required to make sizeable cuts in its actual AMS. Assuming the water due to the price-gap is eliminated simply by taking official price supports off the book, the United States would be left with a required cut of only $2,523 million, far less than the proposed 60 percent nominal reduction.

Figure 1. Water in domestic support

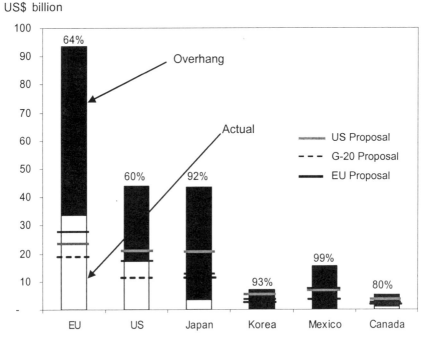

Overall Trade-Distorting Support (OTDS)

US$ billion

Source: Authors calculations based on data from WTO notifications

104

Figure 2. Water in domestic support

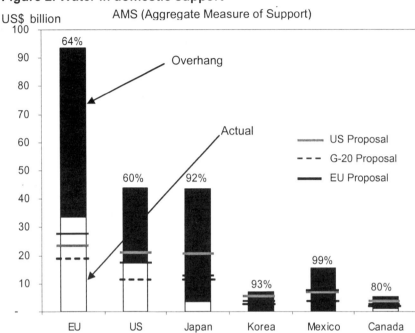

Source: Authors calculations based on data from WTO notifications

While the reductions in actual support required by even the most ambitious of these proposals would be modest, the potential value of such disciplines is perhaps greater than it seems in that it would rule out the possibility of countries' potentially reverting to much higher levels of support in the future.

Suggestions for New Rules

Which formula is finally adopted will be hugely important. In addition, negotiators will need to give careful attention to a number of other issues, either in the current negotiations or in the future, including:

- The 2004 Agriculture Framework proposed a cap on product-specific AMS. This is important as it would limit countries' ability to shift support among sensitive commodities. The WTO also should consider introducing a commitment to reduce support per unit and by sector, along the lines of a tariff, to make reductions more effective.

- Because of the WTO Cotton Panel ruling, product-specific direct-income payments to farmers in the Green Box should be distinguished from expenditures for public goods. The former should be reported as part of a new Amber Box.
- Reduction commitments should be imposed only on the taxpayer-financed portion of the current AMS—plus the Blue Box, product-specific and non-product-specific *de minimis* subsidies, and product-specific, direct farm income payments under the current Green Box. This new (flashing?) Amber Box would report only domestic subsidies that distort trade and that are not border protection. Such a discipline will minimize countries' ability to avoid reductions in support by shifting support from box to box.
- The Green Box should be maintained for expenditures that provide public goods or prevent negative externalities. But programs listed in Annex 2 of the Agreement on Agriculture as non-trade-distorting or minimally trade-distorting must be more tightly defined to screen out abuses. For example, crop insurance programs, which have been found to be very trade-distorting, are currently in the Green Box, and tax concessions are not even considered support. Strict rules, definitions, and monitoring arrangements are required. In recognition of the fact that even these newly defined Green Box expenditures are likely to have some effect on production (and therefore on trade), consideration should be given to introducing a cap on the value of production.

Notes

1. The World Bank–Netherlands Partnership Program and the United Kingdom's Department for International Development provided much-appreciated support for the research reported here. The note was written by Harry de Gorter, Associate Professor of Agricultural Economics at Cornell University in Ithaca, New York, and by J. Daniel Cook, an international trade analyst in the Agriculture and Fisheries Division, Office of Industries of the U.S. International Trade Commission (USITC). This paper's view's do not necessarily represent those of the USITC or any of its individual Commissioners. We are grateful to William J. Martin for the useful comments he provided .

2. All three proposals use the same three tiers of >$60 bil, $10-$60 bil, and < $10 bil.

3. U.S. and G-20 proposals use tiers of >$25 bil, $12-25 bil, and < $12 bil.

4. For purposes of this analysis a 65 percent cut in Japan's AMS will be used as the "additional contribution." It is possible for Japan to make the larger "contribution" and still not have their AMS ceiling binding.

5. In making this calculation, we assume that WTO members would utilize their right under current rules to exclude support provided through Market Price Support from their AMS by abolishing administered support prices while not changing any policies (as Japan did for rice in 1997, thereby eliminating reported support calculated by the "price-gap").

6. Also stated by the EU in their "Statement of EU conditional negotiating proposals – with explanatory annotations". 10 October 2005. Memo/05/357.

References

Baffes, J., J. Daniel Cook, and H. de Gorter. 2005. "Issues in Measuring Domestic Agricultural Support Disciplines in the WTO." Trade Note, International Trade Department, World Bank, Washington, DC.

Josling, Tim. 2005. "The WTO Agricultural Negotiations: Progress and Prospects," *Choices* 20(2): 131-136.

Further Reading

Brink, L. 2005. "WTO 2004 Agriculture Framework: Disciplines on Distorting Domestic Support." International Agricultural Trade Research Consortium Working Paper 05-1. May. http://iatrcweb.org/publications/working.htm

Cook, J. Daniel. 2005. "Issues on Disciplining Domestic Support for Agriculture in the WTO." Unpublished MSc thesis, Cornell University, August.

Hart, C., and J. Beghin. 2006. "Rethinking Domestic Support Disciplines." In *Agricultural Trade Reform and the Doha Development Agenda*, ed. K. Anderson and W. Martin. Washington and New York: World Bank and Palgrave Macmillan.

Jensen, H., and H. Zobbe. 2006. "Consequences of Reducing AMS Limits." In *Agricultural Trade Reform and the Doha Development Agenda*, ed. K. Anderson and W. Martin. Washington and New York: World Bank and Palgrave Macmillan.

Export Subsidies: Agricultural Policy Reform and Developing Countries

Harry de Gorter

The WTO's July 2004 Framework Agreement calls for the elimination—by a credible date certain—of all forms of export subsidy in agriculture and for disciplines on export measures that have the effect of a subsidy, including the subsidy components of export credits and state trading enterprises (STEs). Food aid is to be disciplined to avoid disruption of commercial trade flows, while export taxes and restrictions are to be subject to tighter rules. The elimination of export subsidies and their equivalents will finally put agriculture on an equal footing with manufacturing products, for which export subsidies were banned many years ago.[1]

So-called implicit export subsidies in many forms are disbursed indirectly and nontransparently through food aid programs, STEs (low-interest loans and government underwriting of losses), publicly underwritten export credits (long maturities and below-market interest rates), export promotion activities, and domestic policy levers that can, in combination, function as an export subsidy. Such nontransparent mechanisms were subject to few disciplines in the Uruguay Round Agreement on Agriculture (URAA) and so are key issues for the current negotiations, despite the complexity of calculating their subsidizing effect.

Export taxes, used in periods of high world prices to keep domestic prices low, are not constrained by the URAA. Because they increase the cost of food for net importers, some countries are pressing in the current negotiations for constraints on such taxes and for greater flexibility to protect their own food-crop sectors and so increase self-sufficiency.

This note evaluates the effectiveness of the disciplines imposed on export subsidies in the URAA and presents options for new multilateral rules. We show how countries have circumvented their commitments on explicit export subsidies and explore issues related to indirect export subsidies, as well as some omissions and improper measures associated with commitments to reduce export competition.

Explicit export subsidies in the URAA

Commitments on export competition in the URAA focused mostly on explicit, taxpayer-financed export subsidies. Twenty-five countries agreed to reduce both the volume and value of their export subsidies and to prohibit new subsidies for 23 product categories. Each country committed to reduce the volume of subsidized exports by 21 percent over six years from the level in the 1986–90 base period (14 percent over a 10-year period for developing countries), and to reduce the value of

Table 1. Summary of provisions of the WTO Framework Agreement on export competition, July 2004

Export subsidies	• Eliminate export subsidies by a credible end date. • Agree on schedule and modalities of reductions.
Export credits	• Eliminate export credits, guarantees, and insurance programs with repayment period of more than 180 days.
Food aid	• Eliminate food aid that is not in conformity with disciplines to be agreed. Disciplines will be aimed at preventing commercial displacement. • Negotiate other food aid issues (role of international organizations, humanitarian and development issues, aid in grant form).
State trading enterprises	• Eliminate trade-distorting practices of state trading enterprises. • Negotiate use of monopoly powers.
Special and differential treatment for developing countries	• Allow longer implementation periods for reductions and elimination. • Permit developing countries to continue to benefit from Article 9.4 exceptions. • Make appropriate provisions for export credits in line with Decision on Least Developed and Net Food-Importing Countries. • Accord developing countries special consideration in negotiation of disciplines on STEs. • Allow, in exceptional circumstances, ad hoc temporary financing arrangements relating to exports to developing countries.
Export restrictions	• Strengthen disciplines on export prohibitions and restrictions.

Source: Josling (2005).

export subsidies by 36 percent (24 percent for developing countries). Temporary exemptions for developing countries allow subsidies for marketing, handling, cost reduction, and international transport, while the least developed countries are not subject to reduction commitments at all.

Following adoption of the URAA, the European Union (EU) accounted for more than 90 percent of explicit export subsidies worldwide, which averaged about $5 billion per annum, well below the aggregate limit of approximately $10 billion. Apart from some isolated instances of limit breaches and the addition of export subsidies for some developing countries, the commitments were met. But this was primarily because the base period from which reductions were made was one of low world prices and high levels of export subsidy, making the targets easy to achieve. Abnormally high world prices in 1997–98, exchange rate developments, and domestic policy reforms all contributed to the ease with which countries fulfilled their commitments. Finally, loopholes in the URAA (described below) were amply exploited.

Circumventing explicit export subsidy commitments

The experience of the Uruguay Round has important implications for the current negotiations. Several loopholes in the URAA made commitments to reduce direct export subsidies less effective than they appear to have been.

- Countries were allowed to designate a different base period (1991–92) other than the initial 1986–90 average. In anticipation of this option, some countries actually increased subsidies in the 1991–92 period, a practice known as front-loading.
- Subsidy commitments could be banked across years if unused, a practice known as rollover, or shielded under commodity-group aggregates. Rollover allowed countries to increase subsidies when world prices were low, further depressing the world price to the detriment of producers in developing countries. Because reduction commitments were tied to commodity groups, countries could avoid reductions on selected products while meeting their aggregate commitment by reducing subsidies on other lines in the same group.
- As opposed to the discipline on tariffs, where per unit or *ad valorem* duties are bound, only the total amount spent on export subsidies (or the volume exported) is regulated. This implies less control over the trade distortions caused by export subsidies, because the same value of export subsidy allocated to a commodity can have different effects on the quantities exported, and therefore on world price. The data on export subsidy equivalents confirm that these differences are significant across countries, commodities, and over time (Ruiz 2000).
- Failure to restrict per unit subsidies also allows seasonal subsidies, whereby exports receive high subsidies for part of the year without causing the total of the period to exceed the constraint. During the season of high subsidy, the impact on world price can be substantial.

The objective of eliminating all forms of export subsidies must necessarily close opportunities for avoidance of and delay in implementing trade liberalization.

Issues related to implicit export subsidies

Indirect export subsidies not only are more difficult to measure than direct subsidies, but also involve programs that under some circumstances are beneficial or crucial, such as food aid. Hence, any rules to discipline their use must be carefully designed and will involve more disciplines on reporting and monitoring than will those on more explicit forms of subsidy.

Food aid

Although food aid can have market effects similar to those of export subsidies, it was not included in the URAA schedule of reductions. Crucial in cases of national disaster, food aid has been used by developed countries to dispose of surpluses, provide budget support for the recipient government, and underpin foreign policy. Such uses have created serious problems. When given in kind, food aid may be detrimental to local producers by lowering prices and altering traditional dietary preferences. When distributed outside normal commercial distribution channels— as it usually is—in-kind food aid also disrupts the development of those channels and interrupts the movement of food to the deficit areas from surplus regions in the country and from neighboring countries. Disruption increases the likelihood and severity of future famine. Hence, food aid should be purchased from other developing countries and from food surplus areas of the country assisted, as a first priority. Also, food aid should never be used by industrial countries as a way of disposing of surpluses.

To avoid these risks, food aid in full grant form such as cash or vouchers should be directed to meet the needs of well-defined vulnerable groups or in response to an emergency as determined by the United Nations. This will also support local producers and traders. For these reasons, cash aid is often preferable to in-kind distribution. The exceptions are crisis situations where transportation is severely disrupted or markets are not functioning, or when there are good reasons to believe that in-kind food distribution can be better targeted to those with the greatest need.

Export credits

Officially supported export credit programs average about $6.5 billion per annum, with the United States providing around 50 percent of the world total. The programs involve credit guarantees, public assumption of risk, and subsidization of interest and insurance. It is very difficult to measure the value of the export subsidy associated with these programs because the value of the risk reduction they provide is difficult to estimate. At the same time, export credit programs enhance food security for countries suffering from financial or food crisis, thereby expanding exports to everyone's benefit. However, only about 20 percent of agricultural export credit is extended to poor developing countries. Although the subsidy component of these credit programs is found to be small, disciplines are required for all such public expenditures (with exemptions for poor country importers in emergency situations).

State trading enterprises

STEs and domestic policies that allow for market segmentation and protection of domestic markets can subsidize exports through price discrimination, that is, by using revenues from high domestic prices to subsidize fixed costs for the rest of production, which is then exported (box 1). STEs and domestic marketing arrange-

Box 1. Price discrimination and pooling can combine to create an export subsidy

Export subsidies based on price pooling and price discrimination are quite complex and can occur in different settings. Extra revenues derived from price discrimination are "pooled" and then "averaged" to farmers, thereby acting as a production subsidy, while higher prices to consumers act like a consumption tax. No tax revenues are involved, but the outcome is identical to that of a standard taxpayer-financed export subsidy: supply is increased and demand is reduced at the same time. Such practices are often referred to as "consumer-financed" export subsidies.

Price discrimination with pooling can be carried out by an STE or through legislation fixing domestic prices. Nontraded domestic products (fluid milk, for example) can be used to support implicit export subsidies. Although the milk itself is not traded internationally, its high domestic price can be used to cross-subsidize exports of related products such as cheese or milk powder. If an STE practices price discrimination only in world market segments, without taxing domestic consumers, but pools the revenues, the resulting subsidy is not disciplined in the URAA.

The Dispute Settlement Body of the WTO ruled in 2003 and 2004 for the Canadian dairy and EU sugar sectors, respectively, that price discrimination alone with production quotas have the effect of cross-subsidizing exports and so violate commitments made under the URAA to reduce export subsidies. The WTO panel agreed with Brazil's argument that higher domestic prices for quota production have allowed farmers to expand output and sell the extra output at lower world prices below total average costs of production. The practice constitutes a subsidy because losses in one market (the export market) are offset by profits in another (the domestic quota market).

Why should farmers accept a loss on exports? Because the unit-cost savings they realize from higher output are greater than the marginal losses they incur. Exploiting economies of scale under these circumstances constitutes cross-subsidization, according to the WTO panel. Output is also distorted because some farmers limit their production to the quota amount and would have exited the industry were it not for high domestic prices on the quota. This is output distortion due to "exit deterrence" as opposed to distortions that are due to cross-subsidization (where some farmers produce beyond the quota amount at lower world prices but are able to do so because of higher domestic prices).

Box 1 *(continued)*

These rulings have implications for all production subsidies on limited output (known as "infra-marginal" subsidies), whether financed by taxpayers or consumers. Subsidies on a limited amount of output have been increasing since the URAA was adopted. It is therefore possible that other commodity sectors and countries are in contravention of their export subsidy reduction commitments.

Source: Kropp and de Gorter (2005).

ments can also be used to pool revenues to farmers, a practice that constitutes an export subsidy if domestic consumer prices are higher than world prices. Domestic production expands with pooling, and consumption declines, as in the case of a taxpayer-financed export subsidy. Pooling can occur over time and across markets and commodities.

Some export STEs may counter the power of multinational trading firms and hence may improve competitive conditions in the market. But disciplines are needed to ensure that STEs are more transparent and subject to the same general rules as private firms. In particular, disciplines should be placed on price pooling and on taxpayer support to STEs (for credit guarantees or promotion, for example), with targets for their eventual phasing out. More stringent requirements for reporting acquisition costs and prices are required to ensure that any price discrimination by the STE is within normal business practices and that no product is sold on world markets consistently below domestic prices. There should be no discrimination against private firms' participation in the market; nondiscrimination discourages STEs from using discriminatory practices. Special financing privileges should be also disciplined, with exemptions for poor countries dealing with inadequate institutional infrastructure.

Objectives for negotiators
Some lessons can be drawn regarding the general principles of an effective agreement on export subsidies, and some specific holes can be identified that need to be eliminated.

General principles
* Because countries have committed to eliminate all forms of export subsidy, a firm deadline for phasing them out should be agreed upon. Five years may be reasonable.
* Countries are encouraged to make a gesture of good faith when signing the

agreement by offering a down payment in the form of an across the board cut in export subsidies immediately.

- *Ad valorem* (percentage) limits on the per unit subsidy (as a percentage of the world price) should be introduced on a commodity-by-commodity basis, combined with a ceiling on the total value of exports that may be subsidized. The *ad valorem* limit will place a constraint on the difference between domestic and world prices, while the value limit will constrain the impact of export subsidies on world markets.
- Monitoring of export subsidies should be strengthened by coordinating data collection among organizations (including the OECD and the WTO). One possibility is to consider mandating the WTO Trade Policy Review Mechanism to provide an annual evaluation of the effects of export subsidies, focusing in particular on developing countries.
- The banking of export subsidies, whereby they are rolled over to subsequent years, should be banned.
- All commitments should be made on a per product basis, accompanied by a uniform system of classifying products.
- Delaying or avoiding reductions through practices like front-loading should be anticipated and prevented.
- Special and differential treatment for developing countries should not go beyond Article 9.4 of the URAA, which specifies exclusions for subsidies on marketing, handling and transportation only.

Plugging holes in the URAA
- The URAA lacks rules that directly govern export credits, payment guarantees, and direct financing. As these policies have the effect of subsidizing exports, such rules are needed as part of the disciplines on export subsidies. The methodology developed by the OECD (2001) should be adopted to include the export-subsidy component of such measures; that component would be counted against reduction commitments.
- Specific disciplines on export credits should be established, such as a maximum repayment term, a minimum cash payment by the importer, and premiums based on risk.
- All expenditures involving direct, in-kind disposal of public food stocks in export markets should be subjected to the same rules as normal export subsidies.
- URAA provisions on food aid should be tightened to facilitate genuine food aid while preventing the abuse of aid to circumvent export subsidy restrictions. Proposals include limiting food aid to the form of grants only, and to provision in-kind only in response to appeals from the United Nations or other appropriate international bodies. Donations in cash or channeled through international

agencies should be preferred (WTO 2002).

- Stronger disciplines on STEs are needed. At a minimum, STEs should be subjected to the same export-subsidy rules as private sector enterprises. Notification and transparency requirements must be tightened to prevent disguised export subsidies. Government financing and underwriting of losses should be eliminated, as well as any associated direct export subsidies. One option would be to strengthen and extend the disciplines of GATT Article XVII and Article II on state-trading exports to include limits on *ad valorem* subsidies. Another option is to mandate coexistence with private companies to eliminate the monopoly element of the market.
- Rules are needed to constrain consumer-financed export subsidies, especially revenue-pooling arrangements or cross-subsidization through price discrimination.
- Export taxes should be constrained and eventually phased out. For any developing countries that still depend on these taxes as an important source of government revenue, the phaseout period could be prolonged.

Notes

1. This note was prepared by Harry de Gorter who is an Assistant Professor of Agricultural Economics at Cornell University in Ithaca, New York.

References

Josling, Tim. 2005. "The WTO Agricultural Negotiations: Progress and Prospects," *Choices* 20(2): pp 133.

Kropp, J., and H. de Gorter. 2005. "The Economics of Cross-Subsidization: Implications of the WTO Panels on EU Sugar and Canadian Dairy." Paper presented at the IATRC summer symposium on Pressures for Agricultural Policy Reform, Seville, Spain, June 21.

OECD (Organisation for Economic Co-operation and Development). 2001. July. Paris.

Ruiz, L. 2000. "The Impacts of Export Subsidy Reduction Commitments in the Agreement on Agriculture on International Trade: A General Assessment". M.S. thesis, August, Cornell University.

World Trade Organization Negotiations on Agriculture Committee on Agriculture Special Session TN/AG/6 (02-6943) December 18, 2002.

Further Reading

Messerlin, P. and B. Hoekman. 2005. "Consequences of Removing the Exception of Agricultural Export Subsidies". In *Agricultural Trade Reform and the Doha Development Agenda*, K. Anderson and W. Martin (eds.), New York: Palgrave Macmillan co-published with the World Bank.

de Gorter, H., L. Ruiz, and M. Ingco, M. 2004. "Export Competition Policies." In *Agriculture and the WTO: Creating a Trade Sysytem for Development,* M. Ingco and J. Nash (eds.), Washington, D.C., and New York: World Bank and Oxford Press.

Cotton and the Developing Countries: Implications for Development

John Baffes

When it comes to cotton, rich countries' trade policies negate their development policies. Subsidies paid to producers in rich countries depress world prices and cut into the livelihood of millions in developing countries, where cotton is a typical, and often dominant, smallholder crop.

Cotton's share in world trade is small, but it is an important cash crop for several poor countries at both farm and national levels. For four West African producers (Benin, Burkina Faso, Chad and Mali), for example, cotton represented 20–44 percent of total merchandise exports in 2001-03. The corresponding figures for Uzbekistan, Tajikistan, and Turkmenistan were 32, 15, and 12 percent, respectively. Cotton's contribution to the Gross Domestic Product (GDP) of these countries has been substantial, ranging from 2.4 percent (Chad) to 6.1 percent (Mali). The per capita GDP in most of these cotton-dependent countries is well below $500 (table 1).

This note analyzes the effects of government interventions in the global cotton market.

The market setting

More than two thirds of the world's cotton is produced by developing countries. Over the last four decades production grew at an annual rate of 1.8 percent, reaching 25 million tons in 2005 (from 10.2 million tons in 1960). Most of the growth came from China and India, which tripled and doubled their production during the period. Other countries that significantly increased their shares of the world cotton market were Greece, Pakistan, and Turkey. Some new entrants also contributed to this growth. Australia, for example, which produced only 2,000 tons of cotton in 1960, averaged 650,000 tons during the late 1990s. Francophone Africa produced less than 100,000 tons in the 1960s and now produces ten times as much. The United States and the Central Asian republics of the former Soviet Union, the two dominant cotton producers during the 1960s, have maintained their output levels at about 3.5 and 1.5 million tons, respectively, effectively halving their market shares. A number of Central American countries that used to produce almost 250,000 tons of the fiber now produce virtually none.

A recent survey of costs of cotton production found that Brazil, China, and Pakistan are the lowest-cost producers, followed by Australia, Turkey, and West Africa. High-cost producers are Israel, Syria and the United States (U.S.). In line with most primary commodities, real prices for cotton have declined considerably during the last 40 years; they are currently half their 1960 levels. There is no doubt

Table 1. Cotton's importance to West African and Central Asian economies, 2001-03 Averages

	Cotton exports			Merchandise exports (US$ millions)	Per capita GDP (2000 US$)
	U.S.$ millions	Percentage of merchandise exports	Percentage of GDP		
West and Central Africa					
Burkina Faso	105	44.6	3.3	235	245
Chad	53	29.4	2.4	182	381
Benin	126	27.7	4.5	455	289
Mali	193	22.7	6.1	849	203
Togo	42	8.9	2.7	467	251
Central Asia					
Uzbekistan	727	22.1	4.4	3,295	591
Tajikistan	103	14.1	7.7	729	190
Kyrgyzstan	36	7	2.2	524	295
Turkmenistan	139	4.5	3	3,065	859
Azerbaijan	22	1.2	0.3	1,906	788
Kazakhstan	86	0.8	0.3	10,412	1,534

Source: Food and Agriculture Organization (FAOSTAT) and World Bank (World Development Indicators).

that the low prices seen recently have been influenced by the support provided by major players, which we now examine.

The policy setting

Rich countries protect their cotton industries through domestic subsidies which averaged $4 billion annually between 1997 and 2004 (table 2). Cotton subsidies in the United States have a long history dating from the commodity programs of the Great Depression. The specific provisions of these programs—including the one for cotton—change with each "Farm Bill" passed by the Congress (Farm Bills are introduced approximately every 4 to 5 years), but their chief objective has remained largely unchanged: to transfer income from taxpayers (and to a lesser extent consumers) to commodity producers.

The main channels of support to U.S. cotton producers are price-based payments, decoupled payments, crop insurance, and countercyclical payments (table 3). U.S. cotton users and exporters also receive some support.

* Price-based payments (also known as loan rate payments) are designed to compensate cotton growers for the difference between the market price and the target price when the latter exceeds the former.
* Decoupled payments (renamed direct payments in the 2002 Farm Bill) are predetermined annual payments calculated on the basis of area historically

used for cotton production. Direct payments were introduced with the 1996 Farm Bill to compensate producers for "losses" following the elimination of deficiency payments.

- Crop insurance is a subsidy to weather-related crop failures.
- Countercyclical payments were introduced in 1998 (as "emergency payments") to compensate producers for income "lost" due to low commodity prices. They were made permanent under the 2002 Farm Bill. Payments to cotton exporters and domestic end-users (also known as export subsidies or Step-2 payments) are made when domestic prices exceed world prices, so that U.S. exporters maintain their competitiveness. Implicitly, cotton exporters receive another subsidy through the export credit guarantee program which insures importers of U.S. cotton against potential defaults.

In addition to these transfers there are numerous other publicly funded programs—among them research and extension services and subsidized irrigation.

The European Union's (EU) budgetary expenditure on the cotton sector ranged between €740 million and €903 million in 1996–2000, implying that, on average, EU cotton producers received more than twice the world price (table 2). EU cotton producers receive support even in periods of high prices, since the budgetary allocation to the cotton sector must be disbursed. They received approximately the same level of support in 1995 and 2002, for example, although cotton prices in 1995 were twice as high as in 2002.

The European Union has made adjustments to its cotton program, among them a 1999 reform that effectively capped the budgetary expenditures allocated to the industry. A major reinstrumentation of the EU cotton program will take place in 2006. Under the Luxembourg Council's decision of April 22, 2004 (based on a September 2003 proposal), an estimated €700 million is expected to fund two support measures,

Table 2. Estimated government assistance to cotton producers, 1997–2004

	1997	1998	1999	2000	2001	2002	2003	2004
U.S. $ millions								
US	1,163	1,947	3,432	2,149	3,937	3,075	1,021	2,244
China	2,013	2,648	1,534	1,900	1,217	800	1,303	1,145
Greece	659	660	596	537	735	718	761	836
Spain	211	204	199	179	245	239	233	230
Turkey	—	220	199	106	59	57	22	115
Brazil	29	52	44	44	10	—	—	—
Mexico	13	15	28	23	18	7	6	49
Egypt	290	—	20	14	23	33	9	89

Notes:— No data
Source: International Cotton Advisory committee; US Department of Agriculture; European Union.

Table 3. Budgetary transfers to the U.S. cotton sector, 1995–1996 to 2002–2003
(millions of U.S. dollars)

	1995	1996	1997	1998	1999	2000	2001	2002
Coupled	3	0	28	535	1,613	563	2,507	248
PFC/DP	0	599	597	637	614	575	474	914
Emergency/CCP	0	0	0	316	613	613	524	1,264
Insurance	180	157	148	151	170	162	236	194
Step-2	34	3	390	308	422	236	196	455
TOTAL	217	759	1,163	1,947	3,432	2,149	3,937	3,075

Note: PFC = production flexibility contracts. DP = direct payments. CCP = countercyclical payments.
Source: U.S. Department of Agriculture.

with 65 percent of the support taking the form of a single decoupled payment and the remaining 35 percent taking the form of an area payment. Eligibility for the decoupled payment is limited to growers who produced cotton during the three-year period 1999–2001. The area payment will be given for a maximum area of 380,000 hectares in Greece, 85,000 hectares in Spain, and 360 hectares in Portugal and will be proportionately reduced if claims exceed the maximum area allocated to each country. To receive decoupled payments, cotton growers must keep the land in good agricultural use. To receive area payments they must plant (but not necessarily produce) cotton.

Impact of policies
Numerous models have evaluated the impact of policies on the cotton market, with considerable variation in the results. The International Cotton Advisory Committee (ICAC), for example, concluded from a study based on a short-run partial equilibrium model that in the absence of direct subsidies, average cotton prices during the 2000–01 season would have been 30 percent higher than what they actually were. The ICAC study acknowledged that while the removal of subsidies would result in lower production in the countries that use them (and hence higher prices in the short term), the impact would be partially offset by shifting production to nonsubsidizing countries in the medium to longer terms. Goreux (2003), who extended the ICAC model by replacing the base year with average subsidies for 1998–2002, estimated that in the absence of support the world price of cotton would have been between 3 and 13 percent higher during that period, depending on the value of demand and supply elasticities. Gilson and others (2004), using subsidy data for 1999 and a model similar to Goreux's, estimated that removal of subsidies by the China, the European Union, and the United States, and would increase the world price of cotton by 18 percent.

Reeves and others (2001) used a simple Computable General Equilibrium (CGE) model to find that removal of production and export subsidies by the United States and the European Union would reduce U.S. cotton production by 20 percent and exports by 50 percent, with much higher figures for the European Union. They also estimated that if support were not in place, world cotton prices would be 10.7 percent higher compared to their 2001–02 levels. FAPRI (2002) found that under global liberalization (removal of trade barriers and domestic support in all commodity sectors), the world price for cotton would increase over the baseline scenario by an average of 12.7 percent over the 10-year period. Based largely on the Food Agricultural Policy Research Institute's (FAPRI) data and assumptions, Sumner (2003) estimated that had all U.S. cotton subsidies not been in place during the marketing years 1999–2002, the world price of cotton would have been almost 13 percent higher.

Based on a partial equilibrium model, Tokarick (2003) found that multilateral trade liberalization in all agricultural markets (including cotton) is expected to induce a 2.8 percent increase in the world price of cotton. Tokarick also calculated that global reforms will generate annual gains of $95 million. Poonyth and others (2004) estimated that removal of cotton subsidies (as reported in the World Trade Organization (WTO) notifications) would increase the world price of cotton between 3.1 and 4.8 percent, depending on the assumed value of demand and supply elasticities. Shepherd (2004) and Pan and others (2004) found a negligible impact of subsidies on the world price of cotton.

The models reviewed here produced highly divergent results, partly reflecting the structure of the models and the assumed elasticities. But a number of other reasons are at play as well. First, there are differences in the level and structure of support. For example, some models incorporate China's support to its cotton sector

Table 4. Effect of removal of distortions in world cotton market, 2003-2004 to 2011-2012

(percentage change over baseline)

	2003–2004	2005–2006	2007–2008	2009–2010	2011–2012	Average[a]
World Price	15.6	13.7	13	12.2	11.7	12.7
Exports						
Africa	12.1	15.1	14	13.1	12.3	12.6
Australia	3.9	3	2.7	2.3	2.1	2.7
United States	−8.4	−6.6	−4.0	−1.5	0.9	−3.5
Uzbekistan	5.4	6.9	6.7	6.4	6.2	6
World	3.9	5.6	6.2	6.7	7.3	5.8
Production						
United States	−18.3	−7.9	−5.9	−4.1	−2.3	−6.7
European Union	−77.4	−77.7	−78.3	−78.8	−79.0	−70.5
Uzbekistan	3.1	4.7	4.6	4.4	4.2	4
Africa	4.5	7.5	7.1	6.7	6.3	6

Note: Average is taken over the 10-year period 2001-2002 to 2010-2011.
Source: Food and Agriculture Policy Research Institute (2002).

and hence model its removal; others do not. Second, there are differences in the underlying scenarios. Some models assume liberalization in all commodity markets, whereas others assume liberalization in the cotton sector only. Third, the models use different base years and hence different levels of subsidies. For example, support in the United States during 1999 was three times as high as in 1997.

Setting all differences aside, however, and taking a simple average over all models, it appears that in the absence of support the world cotton price would have been about 10 percent higher than it actually was. Applying that simple average to the cotton-producing countries of Francophone Africa, those countries lost approximately $150 million annually in export earnings due to subsidies.

Not all models reported gainers and losers from the removal of cotton subsidies. The most complete analysis in that respect is offered by the FAPRI study. FAPRI concluded that the largest gains would go to Africa, which would increase its exports by an average of 12.6 percent (table 4). Exports from Uzbekistan and Australia would increase by 6.0 and 2.7 percent, respectively, while exports from the United States would decline by 3.5 percent. The most dramatic impact would come on the production side: the European Union's cotton output would decline by more than 70 percent.

In addition to low prices and a skewing of export shares, support by major players has triggered several noteworthy reactions:

- Many cotton-producing countries have introduced "reactive support." For example, the Arab Republic of Egypt, Brazil, India, Mexico and Turkey provided $0.5 billion in support for their producers in 2001–02.

- Brazil initiated a WTO consultation, claiming losses to its cotton exports from subsidies by the United States. WTO recently ruled in Brazil's favor.

- Four West African cotton producers (Benin, Burkina Faso, Chad, and Mali) are pressing the WTO for accelerated removal of support for cotton (in the so-called West Africa Cotton Sector Initiative).

Implications of cotton policies

Brazil vs. the United States

On September 27, 2002, Brazil requested consultation with the United States regarding U.S. subsidies to cotton producers. On March 18, 2003, the Dispute Settlement Body of the WTO established a panel to examine the issue, and on April 26, 2004, the WTO issued an interim ruling in favor of Brazil. The final ruling (issued on September 8, 2004) concluded that "the United States is under the obligation to take appropriate steps to remove the adverse effects or…withdraw the subsidy" (WTO 2004a).

Brazil argued that U.S. cotton subsidies were inconsistent with provisions of the Agreement on Subsidies and Countervailing Measures, the Agreement on Agriculture, and the General Agreement on Tariffs and Trade and were causing

Figure 1. Assistance to US Cotton Growers (US $ billion)

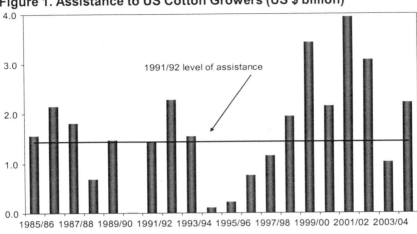

Source: US Department of Agriculture

"serious prejudice to the interests of Brazil" because of a "significant price depression and price suppression" (WTO 2002). Brazil's claims can be summarized as follows (Schnepf 2004):

- During the four marketing years from 1999 to 2002 U.S. domestic support to cotton was in excess of the support provided in 1992, the limit year under the WTO Agreement on Subsidies and Countervailing Measures (figure 1).
- U.S. export subsidies (export credit guarantees and the so-called step-2 payments) violated the Agreement on Agriculture.
- Direct payments to U.S. producers did not qualify for exemption from reduction commitments as decoupled support, because of the associated prohibition against the planting of fruits and vegetables (i.e. direct payments should have been reported under the *Amber Box* instead of the *Green Box* category).

Using the econometric model developed by FAPRI discussed earlier, Brazil claimed that the U.S. subsidies induced a 41 percent increase in U.S. cotton exports, reducing the world price of cotton by 12.6 percent and causing an estimated injury to Brazil of more than $600 million for 2001 alone. The United States appealed the case but the original ruling remained by and large intact. The U.S. announced that it would eliminate the export subsidies. However, it remains unclear what, if any, steps it will take regarding containing the overall level of subsidies and the inappropriate placing of direct payments in the *Amber Box.*

The ruling was issued against the background of the ongoing critical agricultural negotiations, the expiration of the peace clause, the more assertive stance taken by the G-20, and the West African sectoral initiative on cotton (see following section).

125

The ruling has numerous implications for the WTO and the Doha Development Agenda and for developing countries and international institutions (Baffes 2005c):

- As the first case of a developing country challenging an OECD farm subsidy program in the WTO, it may set a precedent. If further cases follow, there may be a shift in the focus of WTO activities from negotiation to litigation.
- The way to avoid a significant increase in such disputes is to make significant progress in the Doha Development Agenda. Hence, the ruling may help agencies such as the EU Commission and the U.S. Trade Representative's Office confront domestic protectionist lobbies.
- The ruling strengthens the claims of many developing countries that OECD subsidies distort global commodity markets and depress world prices.
- This dispute spotlights the importance of models analyzing the effects of subsidies on world prices and export shares, making model developers more accountable for the analysis. The ruling reveals the importance and weaknesses of current measures of support and the differences in WTO, U.S., and EU definitions of "decoupled support."

West African cotton sector initiative

On May 16, 2003, four West African cotton producing countries (Benin, Burkina Faso, Chad, and Mali) submitted a joint proposal to the WTO demanding removal of support to the cotton sector by the United States, China, and the European Union and compensation for damages until full removal of support. The West African countries were aided in this move, often referred to as the "cotton initiative," by IDEAS, a Geneva-based NGO funded by the Swiss government.

The four countries argued that subsidies cost them an estimated $250 million in export earnings during the 2001/02 marketing season—$1 billion when the indirect effects of these subsidies were considered (cotton prices averaged $0.82 a kilogram in October 2001, the lowest since November 1972 with the exception of August 1986). Because the standard WTO remedies (compensation through supplementary concessions or imposition of countervailing duties) were not feasible, the proposal called for "transitional...financial compensation...to offset the injury caused by support of production and export." The compensation would be proportional to the subsidies, declining and ending as the subsidies were reduced and abolished. The proposal argued that the direct and indirect effects of support for cotton production should be taken into account when determining compensation and that "the unit amount and the total amount of subsidies should be taken into account when dividing the compensation among countries which subsidize production" (WTO 2003).

The initiative received considerable attention during the Cancún Ministerial. The director general of WTO urged ministers to consider the proposal "seriously." While numerous countries were sympathetic, there were doubts whether it would benefit the Doha Development Agenda to treat one commodity differently from others. Furthermore, it soon became apparent that direct compensation was unlikely. The inability to deal effectively with the initiative was one reason for the failure to reach agreement in Cancùn.

It was finally determined that while the trade part of the request (subsidies) fell within WTO's mandate, the development part of the request (compensation) should be handled by the multilateral institutions in coordination with the concerned governments. To that end, at a WTO-sponsored conference on March 23–24, 2004, in Cotonou, Benin, both bilateral and multilateral donors reaffirmed their willingness to deal with the development part of the cotton initiative.

On August 1, 2004, the WTO General Council reached a decision to proceed with multilateral trade negotiations, emphasizing that the theme should be addressed "ambitiously, expeditiously, and specifically" (WTO 2004b). The director general was instructed to consult with international organizations, including the Bretton Woods institutions, the Food and Agriculture Organization, and the International Trade Center, to direct existing programs and any additional resources toward development of the economies where cotton is of vital importance. Progress on the "cotton initiative" is being monitored at WTO meetings following the establishment of the sub-committee on cotton (WTO 2004c).

Policy changes

As mentioned above, the European Union reformed its cotton policy recently by replacing its price-support mechanism with two new support measures. With the new support structure expected to be in place until 2011, EU cotton producers will still receive subsidies, albeit with a less distorting effect on production and trade. The 2002 U.S. Farm Bill, on the other hand, which will be in place until 2007 guarantees U.S. cotton producers high prices until 2007. However, part of this subsidy may be removed or altered in response to the recent WTO ruling.

Several cotton-producing countries (especially in Sub-Saharan Africa) that had been taxing their cotton sectors undertook substantial policy reforms in the 1990s to increase efficiency. Although these reforms have been attributed—correctly—to conditions imposed by the World Bank and the International Monetary Fund in the context of structural adjustment programs, the reforms were the only feasible alternative in most cases. Faced with falling world cotton prices and plagued by inefficiencies, poor management, and often outright corruption, the parastatals that handled the marketing and trade of cotton had been staggering under huge debts, remaining afloat only through infusions of state capital. Some had even gone bankrupt.

Substantial reforms were undertaken during the mid-1990s by Tanzania, Uganda, Zambia, and Zimbabwe (Baffes 2001). With the exception of Tanzania (where the reform process was never completed), the reforms generated a considerable supply response. Growers now receive a higher share of export prices and timely payments. There have been numerous reports that the quality of cotton declined after the reforms, but these reports have not been substantiated. West African cotton producers are also contemplating reforms. Central Asian cotton producers, mainly Uzbekistan, still intervene heavily in their cotton sectors; reforms are unlikely to take place soon.

References

Baffes, J. 2001 "Policy Reforms in the Cotton Market." In *Commodity Market Reforms: Lessons from Two Decades*, ed. A. Takamasa, J. Baffes, D. Larson, and P. Varangis. Regional and Sectoral Studies, World Bank, Washington, DC.

_____ 2005. "The Cotton Problem." *The World Bank Research Observer* 20:109-144.

FAPRI (Food and Agricultural Policy Research Institute) (2002). "The Doha Round of the World Trade Organization: Liberalization of Agricultural Markets and its Impact on Developing Economies." Paper presented at the IATRC Winter Meetings.

Goreux, L. 2004. "Reforming the Cotton Sector in Sub-Saharan Africa." Africa Region Working Paper Series 47. World Bank, Washington, DC.

International Cotton Advisory Committee. 2003. *Production and Trade Policies Affecting the Cotton Industry.* Washington, DC.

Pan, S., S. Mohanty, D. Ethridge, and M. Fadiga. 2004. "The Impacts of U.S. Cotton Programs on the World Market: An Analysis of Brazilian and West African WTO Petitions." Department of Agricultural and Applied Economics, Texas Tech University.

Poonyth, D., A. Sarris, R. Sharma, and S. Shui. 2004. "The Impact of Domestic and Trade Policies on the World Cotton Market." Commodity and Trade Policy Research Working Paper, U.N. Food and Agriculture Organization, Rome.

Reeves, G., D. Vincent, D. Quirke, and S. Wyatt. 2001. "Trade Distortions and Cotton Markets: Implications for Global Cotton Producers." Center for International Economics, Canberra.

Schnepf, R. (2004). "U.S.-Brazil WTO Cotton Subsidy Issue." Congressional Research Service Report. Washington, D.C

Shepherd, B. 2004. "The Impact of U.S. Subsidies on the World Market of Cotton: A Reassessment." Groupe d'Economie Mondiale (GEM), Institut d'Etudes Politiques de Paris.

Sumner, D. A. 2003 "A Quantitative Simulation Analysis of the Impacts of U.S. Cotton Subsidies on Cotton Prices and Quantities." Unpublished paper, Department of Agricultural and Resource Economics, University of California, Davis.

Tokarick, S. (2003). "Measuring the Impact of Distortions in Agricultural Trade in Partial and General Equilibrium." International Monetary Fund Working Paper, WP/03/110, Washington, DC.

World Trade Organization (2002). United States—Subsidies on Upland Cotton: Request for Consultations by Brazil. WT/DS267/1. Geneva.

_____ (2004a). United States—Subsidies on Upland Cotton: Report of the Panel. WT/DS267/R. Geneva.

_____ (2004b). Doha Work Programme. WT/L/579. Geneva.

_____ (2004c). Establishment of the Sub-Committee on Cotton. TN/AG/13. Geneva.

Sugar Policies: Opportunity for Change

Donald Mitchell

The source of about 7 percent of the world's calorie supplies, sugar is an important commodity in many countries, accounting for 10 percent or more of total export earnings of 12 developing countries during 1995–2000.[1] However, its importance as a source of export earnings has declined over time, partly because imports by Organization for Economic Co-operation and Development (OECD) countries have declined. In the 1970s, the European Union, Japan, and the United States accounted for half of the world's total sugar imports. Since then, U.S. sugar imports have declined from more than 5 million tons per year to slightly more than 1 million tons per year. The European Union, once a net importer of about 2.5 million tons, is now a net exporter of about 5 million tons. Japan decreased sugar imports from 2.5 to 1.5 million tons between 1970 and 2000. Thus, three of the largest sugar importers in the 1970s have now become self-sufficient (figure 1), slowing the growth of world trade and exports from developing countries.[2]

These countries reduced imports not because of gains in productive efficiencies or a strong comparative advantage in sugar production but because of high protection. Producers in these countries receive more than double the world market price thanks to government guarantees, import controls, and production quotas—a combination of policies that has encouraged production of sugar and sugar substitutes, reduced consumption and imports, and deprived lower-cost producers (many in developing countries) of export opportunities. Total government support to producers in the European Union, Japan, and the United States averaged $6.4 billion in 2004 according to OECD estimates. In comparison, total sugar exports from developing countries were about the same in recent years.

The clout of the U.S. sugar industry was recently demonstrated when it opposed and almost prevented the passage of the Central American-Dominican Republic Free Trade Agreement (CAFTA-DR) because the agreement increased the sugar quotas of these countries (*Wall Street Journal*, July 28, 2005). The U.S. sugar industry had earlier prevented sugar from being included in the Australia–U.S. free trade agreement, even though sugar is an important export for Australia. The *Washington Post* reported (February 9, 2004) that the powerful U.S. sugar lobby and affiliated individuals and political action committees had donated $20.2 million to both U.S. political parties since 1990. Pressures for change are building, however, and the opportunity for sugar policy reform is better now than in several decades.

Figure 1. Inefficient producers in the North are crowding out efficient producers in the South

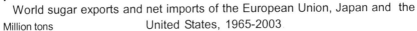

World sugar exports and net imports of the European Union, Japan and the United States, 1965-2003

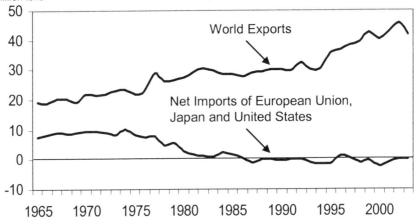

Source: Based on FAO data.

Background

Sugar occurs naturally in most foods, but it is economically extracted from only a few crops—among them sugar beets, sugar cane, and corn. Common sugar, or *sucrose*, is extracted in identical and nearly pure form from sugar cane and sugar beets. *Dextrose* is a sugar derived synthetically from starch (most commonly corn), and *fructose* is a very sweet sugar derived from dextrose. High-fructose corn syrup (HFCS), produced by the enzymatic conversion of a portion of the dextrose in corn syrup to fructose, is used as a sugar substitute in soft drinks. The fact that identical or nearly identical sugars can be produced from different crops provides producers and consumers with a wide range of substitution possibilities. But it also means that sugar policies are often complex, as the different industries vie for government support. For example, the European Union and Japan have legislated quotas on HFCS production in order to limit competition with sugar.

HFCS is a nearly perfect sugar substitute in uses such as soft drinks. It and other corn syrups now account for 40 percent of caloric sweeteners in Japan, and roughly half of U.S. caloric sweetener consumption (figure 2). Discovered in the late 1960s, the technique for commercial production of high-fructose corn syrup was made profitable by high sugar prices in the protected Japanese and U.S. markets. Today, economies of scale, improvements in production techniques, and large installed production capacity (financed under high prices) have made corn syrups competitive with sugar from cane and less costly than sugar from beets.

Costs of production favor producing sugar from cane. Major exporters can produce refined (white) sugar from cane at an average cost of about 13 cents per pound, compared to 26 cents per pound from sugar beets (table 1). The higher cost of production from sugar beets is one of the reasons why protection is high in northern hemisphere countries, which produce sugar mostly from sugar beets. HFCS requires large investments in plant and equipment and a low-cost source of starch. Because producers in the United States, a major producer of corn, have already made such investments, HFCS production costs in the United States are competitive with sugar produced from sugar cane.

Policy changes are inevitable

The European Union proposed major reforms to its sugar regime following a ruling by the World Trade Organization (WTO) Appellate Body on April 28, 2005. That ruling upheld an earlier ruling in a case brought by Australia, Brazil, and Thailand, which charged that the European Union was subsidizing its sugar exports beyond the limits permitted in the Uruguay Round Agreement on Agriculture. The WTO Appellate Body dismissed the EU appeal in full, confirming that all EU sugar exports are subsidized, either directly or indirectly. The European Union, after declaring that it would abide

Figure 2. Sugar supersizing in the U.S.

U.S. consumption of sugar and high-fructose corn syrup, 1970–2004
Million tons

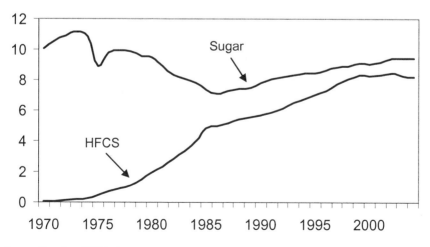

Source: Based on USDA data.

Table 1. Average costs of producing cane sugar, beet sugar, and high-fructose corn syrup by categories of producers, and actual sugar prices, 1997/98–2001/02

Category	1997–1998	1998–1999	1999–1990	2000–2001	2001–2002
	U.S. cents per pound [a]				
Raw cane sugar					
Low cost producers [b]	8.25	8.11	6.84	7.95	6.59
Major exporters [c]	10.55	9.66	8.70	9.51	8.38
Cane sugar, white equiv.					
Low cost producers [b]	11.92	11.77	10.39	11.60	10.11
Major exporters [c]	14.41	13.45	12.41	13.28	12.06
Beet sugar, refined					
Low cost producers [d]	22.44	24.07	23.12	23.56	24.23
Major exporters [e]	25.44	27.02	25.51	24.2	26.19
High-fructose corn syrup [f]					
Major producers [g]	12.62	11.41	11.62	12.87	12.62
Actual Market Prices					
Raw cane sugar [h]	10.76	7.18	6.20	9.81	7.21

a. Measured in nominal U.S. cents per pound, ex-mill, factory basis.
b. Average of six producing regions (Australia, Brazil (Center/South), Guatemala, Malawi, Zambia, and Zimbabwe).
c. Average of seven countries (Australia, Brazil, Colombia, Cuba, Guatemala, South Africa, and Thailand).
d. Average of seven countries (Belgium, Canada, Chile, France, Turkey, United Kingdom, and United States).
e. Average of four countries (Belgium, France, Germany, and Turkey).
f. HFCS-55, dry weight.
g. Average of 22 countries (Argentina, Belgium, Bulgaria, Arab Republic of Egypt, Canada, China, Finland, France, Germany, Greece, Hungry, Italy, Japan, Mexico, Netherlands, Poland, Slovakia, South Korea, Spain, Taiwan (China), Turkey, United Kingdom, and United States).
h. Raw cane sugar price is U.S. cents per pound, July–June average of monthly prices, f.o.b. Caribbean ports.
Source: LMC International as reported in Sugar and Sweeteners Outlook, Economic Research Service, USDA, September 2004. Actual market prices are from World Bank.

by the ruling, tabled a reform proposal on June 22, with a target of getting an agreement before the WTO meeting in Hong Kong in December 2005.

The reform proposed by the European Commission calls for an internal price cut of 39 percent over two years beginning in 2006–07. EU sugar beet producers are to be compensated for 60 percent of the price cut through the Single Farm Payment, which would be linked to environmental and land management standards. The existing A and B quotas are to be merged into a single production quota, and intervention prices are to become a reference price. A private storage system will be introduced as a safety net in case the market price falls below the reference prices.

The European Commission also proposed an assistance scheme for the ACP (Africa, Caribbean, Pacific) countries that includes a broad range of support options that can be tailored to each country.

With successful conclusion of the Doha Round of multilateral trade negotiations expected to require reform on sugar, the proposed reform of the EU sugar regime has had the effect of isolating the United States. The United States has not announced a sugar reform package, but it will face strong internal and external pressures for reform in the next several years. The external pressures will include political pressures in the Doha Round and market pressures stemming from international agreements such as North American Free Trade Agreement (NAFTA) and CAFTA-DR. The U.S. sugar program accounts for a disproportionately large share of the Aggregate Measure of Support (AMS), which is expected to be cut as part of a Doha Round agreement. This will lead to internal pressures for reform as other commodity groups fight to protect their own support programs.

Market pressures will come primarily from Mexico, which will be allowed unlimited duty-free access in 2009 under NAFTA. This could lead to a surge of imports, a build-up of U.S. government stocks, and large budget outlays unless the United States reduces its internal sugar price supports. The next U.S. farm bill, scheduled for 2007, is the most likely occasion for policy reform.

Japan faces less internal pressure for reform, but it provides higher protection to its sugar producers than the European Union and United States. It should be pressured to reform its sugar policy by developing country exporters.

The benefits of reform are substantial

Protection in the world sugar market is imposed by developed countries at great cost to themselves and those developing countries with the economic potential to expand exports.

The welfare benefits of sugar policy reform are substantial—and the gains greatest from multilateral reform. According to recent studies of the global sugar and sweetener markets, the global welfare gains from removing all trade distortions are estimated to be as much as $4.7 billion per year. In countries with the highest protection (Japan, Western Europe, the United States, Indonesia, and Eastern Europe, in descending order) net imports would increase by an estimated 15 million tons per year as production falls and consumption rises. World sugar prices would increase by as much as 40 percent, while prices in countries that heavily protect their markets would decline to the benefit of consumers. The greatest price declines would occur in Japan, where sugar prices would fall 65 percent, followed by a 40 percent decline in Western Europe, and a 25 percent decline in the United States. Brazilian producers stand to gain the most from liberalization: around $2.6 billion per year. Partially offsetting that gain is a loss of $1 billion to Brazilian consumers, who would pay higher prices after liberalization—leaving a net gain of $1.6 billion for Brazil.

If existing polices in the European Union and United States are adjusted to accommodate higher imports under the ACP, Europe's Everything But Arms (EBA) agreement, NAFTA, and other agreements, many low-cost producers, including Brazil, would lose because they do not currently have large quotas and are not among the ACP, EBA, or NAFTA countries. A better alternative is to push for full liberalization of the world sugar market in order to allow efficient producers to expand production and exports, and consumers in protected markets to benefit from lower prices. Full liberalization may also make policy change more palatable because no country would be singled out for reform. It also has the advantage of offering somewhat higher world prices to soften the adjustment for producers in protected markets.

But not all countries stand to gain from reform

A number of countries have preferential access to the EU or U.S. sugar markets through the ACP/EU Sugar Protocol and the U.S. sugar import program (table 2). These countries receive the high internal price on quota exports. Their preferential access is valued at about $800 million per year compared to world market prices—less than it appears, because many of these producers have high production costs and would not produce at world market prices, and because world price increases after full liberalization would partially offset the loss of high prices in preferential markets. The net loss to these exporting countries from full liberalization is estimated to total $450 million per year.

Table 2. Countries with large quotas in the EU and U.S. sugar markets

EU quota holders			U.S. quota holders		
Country	Sugar quota 2003/04	Share of exports from sugar	Country	Sugar quota 2003/04	Share of exports from sugar
Mauritius	491,031	17.3	Dominican	185,335	9.5
Fiji	165,348	20.7	Brazil	152,691	3.3
Guyana	159,410	28.0	Philippines	142,160	0.1
Jamaica	118,696	5.4	Australia	87,402	1.5
Swaziland	117,845	11.9	Guatemala	50,546	7.8
Barbados	50,312	9.5	Argentina	45,281	0.2
Belize	40,349	19.2	Peru	43,175	0.2
Trinidad & Tobago	43,751	0.9	Panama	30,538	2.0
Zimbabwe	30,225	3.2	El Salvador	27,379	2.1
Malawi	20,824	6.0	Colombia	25,273	1.6

Source: European Commission 2004 and USDA 2003.

Low-cost producers with small EU or U.S. quotas relative to their total exports would benefit from policy reform because they would gain more from increased exports and the rise in world market prices than they would lose from eroded preferences. These countries include Australia, which has a U.S. quota of 87,000 thousand tons and total exports of more than 4 million tons; Brazil, with a U.S. quota of 152,000 tons and total exports of more than 17 million tons; and Thailand, with an EU quota of 14,000 tons and exports of 3-4 million tons.

Countries with no quota to the EU and U.S. markets, such as Arab Republic of Egypt and Sudan, would benefit from both higher exports and higher world prices. Other compensations for the loss of quotas may also be available, including broad-based economic supports such as the Economic Partnership Agreements now being negotiated by the European Union.

Employment in sugar industries

Estimates of employment in developing countries' sugar industries have been developed from various reports, surveys, and industry statements (table 3), although no systematic accounting is available. Such estimates show considerable cross-country consistency among high- and low-cost producers. Brazil, Guyana, and South Africa are among the lowest-cost producers; their rates of raw sugar production per industry employee are estimated to range from 16.3 to 19.9 tons per year. Moderately high-cost producers, such as Fiji and Mauritius, produce about 8 tons of raw sugar per industry employee. Jamaica, a very high-cost producer with production costs estimated at about 24 U.S. cents per pound, produces about 5.5 tons of raw sugar per industry employee. Based on these estimates, an additional million tons of sugar production from a low-cost sugar producing developing country would generate about 55,500 direct employment jobs. If the production came from a high-cost producer, the same million tons of production would generate about 128,000 direct employment jobs. (Additional indirect employment would also be generated in transportation and related industries, but no attempt has been made to estimate these jobs.)

Based on these estimates of productivity, full liberalization could generate between 832,500 and 1,920,000 jobs in developing countries by raising imports of developing-country sugar into highly-protected markets by 15 million tons. The net global employment effect would be less because some jobs would be lost in the highly protected markets. In the United States, for example, an estimated 6,000 sugar beet growers produce half of the country's sugar. Many of these jobs would be lost. However, new jobs would be created to accommodate processing of raw cane sugar imported to replace the decline in sugar produced from beets.

Table 3. Raw sugar produced per sugar industry employee, selected developing countries, 1999–2001

Country	Direct employment (growers and factory)	Tons of raw sugar produced average	Tons of raw sugar produced per employee
Low-cost producers			
Brazil	1,100,000	19,485,000	17.7
Guyana	18,000	293,072	16.3
South Africa	130,000	2,589,667	19.9
High-cost producers			
Fiji	40,500	336,333	8.3
Jamaica	38,000	208,351	5.5
Mauritius	65,000	529,299	8.1
Other producers			
Malawi	17,000	200,667	11.8
Mexico	300,000	5,069,233	16.9

Notes and Sources: Production is the three-year average of raw sugar production during 1999–2001 from FAOSTAT. Employment data are from various sources and include total direct employment in sugar factories and the number of growers. Employment data for Brazil are from OECD (1999); Fiji and Guyana data are from F.O.Lichts; data for Jamaica are from the Jamaican Sugar Authority; Kenya data are from the Kenya Sugar Board; Malawi data are from the Malawi Ministry of Commerce and Industry; Mauritius data are from F.O.Lichts; Mexico; and South Africa data are from OECD (1999).

Conclusions

The chances for global reform of sugar policy are better than they have been for several decades. The European Union has already proposed major reforms to its sugar regime following a ruling by the WTO Appellate Body on April 28, 2005. That ruling, upholding an earlier ruling in a case brought by Australia, Brazil, and Thailand, confirmed that all EU sugar exports are subsidized, either directly or indirectly. The EU's proposal in response calls for a 39 percent cut in internal prices and other measures to increase the market orientation of the sugar sector. The United States has not yet proposed reform to its sugar program, but there are strong external and internal market pressures for reform.

The current round of multilateral trade negotiations offer an excellent opportunity for developing countries to push for reform, which would create jobs and raise foreign exchange earnings, while also benefiting consumers in highly-protected markets who pay several times the world market price for sugar.

In anticipation of reform, countries with high protection will need to devise policies to compensate countries for the loss of quotas and producers for the loss of protection. Such compensation should be designed so that it does not continue to support sugar production but rather supports sugar producers during an adjustment period. This type of adjustment was used in the United States for peanut producers facing the threat of increased imports due to WTO and NAFTA agreements. In the 2002 U.S. farm bill, the loan rate for edible peanuts was cut by half (compared to the rate prevailing in the mid-1990s), production quotas were eliminated, and direct cash payments were made to producers. The payments consisted of deficiency payments (paid when prices fell below the new loan rates), decoupled direct payments, and counter-cyclical payments. Quota holders were compensated through direct payments for their loss of quota rights. A similar program is needed for sugar.

Unwinding the system of protection and support will require new policies in some developing countries. Some high-cost producers may be able to raise productivity, but others will have to contract. Policies that encourage investments to increase productivity and assist in the shift of resources to other, more internationally competitive activities, may be in order. Development assistance can play a supportive role in all of these areas.

Note

1. The 12 countries and the average share of export earnings derived from sugar during 1995–2000 were: Gambia (91 percent), Reunion (63 percent), Cuba (41 percent), Saint Kitts and Nevis (37 percent), Fiji (25 percent), Belize (25 percent), Guyana (24 percent), Mauritius (21 percent), Swaziland (17 percent), Dominican Republic (14 percent), Guadeloupe (12 percent), Barbados (11 percent).
2. Donald Mitchell is Lead Economist in the Development Prospects Group of The World Bank. This note is based on "Sugar Policies: Opportunity for Change, World Bank Policy Research Working Paper 3222, February 2004.

Further Reading

Borrell, Brent, and David Pearce. 1999. "Sugar: The Taste Test of Trade Liberalization." Center for International Economics, Canberra and Sydney, September 1999.

Mitchell, Donald. 2004. "Sugar Policies: Opportunity for Change." Policy Research Working Paper 3222, World Bank, Washington, DC.

Sheales, Terry, Simon Gordon, Ahmed Hafi, and Chris Toyne. 1999. "Sugar International Policies Affecting Market Expansion." ABARE Research Report 99.14, Australian Bureau of Agricultural and Resource Economics, Canberra.

Wohlgenant, Michael K. 1999. "Effects of Trade Liberalization on the World Sugar Market." U.N. Food and Agriculture Organization, Rome.

USDA (United States Department of Agriculture). 2003. *Sugar and Sweetener Situation and Outlook Yearbook*. Economic Research Service, Washington, DC.

———. 2004. "Sugar and Sweeteners Outlook." Economic Research Service, Washington, DC. September 28.

Market Access for Nonagricultural Products: In Search of a Formula

Will Martin and Maros Ivanic

Developing countries' exports of nonagricultural products have risen rapidly in recent years, with manufactures leading the way (World Bank 2003). Nonagricultural products now constitute the overwhelming majority of merchandise exports from developing countries.[1] In East Asia, the share of manufactures in total exports has risen from 50 to 90 percent in the past two decades; in Latin America and the Caribbean, it has risen from 20 to 60 percent. Even in Sub-Saharan Africa the share of manufactures has risen from 10 to 25 percent. Other non-agricultural products, such as resources and fishery products, are also important to many developing countries. While many of these exports are subject to low tariffs in the major industrial-country markets, some are subject to high peak tariffs that sharply restrict market access.

The early stages of the Doha negotiations were marked by a flurry of tariff-cutting proposals for nonagricultural market access (NAMA)—among them very concrete proposals from China, the European Union, India, and the United States. Building on these proposals, particularly the proposal from China, the Chairman of the Negotiating Group for NAMA of the World Trade Organization (WTO) proposed in May 2003 the application of a Swiss formula (see equation 1 below and Francois and Martin 2003) that would impose a ceiling tariff based on each country's original average tariff. These proposals were coupled with other proposals for complete elimination of tariffs in certain sectors.

In considering any formula approach to liberalization, WTO members must weigh the formula's implications for their own tariff structure and for their market-access opportunities abroad. Although tariff reductions are based on bound tariffs, which can be substantially above the tariff rates actually applied, countries usually have little trouble assessing the implications of a proposal for their own applied tariffs. Such an evaluation can be undertaken using widely-available software such as EXCEL, and information on bound tariffs (the limits, agreed and recorded at WTO, above which applied tariffs cannot be increased), and applied tariffs. Assessing the implications for tariff revenues is a little more difficult, but still relatively manageable. By contrast, it is a major task for countries to assess a formula's likely effects on their market-access opportunities, since these depend on a range of factors including the nature of the formula; the average and distribution of tariffs; and the importance of exports to *each of the country's export markets*. A particular challenge is posed by the gaps between tariff bindings and the tariffs actually applied. A further complication results from the preferences available on some developing country exports, and the increasing number of preferential trade arrangements, both of which cause applied tariff rates to fall below the scheduled most-favored-nation (MFN) rates on some trade.

Earlier work (World Bank 2003: 89–98) reviewed the key proposals for reform of nonagricultural market access at that time and provided a broad assessment of their market-access implications for several key countries. This note updates that review and assesses the likely effects of current proposals on market access for each developing-country region. Each country's situation will differ from the broad averages that we are able to consider in this note, but we hope these broad assessments will provide an initial guide, and provide an illustration of what can be done in making these assessments.[2]

Three formulas under discussion within WTO

Three formula approaches (modalities) are currently under consideration in the current WTO negotiations on nonagricultural market access (WTO 2005a):

- A single Swiss formula with flexibilities for developing countries,
- A Swiss formula with two coefficients—one for industrial and one for developing countries,
- A Swiss formula with coefficients based on countries' average tariffs.

The Swiss formula has a long history in the multilateral trading system, having been applied in the Tokyo Round of negotiations in the 1970s (Laird and Yeats 1987). It involves setting new tariffs, t_1, using equation (1):

$$(1) \qquad t_1 = \frac{a.t_0}{a + t_0}$$

Where t_0 is the base tariff, and a is the "ceiling" parameter that determines the highest possible tariff in the new tariff schedule. This function has the property of reducing higher tariffs by more than lower tariffs—with extremely high tariffs being reduced to just below the ceiling. It also makes smaller cuts in low tariffs than would a proportional formula—a feature that helps preserve tariff revenues, since low-tariff, high-volume items are often important sources of government revenue.

A stylized representation of the impact of a Swiss formula on tariffs is given in figure 1. The figure is drawn for a ceiling parameter of 16 percent, a value that played an important role in the Tokyo Round (Baldwin 1986). The figure shows three broad features of the formula—small tariffs are cut by less than with a proportional cut that would provide the same reduction in average tariffs; high tariffs are cut more than proportionally; and an initial tariff equal to the coefficient is reduced to half the coefficient value. Three examples are useful to illustrate the potential strength of these effects. By applying the formula illustrated, with a coefficient of 16 percent, an initial tariff of 1 percent would be reduced to 0.94 percent— a 6 percent reduction.

Figure 1. A Swiss formula cuts higher tariffs more

Impacts of a Proportional and a Swiss Formula for Tariff Cutting

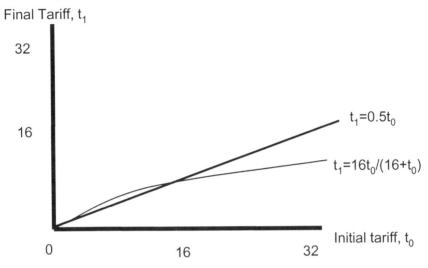

By contrast, an initial tariff of 1,000 percent would be reduced to 15.7 percent—a reduction of more than 98 percent. An initial tariff of 16 percent would be reduced by half.

The top–down nature of the Swiss formula means that it automatically tends to lessen two major concerns of developing countries—tariff peaks and tariff escalation. Its effectiveness in lowering peak tariffs and reducing tariff escalation is consistent with the requirements of WTO's July 2004 Framework (WTO 2004). And it is particularly important for tariff reduction in industrial countries, where average tariffs are low but peak tariffs burden many products of interest to developing countries—among them textiles, clothing, and footwear.

Most attention in the current negotiations seems to be focused on the second and third of the approaches (modalities) under consideration. Pakistan (WTO 2005a) has advocated the second, with the ceiling parameter for industrial and developing countries based on the average bound tariffs in each group—rounded to 6 and 30 percent. Some developed countries, while agreeing with Pakistan's broad approach, seek lower coefficients, particularly for developing countries. Other countries, including Argentina, Brazil, and India (WTO 2005b) favor an approach based on earlier proposals by China and the former chair of the WTO's Negotiating Group for NAMA, in which ceiling parameters are based on average tariffs in individual countries.

Another key issue under discussion is the treatment of tariffs that are currently unbound. Most nonagricultural tariffs are now bound in the industrial countries, but in developing countries binding coverage varies widely. Blackhurst, Enders, and Francois (1996) reported that the import coverage of tariff bindings on industrial products in developing countries rose from 13 to 61 percent as a result of the Uruguay Round, with many countries committing to 100 percent binding. However, coverage rates remain below 10 percent in Mauritius, Zimbabwe, and many other countries.

The binding of tariffs has value, even if applied tariffs are not actually reduced (Francois and Martin 2004), because binding rules out subsequent increases in tariffs, and particularly increases that create costly tariff peaks. With broad agreement on the desirability of achieving 100 percent coverage of tariff bindings in NAMA, as in agriculture, there have been several proposals for dealing with unbound tariffs in the formulas. These include the original proposal by the NAMA chair to use twice the applied rate as the base for cutting and binding tariffs. Another, proposed by Canada, Hong Kong (China), New Zealand, and Norway (CHNN), is to allow countries to add 5 percentage points to each currently applied tariff. A third, proposed by Pakistan, is to add 30 percentage points to each tariff (WTO 2005a).

Effects of NAMA proposals on developing countries' market access

To help relieve the uncertainty surrounding the outcome of the negotiations on binding rates, we experimented with setting the base rates from which cuts are to be made at different multiples of bound rates. Given these choices, we examined the implications of the competing formulas for market access. Our analysis was done using UNCTAD's TRAINS database, taking into account the preferential treatment provided unilaterally by Australia, Canada, the European Union, Japan and the United States. While most earlier studies ignore preferences and hence exaggerate the market access gain from liberalization, our analysis overstates these gains to some degree by assuming full preference utilisation. Our use of weighted average tariffs also understates the benefits since highly restricted products have small initial trade shares.

Highly summarized results are expressed in table 1 as the average tariff facing exporters from each developing-country region, and as the coefficient of variation of those tariffs—a measure that provides an indication of the prevalence of tariff peaks and escalation relative to the mean tariff. The results were obtained (as in World Bank 2003) by cutting bound rates and then assessing the impacts on the corresponding applied rates. Only when bound rates fall below initial applied rates are applied rates cut, and then by only as much as is needed to keep the applied rate at or below the bound rate. In contrast with our earlier results, however, we focus here on the implications for export-market access, rather than on countries' own tariffs.

In generating the numbers presented in the table, we used three basic options that cover the range of possibilities for tariff-cutting formulas and treatment of unbound rates. These range form the Chairman's Proposal to a proposal that provides for much deeper cuts in developing country tariffs through a lower ceiling and smaller increase in unbound tariffs prior to cutting.

Option proposed by the former chair of WTO NAMA Negotiating Group

- Unbound tariffs are first bound at twice the country's applied MFN average.
- Cuts are made using a Swiss formula with a coefficient equal to the country's tariff base average. Least developed countries and those with less than 35 percent coverage do not make cuts.

Option proposed by Pakistan

- Unbound tariffs are bound at MFN rate plus 30 percentage points.
- Cuts use a Swiss formula with a coefficient of 6 for developed countries and 30 for developing countries. Least developed countries and those with less than 35 percent binding coverage do not make cuts.

Option represented by authors' combination of proposals from CHNN and Industrial Countries

- Unbound tariffs are bound by MFN rate plus 5 percentage points.
- Swiss-formula cuts use a coefficient of 5 for developed countries and 15 for developing countries. Least developed countries and those with less than 35 percent binding coverage do not make cuts.

Table 1. Implications of different formula options for average tariffs facing developing countries

| (Percent) | Pre | | Post | | | | | |
| | | | Chair | | Pakistan | | CHNN-Industrial | |
	Average	CV	Average	CV	Average	CV	Average	CV
Sub-Saharan Africa	2.3	560	1.9	510	1.4	340	1.1	270
East Asia, Pacific	3.9	380	2.6	290	1.9	240	1.6	180
Europe, Central Asia	3.6	420	2.6	330	1.9	240	1.6	180
Latin America	4.1	370	2.8	300	2.2	290	1.9	220
South Asia	6.0	420	4.1	330	3.0	290	2.6	240
Mid. East, N. Africa	2.0	400	1.6	360	1.3	290	1.0	200

CHNN = Canada, Hong Kong (China), New Zealand, Norway.
CV = coefficient of variation.

Shaving tariff peaks

Key features of table 1 are the relatively low unweighted average tariffs facing most developing regions once preferences in key markets are taken into account. The very high coefficients of variation of tariffs facing exporters, however, hint at the presence of serious tariff peaks on some products. For Sub-Saharan Africa, for example, the coefficient of variation is 560 percent of the mean, implying a substantial share of tariffs that are five or more times the mean tariff. Many of these are associated with peak tariffs, on which preferences are not available, in key industrial-country markets.

The three proposals all reduce average tariffs and the coefficient of variation of tariffs. However, it is clear that the two proposals that use a single ceiling parameter for developing countries—the Pakistan and U.S.–CHNN approaches—are more effective in reducing the barriers facing developing countries than is the proposal from the former chair of the WTO Market Access Committee, in which the ceiling parameter is based on each country's average tariff.

The CHNN Industrial approach is more effective in reducing market-access barriers than is Pakistan's approach. While Pakistan's proposal would reduce the *pain* that developing countries face in their home markets, it would also reduce their *gain* in market access. The sharp reduction in the coefficient of variation in the tariffs facing each country bears testimony to the success of the approach in reducing tariff peaks and escalation.

Effects on the distribution of high tariffs

Additional insights into the effects of the proposals on the barriers facing each country are given in six plots, one for each region (figure 2). These show the value of trade subject to each level of tariffs. Because tariff peaks reduce the volume of trade in high-tariff categories, we have first estimated the trade that would exist in each category under free-trade conditions, and then plotted those values against the tariff rates.[3] While the precise pattern varies among regions, a key feature of the initial distribution of tariffs is sizeable numbers of tariffs at or close to zero and some peaks associated with rates well above zero. For exporters from Sub-Saharan Africa, for example, there is a substantial peak in the value of exports of products that face tariffs between 30 and 35 percent.

When the tariff-cutting formulas are applied, the entire distribution of tariffs shifts to the left, increasing the share of trade that is subject to tariffs of close to zero. In many cases, that shift is much less marked under the former chair's formula than under the other two.

The difference between the Pakistan and CHNN Industrial proposals in lowering tariffs on large traded-goods categories differs substantially among regions. In South Asia, for instance, the CHNN Industrial proposal is much more effective in reducing high tariffs than the other proposals: virtually all exports from the region would face tariffs of 7.5 percent or less. Pakistan's proposal brings a much smaller fraction of exports into this category. By contrast, in East Asia, all three proposals generate surprisingly similar results, and all are quite effective at reducing the share of exports subject to high tariffs.

Conclusion

The objectives of this note were to provide an outline of the approaches to reform being considered in the ongoing negotiations on nonagricultural market access and to provide some simple estimates of the likely effectiveness of those approaches in expanding market access for developing countries. The results indicate that all of the approaches would have some effect in expanding market access and reducing peak tariffs. The two more aggressive approaches, however, would be more effective in reducing barriers. Although regional averages do not accurately represent the situation of any individual country, the results presented here do illustrate what can be done for any individual country seeking to assess the implications of alternative formulas for market access. They also show that raising the level of ambition in the negotiations on nonagricultural market access has the potential to provide important market access gains to developing countries as a group.

Figure 2: Value of exports by tariff rate by region:

Value of exports by tariff rate from East Asia

Value (in US $ billion)

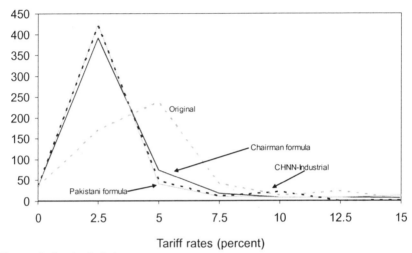

Tariff rates (percent)

Source: Authors' calculations.

Value of exports by tariff rate from East Europe, Central Asia

Value (in US $ billion)

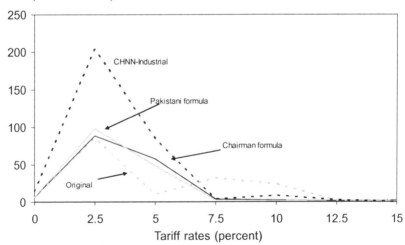

Tariff rates (percent)

Source: Authors' calculations.

Value of exports by tariff rate from Latin America

Value (in US $ billion)

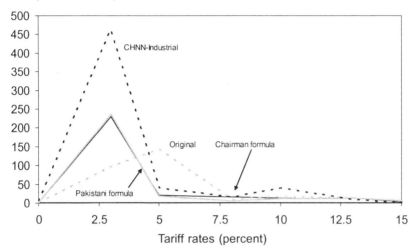

Source: Authors' calculations.

Value of exports by tariff rate from Middle East, North Africa

Value (in US $ billion)

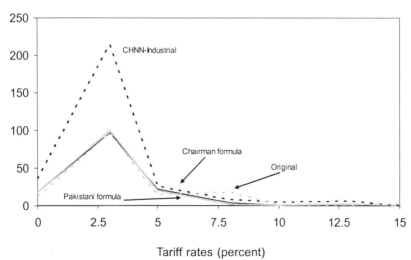

Source: Authors' calculations.

Value of exports by tariff rate from South Asia

Value (in US $ billion)

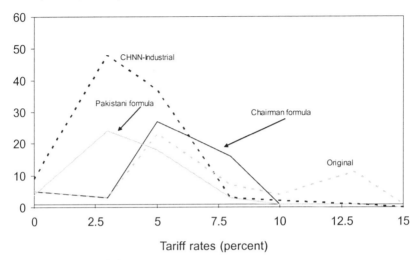

Tariff rates (percent)

Source: Authors' calculations.

Value of exports by tariff rate from Sub-Saharan Africa

Value (in US $ billion)

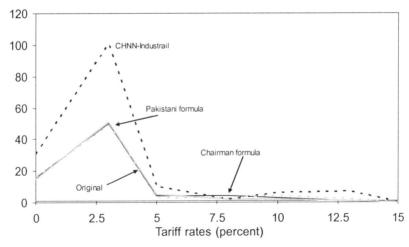

Tariff rates (percent)

Source: Authors' calculations.

Notes

1. The authors would like to acknowledge the important contributions made by World Bank staff Olivier Jammes, Ganesh Kumar Seshan and Jerzy Rozanski on an earlier trade note. Special thanks go to Jurgen Richtering of the World Trade Organization and Marcelo Olarreaga of the World Bank who provided valuable comments on drafts of this chapter.

2. The World Bank and the United Nations Conference on Trade and Development (UNCTAD) have produced a software program—World Integrated Trade Solutions (WITS)—that allows anyone with knowledge of trade and tariff statistics (plus a computer and access to the Internet) to assess the implications of proposed formulas for their own trade regime, and for their market-access opportunities. See http://wits.worldbank.org/witsweb for more information.

3. This adjustment was made using a Constant Elasticity of Substitution demand function with an elasticity of substitution of 3, and taking the tariffs to zero before calculating the country's export volumes.

References

Baldwin, R. E. 1986. "Toward More Efficient Procedures for Multilateral Tariff Negotiations." *Aussenwirtschaft* 41(2–3): 379–94.

Blackhurst, R., A. Enders, and J. Francois. 1995. "The Uruguay Round and Market Access: Opportunities and Challenges for Developing Countries." In *The Uruguay Round and the Developing Countries*, ed. W. Martin and L. A. Winters. Cambridge: Cambridge University Press.

Francois, J., and W. Martin. 2003. "Formula Approaches for Market Access Negotiations." *World Economy* 26(1): 1–28.

Francois, J., and W. Martin. 2004. "Commercial policy, bindings and market access" *European Economic Review* 48: 665–79. June.

Laird, S., and A. Yeats. 1987. The Uruguay Round: A Handbook for the Multilateral Trade Negotiations, Washington DC: World Bank.

World Bank. 2003. Global Economic Prospects 2004: Realizing the Development Promise of the Doha Agenda. Washington, DC.

WTO (World Trade Organization). 2004. "Framework for Establishing Modalities in Market Access for Nonagricultural Products." Annex B in "Doha Work Program: Decision Adopted by the General Council on August 1, 2004." WT/L/579. Geneva,

———. 2005a. "Market Access for Nonagricultural Products: The Way Forward: Communication from Pakistan to the World Trade Organization." TN/MA/W/60. Geneva.

———. 2005b. "Market Access for Nonagricultural Products: Communication to the Negotiating Group on Nonagricultural Market Access from Argentina, Brazil and India." TN/MA/W/54. Geneva.

Laird, S. and de Cordoba, S. eds. 2006. "Coping with Trade Reforms: Implications of the WTO Industrial Tariff Negotiations for Developing Countries." Palgrave-Macmillan, Basingstoke, UK. See www.unctad.org.

WTO 2003. Draft Elements of Modalities for Negotiations on Non-Agricultural Products, World Trade Organization, Geneva, 19 August, TN/MA/W/35/Rev. 1.

Life after Quotas? Early Signs of the New Era in Trade of Textiles and Clothing

Paul Brenton and Mombert Hoppe

On January 1, 2005, the system of quotas that had regulated imports of textiles and clothing into rich countries for 30 years was finally dismantled.[1] That step came despite a last-gasp attempt by certain importing countries, in alliance with a number of developing countries that had benefited from the system's restrictions on China and other Asian countries, to delay the reform. In liberalizing the most protected manufacturing sector, the expiration of the quota system completed a major achievement of the Uruguay Round of multilateral trade negotiations concluded 10 years earlier.[2] Textiles and clothing remain subject to relatively high tariff barriers in both developed and developing countries, and certain developing countries, notably the least developed (LDCs), still receive significant tariff preferences in developed-country markets.

Much has been written about the likely impact of the reforms and the fear that markets will become swamped by Chinese products, with adverse implications for other developing-country producers that export to the developed countries. This note takes a first look at the initial impact of the changes and discusses what they suggest for developing-country strategies in textiles and clothing.

The development significance of exports of textiles and clothing

Although both can be crucial to development, the textiles and clothing sectors are distinct. The modern textiles sector is capital intensive and subject to growing automation. Production has tended to become geographically concentrated, with only a few developing countries having the capacity to export substantial amounts of standardized textile products. The clothing sector remains labor intensive, technology is relatively simple, start-up costs are comparatively small, and scale economies are not important. All of these factors favor production in locations where labor costs are low.

Diversification into export categories with greater value added than traditional agricultural exports is a major objective for many developing countries. Through manufactures of clothing developing countries have been able to significantly increase and diversify exports with positive effects on incomes, employment, and poverty.[3] The relative importance of clothing, in terms of the share of total non-oil exports, exceeds that of textiles in all but the developed-country regions (figure 1). Both textiles and clothing are particularly important in the exports of South Asian and African countries.

Figure 1. Textiles and clothing are important for developing countries

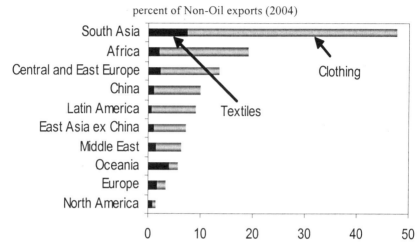

percent of Non-Oil exports (2004)

Source: COMTRADE data accessed through WITS.

Changes in trade following the removal of remaining quotas

Changes in trade in textiles and clothing products hit the newspapers first with predictions that world markets would be swamped with Chinese products and thousands of jobs lost in other developing countries.[4] The issue was back in the headlines after the United States (U.S) and European Union (EU) acted to restore protection (at least temporarily) against certain Chinese products under safeguard agreements negotiated at the time of China's accession to the World Trade Organization (WTO).[5]

Despite the ink spilled over the issue in the media, it is still too early to draw firm conclusions about the impact of the removal of quotas. Here we look at information on imports of textiles and clothing products into the European Union and the United States in the first six months of 2005 and show that the impact is likely to be more nuanced than many commentators have suggested. It is quite likely that many developing countries will have opportunities to continue to export clothing products provided their domestic business climate is favorable.

While U.S. imports from China have increased strongly since the quotas expired, imports from a number of other developing countries also have increased significantly (figure 2). U.S. imports from Bangladesh, a country that many thought would be hit hard, increased by more than 20 percent in the first half of this year. In fact, U.S. imports from a range of countries across Africa, Asia, and South America have increased, while imports from other countries in the same regions, as well as imports from developed countries, have declined. In absolute terms the largest declines in imports are from Hong Kong (China), Republic of Korea, Mexico, Taiwan (China), and Macao, in that order.[6]

A similar situation prevails in the EU market (figure 3). Imports from China have increased strongly, but so have imports from certain other developing countries, including Bangladesh, Cambodia, Arab Republic of Egypt, Madagascar, and Vietnam. Large declines in imports have been recorded for Hong Kong (China) and Macao, while significant reductions in imports are reported from a range of countries in Asia, Eastern Europe, and the Middle East.

Because the initial response to the removal of quotas in the United States and the European Union was far from homogenous, identifying clear patterns is difficult. On balance, removal of quotas appears to have led to a much more competitive global market for textiles and clothing products. After years of suppression, EU and U.S. imports from China have grown strongly, but opportunities remain for efficient suppliers in other countries to expand output and exports.

Chinese exports have increased substantially in many product categories, but

Figure 2. Winners and losers in the US, post ATC

Proportionate change in US textile and clothing imports by supplier (first half 2005/first half 2004), percent

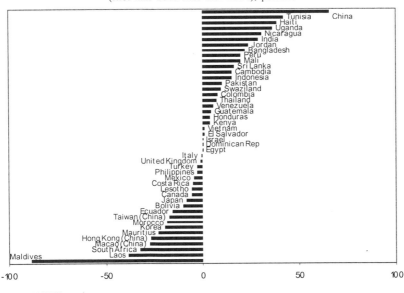

Source: USITC.

Figure 3. Winners and losers in the EU, post ATC

Proportionate change in EU textile and clothing imports by supplier
(first half 2005/first half 2004), percent

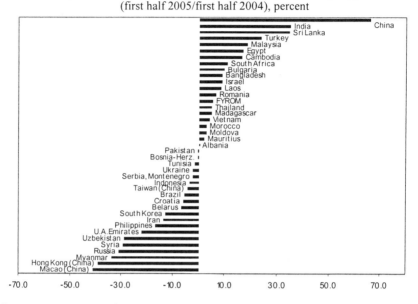

Source: European Commision.

they have declined in others. For example, U.S. imports of T-shirts from China have increased by around 350 percent in the first six months of this year, but imports of certain woven cotton fabrics have declined. Accompanying the surge in U.S. imports of T-shirts from China has been an increase in imports of T-shirts from countries such as Indonesia and Thailand, but not from Vietnam. Imports of T-shirts from South Africa and Lesotho have decreased by 20–35 percent, but imports from Mauritius and Swaziland have shown a modest increase. While U.S. imports of T-shirts from Kenya have declined, imports of men's or boy's cotton shirts from Kenya have increased strongly. Even within product categories such as women's or girl's suits (HS 6104), where overall imports from China have increased by more than 200 percent, the growth of imports from China at a very detailed (10 digit) product level ranges from –45 percent to +1,400 percent. Of the 15 detailed products specified in the trade classification for women's and girl's suits, 7 show a decline in imports from China this year.

It is not yet possible to distinguish clear outcomes even for specific countries. For example, analysis prior to the removal of quotas painted a fairly bleak picture for Lesotho, where the clothing sector dominates exports and has been the major source of employment growth in recent years. Initial reports in the press early in 2005 appeared to confirm those fears, suggesting that at least 10 factories had shut down and at least 10,000 workers (roughly one-fifth of the industry workforce) had lost their jobs.[7] However, exports of clothing to the United States, which accounts for almost all of the output of Lesotho, decreased only slightly (by 5.3 percent, or about $10 million) over the first half of 2005 compared to the same period in 2004. Some commentators suggest that a portion of the job losses reflects substantial improvements in labor productivity. Others report that during the course of this year some factories have reopened and others have opened for the first time. No official data are available on job losses in the clothing sector in Lesotho this year, nor have any official pronouncements been made. The picture is further clouded by the fact that very similar products have exhibited quite different export performance. Exports to the United States of women's and girl's cotton trousers have declined substantially, but exports of men's and boy's cotton trousers have increased significantly. Thus, diagnoses that concentrate on broad sectoral factors will have limited power in explaining developments in the clothing industry in 2005. A careful analysis will need to dig down to identify firm-specific characteristics and responses.

The changes for countries such as Sri Lanka and Bangladesh are in sharp contrast to predictions of the dire impact of the end of quotas. It was suggested that one million jobs would be lost in Bangladesh and that one-half of factories in the industry in Sri Lanka would close down (as reported in Oxfam 2004). It is too early to conclude with confidence that the expiration of quotas will not have a major negative impact on these countries. Buyers in the European Union and United States may be postponing decisions to begin sourcing in China while uncertainty persists concerning official protection against Chinese products. Nevertheless, some countries that were expected to be hit hard by the removal of quotas have managed to *increase* the value of their exports to the European Union and the United States, even in product categories in which Chinese exports have grown the fastest, suggests that opportunities for a range of developing countries to export, especially in the clothing sector, will remain.

While global buyers will review their sourcing strategies, many have indicated that they will not risk placing all their orders with China and will seek to maintain a more diversified sourcing structure. Moreover, China cannot fill every niche. The textiles and clothing sectors have a large number of niches that vary by country to suit vastly differing tastes. Even a small share of a small niche of the United States or a large European country can have a substantial economic impact on a small developing country.

Here it is worth stressing the differences between the European and U.S. markets. Large buyers in the United States, such as Walmart, look to suppliers that can satisfy economy-wide demand for standard products. The EU market, by contrast, remains considerably fragmented along national lines. Footwear is one sector in

Table 1. Applied import duties on cotton yarns, cotton fabrics and sewing needles in selected countries, 2005

Percent

	Bangladesh	Brazil	Ethiopia	Kenya	Mexico	Morocco	Nigeria	Pakistan
Cotton yarns	15.0	14.0	20.0	20.0	15.0	32.5	40.0	5.0
Cotton fabrics	30.0	18.0	40.0	25.0	15.7	40.0	75.0	25.0
Sewing needles	30.0	17.5	20.0	15.0	20.0	10.0	20.0	10.0

Source: TRAINS database on WITS.

which the European Union and United States imposed quantitative restrictions against China and other East Asian suppliers in the late 1980s. Those restrictions were removed in the 1990s. In the United States, China now accounts for around 70 percent of U.S. imports. Its share of EU footwear imports, however, is less than 15 percent. As a last observation, China and India are experiencing high growth rates. Rising domestic demand will reduce some of the excess supply that can be exported. At the same time, rising wages will shrink competitive margins.

A strategy to support competitiveness of the clothing sector

What elements are likely to comprise a successful strategy to support the clothing sector in developing countries?

Review domestic trade policies to remove constraints that act against clothing exports

For clothing producers the ability to source fabrics and other inputs from the global market is a crucial competitive factor. Many developing countries apply high import duties on products used as inputs in textile and clothing industries, thereby limiting the capacity to export competitive final products. Producers in many developing countries pay considerably higher than world prices for yarns, fabrics, sewing needles, and other inputs (table 1). In many cases drawback schemes reimburse exporters for these duties, but poor implementation often leads to delays in payment, while exporters bear the cost of compliance with the schemes.[8]

The ability to fill orders quickly is a significant competitive advantage in the clothing sector. That makes the efficiency of customs procedures on both imported inputs and the exported product, and the availability, cost, and speed of transport services, important determinants of competitiveness. In many developing countries, and especially in Africa and South Asia, long delays in customs and poor transport infrastructure keep producers away from key global markets. Compared with China, the documentary requirements and customs procedures of many developing countries are onerous and complicated, thereby slowing imports and exports (table 2). Customs reform, improvements to ports and transport infrastructure, and the stimulation of competition among transport companies are all important measures to support the competitiveness of the clothing sector.

Improve the business environment

Many countries have lower labor costs than China in the production of clothing (the relevant metric is the price per one standard minute). Moldova, for example, has per minute costs that are two-thirds of those in China. Labor costs are also lower in Bangladesh and in many countries in Africa than in China. In many of these countries, however, the advantage of low labor costs is undermined by high indirect costs resulting from a hostile business environment. The World Bank estimates that the cost of doing business in Africa, for example, is as much as 40 percent higher than in other developing regions (World Bank 2005). Countries that implement policies to provide a favorable business climate can help their firms compete in both domestic and overseas markets.

Exploit cost advantages in areas other than labor

Labor cost is just one of the elements that influence the sourcing decisions of global buyers. The value of proximity and turnaround increases the competitive importance of efficiency in customs, handling, and transport. Many buyers, particularly in Europe, are turning to products with very limited shelf life and hence short production runs, so flexibility and responsiveness can give firms a critical competitive edge. At the same time, environmental and labor standards affect the sourcing decisions of growing numbers of buyers.[9]

Advocate for more effective trade preferences

The European Union, United States, and other developed countries offer substantial preferences on clothing products. Full preferences are available in the European Union to all LDCs and ACP (Africa-Caribbean-Pacific) countries. Partial preferences are available to other developing countries. The United States offers preferences on clothing products to Central and South American countries and to African countries under the African

Table 2. Average time required to satisfy import and export procedures in selected countries, 2004

Days	Bangladesh	Brazil	Ethiopia	Kenya	Morocco	Nigeria	Pakistan	China
Imports	57	43	57	62	33	53	39	24
Exports	35	39	46	45	31	41	33	20

Source: World Bank, Doing Business Database, www.doingbusiness.org.

Growth and Opportunity Act (AGOA),[10] but not to Asian LDCs such as Bangladesh and Cambodia.

But preferences typically are severely curtailed by restrictive rules of origin. In particular, EU and U.S. rules of origin (with the notable exception of imports from most African countries under AGOA) severely limit the ability of clothing producers to source fabrics from the global market, thus reducing the economic potential of available preferences. To obtain preferences, firms must use more expensive inputs from local firms or from the European Union or the United States, which usually negates the benefit of preferential access. In fact, it is apparent that for many producers of clothing in countries that receive preferences the higher cost of having to use inputs dictated by the rules of origin exceeds the margin of tariff preference. The result is that firms source their inputs globally and forgo preferences.[11] A significant liberalization of rules of origin would allow developing countries to take advantage of available preferences and thus soften the shock of the removal of quotas.

Conclusions

The end of three decades of quantitative restrictions on textiles and clothing products in developed countries entails both challenges and opportunities for many developing countries.

Countries that have a favorable business environment, efficient customs and transport systems, and competitive firms that are flexible enough to meet the requirements of overseas buyers can prosper—even in the face of unfettered competition from China. Developed countries can assist by (a) providing a stable trade-policy environment in which investors can make effective long-term decisions, (b) ensuring that all LDCs have access to preferences on clothing products, and (c) liberalizing the rules of origin governing those preferences in ways that better support development.

The early data discussed in this analysis give a preliminary and partial indication of the outcome of the removal of quotas on textiles and clothing products in the EU and U.S. markets. The analysis suggests that certain countries have seen large declines in the value of their exports of textiles and clothing products, declines that may entail substantial adjustment. Even countries that have continued to increase exports may experience significant adjustment toward more efficient firms in the textile and clothing sectors. A clear view of these adjustment pressures requires more detailed information on the impact on firms and workers of the expiration of the quota system. Nevertheless, it is clear that in the absence of other employment opportunities workers made redundant from the textile and clothing sectors may fall back into poverty. Thus, minimizing the costs incurred by released workers and their families and facilitating their adjustment into alternative employment will be a major challenge in a number of countries.

International organizations and bilateral donors can support developing countries, especially the least developed, in adjusting to the substantial trade shocks that may arise from the expiration of quotas on textiles and clothing. That support must include analytical work to lay the basis for effective decision-making, as well as technical assistance and capacity building in the areas of customs reform, trade facilitation, and improving the investment climate. In some cases, it should include financial assistance. The IMF's Trade Integration Mechanism may play a role in cases of large, adverse effects on countries' balance of payments.[12]

In sum, the paramount challenge facing international organizations, bilateral donors, and national governments is to provide a favorable business environment in which companies can restructure their operations and access the financing they need to compete more effectively, and to assist workers who lose their jobs as the textile and clothing sectors adjust to new global realities.

Notes

1. The authors are Paul Brenton, Senior Economist in the International Trade Department of the World Bank, and Mombert Hoppe, Junior Professional Associate in the Trade Department of the World Bank. They are grateful for the comments and suggestions of Richard Newfarmer.

2. From January 1995 to January 2005, international trade in textiles and clothing trade operated under the 10-year transitional program of the WTO's Agreement on Textiles and Clothing (ATC). Before the Agreement took effect at the end of the Uruguay Round, a large share of exports of textiles and clothing from developing countries to the industrial countries was subject to quotas under a special regime known as the Multifibre Arrangement (MFA), which operated outside the normal rules of the General Agreement on Tariffs and Trade (GATT), notably the rule against discrimination in trade. The MFA provided for the application of quantitative restrictions against specific countries for a wide range of textile and clothing products. The purpose of ATC was to gradually integrate textiles and clothing into GATT (now WTO) rules through the progressive removal of quotas.

3. Kabeer and Mahmoud (2004) suggest that the production of garments for export in Bangladesh has generated 1.6 million new jobs, most of which were captured by women. Many of these workers tend to be migrants from poorer areas. Kabeer and Mahmoud also find that wages for garment workers are double those of other workers involved in nontradable activities. There is, however, some evidence to suggest that workers in this sector are vulnerable to changing employment contracts and the increasing "casualization" of work (Nadvi 2004).

4. "Thirty Million Jobs Could Disappear with the End of Apparel Quotas." *Business Week*, December 15, 2003.

5. Both the European Union and the United States have introduced new trade restrictions against imports from China since early 2005, and China has "voluntarily" sought to limit certain exports by levying an export tax. In the European Union, new quota restrictions on 10 categories (8 of which refer to clothing products) have been justified on the basis that the rapidity of the change in trade "made effective adjustment impossible." Initially this argument was made in relation to EU producers, although it is not clear how many producers in the European Union really compete directly with Chinese products; recently it has been extended on the grounds that it is important for producers in the Maghreb and other developing countries. On the other hand, some commentators suggest that the restrictions in the European Union and United States are diverting Chinese products to large developing-country markets such as South Africa. In the United States safeguard cases have concluded that Chinese imports "are disrupting

and threatening to disrupt" U.S. markets. These arguments have been accepted despite the fact that the agreement to phase out quotas allowed for a 10-year period of adjustment.

6. The declines for Hong Kong (China), Macao, and Taiwan (China) may reflect that under quotas a portion of mainland China's exports were handled by middlemen in these countries and recorded as their exports. Hence some of the recorded increase in China's exports reflects the reorganization of trade. Similarly, part of the falling price of imports from China results from the elimination of middlemen (Mayer 2005).

7. "Southern Africa: Textile Industry Undone by Globalisation." IRINnews.org, September 26, 2005.

8. In Bangladesh, for example, it has been reported that reimbursement takes 58 days on average and requires 6 percent of additional expenditure to obtain the refund check (WTO 2005).

9. Reports in the press conjecture that the continued success of the clothing industry in Cambodia (where exports to the European Union and United States increased substantially in 2005) reflects a strategy of enhancing labor standards. That strategy has improved quality and captured the attention of international buyers. In addition, it has been suggested that constraints on cutting labor costs have led factory owners to push the government to tackle corruption and unnecessary bureaucratic rules. See, for example, "Labor Standards Help Cambodia Keep Customers." *International Herald Tribune*, May 11, 2005. This issue is ripe for detailed analysis and assessment.

10. See Brenton and Ozden (2005).

11. Thus, for example, in 2002 only 50 percent of the exports of Bangladesh to the European Union that were eligible for preferences under the Everything But Arms program actually requested preferences due to rules of origin. Similarly, only 36 percent of Cambodia's eligible exports requested EU preferences. A key feature of AGOA is that many African countries can export to the United States using globally sourced fabrics. This has led to substantial supply responses and higher exports to the United States in a number of cases including Lesotho, Swaziland, Kenya, and Uganda. South Africa, however, faces restrictive rules of origin requiring the use of domestic or U.S. fabrics. In 2004 exports of clothing from South Africa to the United States where almost 20 percent lower than in 2001.

12. See http://www.imf.org/external/np/exr/facts/tim.htm. However, certain countries, such as Lesotho and Haiti, have substantial clothing sectors but do not have immediate access to the IMF's Trade Integration Mechanism (TIM) as they are not engaged in an IMF program, and their sectors, unaided, could founder. (see WTO (2005) for more details).

References

Brenton, P., and C. Ozden. 2005. "Trade Preferences and Apparel and the Role of Rule of Origin: The Case of Africa." Presented at the WTO conference on Preference Erosion: Impacts and Policy Responses, Geneva, June.

Kabeer, N., and S. Mahmud. 2004. "Globalisation, Gender, and Poverty: Bangladeshi Women Workers in Export and Local Markets." *Journal of International Development* 16.

Mayer, J. 2005. "Not Totally Naked: Textiles and Clothing Trade in a Quota-free Environment." *Journal of World Trade* 39: 393–426.

Nadvi, K. 2004. "Globalisation and Poverty: How Can Global Value Chain Research Inform the Policy Debate?" *IDS Bulletin* 35: 20–28.

Oxfam. 2004. "Stitched Up: How Rich-Country Protectionism in Textiles and Clothing Trade Prevents Poverty Alleviation." Briefing Paper 60. http://www.oxfam.org.uk/what_we_do/issues/trade/downloads/bp60_textiles.pdf

World Bank. 2005. *Meeting the Challenges of Africa's Development: A World Bank Group Action Plan*. World Bank: Washington, D.C.

WTO. 2005. "Options for Least-Developed Countries to Improve their Competitiveness in the Textiles and Clothing Business." WT/COMTD/LDC/W/37, Geneva.

Services in a Development Round: Proposals for Overcoming Inertia

Aaditya Mattoo

Much of the public discourse on the Doha Development Agenda has focused on trade in goods, particularly protectionist policies in agriculture. Negotiations on trade in services have received much less attention. The neglect matters. The potential benefits of services trade reform are huge, but services negotiations in the World Trade Organization (WTO) are making little progress.

One problem, of course, is that services negotiations are part of a stagnant whole. Progress in other areas, notably agriculture, is a necessary condition for progress in services. But it is not a sufficient condition. To produce a services outcome that supports broader development goals will require extraordinary intellectual, technical, and political effort.

This note first describes the current, sad state of negotiations. It then argues that the negotiations could be galvanized by agreement on three goals that should appeal equally to the development and business communities. Finally, the note advances three proposals that may help achieve those goals: the first pertains to a reform of the negotiating process; the second and third argue for the negotiations to be complemented by broader cooperation to remedy regulatory inadequacies and to deal with the particular issues raised by labor mobility.

Where do things stand?

At Cancún, services were not an area of disagreement. Ministers recognized the progress made in the negotiations and urged participants to intensify efforts to reach a successful conclusion. As we approach Hong Kong, the mood is less sanguine. The progress so far consists of a large number of confidential but reportedly highly ambitious *requests* that WTO members (including several developing countries) have made to each other for greater market access, and reportedly disappointing *offers* of improved access submitted so far by more than 60 WTO members (including many developing countries). The chair of the WTO Services Trade Negotiations Committee, Alejandro Jara, concluded in July 2005 that

> Notwithstanding the fact that the number of offers has improved since my last report, it was widely acknowledged that the overall quality of initial and revised offers is unsatisfactory. Few, if any, new commercial opportunities would ensue for service suppliers. Most members feel that the negotiations are not progressing as they should. It is clear that much more work will be necessary in order to bring the quality of the package to a level that would allow for a deal.[1]

There is a growing perception that the request-and-offer process is not proving to be fruitful and that there is a need for complementary negotiating methods. In particular, some WTO members have suggested the adoption of numerical benchmarks to secure wider sectoral coverage, as well as qualitative criteria to ensure that commitments embody a certain degree of openness. Meanwhile, negotiations on completing the General Agreement on Trade in Services (GATS) framework of rules (on safeguards, government procurement, subsidies, and domestic regulation)— underway since the conclusion of the Uruguay Round—have borne little fruit.

What should the goals be?

The negotiations have fallen into a low-level equilibrium trap: little is expected and less offered. Members need to identify a set of desirable and feasible goals to give direction and momentum to the negotiations. These goals must be articulated not in arbitrary and opaque numerical terms, but in terms that resonate equally with the development and business communities.

Realizing the development benefits of services reform

Recent research concludes that the increase in real income from a cut in services protection by half would be five times larger than that generated from comparable goods trade liberalization (Robinson and others 1999). Countries that successfully reformed their financial and telecommunications services sectors have grown, on average, about a percentage point faster than other countries (box 1). This reflects the key role of services such as finance, transport, and telecommunications in determining economic performance, and the spillover benefits of liberalization as factors move across countries.

It would be wrong, however, to assume that these gains can be realized by a mechanical opening up of services markets. A flawed reform program can undermine the benefits of liberalization. For example, if privatization of state monopolies to private owners (sometimes foreigners) is conducted without creating conditions of competition, the simple result may be transfers of monopoly rents to private owners. Similarly, if increased entry into financial sectors is not accompanied by adequate prudential supervision, the result may be insider lending and poor investment decisions. Also, if policies to ensure universal service are not put in place, liberalization need not improve access to essential services for the poor. Managing reforms of services markets therefore requires integrating trade opening with a careful combination of competition and regulation.

The challenge is to ensure that international commitments reflect good economic policy rather than the dictates of domestic political economy or international negotiating pressure. In particular, it is essential to distinguish between the areas where liberalization is prevented solely by the political power of vested interests—to which the WTO's reciprocal market opening is an antidote—and those

Box 1. Dynamic benefits of services trade reform

Certain services industries clearly possess growth-generating charac-teristics. Thus, financial services play a central role in the transformation of savings to investment, telecommunications in the diffusion of knowl-edge, transport in a country's ability to participate in global trade, education and health services in building up the stock of human capital, and business services in reducing transactions costs and adding value to products. Barriers to entry in several services sectors, ranging from telecommunications to professional services, often are maintained not only against foreign suppliers but also against new domestic suppliers. Full liberalization can, therefore, lead to enhanced competition from both domestic and foreign suppliers. Greater foreign factor participation and increased competition together imply a larger scale of activity, and hence greater scope for generating the growth-enhancing effects. Even without scale effects, the import of foreign factors that characterizes services sector liberalization could still have positive effects because they are likely to bring technology with them.

Econometric evidence suggests that openness in services improves growth in the long run (figure 1a). After controlling for other determinants of growth, countries that fully reformed the financial services sector grew, on average, about 1 percentage point faster than other countries. An even greater impetus on growth was found to come from fully reforming[a] both the telecommunications and the financial services sectors. Estimates suggest countries that fully liberalized both sectors grew, on average, about 1.5 percentage points faster than other countries (figure 1b).

While these estimates indicate substantial gains from liberalizing key services sectors, it would be wrong to infer that those gains can be realized by a mechanical opening up of services markets. Managing reforms of services markets requires that trade opening be accompanied with a careful combination of competition and regulation (see text on the second page of this note).

a. The measure of reform included not just liberalization but also regulatory improvements.

Box 1. *(continued)*

Figure 1a. Developing countries lag in services liberalization

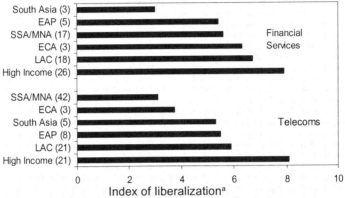

Note: Number of countries in sample in parenthesis

a) The openness index for telecommunications captures the degree of competition, restrictions on ownership and the existence of an independent regulator (needed to enable competitive entry), and draws on an ITU-World Bank database for 1998. The index for financial services captures the restrictions on new entry, foreign ownership and capital mobility, and draws primarily upon commitments made by countries under the GATS, which are known to reflect closely actual policy, and data in the IMF's Annual Report on Exchange Arrangements and Exchange Restrictions.

Source: Mattoo, Rathindran, and Subramarian (2005).

Figure 1b. Greater liberalization in services is associated with more rapid growth

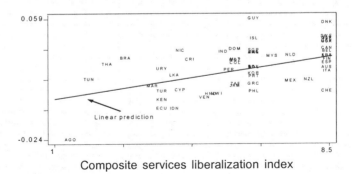

Composite services liberalization index

Source: Mattoo, Rathindran, and Subramarian (2005).

where regulatory or other problems need to be remedied before the full benefits of liberalization can be reaped. Even in the latter case, if the time frame for reform could be predicted, a government would be in a position to decide whether to precommit in the WTO to future liberalization in order to lend credibility to the reform program and obtain a negotiating benefit.

The evidence of benefits conditional on appropriately designed reform programs points to our first goal:

Goal 1: WTO members will eliminate barriers to foreign participation in sectors where there is adequate regulatory preparedness, and consistent with their development goals. They will precommit to eliminating barriers where the necessary conditions for successful market opening can be fulfilled in a predictable time span.

Preempting protection in cross-border trade in services

The shared interest in an open services markets is vividly illustrated by the pattern of cross-border trade in business services. While industrial countries are still the largest exporters of such services, several developing countries are among the most dynamic (box 2). Since the mid-1990s, the business-services exports of 20 developing countries, including Brazil, Costa Rica, India, Israel and Mauritius have grown by more than 15 percent per year.

Many countries, rich and poor, are reaping large efficiency gains from this enhanced international division of labor. The U.S. banking industry alone is estimated to have saved more than $8 billion over the last four years, and the cost savings for the world's top hundred financial institutions could be as high as $138 billion annually. And the development potential of cross-border trade in services is being felt in an ever-widening group of developing countries that are equipping themselves with the appropriate skills, infrastructure, and institutions.

But such trade will also create adjustment pressures and could provoke a protectionist backlash—signs of which are already visible in recent procurement restrictions and regulatory impediments. It would therefore be wise to preempt protectionism, to ensure that any adjustment pressures are dealt with through desirable domestic assistance rather than inefficient barriers to trade. That points to our second goal.

Goal 2: WTO members will lock in the current openness of cross-border trade for a wide range of services. Certain services, such as those that involve the mobility of capital, may be exempted.

Reaping the gains from the temporary migration of service providers

The most stringent barriers to service trade are those involving the mobility of individual service providers, known as "mode 4" in the GATS context. Such temporary movement offers arguably the neatest solution to the problem of how some forms of international migration are best managed, enabling mutual gains from trade while averting to a large extent social and political costs in host countries and brain drain from poor countries. Recent research finds that if industrial countries were to allow temporary access to foreign service providers equal to just 3 percent of their labor force, the global gains would be over $150 billion—more than the gains from the complete liberalization of all trade in goods (Winters and others 2003). Those gains would be shared equally by the industrial and developing countries.

The challenge is to define a package that can liberate at least some forms of movement from the prohibitive political difficulties that have prevented any progress on mode 4. First of all, in order to harness the coincidence of interest between industrial and developing countries, the package would include both intracorporate movement and the movement of personnel independently of commercial presence. Second, in order to remain politically feasible, the proposed liberalizing commitments might be required to apply (a) only above specified skill thresholds, (b) to strictly temporary presence of a specified duration (say, less than one year), and, for independent movement, (c) to the fulfillment of services contracts to the exclusion of other employment arrangements. Countries would of course be free to adopt more flexible and liberal regimes for other types of movement; for example, it might be possible to make greater progress on the movement of the unskilled through bilateral agreements. But the GATS negotiations would focus most fruitfully on the type of movement for which there seems to be an emerging international market, and for which *multilateral* negotiations can help eliminate explicit restrictions and create streamlined procedures. This leads to our third goal.

Goal 3: WTO members will allow greater freedom for the temporary presence of at least some categories of individuals, such as intracorporate transferees and service providers to fulfill specific services contracts.

How do we get there?

In principle, the traditional WTO mechanism of reciprocal market opening could help attain all three goals. In practice, the mechanism has not functioned in services because of inadequacies in the negotiating process and failure to win the consent and support of regulators. To revive reciprocity, the negotiating process must be reformed; more importantly, regulators must be reassured that regulatory weaknesses will be remedied and regulatory cooperation facilitated. Each of these actions is relevant for all modes of service delivery, but in some cases it is convenient to illustrate the significance of each with regard to a particular mode.

Reforming the services negotiating process to further desirable goals

Between identifying worthwhile goals and making them an integral part of the Doha negotiations, falls the shadow. How can negotiations be informed by and lead toward desirable goals?

Box 2. Developing countries' growing stake in cross-border trade in business services

"Other business services" in the IMF balance-of-payments system includes a range of services (other than services like banking, insurance, and telecommunications) that provide intermediate inputs throughout the production processes for goods and services. As the figure 2a below shows, the bulk of such exports still originate in OECD countries. But as the exports of the EU and the U.S. grew by 3.5 and 11.2 percent per annum in the second half of the 1990s, those of India, Peru, Israel, Romania, and Brazil and several others grew at annual rates in excess of 30 percent. Moreover, many other developing countries—including Nicaragua, Argentina, Jamaica, China and Barbados—have witnessed high rates of growth (figure 2b).

2a. Regional distribution of other business services exports, 1995–2000

US $ billion

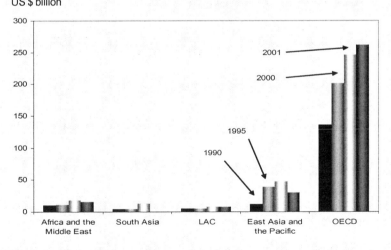

Box 2 . *(continued)*

2b. Average growth rates of exports of other business services for selected countries, 1995–2000

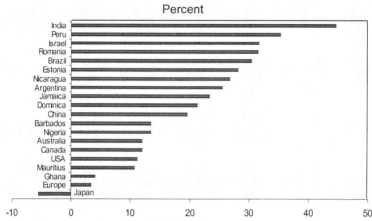

Note: "Other business services" includes: "merchanting and other trade related services," "operational leasing services," and "miscellaneous, business, professional and technical services," which include: "legal, accounting management, consulting, public relations services," "advertising, market research, public opinion poll services," "research and development services," "architectural, engineering, other technical services."

The current bilateral request-and-offer approach, adopted as the dominant negotiating method in the services negotiations, is leading nowhere. There is a strong case for complementing it with certain collective approaches to negotiations. In a world of unequal bargaining power, multilateral approaches (which must be seen to be equitable and efficient if they are to produce agreement) are likely to yield a more desirable outcome than bilateral negotiations. Avoiding sector-by-sector and country-by-country bartering of commitments can substantially reduce the transactions costs of negotiations. Formulae, applied multilaterally, can help overcome the free-rider problem that arises in negotiations conducted under most-favored-nation (MFN)-based system.[2] Use of such formulae is perhaps the only credible way to grant credit to unilateral liberalizers. In contrast, it is much more difficult to ensure compensation for the loss of negotiating coinage caused by unilateral liberalization in a bilateral request-and-offer negotiation.

In goods negotiations, collective approaches have typically taken the form of formula cuts in tariffs and subsidies. In services, quantitative assessments of offers or numerical targets would be an unhelpful distraction because even the best available methods of quantifying barriers to trade are hopelessly inadequate (Findlay and Warren 2003). At best, it would be possible to measure differences in the sectoral coverage of commitments, possibly weighted by some crude measure of the level of openness.[3] To get agreement on any such target, however, would be extremely difficult and consume valuable negotiating time and energy. Even if agreement were reached on a target, it may merely invite a spate of dubious entries along the lines of "economic needs tests" to create the illusion of coverage. Such a result would confirm the high level of cynicism about the GATS process.

Any goals must be articulated not in arbitrary and opaque numerical terms, but in terms that resonate with the development and business community. A far more fruitful collective approach would be for groups of members, akin to the "friends" groups that already exist, to champion clearly specified goals—possibly similar to those identified above. These goals could be embodied in model schedules (or model regulatory principles) along the lines of the Understanding on Financial Services, the Telecommunications Reference Paper, and the Model Schedule for Maritime Transport. The building blocks of model schedules are relatively straightforward, and some have already been proposed for specific modes (Chaudhuri and others 2004) ; (Mattoo and Wunsch 2004).

By an appropriate choice of sectors and levels of openness, it should be possible to strike a balance between collective commitment and individual flexibility, as well as between sound policy and negotiating imperatives. Different levels of ambition are possible. At the very least, this approach can provide a framework for negotiations. Or it could help establish a presumption in favor of a certain threshold level of commitments. Or it could represent a formula for liberalizing commitments, analogous to the "zero-for-zero" goods formulae, with the objective of securing acceptance by at least a *critical mass* of members—defined as a group of members each of whom would be willing to accept the commitments provided all others in the group do so.

Proposal 1: Members will adopt, or at least complement, the current request-and-offer approach with, a collective approach to negotiations. Groups of members will champion clearly specified goals and articulate them in model schedules (or model regulatory principles). By appropriate choice of sectors and level of commitments, agreement will be secured among a critical mass of members.

An individual member's incentive to participate in a particular sector or mode will, of course, depend on the willingness of its trading partners to make commitments in modes and sectors (within and outside services) in which the member has an export interest. A reformed negotiating method can help, but ultimately members will need to make the hard political bargains necessary for a successful outcome.

The next two proposals address the substantive concerns that inhibit commitments in the GATS context.

Policy advice, and diagnosing and remedying regulatory inadequacies
Market access in services is negotiated within the WTO. Policy advice and
assistance for regulatory reform, by contrast, are provided by multilateral institutions
and other agencies. There is virtually no link between the two processes.[4]

This disconnect persists even though it is clear that improved
regulation—ranging from prudential regulation in financial services to
procompetitive regulation in a variety of network-based services—will be critical to
realizing the benefits of services liberalization in many sectors. Policy intervention
will also be necessary to ensure universal service because liberalization per se will
not always deliver adequate access to the poor. Regulatory institutions can be
costly and require sophisticated skills. For example, even a bare-bones
telecommunications regulatory authority is likely to cost around $2 million each
year, or 5 percent of the government budget in a country like Dominica. The Doha
Declaration contains innumerable references to technical assistance, but not one of
these is binding.

It is desirable to establish a credible link between policy advice and regulatory
assistance, on the one hand, and liberalization commitments, on the other. Added
urgency is lent by negotiating deadlines—improved offers to liberalize were to be
submitted by the end of May this year—but negotiating pressure alone is hardly
likely to produce the best responses. In the Uruguay Round negotiations, most
countries erred on the side of caution and made few commitments to genuine
liberalization, while some may have gone too far. For example, the Gambia and
Guyana have allowed unrestricted cross-border trade in financial services in their
GATS commitments—and hence capital mobility—while the United States and the
European Union have not. Malaysia, Pakistan, the Philippines and others agreed to
protect foreign incumbents while they offered new entrants inferior conditions of
operation—leading to less rather than more contestable markets. A decision on
"duty-free" electronic commerce created the legal illusion of a liberated medium,
while the much greater threat of discriminatory quantitative and regulatory barriers
was not addressed. The liberalization of maritime and air transport has not been
seriously negotiated, and exemptions from competition law continue because of
the power of vested interests in industrial countries, even though Sub-Saharan
African countries pay transport costs that are on average more than five times
greater than the tariffs they face.

Development institutions have a stake in the outcome of the services
negotiations, because GATS negotiations can be harnessed to deliver much-needed
reform and also because unbridled mercantilism could produce outcomes that are
antithetical to development. Thus the following question requires an answer: Is
there a good reason to defer liberalization, or not to make binding commitments?
Weaknesses in existing mechanisms for prudential or procompetitive regulation,
the need to alleviate adjustment costs, and the desire to ensure universal access in

liberalized markets may be good reasons for gradual rather than abrupt opening.

Service exporting firms in industrial countries also have a stake, not only in ensuring that markets are opened, but also that such opening is sustainable and in a sound regulatory environment. These objectives can be served by support for improved regulatory institutions and universal access policies. Just as in a national context the private sector is required to contribute, directly or indirectly (through taxation) to financing the regulator without compromising the arms-length relationship, it should be possible for the private sector to contribute resources for regulatory reform in developing countries. Private sector contributions could also help ensure that assistance is genuinely additional and not diverted from other forms of public assistance.

Proposal 2: The international development community will establish a mechanism, funded by public and private donors, to provide policy advice and to diagnose and remedy regulatory inadequacies for developing countries that are considering liberalizing commitments. Recourse to the mechanism will be voluntary.[5]

If such a mechanism is to work, then there must be a *demand* for assistance, which will emerge only if there are fewer suspicions and greater appreciation of its value. On the one hand, countries must be confident that the mechanism will serve their needs and not be a Trojan horse designed for the sole purpose of inducing them to make market-opening commitments. The mechanism must therefore be established in consultation with the relevant countries; credible funding must be provided for diagnostics and remedial action; and it must be clearly understood that recourse to the mechanism will not create an obligation to make commitments. On the other hand, user countries must also see the usefulness of establishing a link between negotiations and assistance in order to foster desirable reform.[6]

Facilitating regulatory cooperation

Facilitating regulatory cooperation could help deal with apprehensions about liberalization of all modes. For example, in financial services, confidence in cooperation by the home-country regulator could lead to openness to both commercial presence and cross-border trade. Similarly, in international transport services, confidence in the enforcement of home-country competition law may increase the willingness to liberalize in importing countries. We focus here on the presence of natural persons, or mode 4. Progress in these negotiations has become a precondition for more meaningful developing-country participation in the process of reciprocal market opening. And it is proving extremely difficult for some countries to make meaningful concessions in this area.

How can we make mode 4 a milestone rather than a millstone for the services negotiations? First of all, members need to recognize that simply asserting that mode 4 is about trade in services and not about migration cannot dispel deep-rooted fears raised by the entry of foreign providers. These fears have to be acknowledged and addressed. One way forward may be to take a more cooperative and less antagonistic approach to mode 4, drawing upon the experience of a few relatively successful bilateral and regional agreements.[7]

The inclusion of labor mobility in the framework of a *multilateral trade agreement* implies that obligations are assumed by host countries to provide market access on an MFN basis regardless of conditions in source countries. In contrast, the assumption of obligations by source countries also is a key element of regional trade agreements North American Free Trade Agreement (NAFTA) and Asia-Pacific Economic Cooperation (APEC) that have facilitated mobility of the skilled, and of bilateral labor agreements (such as those between Spain and Ecuador, Canada and the Caribbean, and Germany and Eastern Europe) that have to a limited extent improved access for the unskilled. Source-country obligations include premovement screening and selection, accepting and facilitating return, and commitments to combat illegal migration. In effect, cooperation by the source can help address security concerns, ensure temporariness, and prevent illegal labor flows in a way that the host cannot accomplish alone—and constitute a service for which the host may be willing to pay by allowing increased access.

Can these elements be incorporated in a multilateral agreement? One possibility is that host countries commit under the GATS to allow access to any source country that fulfills certain specified conditions—along the lines of mutual-recognition agreements in other areas. Even if these conditions were unilaterally specified and compliance determined unilaterally, it would still be a huge improvement over the arbitrariness and lack of transparency in existing visa schemes. Eventually, it would be desirable to negotiate these conditions (and even establish a mechanism to certify their fulfillment) multilaterally rather than in an unequal, nontransparent, and potentially labor-diverting bilateral context.

In the current GATS framework, when a country makes a market access commitment, it is obliged to grant a fixed level of access every year in the future regardless of domestic economic conditions. In contrast, bilateral labor agreements allow host countries to vary the level of access depending on the state of the economy. One example is the bilateral agreement between Germany and certain Eastern European countries, under which the quota on temporary migrants increased (decreased) by 5 percent for every one percentage point decrease (increase) in the level of unemployment. It may be desirable to consider GATS commitments along these lines, which allow necessary flexibility, albeit in a transparent, predictable, and objectively verifiable manner—a big improvement over the opaque economic needs tests that infest GATS schedules.

Proposal 3: Immigration authorities in member countries would be requested to define a set of conditions that source countries need to fulfill—in terms of screening services providers, accepting and facilitating their return, and making efforts to combat illegal migration—to be eligible for an allocation of temporary visas. These conditions could be the basis for a dialogue between immigration authorities in host and source countries. GATS commitments on mode 4 would be transparently and predictably conditional on source-country cooperation and host-country economic conditions.

Conclusion

There is considerable scope for the WTO to play its traditional role of facilitating reciprocal liberalization, not only by exploiting trade-offs across goods and services but also within services. But for the process to work, the negotiating process must be reformed and regulators reassured. These steps may help generate a virtuous cycle of mutually beneficial liberalization rather than a bitter round of grudging concessions.

To summarize the main proposals in this paper:

- First, members should adopt, or at least complement the current request-and-offer approach with, a collective approach to negotiations. Groups of members should champion clearly specified goals and articulate them in model schedules (or model regulatory principles). By appropriate choice of sectors and level of commitments, agreement should be secured among a critical mass of members.
- Second, a critical mass of members should lock in the current openness of cross-border trade in a wide range of services, while retaining the right to impose any regulation or restriction that does not discriminate against foreigners.
- Third, a critical mass of members should eliminate barriers to foreign participation in sectors where there is no good reason to defer liberalization. The same members should precommit to eliminating barriers where the necessary preconditions can be fulfilled in a predictable time span. To complement this effort, a multilateral commitment should be made to provide policy advice and to help poor countries establish regulatory mechanisms necessary for successful liberalization.
- Finally, a critical mass of members should allow greater freedom for the temporary presence of intracorporate transferees and of service providers to fulfill specific services contracts. Commitments in this area could be made transparently and predictably conditional on the unemployment rate in host countries and on source countries' assumption of certain obligations related to certification, expatriation, and illegal immigration.

Notes

1. WTO Document TN/S/20.

2. The problem arises in bilateral negotiations because each of the beneficiaries of a concession from a trading partner may be tempted to understate their willingness to pay for it, hoping that offers of reciprocal concessions from other members will be sufficient to induce the concession.

3. See, for example, Hoekman (1996) and Mattoo (1999).

4. The exception are certain countries that recently acceded to or are acceding to the WTO— among them China, the Russian Federation, and Vietnam.

5. Such a mechanism could be part of a broader "aid for trade" initiative of the type called for in the United Nations Millennium Project (2004) and by the G-8 at Gleneagles in 2005. See also Hoekman (2005) and Prowse (2005).

6. In the past, many developing countries either did not engage at all in the negotiations, or succumbed to the bandwagon effect, as in the basic telecommunications negotiations, where many rushed forward to submit schedules of commitments at the last minute; the only directly linked assistance they received (including from the World Bank) was in drafting their schedules.

7. This section draws on joint work done with Julia Nielson.

References

Chaudhuri, S., A. Mattoo, and R. Self. 2004. "Moving People to Deliver Services: How Can the WTO Help?" *Journal of World Trade* 38: 363–93.

Findlay, C., and T. Warren (eds.). 2000. *Impediments to Trade in Services: Measurement and Policy Implications.* London and New York: Routledge.

Hoekman, B. 1996. "Assessing the General Agreement on Trade in Services." In *The Uruguay Round and the Developing Countries,* ed. W. Martin and L. A. Winters. Cambridge: Cambridge University Press.

Hoekman, B. 2005. "Expanding WTO Membership and Heterogeneous Interests." *World Trade Review.*

Mattoo, A. 2000. "Financial Services and the WTO: Liberalization Commitments of the Developing and Transition Economies." *World Economy* 23(3): 351–86.

Mattoo, A., R. Rathindran, and A. Subramanian. 2005. "Measuring Services Trade Liberalization and Its Impact on Economic Growth: An Illustration." *Journal of Economic Integration.*

Mattoo, A., and S. Wunsch. 2004. "Pre-Empting Protectionism in Services: The WTO and Outsourcing." *Journal of International Economic Law* 7: 765–800.

Prowse, S. 2005. "Aid for Trade: Increasing Support for Trade Adjustment and Integration—A Proposal." Unpublished paper, Department for International Development, London.

Robinson, S., Z. Wang, and W. Martin. 1999. "Capturing the Implications of Services Trade Liberalization." Paper presented at the Second Annual Conference on Global Economic Analysis, Gl. Avernaes Conference Center, Ebberup, Denmark, June 20–22.

U.N. Millennium Project. 2004. "Trade for Development." Task Force on Trade New York, United Nations, New York.

Winters, L. A., T. L. Walmsley, Z. K. Wang, and R. Grynberg. 2003. "Liberalising Temporary Movement of Natural Persons: An Agenda for the Development Round." *World Economy* 26(8): 1137–61.

WTO Document TN/S/20.

Trade Facilitation: Progress and Prospects for the Doha Negotiations

Gerard McLinden

It is widely acknowledged that lowering the costs of trading can be as important as lowering tariffs in foreign markets.[1] Too often, outdated and inefficient processing systems, procedures, and infrastructure can result in high transaction costs, long delays in the clearance of goods, and opportunities for administrative corruption. Hummels (2001) estimates that cutting delivery times by one day (by reducing waiting time in ports or delays in customs) would reduce the average landed costs of goods around the world by 0.8 percent. Inefficiencies in the processing of trade adversely affects a country's competitiveness by raising the cost of imported inputs and saddling exports with dead weight inefficiencies. Countries that facilitate the movement of imports and exports, by contrast, are likely to attract investment and help their small and medium-sized enterprises participate and compete in the international trading system.

Most developing countries could do better

Many developing countries lag far behind the Organization for Economic Cooperation and Development (OECD) average in the time it takes to process imports and exports (figures 1a and b), putting their traders at a significant disadvantage and further pressuring already stretched port and transport infrastructure.

Evidence suggests that improvements in border clearance systems and procedures can significantly reduce delays and lower traders' transaction costs. At the same time, such improvements typically enhance revenue collection and the level of community protection provided by border institutions (Table 1). For these reasons, trade facilitation reform based on better customs processing and improved border management procedures has become an important development issue in recent years, as reflected in increased levels of investment by governments and donors alike. Its importance is also reflected in numerous provisions related to trade facilitation in recent bilateral and regional trading agreements and in the push by many countries for multilateral rules on trade facilitation within the World Trade Organization (WTO).

The decision of the WTO General Council in July 2004 to launch negotiations on trade facilitation was not taken lightly. Many developing countries had serious reservations about whether new WTO disciplines were a good way to promote reform. This note examines progress in the negotiations and argues that developing countries can use new WTO obligations to further their domestic reform agenda

Figure 1a. Port and customs inefficiency drive up the cost of imports

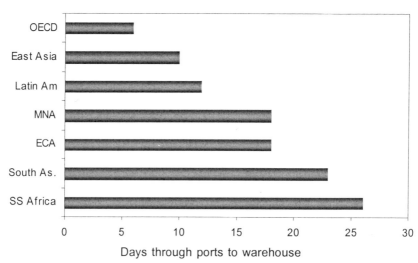

Days through ports to warehouse

Source: World Bank, Doing Business 2006.

rather than distort it—provided they develop a coherent negotiating strategy based on securing agreement to a range of practical measures to facilitate trade and make it easier for traders to compete in regional and international markets.

Trade facilitation has always been a WTO concern

Provisions and obligations related to trade facilitation have been a central part of the GATT/WTO system since 1948 (Box 1).

The desirability of revisiting the WTO's existing trade-facilitation measures was first proposed in 1996 at the Singapore Ministerial Conference. Five years later, at the 2001 Ministerial meeting in Doha, WTO members decided to launch negotiations on trade facilitation provided that members could reach explicit consensus on the modalities for negotiation at the 5th ministerial meeting in Cancun, Mexico, in September 2003. The negotiations in Cancun broke down in acrimony when members could not reach agreement on the four so-called Singapore issues, one of which was trade facilitation.[2] At a meeting of the WTO General Council in July 2004, agreement was finally reached to launch negotiations on trade facilitation.

But it was a reluctant consensus. While almost all WTO members acknowledge the benefits to be obtained by investing time and energy in improving trade facilitation, several were reluctant to commit to a series of new multilateral rules while they are still struggling to implement existing commitments. Several members believed that they lack the necessary capacity and resources to implement additional obligations. Moreover, many developing country members were concerned that new rules on trade facilitation may expose them to action under the WTO's dispute-settlement mechanisms.

Modalities for negotiations on trade facilitation

The modalities for negotiations on trade facilitation—Annex D of the package that emerged from the July 2004 WTO Council meeting—were therefore constructed in such a way as to address and protect the interests of developing-country members, particularly least developed countries (LDCs), through four unique features.

- The scope of the negotiations is limited to clarifying and improving the relevant aspects of Articles V, VIII, and X of the General Agreement on Tariffs and Trade (GATT) with a view to further expediting the movement, release, and clearance of goods, including goods in transit. Members explicitly narrowed the definition of trade facilitation to "the simplification and harmonization of international trade procedures."[3]
- The modalities do not necessarily envisage binding rules as the outcome of negotiations. "It is understood that [the negotiations are] without prejudice to the possible format of the final result of the negotiations and would allow consideration of various forms of outcomes" .
- Any commitments ultimately negotiated are to be calibrated to the implementation capabilities of developing-country members. LDC members will not be expected or required to undertake commitments that are inconsistent with their individual development, financial and trade needs, or their administrative and institutional capabilities. Likewise, they will not be obliged to undertake investments in infrastructure beyond their means.

Table 1. Some benefits of enhanced trade facilitation for governments and traders

Governments	Traders
• Increased effectiveness of control methods	• Lower costs and shorter delays
• More effective and efficient deployment of resources	• Faster customs clearance and release through predictable official intervention
• Correct revenue yields	• Simpler commercial framework for domestic and international trade
• Improved trader compliance	• Enhanced competitiveness
• Encouragement of foreign investment	

Source: UNECE 2002. Trade facilitation: An introduction to the basic concepts and benefits, 2002 (www.unece.org).

Box 1. Existing GATT Trade Facilitation-Related Articles

Article I (*most-favored-nation treatment*) requires that imports from, or exports to, any WTO member must receive nondiscriminatory treatment in the application of customs duties and customs formalities.

Article V (*freedom of transit*) provides a basis for an environment in which the transit of goods is free from barriers to transport and discrimination among suppliers, firms, and traders from different countries.

Article VIII (*fees and formalities connected with importation and exportation*) relates in general to customs clearance procedures and includes a general commitment to nondiscrimination and transparency in fees and rules applied to goods crossing borders.

Article X (*publication and administration of trade regulations*) contains general commitments to assist in ensuring timely publication of regulations regarding imports, including fees, customs valuation procedures, and other rules. It also provides general obligations to maintain transparent administrative procedures for review of disputes in customs.

Trade facilitation is addressed in other WTO obligations and provisions, as well, including special agreements on matters such as Customs Valuation, Import Licensing, Preshipment Inspection, Rules of Origin, Technical Barriers to Trade, Sanitary and Phytosanitary Measures, and Intellectual Property Rights.

• The modalities duly link implementation of any commitments to the receipt of technical assistance and support for capacity building both during the negotiations and in the course of implementation. Indeed six of Annex D's ten paragraphs are devoted to the issue of technical assistance and capacity building.

In one sense, the content of the Annex D document, developed in the weeks leading up to the July 2004 General Council meeting, was a victory for the developing-country members in that its provisions clearly shelter them from obligations that are beyond their means and capacity. At the same time, the document commits the developed countries to providing appropriate technical assistance. However, these same provisions may leave LDCs in a position where they are required to implement almost nothing of substance, which may encourage them to postpone necessary improvements to their border processing regimes and so prolong their marginal status in the international trading system.

The trade-facilitation negotiations—progress to date

In October 2004 the WTO Trade Negotiations Committee established a Trade Facilitation Negotiating Group (TFNG) under the chairmanship of Ambassador Yacob Muhamad Noor of Malaysia. Since beginning its work in November, the group has met at four- to six-week intervals. As of the end of September 2005, WTO members had submitted more than 50 proposals, focused on clarifying and improving Articles V, VIII and X. To assist members to analyze the proposals and to provide a basis for further discussion within the TFNG, the WTO Secretariat has prepared a compilation or summary document (TF/TN/W43) that is updated after each meeting of the TFNG.[4]

The proposals submitted to date, covering all aspects of GATT Articles V, VIII, and X, have stimulated productive discussion and debate within the TFNG. Proposals range from relatively straightforward issues that are likely to be incorporated in any possible new agreement (such as employing risk-management principles to assess the risks posed by imported cargo), to more difficult and resource-intensive measures, such as the implementation of electronic single-window regimes. Significant time has been devoted to discussing the needs and priorities of developing-country members for technical assistance and capacity building.

Overall, the negotiations have been conducted in a spirit of cooperation and compromise not always evident in other areas of negotiation within the WTO. With

Figure 1b. Port and customs in efficiency drive up the cost of export

Signatures required to export

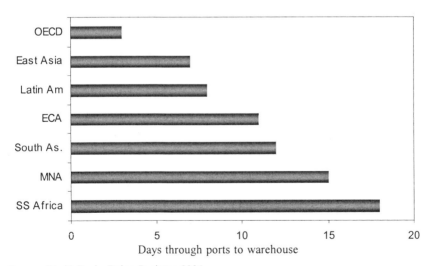

Days through ports to warehouse

Source: World Bank, Doing Business 2006.

most of the key proposals now in hand, negotiations will shift toward a process of clarifying those proposals, and then narrowing and refining the list of measures that are likely to be agreed on.

Support from international organizations

The modalities encouraged international organizations—including the International Monetary Fund, OECD, UNCTAD, World Customs Organization (WCO), and the World Bank—to "undertake a collaborative effort." To date, the international organizations have focused on three key areas: (a) promotion and advocacy to highlight the benefits of trade facilitation and encourage members to seek a positive and ambitious outcome; (b) sharing of information on relevant tools, instruments, and international standards; and (c) providing advice and assistance to help members determine needs and priorities for technical assistance related to the negotiating agenda.

Noteworthy in this regard is OECD's ongoing work on the cost of introducing and implementing trade-facilitation measures. The WCO, too, has supported the negotiations by providing information on its instruments and tools, including the Revised Kyoto Convention and its Time Release Study methodology. The WCO also has partnered with the WTO secretariat, UNCTAD, and the World Bank to contribute its expertise through workshops, seminars, and other events throughout the world. UNCTAD has been equally active, providing advice and guidance to

Figure 2. Governments should look for high benefits, low cost reforms

WB/WCO proposal analysis grid

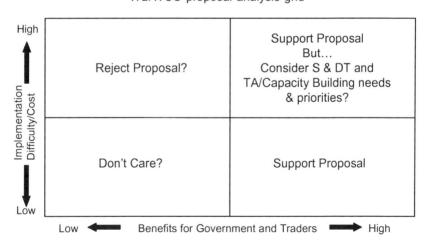

Source: World Bank and World Customs Organization.

members based on its capacity building experience and hosting or contributing to a range of relevant educational and informational events in Geneva and around the world. The World Bank's support for negotiations has been focused on providing balanced advice to negotiators on the benefits and consequences of an ambitious trade-facilitation agreement. It has also helped developing-country negotiators overcome some of the practical constraints they face.[4] The World Bank's engagement has been premised on the view that much of the technical expertise necessary to examine and assess proposals as they are tabled within the TFNG already exists in members' capitals and that real-time contact between Geneva-based negotiators and content specialists in the capital will help developing-country members gain confidence in their ability to implement the measures under negotiation.

Several points of nascent agreement have emerged from the discussions of technical assistance and capacity building:

- Although needs, priorities, and capacities vary enormously from region to region and from country to country, there is a significant degree of commonality and much agreement about the potential benefits of the proposals tabled to date.
- Most proposals are positive and have been welcomed by government officials and private sector representatives. Fears of excessive costs and a lack of technical capacity associated with implementation may have been overstated. This not to suggest that members would not benefit from well-targeted capacity building support, but that many of the measures currently proposed can be implemented with relatively modest amounts of technical assistance and capacity building support. The assessments of members' home-based specialists have revealed that many of the measures proposed to date within TFNG would ultimately have been introduced by members' customs administrations as they represent best practice in customs and border management and are frequently included in existing internationally agreed instruments.[5]
- Content-matter specialists have also noted that many of the barriers to implementation are domestic (insufficient political commitment to reform and poor interagency cooperation are two examples) and thus not susceptible to resolution through the sort of technical assistance and capacity building that have been under discussion.
- Few countries are starting from scratch as most are already engaged in some form of reform and modernization of their border processing regimes (often supported by significant donor support) and therefore any technical assistance and capacity building support that is ultimately provided will need to complement rather than displace existing efforts.

With respect to the proposals tabled within the TFNG, many participants have noted that it is easier to identify needs for assistance than it is to ascertain the precise form and cost of that assistance. Donor organizations have a comparative advantage in this area, because they possess much more experience and expertise in developing and costing technical assistance and capacity building activities. Clearly, concerns about the potential costs associated with implementing a new agreement have been at the center of the debate within the TFNG and a clearer understanding of exactly what is required will greatly facilitate negotiation of a meaningful agreement.

Inspired in part by the above conclusions, the World Bank will undertake, in the first half of 2006, a series of studies to provide more detailed information to members about the actual costs of closing the gap between existing systems and procedures and those envisaged under a new trade-facilitation agreement.

In the coming months negotiators within the TFNG will focus on refining the measures that have been proposed to date. Essentially, they will weigh up the costs and benefits of individual proposals and measures based on their own needs and priorities. Although this is often a complex process involving the participation of many national stakeholders the basic decisions that can be made are illustrated by the proposal-analysis grid prepared by the WCO and the World Bank (figure 2). Members must decide whether the potential benefits to their governments and traders justify the cost and effort of implementation. To date, when content-matter specialists have been involved in the assessment of the various proposals, the vast majority of proposals have been deemed worthy of support; that is, the specialists placed them in one of the two right-hand quadrants of the grid.

Challenges ahead: prospects for a new WTO trade-facilitation agreement

The key to a positive outcome will depend in large part on the capacity of developed country members and the international organizations to deal with the remaining concerns of developing and LDC members about the potentially high costs of implementation and the availability of technical assistance and capacity building support. The difficulty is complicated by the fact that the precise content of a new agreement is not yet clear. For example, several countries have submitted proposals relating to the implementation of a "single window" at which traders might obtain all of the permits and clearances required for the importation or exportation of goods. Depending on the definition ultimately employed in a new agreement, members' needs for technical assistance and capacity building related to the single window could vary from almost nothing to many millions of dollars.[6] Likewise, the scale of a country's needs for technical assistance and capacity building will depend on the provisions for special and differential STDT treatment that might apply to specific measures.

In the continuing absence of precise information on the scope, content, and magnitude of the technical assistance needs facing members it will be difficult for developed-country members and international organizations to make open-ended commitments about the provision of technical assistance and capacity building. A second complication is related to donors' concerns that the imperatives of a new WTO agreement on trade facilitation might subsume or displace their existing projects and development assistance activities agreed though existing bilateral and multilateral channels. To move away from this approach would be to ignore the focus on "demand driven" assistance that has characterized donor support in recent years.

Differentiating between the specific issues on the negotiating agenda and comprehensive trade-related reform is sometimes extremely difficult. For example, many customs and border clearance systems involve a series of separate but interdependent activities; several members have expressed concerns about accepting new obligations that may require changes in underlying technical and administrative systems. Identifying critical interdependencies among the specific WTO measures under negotiation will be an important element of the work being done by members and international organizations to determine needs and priorities for technical assistance and capacity building support.

The World Bank and other multilateral and bilateral donors have reported on the scale and scope of their trade-facilitation activities in meetings of the TFNG. Such information has raised members' awareness of the scope and scale of donor support already available. The process of sharing such information will have to continue in the coming months, because obtaining an ambitious agreement will require universal confidence that developing-country members will be able obtain the help they need to implement the agreement.

While the nature and shape of a suitable international mechanism to coordinate and manage this process is still being discussed within the TFNG, it is generally accepted by WTO members that it will need to ensure effective cooperation and coherence between all the different players and meet certain key criteria. In essence, to allay the concerns of developing-country and LDC members, the coordination mechanism must have the following attributes:

- A robust process for identifying needs and priorities and matching those needs and priorities with technical assistance and capacity building support; and
- Sufficient flexibility to allow bilateral and multilateral donors to contribute according to their capacity, resources, priorities, and comparative advantage[7]; and
- The ability to build on or complement, rather than replace or duplicate, existing bilateral and multilateral mechanisms developed by donors over many years and established in close consultation with client governments; and
- Economies of scale (for example, if many countries determine that they need technical assistance to introduce a measure such as risk management, it would seem sensible to develop a core package that can then be tailored to meet the specific needs of individual members); and

- Compatibility with other relevant international tools, standards, and trade facilitation developments;[8] and
- As least resource intensive as possible to ensure scarce resources are not wasted on unnecessary administrative activities; and
- Incorporate some form of robust evaluation and review mechanism.

The need to develop effective mechanisms to coordinate and manage the delivery of technical assistance associated with the implementation of the TF agreement is well acknowledged by all donors. Such mechanisms should build on existing initiatives at the multilateral and bilateral levels and be consistent with the broad Aid for Trade initiative that is underway. Of critical importance at the moment is that members continue to define the content of a new trade-facilitation agreement in full confidence that their concerns about the long term availability of technical assistance needs are understood and that a suitable mechanism will be developed to deal with their legitimate concerns about implementation capacity.

Conclusion

The decision taken by the WTO General Council in July 2004 to launch negotiations on trade facilitation reflects a widely shared view that reforms to facilitate the movement of imports and exports and reduce costs and delays make good development sense. To make the most of the opportunity presented by the launch of negotiations, developing countries (and particularly the least developed) should view the WTO negotiations as an opportunity to further their domestic reform agenda and accelerate the implementation of measures already accepted as good practice and incorporated in a range of internationally agreed instruments. To reinforce that view of the negotiations, developing-country negotiators in Geneva should work closely with content matter specialists at home to develop a coherent negotiating strategy that focuses on securing agreement on a range of practical measures that will make it easier for their traders to compete in regional and international markets.

Notes

1. The author is a Senior Trade Facilitation Specialist–in the International Trade Department of the World Bank.

2. The other Singapore issues were trade and investment, trade and competition policy, and transparency in government procurement.

3. A wider definition of trade facilitation could include all aspects of the supply chain including government regulations, business competency and efficiency, the performance of customs and other regulatory agencies, the quality and availability of transport infrastructure, such as roads, airports, ports, etc., information and communications technology, and trade-related finance and insurance services, among other things.

4. See WTO Document TN/TF/W/43/Rev 3.

5. The Bank launched a Trade Facilitation Negotiations Support Project in February 2005. It is designed to assist members who have limited resources in Geneva to provide their negotiators with real-time analysis and advice on the content and implications of proposals tabled in Geneva. The project has three components. Component I involved the development of a Trade Facilitation Negotiation Support Guide (available in English, French, and Spanish) to help members establish negotiation-support groups in their capitals and improve the level of communication between content specialists and Geneva-based negotiators. Component II consists of a series of pilot workshops designed to promote the use of the guide and to demonstrate the usefulness of capital-based support groups to Geneva-based negotiators. Pilot workshops have been conducted in Jamaica, Uganda, and Sri Lanka and the results shared with WTO members. Three more pilot workshops will be conducted in the second half of 2005. Component III will consist of a series of in-country studies of the cost of compliance focused on determining the cost of implementing a new agreement.

6. Such as the WCO's Revised Kyoto Convention on the Simplification and Harmonization of Customs practices.

7. Recent World Bank projects that have included the development of a genuine electronic single window to connect traders with relevant government agencies have ranged in cost from $5.6 million to more than $30 million.

8. For example, Malaysia has recently offered its customs academy for use for regional workshops, seminars, and other events during the negotiations and later implementation. Likewise, India has indicated its willingness to make its training facilities and expertise available to other countries in the region to assist with implementation of commitments that may flow from a new trade-facilitation agreement.

9. For example, at the WCO Council sessions in June 2005, the directors-general of 164 customs administrations agreed on a Framework of Standards to Secure and Facilitate Global Trade (www.wcoomd.org). The framework overlaps many of the measures under consideration in the WTO negotiations.

References

Hummels, D. 2001. "Time as a Trade Barrier." Mimeo. Department of Economics, Purdue University, Lafayette, Ind.

UNECE. 2002. "Trade Facilitation: An Introduction to the Basic Concepts and Benefits." Geneva:United Nations, ECE/TRADE/289. www.unece.org.

World Bank. 2006. *Doing Business*. Washington, D.C.

Intellectual Property and Public Health: The WTO's August 2003 Decision in Perspective

Carsten Fink

In August 2003, members of the World Trade Organization (WTO) agreed on a waiver to certain WTO intellectual property rules. The waiver was designed to improve access to generic drugs for countries in need. Promoting poor people's access to medicines and vaccines is central to alleviating poverty and fighting the HIV/AIDS epidemic. Only 5 percent of infected patients in the developing world receive the antiretroviral (ARV) drugs that have made AIDS a treatable disease in rich countries. Better access to drugs is equally important for combating malaria, tuberculosis, diarrhea, cancer and many other diseases that annually kill millions of children and working-age adults in poor countries. This note outlines the main elements of the so-called August 2003 Decision and explores how it may affect access to medicines in poor countries.[1]

Patents, generics, and drug prices

Newly developed medicines are generally protected by patents that offer time-limited market exclusivity to the patent holder, usually a research-based pharmaceutical company. The patent system provides incentives for pharmaceutical innovation. It allows patent holders to charge prices in rich-country markets that recoup investments in research and development (R&D). But rich-country prices for new drugs can be unaffordable to poor people in the developing world. For example, the cost of an ARV drug therapy in developed nations can easily exceed $30 a day, whereas three billion of the world's people live on less than two dollars a day.

Efforts have been made to reduce drug prices in poor countries. In the case of ARVs, pharmaceutical companies have offered steep price discounts to developing-country governments. In selected countries, they also have offered drugs for free and provided the health infrastructure needed to make antiretroviral treatments effective. While such actions are laudable, they are not systematic and depend on the good will of private firms. Clearly, the scale of the health crisis in the developing world is too large to be solved by private philanthropy alone.

Another strategy is to rely on manufacturers of generic drugs to produce copycat versions of patented products and so force down prices through market competition. Indeed, the price discounts on ARVs offered by the originator companies were probably brought about as much by competition from generic producers as by voluntary decision (figure 1). As of June 2005, generic manufacturers—especially from India, but also from other developing countries—offered the lowest prices for most AIDS drugs.[2]

Figure 1: Originator and Generic Drug Prices for a Sample ARV Triple - Combination

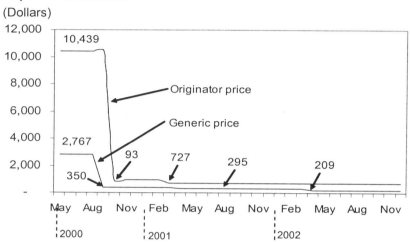

(Dollars)

Notes: Sample of ARV triple-combination: stavudine (d4T) + lamivudine (3TC) + nevirapine (NVP). Lowest world prices per patient per year.
Source: Médicines sans Frontières, "Untangling the Web of Price Reductions," various editions, available at www.accessmed-msf.org.

TRIPS, compulsory licenses, and the Doha Declaration

Generic production is possible for the great majority of essential medicines, which currently are not protected by patents in developing countries.[3] However, this practice may become more difficult as stronger patent rules required by the WTO have come into effect. As part of the Uruguay Trade Round (1986–94), members of (what is now) the WTO negotiated the Agreement on Trade-Related Aspects of Intellectual Property Rights (TRIPS). That agreement obliges countries to extend patent protection to pharmaceutical products and processes. While TRIPS foresees various periods of transition for developing countries, the supply of generics may be significantly curtailed in the near future (box 1).

In principle, governments have the option of overriding the market exclusivity of patents by granting so-called compulsory licenses to generic manufacturers. TRIPS allows the use of compulsory licenses. In cases of "national emergency or other circumstances of extreme urgency," and in cases of public, noncommercial use, it does not even require that the proposed user first make efforts to obtain a voluntary license from the patent holder.[4]

Responding to concerns that the TRIPS patent rules could undermine access to medicines in poor countries, WTO members issued a declaration at their ministerial meeting in Doha, Qatar in 2001, reaffirming the right of governments to use compulsory licenses. Indeed, several developing country governments have granted compulsory licenses on different AIDS drugs in the past few years—for example, Malaysia, Mozambique, and Zambia.[5] Notwithstanding these recent cases, compulsory licenses have not been used frequently in the past, for two reasons. First, as pointed out above, most medicines in developing countries have been free of patents, so there has been little need to override market exclusivity. Second, the threat of permitting the production of competing generic medicines has led pharmaceutical companies to offer the drugs at cheaper prices. This arguably happened when some in the U.S. government advocated overriding the patent of the drug Ciprofloxacin during the 2001 anthrax crisis.[6] Similarly, the pharmaceutical company Roche offered a 40 percent price reduction on its AIDS drug, Viracept, to Brazil after the Brazilian government publicly announced in 2001 that it would issue a compulsory license to a local laboratory.[7]

In the future, as more products in more places will be protected by patents, granting compulsory licenses to local producers may emerge as an effective strategy to promote generic competition in developing countries that have the capacity to manufacture pharmaceuticals. Well-developed pharmaceutical industries can be found, for example, in Argentina, Brazil, China, India, and Thailand. Yet many other developing countries—especially the least developed countries of Africa—do not possess pharmaceutical manufacturing capabilities. These countries can effectively use the compulsory licensing option only if they are allowed to import generic drugs. Yet it was legally uncertain whether this would be allowed under TRIPS (Box 2). Acknowledging the difficulties that countries with insufficient or no manufacturing capacity face in using the compulsory licensing mechanism, the Doha Declaration called for negotiations to solve the problem.

The August 2003 decision

Post-Doha negotiations on implementing the declaration lasted almost two years and were marked by acrimonious debate. Several points of contention emerged—among them which countries should be eligible importers, whether to limit the range of diseases to which the new system would apply, and what kind of reporting requirements and safeguards should be established (Abbott 2005). WTO members were not able to strike a deal by the December 2002 deadline specified in the Doha Declaration, with the United States alone blocking the proposed compromise. Another attempt at consensus failed in February 2003. But in August, amid concerns that the stalled negotiations would risk failure of the September 2003 WTO Ministerial Meeting in Cancún, Mexico, an agreement was reached.[8]

The August 2003 deal consists of a decision by WTO members, accompanied by a statement from the chair of the WTO General Council that spelled out certain shared understandings on the interpretation and implementation of the decision. Key elements of the new system are as follows:

Box 1. Untangling the TRIPS transition periods

The provisions of TRIPS entered into force on a staggered schedule—with the main obligations applicable to developed countries at the beginning of 1996, and most obligations applicable to developing countries as of January 1, 2000. Developing countries were allowed to delay the introduction of pharmaceutical patent protection until the beginning of 2005, and the least developed countries are still entitled to a transition period ending in 2016 (with the possibility of a further extension). At the same time, a convoluted compromise negotiated during the Uruguay Round obliged developing countries that did not immediately provide for patent protection to accept applications for pharmaceutical product patents during the transition period (so-called mailbox patents) and grant "exclusive marketing rights" to those products for five years or until the patent is granted or rejected, whichever is shorter.

In practice, these transition periods mean that pharmaceutical compounds for which patents were filed before the entry into force of the TRIPS agreement (January 1, 1995) will not receive patent protection in those countries that previously excluded pharmaceutical products from the scope of patentability. The compounds that will remain open to generic competition include the great majority of medicines on essential drug lists, among them a number (but not all) of the ARVs. Drugs patented after developing countries implemented their TRIPS obligations—including some of the most effective new treatments to combat HIV/AIDS, malaria, and tuberculosis—are now coming into markets. As time goes by, they will make up a growing share of pharmaceutical sales.

Of special relevance is the situation of India—the most important supplier of generic drugs. Following the conclusion of the Uruguay Round, India opted for the mailbox transition mechanism to fulfill its TRIPS obligation. Full pharmaceutical product patent protection became available only with the 2005 amendments to the Indian Patents Act. However, the March 2005 amendment contains a provision allowing Indian manufacturers to continue generic production of drugs for which mailbox patents are granted. This provision would appear to delay the arrival of medicines supplied under market exclusivity in India.

Least developed countries in Africa and elsewhere will not be required to protect drug patents for the foreseeable future. While many of these countries do not possess generic manufacturing capabilities in the first place, some do, and the staggered structure of the TRIPS transition periods may encourage generic pharmaceutical production in the least developed countries. Pharmaceutical manufacturers in Bangladesh, for example, are seeking to build on this advantage.

- Its applicability is not limited to a predefined set of diseases (as was favored by some WTO members during negotiations) or to emergency situations.[9] At the same time, members acknowledged that the system should not be used "as an instrument to pursue industrial or commercial policy objectives."
- Eligible importing members are defined as any least developed country as well as any other member that finds that it has insufficient pharmaceutical manufacturing capacity for the product in question. However, several developing countries indicated that they would use the system only in situations of national emergency or other circumstances of extreme urgency.[10] The majority of OECD countries and the countries that recently acceded to the European Union opted out of the system altogether.[11]
- The importing member must notify the WTO of its grant of a compulsory license (or its intention to make such a grant) and the names and expected quantities of the pharmaceutical products needed.[12] The exporting member must notify the WTO of the name of the generic manufacturer(s), the products and quantities for which the license is granted, and the countries to which generic drugs are to be exported. In addition, the exporting manufacturer has to post detailed information about its shipments on a dedicated website.
- A number of safeguards minimize the risk that drugs produced under the system and destined for poor countries should leak into rich countries' pharmaceutical markets. Prices of patented medicines are substantially higher in the developed world, creating opportunities to profit by illegally diverting drugs. Thus, pharmaceutical products produced under the system have to be appropriately labeled and, to the extent possible, distinguished through special packaging, coloring, and shaping (provided this does not significantly affect prices). In addition, importing countries must take reasonable measures to prevent reexportation of the products in question.

The August 2003 Decision takes the form of a waiver of existing TRIPS rules. It also instructs WTO members to adopt a permanent amendment to the TRIPS agreement that would be based, "where appropriate," on the decision. This has not happened, because WTO members still hold different views on the amendment. The United States—supported by Japan and Switzerland—would like it to include a reference to the statement by the chair of the General Council, a step opposed by many developing-country members, which argue that such a reference would elevate the legal status of the chair's statement, which they view as separate from the decision.

Several of the members that said they would use the system only in emergencies have emphasized that their undertaking was voluntary. They oppose an amendment that would formally incorporate a list of countries opting out of the system. The group of African WTO members has proposed an amendment that does not refer to the chair's statement and that eliminates several provisions of the decision that the group views as redundant—for example, certain notification requirements. Several developed-country members have criticized the proposal as upsetting the delicate balance achieved in the August 2003 Decision.

Meanwhile, the August 2003 Decision retains its full legal effect. Several WTO members have begun to implement it in national laws and regulations. Canada and Norway were the first countries to amend their patent laws in 2004, allowing generic manufacturers from these countries to become exporters under the new system. India also implemented the decision as part of its March 2005 amendment to its patent act—an important step because some of the world's most competitive generic manufacturers are located in there. In addition, legislative changes are under way in the European Union, Republic of Korea, Switzerland, and elsewhere.

How important is the new system?

To date, the sysytem has not been used, and it may not be used for some time, as most drugs are not covered by patents in key producer countries—notably India (see box 1). In addition, there is no need to invoke the system if an exporting

Box 2. Imports of generic drugs under compulsory license and TRIPS rules

The TRIPS agreement does not prohibit governments from *importing* generic drugs under a compulsory license. Instead, the conflict arises in the exporting country. Article 28 of TRIPS confers on patent holders the exclusive right to *make* patent protected products. Thus if a generic manufacturer in country A produces a drug for export to country B (where the government has issued a compulsory license), it may infringe on the rights of the patent holder in country A.

A special case arises if the drug in question is already produced under a compulsory license in country A. Article 31(f) of TRIPS mandates that compulsory licenses "shall be authorized *predominantly* for the supply of the domestic market of the Member authorizing such use." (Emphasis added.) If compulsory licenses are granted in large developing countries such as Brazil, China, and India, a nonpredominant share of production could still represent a significant supply for least developed countries. However, there may well be situations in which an exporter in a member country, acting in response to a compulsory license issued by another member (with insufficient capacity), would not intend to sell a predominant part of its production in the local market. Finding a solution to that problem was the crux of the post-Doha negotiations on TRIPS and public health.

country grants a compulsory license to supply the domestic market and a "nonpredominant share" of production is exported (see box 2). But as more patented drugs come onto developing-country markets, there may well be situations in which countries with no or insufficient manufacturing capabilities seek to import under compulsory license medicines that are not available abroad as generics. While compliance with the decision's notification and safeguard requirements seems manageable, there are other barriers to overcome. In particular, it may take more than a year and significant up-front investments for a generic supplier to deliver quality medicines. Ensuring interim supplies from the patent holders and finding foreign manufacturers willing to take on the business risk involved—especially if the quantities involved are small—may not be easy. In any case, even if the system is not used frequently, countries with insufficient manufacturing capability are now in a more credible position to break the price hold of pharmaceutical patents when negotiating drug prices. As pointed out above, the threat of compulsory licenses has been a valuable bargaining tool for governments in the past.

Moving forward: the need for further action

The August 2003 Decision was an important landmark in ensuring consistency between multilateral intellectual property rules and public health objectives. Yet progress in resolving intellectual property–related conflicts is insufficient to widen access to medicines in poor countries. Complementary action is needed in several areas.

First, sufficient financial resources are needed to fight the developing world's health crisis. While substantial funding has become available in recent years, UNAIDS projects a gap between pledged funds and real needs totaling more than $18 billion over the next three years. The agency says that annual spending of $22 billion will be needed by 2008.[13]

Second, to effectively treat patients in poor countries, large investments in complementary health infrastructure are necessary, including hospitals, roads, warehouses, and medical personnel. In addition, the procurement of generic drugs requires the development of quality control mechanisms. In the case of ARVs, drugs of inferior quality can cause AIDS patients to become resistant, even to drugs of better quality. A WHO program to prequalify generic producers of ARVs already helps governments in selecting quality generic medicines. That program needs to be complemented by quality assurance regulations at the national level—and by greater capacity to implement and monitor those regulations.

Third, relatively little research has been done on diseases that are prevalent in the developing world but not common in rich countries. For such diseases, the low purchasing power of patients in poor countries limits the incentives for research-based pharmaceutical companies to invest in such research (even if the economic value of patents remained undiluted by compulsory licenses.) In 2003, North America, the European Union, and Japan alone accounted for 88 percent of the $466 billion of global pharmaceutical sales. The low-income countries with the heaviest disease burden probably account for less than 2 percent of global sales. It is therefore important to find alternative incentive mechanisms and funding sources to encourage more R&D specific to developing countries.[14]

Conclusion

The WTO's August 2003 Decision has established a new system for countries with insufficient manufacturing capabilities to import generic medicines under compulsory licenses. Fully operational until replaced by a formal amendment to the TRIPS agreement, it may develop into a useful policy option as the share of drugs patented in the developing world grows over the next five to ten years. Meanwhile, it will be important to address other barriers to promoting access to medicines—notably insufficient funding, weak health infrastructures, and inadequate incenives to engage in R&D specific to the diseases of the poorest countries.

Notes

1. This Trade Note was written by Carsten Fink, Senior Economist at the World Bank Institute. It is a revised version of Trade Note No. 5, which was published in May 2003. Comments by Frederick Abbott, Carlos Braga, Philip John Hedger, Manjula Luthria, Richard Newfarmer, Juan Rovira, Beata Smarzynska Javorcik and Arvind Subramanian are gratefully acknowledged.

2. Comparing prices of originator and generic drugs is a tricky business. For example, some of the generic manufacturers listed in the pricing guides published by Médecins Sans Frontières are not prequalified by the WHO as meeting standards of quality and compliance with good manufacturing practices. These manufacturers do not necessarily produce substandard medicines, as exclusion from the WHO list does not mean that a drug has failed to gain approval from a national drug regulator. Different price quotation practices with regard to transportation and distribution costs, as well as currency fluctuations, further complicate price comparisons.

3. The World Health Organization's Model List of Essential Drugs has excluded many drugs protected by patents, as affordability is one of the criteria used in designating medicines as essential. However, WHO's latest list includes a significant number of patented drugs (particularly for treatment of HIV/AIDS).

4. The term "compulsory license" is often used loosely. As a matter of domestic policy, there is an important distinction between use of a patent by third parties (private firms) and use by governments.

5. See WHO Document EB115/32 ("Antiretrovirals and Developing Countries"). In the case of Malaysia, the license in question was for the import of antiretroviral drugs from India for use in public hospitals only.

6. According to a October 2001 press release of the U.S. Department of Health and Human Services, Bayer agreed to supply ciprofloxacin at $0.95 per tablet, much less than the previous discounted price of $1.77 (http://www.os.dhhs.gov/news/press/2001pres/20011024.html). In a January 2002 "Form 20-F" filing with the U.S. Securities and Exchange Commission, Bayer informed investors that "in response to the recent bioterror attacks in the United States, the

U.S. and Canadian governments contemplated compulsory licensing of our ciprofloxacin antibiotic—in effect, permission to generic manufacturers to market ciprofloxacin before the expiry of our patent rights."

7. See the press release by Roche, dated August 31, 2001. http://www.roche.com/media-news-2001-08-31-e.pdf.

8. The Cancún WTO Ministerial Meeting failed anyway, for different reasons.

9. The decision refers to the public health problems recognized in paragraph 1 of the Doha Declaration. That paragraph reads: "We recognize the gravity of the public health problems afflicting many developing and least-developed countries, especially those resulting from HIV/AIDS, tuberculosis, malaria and other epidemics."

10. These countries are Hong Kong (China), Israel, Republic of Korea, Kuwait, Macao (China), Mexico, Qatar, Singapore, Taiwan (China), Turkey, and the United Arab Emirates.

11. These countries include all 30 members of the OECD (except Republic of Korea, Mexico, and Turkey) as well as Cyprus, Estonia, Latvia, Lithuania, Malta, the Slovak Republic, and Slovenia

12. This notification is required only if the drug in question is protected by patent in the importing country.

13. See "Resource Needs for an Expanded Response to AIDS in Low and Middle Income Countries," presented to the UNAIDS Programme Coordinating Board in 2005 (available at www.unaids.org).

14. The World Health Organization's Commission on Intellectual Property Rights, Innovation, and Public Health is collecting proposals to this effect (see www.who.int/intellectual property).

References

Abbott, Frederick M. 2005. "The WTO Medicines Decision: World Pharmaceutical Trade and the Protection of Public Health." *American Journal of International Law* 99: 317–58.

Data sources

Data on the number of people infected by HIV/AIDS and the number who receive antiretroviral drugs are from UNAIDS. The $30 figure on the estimated costs of antiretroviral therapy in developed countries is approximately equivalent to the $10,439 figure shown in figure 1. The figure on global pharmaceutical sales in 2003 and the share of North America, the European Union and Japan in these sales are from the IMS Health Review 2004.

The Debate on Geographical Indications in the WTO

Carsten Fink and Keith Maskus

New rules and mechanisms for the protection of geographical indications (GIs) have been a subject of lively discussion in the current multilateral trading round—the Doha Development Agenda (DDA). Some WTO members advocate stronger multilateral protection for GIs and view progress on the issue as an important *quid pro quo* for advancing negotiations in other areas. Other members favor a less ambitious outcome as part of an eventual Doha Round package, and, in particular, argue that the negotiating mandate on GIs is limited in scope and ambition. Differences do not break along the typical North–South divide associated with intellectual property discussions in the WTO, nor along the lines of some of the main negotiating alliances in the DDA. Proponents of a stronger GI system include, Bulgaria, the European Union, Kenya, India, Sri Lanka, Switzerland, and Thailand. Members favoring a less ambitious outcome include Argentina, Australia, Canada, Chile, Costa Rica, Guatemala, Japan, Namibia, Taiwan (China), and the United States.[1]

This note will take stock of the discussion on GIs stands as WTO members prepare for the Sixth WTO Ministerial Conference in Hong Kong in December 2005. It also will put this discussion into a broader economic perspective and highlight some of the key issues at stake.

What are geographical indications?

Geographical indications are signs that link a product to a particular place, such as a city or region. Their use indicates that a product possesses certain qualities or enjoys a reputation associated with its geographical origin.[2] Many GIs pertain to food products, for which quality is often directly linked to a region's inherent characteristics, such as soil attributes or climatic conditions. But a GI may also reflect certain manufacturing skills or production processes that are associated with a particular place. Box 1 presents examples of geographical indications from around the world.

Governments have long used various legal instruments to protect GIs from misappropriation by nonoriginal producers. Historically, protection was first afforded through consumer protection laws, such as regulations against false trade descriptions. In many countries, GIs have also been recognized as a form of intellectual property—either as part of the trademark system or through dedicated laws for their protection. To obtain protection through the intellectual property system, interested parties must register their GIs with a designated public body.

Box 1. A few examples of geographical indications[a]

Country of origin	Products
Chile	Valle del Maipo (wine)
Colombia	Colombian coffee
India	Darjeeling (tea), Basmati (rice)
European Union [b]	Chablis (wine), Ouzo (spirit), Roquefort (cheese), Solingen (steel products)
Mexico	Tequila (spirit)
New Zealand	New Zealand lamb
Sri Lanka	Ceylon (tea)
Switzerland	Swiss watches, Etivaz (cheese)
Thailand	Thai silk
United States	Washington State apples, Idaho potatoes, Florida oranges

a. Not all of the products listed here have necessarily been registered as GIs.
b. Or individual member states.

Economic Considerations

Like other forms of intellectual property, GIs arise as a solution to certain failures in markets for information.[3] They are used primarily for products that are known in economics as "search goods" or "experience goods." Simple commodities, such as wheat and sugar, generally do not command GI protection because they can be produced with a reasonable degree of homogeneity in many locations. Accordingly, consumers need not worry too much about searching for specific quality characteristics. However, products with known quality variations (and therefore differentiated or heterogeneous), do carry significant search costs for consumers. By providing a signal to potential buyers, GIs can lower those costs and make markets more efficient. Such a signal can be particularly important in the case of experience goods, such as wine and cheese, where consumers understand the quality from prior consumption but cannot distinguish quality simply by inspecting the product.

The signaling function of GIs is valuable not only for consumers in the domestic economy, but also for those in foreign countries. In fact, their role in international trade may be greater than in domestic commerce, because informational problems are likely to be more pronounced when producers and consumers are located in different countries.

Conceptually GIs are closely related to trademarks, which identify a product as having been produced by a particular enterprise. Because firms wish to protect the value of their trademarks, and reputation associated with them, they have a strong incentive to produce goods of a particular and predictable quality. Many food products bear both a GI and a trademark to signal the quality of the geographic origin and the quality of the individual producer.

Trademarks and GIs differ in two significant respects. First, a trademark is usually the property of a particular firm; other firms cannot compete under the same mark.[4] In contrast, a GI is a piece of property shared by several or many firms. The shared nature of a GI can raise problems of collective action. Free-riding by low-quality producers is one concern, but this is usually overcome by linking the use of a GI to achievement of specific attributes detailed in the GI registration. Still, establishing, defining, enforcing, and jointly marketing GIs requires coordination and can involve nontrivial transaction costs. This explains why GIs are sometimes managed or supported by (quasi-)public institutions, such as the "Consorzio del Prosciutto di Parma" representing producers of Parma ham in Italy (Rangnekar 2004).

A second, related difference is that trademarks do not attach to a location, whereas GIs do. Accordingly, a good protected by trademark can be produced anywhere, whereas at least some significant portion of a good protected by GIs must be produced within the indicated location. It is at this point that conflicts between protection systems can arise, as discussed below.

From the perspective of producers, GIs offer a means of attaching a reputation for quality to a place name that may then be marketed and used on labels. In this context, GIs can encourage firms to add value to their products, either by investing in higher-quality production techniques or by marketing.

Studies have quantified the price premia associated with certain GI-protected products. A 1999 EU consumer survey found that 40 percent of consumers would pay a 10 percent premium for origin-guaranteed products (WTO 2004). Econometric models employing so-called hedonic pricing techniques support the willingness to pay more for GI products. One econometric study found that certain regional designations for Bordeaux wines command a large price premium—as much as $15 per bottle in the case of the "Pomerol" designation (Landon and Smith 1998). Another such study found that wines with a "Napa Valley" designation were priced 61 percent higher than wines with a "California" designation (Bombrun and Sumner 2003). Evidence for price premia is not limited to wines. Econometric work on the Spanish market for meat products showed, for example, that products bearing the "Galician Veal" label commanded a premium of $0.21 per kilogram (Loureiro and McCluskey 2000).

From this evidence, there is little doubt that protection through GIs can support significant increases in value-added through premium pricing. In this context, enterprises in some developing countries may be able to gain by using GIs in national and international markets.

Where does the controversy lie?

Like other intellectual property rights, it may be difficult to strike an optimal balance between consumer needs and producer gains in designing GIs. The economic considerations outlined above indicate that one key criterion in assessing the adequacy of a particular GI regime is its ability to reduce consumer confusion and search costs. From this perspective, exclusive rights attached to a GI can be overly strong if they exclude alternative users that could enter the market and compete without confusing consumers.[4] This is especially relevant for geographical expressions that have evolved as product descriptions in the common language of certain countries—consider, at the extreme, expressions such as "china" for porcelain wares or "parmesan" for hard, dry, sharply flavored cheeses.

Policymakers' views on how best to strike a balance in the protection of GIs differ markedly across countries. For example, in the United States nonoriginal producers have been allowed to use GIs on certain products as long as the true geographical origin of the products is made clear. This has given rise to so-called semi-generic expressions (such as "American-made Pecorino cheese"). By contrast, the European Union has a strong set of GI rules that give owners stronger exclusive rights than do U.S. rules. In addition, EU laws protect so-called traditional expressions that describe certain methods of production (such as "ruby" for a class of port from Portugal).

The more lenient U.S. approach to GIs system is arguably more conducive to entry than the EU system. Little systematic evidence exists about whether it may confuse consumers. Complicating an economic assessment of different protection regimes is that certain GI products are likely to have significant status value. Economists view "status goods" as products for which the mere use or display of a particular label confers prestige on their buyers—regardless of a product's quality.[6] "Champagne," "Beluga caviar," and "Kobe beef" may fall into this category. Use of these GIs by nonoriginal producers may undermine the status value attached to products, eroding the price premia of original producers—even if consumers are not confused about the true origin of their purchases.[7]

As a matter of law, GIs receive protection at the level of national jurisdictions; international conflicts result from different national approaches to protection. In particular, constituencies such as those in the European Union, which hosts many GIs and provides strong protection, view weaker standards of protection abroad as a barrier to their exports. Even if there is little direct competition from producers in foreign countries, standards of GI protection can still matter because they may influence competition from third countries. For example, Singapore's GI rules affect the extent to which European producers face competition from American producers using semi-generic expressions. To resolve such conflicts, various international agreements for the protection of GIs have emerged over time.

The existing international system for protecting GIs

International rules for the protection of GIs were first established in several intellectual property conventions, notably the Paris Convention (originally signed in 1883) and the Madrid Agreement (originally signed in 1891). However, these conventions were primarily concerned with repressing deceptive indications of origin in international trade and did not provide for harmonized standards. The Lisbon Agreement (originally signed in 1958) went further, requiring signatories to protect "appellations of origin" against usurpation (wrongful appropriation) or imitation and by establishing a system through which signatories to the agreement can register their appellations of origin.[8] However, only 23 countries have become contracting parties to the Lisbon Agreement.[9]

An important shift in international GI rulemaking was brought about by the coming into force of the WTO's Agreement on Trade-Related Aspects of Intellectual Property Rights (TRIPS) in 1995. The TRIPS Agreement sets minimum standards of intellectual property protection, which all 148 WTO members as well as countries acceding to the WTO must, in principle, respect.[10] In the area of GIs, it establishes the following rules:

- Members must establish the legal means to prevent GIs from being used by nonoriginal producers in a way that would mislead the public as to the geographical origin of a good or would constitute an act of unfair competition.
- A higher level of protection is reserved for GIs relating to wines and spirits. For these two classes of products, members have to prevent the use by nonoriginal producers of a GI, even where the true origin of the good is made clear or use of the GI is accompanied by expressions such as "kind," "type," "style," or the like.
- These obligations are subject to certain exceptions. For instance, members are not required to protect GIs that were used in good faith before the TRIPS Agreement was signed. Similarly, members are not required to protect GIs that are considered to have become part of the common language.[11] Whether a geographical name is considered generic depends on its historical use in the language of a WTO particular member and may require domestic judicial interpretation.

TRIPS provisions on GIs reflect a negotiating compromise reached in the Uruguay Round of trade negotiations. Accordingly, they did not fully satisfy the proponents of stronger GI protection. The European Union, in particular, has pursued stronger protection in the context of bilateral trade agreements and in dedicated bilateral GI agreements. For example, additional obligations for the protection of GIs pertaining to wines and spirits exist in bilateral agreements between the European Union and Australia, Canada, Chile, Mexico, and South Africa. Most notably, these agreements contain lists of specific GIs to which signatories are required to apply the higher level of protection mentioned above. Several of the European GIs listed—especially for spirits—had been used by local producers; such use had to be (or will have to be) phased out, even though it would likely have fallen under the exceptions of the TRIPS Agreement.[12]

In September 2005, the European Union and the United States concluded an Agreement on Trade in Wines settling certain longstanding disputes on wine names and wine-making practices. As part of this agreement, the Unites States promised to seek legislative changes to limit the use of 17 semi-generic names—among them Chablis, Champagne, Chianti, Port, and Sherry. However, current use of these names will be grandfathered such that U.S. producers can continue to sell their wines under their present names. In return, the European Union pledged to recognize U.S. wine-making practices, thereby facilitating access of U.S. wine producers to the European market.

Geographical indications in the Doha Development Agenda

Discussions on GIs in the DDA have centered on three elements: the establishment of a multilateral system of registration for geographical indications; the extension of the higher level of protection to products other than wines and spirits; and the protection of product names as established through a list of geographical indications currently used by nonoriginal producers (often referred to as the "claw-back" of GIs).

Table 1. WTO members with more and less ambition to strengthen GI protection

	More ambitious members	Less ambitious members
Multilateral GI register	Bulgaria, European Union, Georgia, Iceland, Mauritius, Moldova, Nigeria, Romania, Sri Lanka, Switzerland, Turkey	Argentina, Australia, Canada, Chile, Colombia, Costa Rica, Dominican Republic, Ecuador, El Salvador, Guatemala, Honduras, Japan, Mexico, Namibia, New Zealand, Philippines, Taiwan (China), United States
Extension of higher level protection	Bulgaria, Cuba, European Union, Georgia, Guinea, Iceland, India, Jamaica, Kenya, Kyrgyz Republic, Liechtenstein, Macedonia, Madagascar, Mauritius, Morocco, Pakistan, Romania, Sri Lanka, Switzerland, Thailand, Tunisia, Turkey	Argentina, Australia, Canada, Chile, Colombia, Dominican Republic, Ecuador, El Salvador, Guatemala, Honduras, New Zealand, Panama, Paraguay, Philippines, Taiwan (China), United States
"Claw-back"	European Union	

Source: Based on submissions of WTO members since 2001 (TN/IP/W/3, TN/IP/W/5, TN/IP/W/10, and as summarized by the WTO Secretariat in Document TN/C/W/25).

Table 1 depicts the differential level of ambition of WTO members to strengthen GI protection along these three dimensions. The European Union is generally the member with the greatest ambition on all three, though several other developed and developing countries also see themselves as having offensive interests in the protection of GIs. The group of less ambitious members is often associated with the "New World"—which refers primarily to countries in the Western Hemisphere. However, the group also includes countries in other regions (e.g., Namibia, the Philippines).

The creation of a *multilateral GI register* is the least controversial in that it has an explicit negotiating mandate. The TRIPS agreement called for negotiations to establish such a register for wines, and the ministerial declaration launching the DDA in 2001 broadened that mandate by widening the scope of the envisaged register to include spirits. Several explicit proposals for the design of a multilateral GI register have been put forward, but WTO members were not able to reach agreement by the original 2003 deadline. Substantial differences remain on several features of the registration system, including:

- *Scope of coverage.* The more ambitious members would like the register to cover products other than wines and spirits, whereas other members would prefer to adhere to the more limited negotiating mandate.
- *Legal effect of registered GIs.* According to TRIPS, the purpose of the multilateral register is to "facilitate the protection of geographical indications." The more ambitious members believe that effective facilitation requires a legal presumption that registered GIs are protected in the territory of WTO member states. Moreover, unless members were to lodge a reservation against a multilaterally notified GI within 18 months, they should not be able to refuse protection of that GI–even if protection was not required by a country's obligations under TRIPS. Other members believe that requiring WTO members simply to consult the multilateral register when making decisions about registration and protection at the domestic level would suffice in facilitating protection.
- *Legal effect in nonparticipating member countries.* The TRIPS mandate makes clear that participation by WTO members in the registration system will be voluntary. However, under the proposal put forward by the European Union, there would still be a legal effect of registered GIs in nonparticipating member countries. While there would be no legal presumption of protection, nonparticipating members—just like participating members—could not refuse protection of a multilaterally registered GI unless they objected to the notification within 18 months. Other members favor a system in which multilateral registration has no legally binding effect whatsoever in nonparticipating countries. As for the question of *extending the higher level of protection* to products other than wines and spirits, differences of WTO members center on

whether the Doha Ministerial Declaration establishes a negotiating mandate for such a move. Members with more defensive negotiating interests on this issue argue that negotiations can take place only if the WTO's Trade Negotiating Committee so decides, whereas the European Union and other members believe a negotiating mandate exists already.[13]

Substantively, the proponents of extension argue that the current system discriminates against countries that are not significant producers of wines and spirits but that possess valuable GIs on other products that may be subject to usurpation in foreign jurisdictions. This explains why developing countries such as India, Kenya, Pakistan, and Thailand support extension. The opponents of extension contend that certain uses of GIs by nonoriginal producers can improve consumer choice, as long as the true origin of products is made clear. They also argue that there is no proof that the existing level of protection under TRIPS is insufficient. Finally, New World producers have pointed out that, in many cases, production methods and product names were brought in by immigrants decades ago. Some reference to the original geographical names is therefore justified and should not be regarded as usurpation.

Probably the most controversial element in the current discussions is the *"clawback" initiative.* In 2003, the European Union advanced a list of geographical names for which it wished to prohibit use by nonoriginal producers—mirroring the approach taken in some of the European Union's bilateral agreements. Many of the names on the list do not enjoy GI protection in certain jurisdictions, as they are considered to be generic terms falling under the common-language exception of the TRIPS Agreement. The European Union (acting alone) put forward the claw-back initiative in the DDA's agricultural negotiations, and not in the TRIPS Council—the WTO forum normally responsible for trade-related intellectual property issues. That move has been criticized by some members because the negotiating mandate on agriculture set by the Doha Ministerial Declaration does not mention GIs.[14] The European Union's GI list includes wines and spirits as well as other products such as Gorgonzola, Parmigiano Reggiano, Prosciutto di Parma, and Roquefort. If accepted, it would imply new obligations even for those countries that have entered into bilateral agreements on wines and spirits with the European Union.

Conclusion

GIs may become a contentious topic in the run-up to the Hong Kong WTO Ministerial Conference in December 2005. The European Union and other European countries view progress on GIs as an important *quid pro quo* for improved market access and reduction of subsidies in agriculture. The Hong Kong Ministerial Conference may be the moment to strike a bargain, as one of its key aims is the conclusion of modalities for the DDA's agriculture negotiations. At the same time,

WTO members remain deeply divided on the three elements outlined above. Progress on any one of them would require significant movement by those members with opposing interests, which seems possible only with substantial political impetus.

From an economic perspective, the "claw-back" of geographical names currently not receiving protection would likely bring the greatest and most immediate economic benefit for the European Union. But it would also require the largest adjustments by nonoriginal producers who currently use European GIs. The scale of adjustments remains uncertain, however. For example, while nonoriginal producers may experience a temporary decline in market share, the experience of Australian wine producers suggests that the cessation of semi-generic terms under the Australia-EU bilateral agreement did not harm local products. To the contrary, it has been argued that the rebranding of affected products and associated marketing efforts provided a boost for Australian producers.[15] Aside from such anecdotal evidence, there is little systematic evidence on the size of adjustment costs. Similarly, there is little evidence about the effects—in direction and size—of a GI "claw-back" on consumer welfare.

Some developing countries stand to gain from stronger WTO rules for GI protection. However, benefiting commercially from GIs requires complementary efforts to identify valuable GIs and to build an international reputation for them. Many developing countries have only recently begun to develop national GI systems; it will take time before substantial commercial benefits will arise. Meanwhile, there are difficult questions to resolve in delineating the geographic boundaries of a GI, defining its quality attributes and other characteristics, establishing quality control mechanisms, and collectively managing and promoting an indication. In addition, there is the risk that certain rent-seeking producers may use GIs as devices for excluding competitors capable of producing goods of comparable quality. Addressing these challenges will require concerted efforts regardless of what emerges from the GI discussions in the DDA.

Notes

1. This Trade Note was written by Carsten Fink, Senior Economist at the World Bank Institute and Keith Maskus, Professor of Economics and Chair of the Economics Department at the University of Colorodo in Boulder. Comments by Antonio Berenguer, Lauro Locks, Wolf Meier-Ewert, Pedro Roffe, Maximiliano Santa Cruz, Christopher Spenneman, Thu-Lang Tran Wasescha and David Vivas are gratefully acknowledged.

2. The WTO's Agreement on Trade-Related Aspects of Intellectual Property Rights defines GIs as "indications which identify a good as originating in the territory of a Member, or a region or locality in that territory, where a given quality, reputation or other characteristic of the good is essentially attributable to its geographical origin." There are two instruments related to GIs: indications of source and appellations of origin. Indications of source are broader than GIs, in that goods do not necessarily have to exhibit a quality, reputation, or other characteristic attributable to its geographic origin. Appellations of origin are narrower than GIs in that they necessitate a link to quality or some other special characteristic directly attributable to a good's geographic origin. Reputation alone is insufficient.

3. The failure of the market to provide for an efficient allocation of resources when consumers are unable to assess the quality of products was first observed by Akerlof (1970).

4. Exceptions are so-called collective marks and certification marks, which can be owned by an association of companies. In fact, these types of marks are used in some jurisdictions as an instrument for the protection of GIs.

5. Josling (2005) argues that an overly strict GI regime that prohibits the use of place names in ways that have no possibility of confusing consumers may be considered protectionist from a trade policy perceptive.

6. Fink and Smarzynska (2002) discuss status goods more extensively.

7. Such an outcome is not certain, however. It is equally possible that clearly distinguishable and low-quality copycat products enhance the perceived exclusiveness of the original products.

8. See note 2 for the difference between appellations of origin and GIs.

9. The 23 countries are Algeria, Bulgaria, Burkina Faso, Congo, Costa Rica, Cuba, Czech Republic, Democratic People's Republic of Korea, France, Gabon, Georgia, Haiti, Hungary, Israel, Italy, Mexico, Peru, Portugal, Republic of Moldova, Serbia and Montenegro, Slovakia, Togo, and Tunisia.

10. Least developed countries (LDCs) are exempted from most TRIPS disciplines—including the specific obligations on GIs—until December 31, 2005, although this deadline can be postponed upon duly motivated request. The two LDCs that have acceded to the WTO since 1996—Cambodia and Nepal—were granted a transition period until December 31, 2006.

11. In addition, WTO members are not required to protect foreign GIs that are not protected in their country of origin. Thus, any country seeking to promote a GI has to provide domestic protection before seeking to have the indication protected internationally. For an in-depth discussion of the TRIPS provisions on GIs, see chapter 15 in UNCTAD-ICTSD (2005).

12. For a more detailed discussion of the European Union's bilateral agreements, see Vivas and Spennemann (2005).

13. According to the ministerial declaration launching the DDA, the question of GI extension is considered an "outstanding implementation issue" to be dealt with "as a matter of priority" by the TRIPS Council, "which shall report to the Trade Negotiations Committee [...] by the end of 2002 for appropriate action."

14. The framework for agriculture negotiations adopted by WTO members in July 2004 identifies GIs as an issue "of interest but not agreed."

15. See Battaglene (2005). In addition, Schamel and Anderson (2003) find that regional origin has become a major determinant of prices in the Australian wine industry, with price premia averaging about 31 percent for wines carrying Australian GIs.

References

Akerlof, G. A. 1970. "The Market for Lemons: Qualitative Uncertainty and the Market Mechanism." *Quarterly Journal of Economics* 84: 488–500.

Battaglene, Tony. 2005. "The Australian Wine Industry Position on Geographical Indications." Paper presented at the Worldwide Symposium on Geographical Indications in Parma, Italy, June 27–29.

Bombrun, Helene, and Daniel A. Sumner. 2003. "What Determines the Price of Wine?" AIC Issues Brief 18, University of California, Davis.

Fink, Carsten, and Beata Smarzynska. 2002. "Trademarks, Geographical Indications, and Developing Countries." In *Development, Trade, and the WTO: A Handbook* (pp. 403–12), ed. Bernard Hoekman, Aaditya Mattoo, and Philip English. Washington, DC: World Bank), pp. 403-41.

Josling, Timothy. 2005. "Geographical Indications: Protection for Producers or Consumer Information?" Unpublished paper. Stanford Institute for International Studies, Palo Alto, CA.

Landon, Stuart, and Constance E. Smith. 1998. "Quality Expectations, Reputation, and Price." *Southern Economic Journal* 64(3): 628–47.

Loureiro, Maria Luz, and Jill J. McCluskey. 2000. "Assessing Consumer Response to Protected Geographical Identification Labeling." *Agribusiness* 16(3): 309–20.

Rangnekar, Dwijen. 2004. "The Socio-Economics of Geographical Indications: A Review of Empirical Evidence from Europe." UNCTAD-ICTSD Project on IPRs and Sustainable Development, Issues Paper 8. www.iprsonline.org.

Schamel, Günter, and Kym Anderson. 2003. "Wine Quality and Varietal, Regional and Winery Reputations: Hedonic Prices for Australia and New Zealand." *Economic Record* 79(246): 357–69.

UNCTAD-ICTSD. 2005. *Resource Book on TRIPS and Development.* Cambridge: Cambridge University Press.

Vivas-Eugui, David, and Christoph Spennemann. 2005. "The Treatment of Geographical Indications in Recent Regional and Bilateral Free Trade Agreements." In *The Intellectual Property Debate: Perspectives from Law, Economics and Political Economy*, ed. Meir Pugatch. Cheltenham, England: Edward Elgar.

World Trade Organization. 2004. *World Trade Report 2004.* Geneva: WTO.

More Favorable Treatment of Developing Countries: Ways Forward

Bernard Hoekman

Although the principle of more favorable treatment for developing countries has a long history and is firmly embedded in the World Trade Organization (WTO),[1] the existing system of differential treatment has left both developed and developing countries dissatisfied. In the current Doha trade negotiations, as in the implementation of multilateral trade rules, it is among the more important issues to be resolved.[2]

Currently, "special and differential treatment" (SDT) provisions in the WTO rules call for preferential access to developed country markets, exemptions (transitory and permanent) from certain rules, and promises of development assistance. There are good reasons for SDT. One is that very small and low-income economies lack the institutional strength to manage the full panoply of WTO rules and might well find the returns to developing the necessary strength outweighed by the costs. Small and poor countries may also lack the resources to overcome natural obstacles to trade or to pursue policies to address market failures.

The Doha Declaration called for a review of SDT provisions, with a view to "strengthening them and making them more precise, effective, and operational." During 2001-02, developing countries made some 88 specific suggestions to strengthen SDT—among them improved preferential access to industrialized country markets, exemptions from specific WTO rules, binding requirements to provide technical and financial assistance to help developing countries implement multilateral rules and benefit from negotiated rights, and an expansion in aid to address supply-side constraints. Despite intensive talks and numerous meetings, however, no agreement has yet proved possible on strengthening SDT provisions.

One reason for this is that a common element of many of the proposals was to convert existing "best-endeavors provisions" into binding obligations that could be enforced through WTO dispute settlement procedures. Another is the difference in views on what types of exemptions make economic sense. Indeed, the debate on strengthening SDT overlaps to a significant extent the broader issue of making the WTO more supportive of development—perhaps the most serious challenge confronting the WTO, given the huge differences in the level of development among WTO members.

Breaking the deadlock will require actions by developed and developing countries alike to bolster the three major pillars of SDT:
- Greatly improved market access for developing countries.
- Mechanisms to ensure that WTO rules and disciplines support development

- Increased development assistance ("aid for trade").

The outlines of a possible package of measures to make SDT more effective are sketched out below.

Market access for disadvantaged countries

Trade preferences have been a mainstay of SDT since the late 1960s. Unfortunately, evidence suggests that preferences generally deliver less than expected. First, for most goods, particularly manufactures, the margin of tariff preference granted to developing countries is often small. For example, Amjadi, Reinke and Yeats (1996) show that, at the end of the Uruguay Round transition period, Sub-Saharan African countries would have preference margins averaging slightly less than 2.5 percentage points.[3]

Of course, there are cases where tariffs are higher or where quotas provide preferred partners with deeper preferences that are potentially more valuable. But these are not as common as they may appear on the surface. Consider, for example, textiles and clothing. This simple and labor-intensive sector is one in which developing countries clearly have comparative advantage. It also has some of the highest most-favored-nation (MFN) tariffs, potentially offering the greatest margins of preference. But the United States, for example, grants no general preferences on textiles and clothing, although it does offer some to particularly favored partners—such as the African nations covered by the African Growth and Opportunity Act. The European Union does grant tariff preferences on textile and clothing exports under its general system of preferences (GSP), the Cotonou Agreement, and various regional agreements—and, since 2001, to the Least-Developed Countries (LDCs) under the Everything But Arms (EBA) initiative—but all of these are subject to restrictive and cumbersome rules of origin.

In key product categories in which they have a comparative advantage, developing countries receive no significant tariff preferences (table 1). In general, preferences tend to be the most limited where tariff peaks exist (Hoekman, Ng, and Olarreaga 2002). This has been changing—for example, the EBA gives duty- and quota-free access to LDCs for virtually all products. But the countries that are home to most of the world's poor, including Brazil, China, India, Indonesia, Malaysia, Pakistan and Thailand, are granted only limited preferences, if any.

In summary, research suggests that preferences are often of little value (a) because they exclude textiles, agricultural products, or other important items, (b) because they place limits on the value of exports eligible for preferential treatment (including so-called competitive needs tests), or (c) because other nontariff measures are used to restrict access. Combined with complex administrative requirements and red tape, notably restrictive rules of origin, the effect is to reduce investment in activities that could otherwise benefit from preferences.

One way to strengthen SDT would be for developed countries to extend duty- and quota-free market access, as under the EBA, to *all* developing countries. From the perspective of the Millennium Development Goals, a good case can be made that preferences should focus on the poor, wherever they are located, and not on a limited set of countries. In absolute terms, most poor people live in countries that are not LDCs—such as China and India. Limiting preferences to the poorest countries—while appropriate in light of limited institutional and infrastructure weaknesses in these countries—ignores the majority of the poor in the world today, who confront tariffs on world markets that are more than twice as high as those confronting nonpoor producers (World Bank 2002).

But deep trade preferences for larger economies are not politically feasible. Therefore, action is required to liberalize, on a nondiscriminatory basis, trade in goods and services in which developing countries have a comparative advantage. A binding commitment by developed countries to abolish export subsidies, decouple agricultural support and significantly reduce—or abolish—tariffs on labor-intensive products of export interest to developing countries would provide a strong signal of commitment to poverty alleviation by developed countries. A corresponding commitment to expand temporary access for developing country service providers by a specific amount—say by 1 percent of the workforce—and not to restrict cross-border trade in services would also bring substantial benefits (Mattoo 2005).

MFN-based market access is not traditionally considered an element of SDT. But it may well have the greatest impact on development. For one thing, it could rebalance the WTO by removing "reverse SDT"—special opt-outs and exemptions

Table 1. Key products lacking GSP preferences in the European Union and United States

	United States				European Union			
	Total imports ($bn)	GSP recipients' market share (percent)	Average tariff rate (percent)	Average tariff rate faced by GSP recipients (percent)	Total imports ($bn)	GSP recipients' market share (percent)	Average tariff rate (percent)	Average tariff rate faced by GSP recipients (percent)
Dairy products	1.1	13.0	13.4	19.7	1.0	16.0	9.9	15.9
Textiles & yarn	9.8	21.0	7.8	7.2	16.1	42.0	5.4	4.6
Apparel & clothing	58.5	47.0	15.3	15.9	43.4	56.0	10.2	8.8
Leather products	7.2	24.0	10.4	11.5	5.6	80.0	2.3	1.9
Footwear	15.3	18.0	10.6	10.0	8.5	67.0	7.5	7.4
Ceramics & glassware	7.9	13.0	6.3	8.2	5.5	28.0	5.1	3.8

Note: GSP countries only; LDCs obtain deeper preferential treatment. China is included in the European Union's GSP but excluded by the United States.
Source: WITS.

that benefit interest groups in industrialized countries at the expense of developing countries. Examples include agricultural subsidy programs, high protection for textile products, and tariff peaks and escalation that imply high rates of effective protection for developed country industries. Removing such distortions would not only benefit developing countries (and developed country consumers), but would also promote further trade reforms in developing countries.

Implementation of WTO rules

SDT includes derogations or exemptions from certain WTO rules. Is this a good thing? Not if poor countries would derive a positive net benefit from implementing the rules. While governments presumably consider that possibility in the course of negotiations, past experience suggests that the necessary analysis and consultations often are not undertaken, explaining why there is now a lack of "ownership" of—support for—some WTO rules in many of these nations.

In considering the net benefit of WTO rules, it is important to make a distinction between trade-policy disciplines and rules that require significant upfront investment of resources to establish or strengthen institutions. Trade-policy disciplines should apply uniformly to all WTO members (Hoekman, Michalopoulos, and Winters 2004), but when it comes to trade institutions and domestic regulation, one size does not necessarily fit all. A given country's development priorities may not leave room for effective compliance with some aspects of WTO agreements. Certain measures may require many preconditions before implementation will be beneficial. Some disciplines may not be appropriate for very small countries, in that the regulatory institutions that they require may be unduly costly—countries may lack the scale needed for benefits to exceed implementation costs.

These observations suggest there is a need to differentiate among developing countries when determining the reach of resource-intensive WTO rules. Possible approaches to differentiation are:

- Total flexibility for developing countries to invoke exemptions as long as these do not harm any other member country.
- Country-specific determinations of eligibility for rule-related SDT provisions that would apply to a predefined set of agreements, so as to limit SDT to countries that need it most—the poorest countries and very small states.
- An agreement-specific approach in which objective criteria in each agreement would link implementation by developing countries to local conditions, priorities, and capacities (based on an audit of costs), and to availability of technical assistance.

Of these approaches, the first is clearly discernible in many countries' current proposals. As the status of the negotiations suggests, it is unlikely to prove fruitful. The second would require renegotiating the three country classifications currently used in the WTO—LDCs, all other developing countries, and developed countries.

A good case can be made for reclassification, given that many countries that define themselves as developing have per capita incomes that are many multiples of the poorest countries. However, this has been a politically sensitive issue in the WTO. The third option would allow the issue of defining general eligibility to be avoided, but it involves significant transaction costs.

Any approach to strengthening rule-related SDT will require substantial thought and discussion among WTO members, as well as recognition that capacities and priorities differ hugely across the membership. Given the steady expansion of the WTO into regulatory areas, a serious discussion of rule-related SDT is critical if development-relevance is to be more than a slogan. A first step discussed in Hoekman (2005) could be to allow for greater policy flexibility for developing countries, accompanied by greater efforts on the part of WTO members to assist developing countries attain their trade objectives, with a regular multilateral monitoring of outcomes and effects of the policies pursued.

Renegotiation of certain WTO disciplines
Many developing countries believe that the rules in some WTO agreements are not development friendly. Rather than seek opt-outs through SDT, however, it may be preferable to renegotiate the agreements. For example, in agriculture, it may be useful to introduce new rules to ensure that developing countries have the freedom to pursue policies that support the rural poor. With respect to intellectual property, the world as a whole has an interest in ensuring that developing countries have the flexibility to provide their poor with access to drugs at affordable prices and that traditional knowledge is protected and properly remunerated. Two examples of direct relevance to the SDT and development debate where WTO disciplines can be improved are rules of origin and the requirements for regional integration. On the first, there is a strong case for substantial relaxation of such rules to allow goods to benefit from preferential access programs as long as a minimal amount of labor value has been added. Current rules of origin for processed goods tend to require too high local content in terms of intermediates, or else require that such inputs are sourced from the country granting the preference. This works against the exploitation of comparative advantage and the need to specialize in narrow parts of the value chain—a key requirement for firms and countries as the world economy becomes more integrated. The experience with AGOA for those countries benefiting from relaxed rules of origin has illustrated that such rules can be a binding constraint on the development and expansion of manufactured exports. The second example concerns the design of North-South regional integration. Here a beneficial rule change would require Southern members of such agreements to pursue partial MFN liberalization as opposed to requiring complete preferential (discriminatory) liberalization in favor of the high-income partner. This would avoid trade diversion costs while also attenuating the fiscal impacts—giving more time to put in place alternative tax collection mechanisms.

Aid for trade

Development assistance can play an important role in building the institutional and trade capacity that developing countries need if they are to benefit from better access to markets. But the desire of donors to see developing countries implement certain WTO agreements should not divert assistance from recipients' own priorities. The risk of such diversion is one of the downsides of proposals to make technical assistance mandatory under the WTO and to link implementation of WTO agreements to the provision of such assistance. To ensure that trade priorities are identified for funding, a better approach is to support efforts to embed trade-related technical assistance in national priority-setting processes, such as the Poverty Reduction Strategy Paper (PRSP), used by governments and the donor community. Once trade-related needs have been embedded in national priorities, donors and international financial institutions must stand ready to expand assistance to help bolster trade capacity and strengthen trade-related institutions in developing countries.

Export diversification was the primary motivation for preferences. But many of the poorest countries have not managed to use preferences to diversify and expand exports. Benefiting more from integration into the trading system requires improving the productivity and competitiveness of firms and farmers in the poorest countries. Supply constraints are the primary factors that have constrained the ability of many African countries to benefit from preferences. Improving trade capacity can be pursued through a shift to more (and more effective) development assistance that targets domestic supply constraints as well as measures to reduce the costs of entering foreign markets.

Recognizing the importance of complementary policy actions and the need for support for adjustment and integration to achieve successful trade reform in low-income economies does not imply that the Doha Round should be any less ambitious or deliberately slowed. The reverse is true. But it should be complemented by actions to redistribute some of the global gains from trade reform to help address the trade and growth agenda in the poorest countries—in the process helping to attain the original objective motivating preferential access regimes.

The *quid pro quo*

Reciprocity is the engine of WTO negotiations. In the past, however, the lure of nonreciprocal preferences has kept developing countries from exploiting the major source of gains from trade liberalization—namely the reform of their *own* policies.[4] Unilateral liberalization could be linked to market access by granting negotiating "credit" to developing countries that make significant autonomous reforms. One way to achieve this would be through a formula approach to tariff negotiations that used the level and extent of reduction in tariff bindings as the focal point of liberalization commitments.[5] Given that many developing countries either have not bound tariffs at all or have high tariff bindings, such an approach would ensure that credit was given for past reductions in applied tariffs.

On the rules side, an important *quid pro quo* to shore up the trading system would be for developing countries to accept that core WTO trade policy rules are beneficial. This does not imply that developing countries should be forced to sign away all flexibility to use trade policies. But the economic literature has shown that tariffs and other traditional trade policy tools are poor instruments for the achievement of economic development objectives (Hoekman and others 2004). Abiding by WTO procedural rules on the use of such instruments will benefit consumers and enhance welfare in developing countries. It will also help focus attention on areas where SDT could make a real difference.

Conclusion

Moving forward on SDT requires a mechanism to enable developing countries, particularly the poorest, to benefit more fully from participation in the multilateral trading system. Greater differentiation among developing countries arguably must be part of a new grand bargain within WTO. The existing country classification system of LDCs (as defined by the United Nations) and other developing countries (self-declared) has resulted in a mechanism that is ineffective for all.

Of the three major dimensions of SDT—better market access for developing countries' exports of goods and services, implementation and enforcement of WTO rules, and expanded development assistance ("aid for trade")—rapid movement is possible on the first and last. Agreement on how to deal with implementation constraints and define the reach of resource-intensive rules, however, will take time. The formation of a high-level group operating under the auspices of the WTO General Council to discuss options for a new mechanism for rule-related SDT, could be a first step forward.

SDT cannot be a one-way street. Differentiation implies that only a subset of developing countries should be eligible for SDT, and that the more advanced should accept that they are not eligible. All developing countries, even those that qualify for SDT, should engage in the exchange of trade policy commitments (market access). Providing credit for past autonomous reforms can and should figure in the negotiating modalities that are adopted, but the viability of the trading system requires that the core principles and rules apply to all members.

Notes

1. In 1965, developing country demands for special status in the multilateral trading system led to the drafting of a new Part IV of the GATT. This introduced the concept of SDT for developing countries. In 1979 a Framework Agreement was negotiated, which included the so-called Enabling Clause. Officially called Differential and More Favorable Treatment, Reciprocity and Fuller Participation of Developing Countries, the Enabling Clause provided for departures from MFN and other GATT rules. It also created a permanent legal basis for the operation of the general system of preferences (GSP) established under UNCTAD auspices and codified principles, practices, and procedures regarding the use of trade measures by developing countries, giving developing countries more flexibility in applying trade measures to meet their "essential development needs."

2. This Trade Note was written by Bernard Hoekman, Manager, World Bank. It draws on joint work done with Caglar Ozden, Costas Michalopoulos, Susan Prowse and Alan Winters.

3. Preferences should be assessed in terms of the price advantage they confer rather than, as is quite common, the percentage of the tariffs they remit. To have 100 percent remission of a 1 percent tariff is worth far less—1 percentage point—than a 50 percent remission of a 10 percent tariff—5 percentage points.

4. Ozden and Rheinhart (2005) argue that countries with preferential access to developed country markets—even if it is of limited value due to administrative requirements and exceptions—have less of an incentive to pursue trade liberalization. Nonreciprocity also helps to explain why tariff peaks today are largely found on goods produced in developing countries. In the absence of a willingness by developing countries to open access to their own markets there was less incentive for OECD countries to reduce barriers in areas of export interest to developing countries.

5. See Francois and Martin (2003) for an in-depth analysis of alternative formula-based approaches.

References

Amjadi, A., U. Reinke, and A. Yeats. 1996. "Did External Barriers Cause the Marginalization of Sub-Saharan Africa in World Trade?" Policy Research Working Paper 1586, World Bank, Washington, DC.

Francois, J., and W. Martin. 2003. "Formula Approaches for Market Access Negotiations." *The World Economy* 26:1–28.

Hoekman, B. 2005. "Operationalizing the Concept of Policy Space in the WTO." *Journal of International Economic Law* 8(2): 405-24.

Hoekman, B., F. Ng, and M. Olarreaga. 2002. "Tariff Peaks in the Quad and Least Developed Country Exports." *World Bank Economic Review* 16:1–22.

Hoekman, B., C. Michalopoulos, and L. A. Winters, 2004. "Special and Differential Treatment for Developing Countries." *The World Economy,* 27: 481-506.

Mattoo, A. 2005. "Services in a Development Round: Three Goals and Proposals." *Journal of World Trade* 39(6): 1223-37

Ozden, Caglar, and E. Rheinhart. 2005. "The Perversity of Preferences." *Journal of Development Economics*, 78 (1): 1-21.

World Bank. 2002. *Global Economic Prospects and the Developed Countries: Making Trade Work for the Poor.* Washington DC: World Bank.

Further Reading

Brenton, Paul. 2003. "Integrating the Least Developed Countries into the World Trading System: The Current Impact of EU Preferences under Everything But Arms." *Journal of World Trade,* 37 (3): 623-46.

Mattoo, Arvind, Devesh Roy, and Arvind Subramanian. 2003. "The Africa Growth and Opportunity Act and Its Rules of Origin: Generosity Undermined?" *The World Economy,* 26 (6): 829-52.

Oyejide, T. Ademola. 2002. "Special and Differential Treatment." In *Development, Trade and the WTO: A Handbook,* ed. B. Hoekman, Aaditya Mattoo and Philip English. Washington, DC: World Bank.

Prowse, Susan. 2005. "Aid for Trade: Increasing Support for Trade Adjustment and Integration," in Simon Evenett and Bernard Hoekman (eds). *Economic Development and Multilateral Trade Cooperation.* Palgrave, World Bank.

Stevens, Christopher. 2002. "The Future of SDT for Developing Countries in the WTO." Unpublished paper, Institute for Development Studies, University of Sussex. May.

Winters, L. A. 2001. "Post-Lomé Trading Arrangements: The Multilateral Option." In *Regionalism in Europe: Geometries and Strategies After 2000,* ed. Jürgen von Hagen and Mika Widgren. Leiden: Kluwer Academic Press.

The Value of Trade Preferences for Africa

Paul Brenton and Takako Ikezuki

mproving the ability of the least developed countries (LDCs) to participate in world markets can stimulate growth and reduce poverty. To help achieve those goals, industrial countries offer developing countries preferential access to their markets through lower duties. In this note we discuss the magnitude of the preferences granted by the European Union, Japan, and the United States to Sub-Saharan African countries and show that only a small number of countries actually receive substantial preferences.[1]

The role of trade preferences

Tariffs introduce a wedge between the world price of a product and the price in the domestic market. The premium normally accrues to the government of the importing country as tariff revenue. Under preferences, however, it may go to the developing country beneficiary, thereby raising returns to the activity that enjoys the preference and, depending on the nature of competition in domestic product and factor markets, stimulate expansion of that activity, with implications for wages and employment.

However, if there is little effective competition among buyers/importers in the developed country then the suppliers/exporters in the developing country may be unable to acquire much of the price premium. Ozden and Olareaga (2005) find that only one-third of the available rents for African exports of clothing to the U.S. under The African Growth Opportunity Act (AGOA) actually accrue to the exporters. In addition, as will be discussed below, the costs of satisfying the rules governing preferences reduces the extent to which they raise actual returns in developing countries.

The arguments underlying trade preferences are that the small scale of industry and low level of development in developing countries lead to high costs, which reduce countries' ability to compete in global markets, and to a lack of diversification, which increases risks. Developing countries, especially least developed countries, face much higher trade-related costs than other countries in getting their products into international markets. Some of these costs may reflect institutional problems in the exporting countries, such as inefficient practices or corruption, which require a domestic policy response. They may also reflect weak transport infrastructure and firms' lack of access to standard trade facilitating measures such as insurance and trade finance.

Trade preferences are expected to provide a premium over the normal rate of return and so encourage investment in these economies. The increase in trade due to preferences leads to more output and, if there are scale economies, to lower costs, further stimulating trade. It is important, however, that the sectors that receive preferences and investment should be those in which the country has a comparative advantage in the long term and that investment not be based on a false comparative advantage derived from the margin of preference.

Adverse effects

Tariff preferences can lead to several adverse effects. When rents do accrue to the developing country, they tend to accrue not to the poorest constituents but to the owners of the most intensively used factors. With agricultural preferences, the main beneficiaries are typically the owners of land. Preferences will typically have a strong impact on poverty only if the landowners are poor. So, even when preferences create substantial transfers for producers in developing countries, they may not stimulate the long-term growth of exports or reduce poverty, and may lead to a less diversified export base. Preferences can create a degree of dependence that constrains flexibility and diversification and results in high-cost production of preferred products (Topp 2001).

Finally, negotiations under the Doha Round have shown that preferences can be used to bolster external support for protectionist policies in industrial countries and to weaken proposals to reduce protection.

The value of preferences offered by the European Union, Japan, and the United States

Table 1 summarizes the calculated value of the preferences of the European Union, Japan and the United States for Sub-Saharan African countries in 2002. We allow for the fact that both the European Union and the United States have schemes that offer enhanced preferences to exporters in Sub-Saharan Africa beyond those of the standard Generalized System of Preferences (GSP). The United States has introduced the African Growth and Opportunity Act (AGOA), while the EU has the Cotonou Agreement and Everything But Arms (EBA) arrangement (a special provision in the EU's GSP scheme) for the least developed countries. The value of the preferences obtained under those arrangements is derived from the value of exports for which preference is actually requested multiplied by the preference margin. This is the implicit transfer of tariff revenue due to the preference scheme, all of which we assume goes to the developing country. This is presented in table 1 as a share of the total value of exports to each market.

The overall value of EU preferences to Sub-Saharan African countries under the Cotonou Agreement and the EBA amounted to just 4 percent of the value of the affected countries' exports to the European Union in 2002 (table 1). The value of

Table 1. Summary of the impact of trade preferences for Sub-Saharan Africa, 2002

Percent	Sub-Saharan Africa (total)			LDCs			Non-LDCs		
	EU	US	Japan	EU	US	Japan	EU	US	Japan
Value of preferences/ total exports	4.0	1.3	0.1	2.3	2.1	0.4	5.1	1.1	0.1
Share of top 5 beneficiaries in total value of preferences requested	59.9	73.9	88.9	73.8	98.8	95.8	76.9	92.9	98.7
Share of top 10 beneficiaries in total value of preferences requested	80.1	95.4	97.7	91.2	100.0	100.0	97.5	99.3	100.0
Share of top sector[a] in total value of preferences	31.3	31.9	41.0	37.1	51.5	70.9	34.5	33.4	31.9
Share of top 3 sectors[a] in total value of preferences requested	56.5	79.6	63.6	68.5	91.3	92.2	65.2	71.3	56.8

[a] Defined at the two-digit level of the harmonized system.
Source: Calculated using data from USITC, EUROSTAT and Japanese Ministry of Trade.

U.S. preferences for Sub-Saharan African countries under AGOA and the GSP amounted to 1.3 percent of the value of exports to the United States. Japanese preferences to Sub-Saharan African exporters amounted to 0.1 percent of the value of exports. The value of preferences to non-LDCs is higher than that for LDCs in the EU schemes, while this situation is reversed for the U.S. and Japanese schemes.

The benefits of preferences are highly concentrated on a small number of beneficiaries. Under the EU schemes, 60 percent of the benefits accrue to five countries. For the United States, the top five beneficiaries account for almost three-quarters of the value of preferences, while for Japan the top five account for nearly 90 percent. For the LDCs, the top 10 beneficiaries account for 100 percent of the benefits under the U.S. and Japanese schemes and more than 90 percent of the benefits offered by the EU schemes. Thus, the value of preferences for the remaining 37 countries (although they are not the same countries in each case) is very small.

Preferences are also concentrated on a small number of sectors, especially for the LDCs. In the EU schemes these are mainly agricultural products (sugar, fruits, and processed meat and fish). U.S. preferences are dominated by clothing and mineral fuels. Fish, iron and steel, and nickel dominate Japanese preferences. Almost one-third of the value of EU preferences is derived from sugar, the market for which is highly distorted. These preferences will be affected by the EU's reform of

Table 2. Classification of Sub-Saharan African countries by magnitude of the value of combined (non-oil) preferences in the European Union, Japan, and United States relative to total (non-oil) exports, 2002

Less than 1 percent	Angola, Burundi, Central African Republic, Chad, Congo, Democratic Republic of Congo, Djibouti, Equatorial Guinea, Gabon, Guinea, Liberia, Mali, Niger, Nigeria, Rwanda, Sao Tome and Principe, Somalia, South Africa
Between 1 percent and 5 percent	Benin, Botswana, Burkina Faso, Cameroon, Cape Verde, Comoros, Eritrea, Ethiopia, Ghana, Ivory Coast, Mauritania, Sierra Leone, Sudan, Tanzania, Togo, Uganda, Zambia
Greater than 5 percent but less than 10 percent	Gambia, Guinea-Bissau, Kenya, Madagascar, Mozambique, Namibia, Senegal, Zimbabwe
Greater than 10 percent	Lesotho, Malawi, Mauritius, Seychelles, Swaziland

*Source:*Based on calculations using data from USITC, EUROSTAT and Japanese Ministry of Trade.

its sugar policies; they should be distinguished from general trade preferences that arise from a tariff preference in otherwise undistorted sectors.

For only five countries do the combined preferences requested in the EU, Japan and U.S. account for more than 10 percent of the value of total non-oil exports (table 2). For 35 of the countries—73 percent of the total in Sub-Saharan Africa—preferences amount to less than 5 percent of the value of exports. For 18 countries preferences are negligible, amounting to less than 1 percent of exports.

Because the trade preferences obtained in the EU, Japanese, and U.S. markets amount to a very small proportion of the value of exports of all but a few countries of Sub-Saharan Africa, the impact of those preferences is likely to be very muted. Only a small number of countries receive substantial transfers under current schemes. These are driven mainly by preferences for sugar in the European Union and for clothing in the United States.

Why do trade preferences fall short of their potential?

Trade preferences have not transformed the export and growth performance of most developing country beneficiaries, although performance may have been worse without them and a few countries may have benefited substantially. Trade preferences have not enabled beneficiaries as a group to increase their market shares in the main preference-granting markets. Why?

First, many products produced in developing countries are subject to zero MFN duties in industrial countries, and therefore no trade preference can be given. Second, products with high duties are typically excluded from preferences or the preference margin is very small. For a small number of products, preference margins are substantial, though usually within strict quantitative limits and only for certain countries. Some countries that have been granted preferential access for sugar and tobacco, for example, have received large transfers due to preferences.

Third, many of the schemes are surrounded by uncertainty concerning their duration and the discretion that the donors have to exclude countries and products. That uncertainty limits incentives to invest in the beneficiary countries to take advantage of preferences.

Fourth, exporters in developing countries are often hampered in their ability to take advantage of preferences by complex rules of origin, which impose two types of costs: (a) the additional costs of sourcing inputs and designing production structures to ensure compatibility with the rules of origin, and (b) the costs of demonstrating conformity with the rules, in terms of documentation, accounting, and obtaining the relevant certificate.

Here we have concentrated on aspects of the preferential schemes that limit their impact, rather than on limitations in the beneficiaries' capacity to satisfy other requirements for market access, such as public and private standards related to health, safety, and quality, as well as broader constraints relating to transportation, energy, and so on, all of which constrain the supply response to preferences in developing countries, just as they do trade opportunities in general.

Conclusions

Trade preferences are not a panacea for success but rather should be seen as just one part of a strategy for export-led growth. In principle, trade preferences can promote development by providng temporary margins of preference to enable industries to adjust and compete more effectively in global markets. Multilateral trade liberalization contributes to this outcome by ensuring that preferences have a short half-life and that inefficient, high-cost industries with entrenched lobbies do not constrain flexibility and adjustment. Multilateral liberalization is also important for limiting the trade-diverting impact of preferences on other countries (usually other developing countries).

In practice, only a small number of countries receive large transfers as a result of preferences in developed country markets. The values of preferences are largest in the EU market, driven by a narrow range of products and the very high EU price for sugar. In a very few countries, such as Mauritius, preferences appear to have contributed to a relatively strong economic performance and economic diversification (Subramanian and Roy 2003). In some other countries, preferences have led to large transfers, but domestic industries have experienced rising costs and declining output and have accumulated large debts.[2] But most beneficiaries of European, Japanese, and U.S. preferences have experienced little or no impact. Preferences have done little to stimulate the export of a broader range of products.

Preference schemes would be enhanced by

- Extending coverage to all products and making schemes permanent (as with the EBA).
- Liberalizing rules of origin and simplifying the process of certifying compliance. If all schemes had the same simple and easy-to-apply rules, a producer in a least developed country could make production and investment decisions on the basis of equal and predictable access to all industrial markets.

The impact of preferences on developing countries would be facilitated by

- Improving the domestic investment environment.
- Addressing the internal barriers that raise the costs of trade for developing countries—inadequate and high-priced transport services, inadequate and unreliable energy supplies, inefficient customs practices, and lack of trade-supporting financial and telecommunications services.

The challenge is to find preference schemes that complement the domestic reforms that developing countries must undertake to improve the returns to exports without stifling diversification and multilateral trade liberalization.

Developed countries should not treat trade preferences as a substitute for direct development assistance, which remains crucial in alleviating internal barriers that constrain supply responses to trade opportunities. Nor should they allow allocations of development assistance to be distorted by preferences. While there is a need to address the difficulties that a small number of countries may face from the erosion of preferences under multilateral liberalization, such needs must not be met by redirecting assistance away from the large number of low-income countries that do not benefit from preferences. At the same time, developing countries must not view preferences as an alternative to domestic reforms that are needed to improve investment conditions, promote effective competition, and facilitate integration into the global economy.

Notes

1. This chapter was written by Paul Brenton, Senior Economist, and Takako Ikezuki, Junior Professional Associate Economist, of the International Trade Department of the World Bank. Comments from Elke Kreuzwieser and Faezeh Foroutan on the paper underlying this chapter are gratefully acknowledged. -

2. For example, Mitchell (2005) concludes that despite substantial preferences, most Caribbean sugar producers are not competitive and will need to close or restructure once the European Union reforms its sugar policies.

References

Mitchell, D. 2005. "Sugar in the Caribbean: Adjusting to Eroding Preferences." Policy Research Working Paper, World Bank, Washington, DC.

Ozden, C., and M. Olarreaga. 2005. "AGOA and Apparel: Who Captures the Tariff Rent in the Presence of Preferential Market Access?" World Economy 28, 63-77.

Subramanian, A., and D. Roy. 2003. "Who Can Explain the Mauritian Miracle: Meade, Romer, Sachs or Rodrik?" *In Search of Prosperity - Analytical Narratives on Economic Growth*, ed D. Rodrik. Princeton University Press, Oxford.

Topp, V. 2001. "Trade Preferences: Are they Helpful in Advancing Economic Development in Poor Countries?" ABARE, Canberra.

Further Reading

Brenton, P., and T. Ikezuki. 2005. "The Impact of Agricultural Trade Preferences, with Particular Attention to the Least Developed Countries." In Global Agricultural Trade and Developing Countries, ed. A. Aksoy and J. Beghin. Washington DC: World Bank.

Hoekman, B., and C. Ozden. 2005. "Trade Preferences and Differential Treatment of Developing Countries: A Selective Survey." Policy Research Working Paper 3566, World Bank, Washington, DC.

Stevens, C., and J. Kennan. 2005. "Making Trade Preferences More Effective." Trade Note, Institute of Development Studies, University of Sussex, http://www.ids.ac.uk/IDS/global/pdfs/CSJKTradePreferences.pdf.

WTO Accession: Moving the Goalposts?

Simon J. Evenett and Carlos A. Primo Braga

Since it was created a decade ago, the World Trade Organization (WTO) has welcomed 20 new members. On October 13, 2004, Cambodia became the WTO's 148th member, almost 10 years after it had first applied and just over a year after its membership package was approved at the Cancún Ministerial Conference. Cambodia is the second least developed country (LDC) to join the WTO, following Nepal's accession on April 23, 2004.[1]

Countries applying for WTO membership face a long and complex process. Some pending applications date back to the late 1980s (Algeria's, for example) and early 1990s (those of Belarus, Russian Federation, Saudi Arabia, Ukraine). Applicants often need to implement substantive reforms to align their domestic institutions and policies with WTO disciplines. Many cannot engage effectively in accession negotiations for lack of trained personnel or because of institutional and financial constraints. Roughly one-third of the 30 governments now in the process of accession are LDCs. (See Annex 1 for a list of current applicants.)[2]

Notwithstanding these concerns, the demand for WTO accession remains strong. Moreover, as illustrated by the experiences of China and, more recently, Cambodia, WTO accession can be an effective lever to promote trade liberalization and substantive regulatory reform. In this note, we discuss the experience of developing countries with the WTO accession process and highlight the implications for policymakers in applicant countries and in existing WTO members.[3]

Why do nations join the WTO?

Policymakers from countries seeking to join the WTO give a range of economic, legal, and political reasons for doing so. For some, the rationale is to further integrate their country into the world economy. The expectation is that more predictable access to foreign markets, which WTO membership can bring, will result in higher exports. Another economic rationale is to attract more foreign direct investment and, more generally, to use WTO membership as a seal of approval recognized by the international business community. The legal advantages of accessing a rules-based system and of using the WTO dispute-settlement process are often mentioned as well. Many nations join the WTO for political reasons. Transition economies, for example, often see WTO membership as a means to signal their commitment to joining the international community of market-based economies.

There is some overlap between these rationales and the potential benefits of WTO accession identified in economic research—particularly with regard to bolstering exports and foreign direct investment.[4] Economists would point to the benefits that flow from better foreign access to the acceding nation's markets, specifically in terms of price and variety of imports. By binding national tariffs, committing to eliminate quotas on imports, and reforming other state measures, WTO membership can enhance the credibility of an acceding nation's policies and thus reduce the uncertainty faced by the private sector. It can also improve important components of the national business environment, which, in turn, has sizeable domestic payoffs.

The reality of the WTO accession process

The experience of 20 members that have joined the WTO since 1995, and of the 30 countries and custom territories now seeking to join, form the basis of much of what is known about the WTO accession process. Not every aspect of the process is publicly documented. In particular, little is known about the numerous bilateral negotiations between an applicant and existing WTO members. Because of these lacunae, a certain amount of folklore has arisen concerning the accession process. Recently, studies have shed some light on the validity of the folklore. The main findings of those studies are described below.[5] However, readers, particularly stakeholders in applicant countries, should bear in mind that key steps in the WTO accession process remain confidential. It is also important to keep in mind that noneconomic considerations can play a role in shaping the process.[6]

The formal procedures that an applicant must follow to become a WTO member are well established. They involve at least 20 distinct steps.[7] The most important are the creation of a Working Party of WTO members to consider the application for membership,[8] the drafting of a memorandum on the applicant's foreign trade regime, satisfactory responses to questions about the memorandum posed by existing WTO members, the conclusion of bilateral negotiations with each of the Working Party members, and the adoption of the Protocol of Accession by the Working Party and then by the WTO's General Council or Ministerial Conference.

Throughout this process the onus is on the applicant to satisfy the demands of existing WTO members. This apparently one-sided procedure has given rise to the following perceptions:

- The WTO accession process is increasingly costly and complex and takes longer and longer to complete.
- The price of joining the WTO now includes commitments that go beyond the General Agreement on Tarriffs and Trade (GATT)/WTO agreements.
- The accession process takes little account of the specific circumstances of applicant countries or their needs for special and differential treatment.

The underlying reason for the emergence of these perceptions is that the terms, rather than the procedures, of WTO accession are not well defined. Paradoxically for a rules-based organization, the WTO has no clear rules governing

Figure 1. The lengthening process of WTO accession

Countries in order of accession to WTO

Number of months

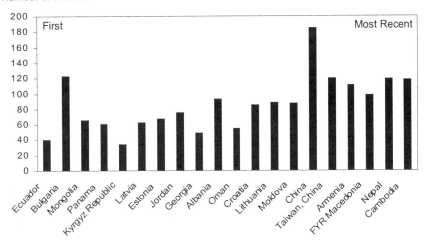

*Source:*Compiled by the authors on WTO data (2004a).

Note: All 20 countries in question are those identified in Annex 2.

the "price" of membership. Article XII of the Marrakesh Agreement, the legal instrument covering the accession process, merely states that new members may join the WTO "on terms to be agreed." This sparse guidance leaves the door wide open for an expedited, hassle-free accession or a drawn-out, decade-long, and burdensome one. The latter occurs more often. The time required to complete the WTO accession process has steadily grown over the past decade (figure 1). Recently acceded countries have needed approximately a decade to negotiate their WTO entry.[9]

Turning to the price of accession, it is important to distinguish between the two broad types of commitments made by acceding countries: those relating directly to market access and commitments on rules.

With respect to market access for agricultural and nonagricultural (i.e., manufacturing) products, there is clear evidence that the price of accession—expressed in terms of the concessions made by acceding countries—has grown over time. Separating out the accession of LDCs (which happen to be the last two countries to join the WTO) from other acceding developing countries, a clear pattern emerges (figures 2a and 2b). For both agricultural and nonagricultural goods the average tariff binding allowed to acceding countries has fallen over time, standing now at levels well below those agreed by developing countries in the Uruguay Round.[10] From a mercantile perspective,

Figure 2a. Recent WTO members face tighter commitments on agricultural products

Countries in order of accession to WTO

Average tariff bindings

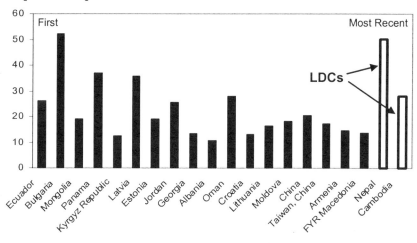

Figure 2b. ...and on manufacturing products

Average tariff bindings

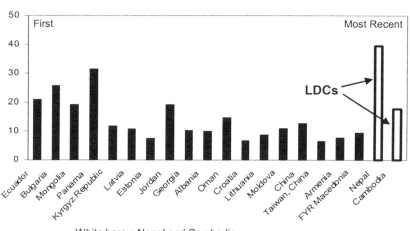

White bars = Nepal and Cambodia.

Source: Compiled by the authors on WTO (2004a).

therefore, the relative price of WTO accession is high in comparison to Uruguay Round commitments made by peer nations—and it is growing over time. The picture that emerges concerning services commitments under the General Agreement on Trade in Services (GATS) tells a similar story. Taking the number of services subsectors (of the 160 identified in the WTO's classification list) committed by countries as a proxy for the price of becoming a WTO member, one observes that LDCs that were founding members of the WTO committed on average 20 subsectors. The averages for founding members in the developing and developed categories were 44 and 108. Countries in all categories that have acceded since 1995, by contrast, have committed an average of 104 subsectors.[11] This figure is a crude measure of the services-related price of accession because it does not capture either the depth (for example, the extent of explicit limitations) or the breadth (modes of delivery) of the commitment. Still, it is illustrative that countries that went through the WTO accession process typically committed a much higher number of subsectors than did GATT contracting parties at a similar level of development in the Uruguay Round negotiations (1986–94).[12]

Turning to rules commitments that countries have made when joining the WTO, the picture is more mixed. With the exceptions of China and Taiwan (China), accession countries signed around 25 such commitments related to a wide range of state measures, some of which are not obviously trade-related. Bulgaria, for example, made commitments with respect to domestic price controls, the privatization of state-owned enterprises, and excise taxes on alcohol, as well as many other measures related to trade policy.

A controversial question is whether these commitments go beyond those agreed during the Uruguay Round (so-called WTO+ commitments) or require an accession country to forgo rights available to other WTO members (so-called WTO–commitments). Whether an accession commitment goes beyond an existing WTO agreement depends in large part on how the latter is interpreted, and so it should not be surprising that disagreement is rife on the extent of WTO+ commitments. Some WTO+ obligations may involve no more than consultation with, or reporting to, existing WTO members and thus are of limited developmental significance. Others may be more fundamental, such as Jordan's commitment that if any of its laws or state acts are subsequently found to contradict international treaties (not just WTO agreements), then the latter will have precedence. WTO–commitments are easier to identify, such as Ecuador's commitment to eliminate all subsidies before the date of accession and its commitment never to introduce them afterwards. China's acceptance of product-specific transitional safeguard provisions, which can be more easily triggered than regular WTO safeguards, provides another example. WTO+ and WTO–commitments differentiate WTO members and could be interpreted as contributing to a multi-tier multilateral trade system. Also of concern are the adverse developmental effects that may result from these commitments.[13]

In sum, there is evidence that the accession process is becoming more demanding in terms of market access commitments. WTO's "July package" (WTO 2004c) recognizes as much by stating that new members should be granted more flexibility in market access negotiations under the Doha Round in consideration of the extensive commitments already made in the WTO accession process. Whether there are trends in WTO+ or WTO–commitments is unclear, but the very fact that existing WTO rules allow for them is a source of concern.

Any evidence of trends should be interpreted with care in view of the possibility of an adverse-selection bias in the sample of recently acceded countries. After all, most of these countries were transition economies with highly distorted trading regimes. It could be argued that the higher demands of WTO members reflect this reality rather than a systemic trend.

Tough love or power plays?
The critical question, however, is not whether the price of WTO accession is rising, but whether the price is worth paying given the developmental impact of WTO membership. If it is, then the demands made by existing WTO members might be characterized as "tough love." Otherwise, the WTO accession process may be seen as a one-sided power play in which current WTO members wring commercial advantage out of weaker economic partners.

When considering the developmental impact of WTO accession, two important points should be borne in mind. The first is that a comprehensive evaluation of WTO accession should examine post-accession performance on many metrics and should consider the state measures taken before and after WTO accession. At present, few accession countries have five or more years of post-accession data to use in identifying the effect of WTO accession, so the available evidence is necessarily limited. Second, most of the country-specific studies on WTO accession relate to China and involve predictions of the likely effects of its accession, rather than evaluations of actual impact.

Much of the available evidence concerns the impact of WTO accession on national exports and imports. This evidence is useful for assessing whether accession really does help integrate developing countries into the world's trading system. There are two main strands of recent literature analyzing aggregate studies of trade flows and the role of the WTO/GATT in influencing them. In a series of papers, Andrew Rose (2003 is a prominent example) has called into question whether membership in the GATT/WTO has actually increased trade above the levels expected from the "standard gravity" determinants of bilateral trade.[14] Analyzing the same data in a different way, Subramanian and Wei (2003) find that GATT/WTO membership has been associated with a significant increase in the imports of industrialized countries, although the same cannot be said for developing country members.

There is little reason, however, to expect that exporters in acceding countries respond similarly to the different opportunities created by their nation's WTO accession—an assumption implicit in the above two analyses. Recent country-by-country estimates of the impact of WTO accession on imports and exports vary a great deal, probably because national experience varies a great deal.[15] For example, after stripping out the effects of nontrade policy determinants on its trade, Ecuador's manufacturing imports fell after its WTO accession in 1996. This apparently surprising finding is easy to understand when one notes that Ecuador raised its applied tariffs across the board in the years after WTO accession, something that was possible in view of the binding overhang of its WTO tariff commitments. Another problem with these aggregate studies is that they do not shed light on the mechanisms by which WTO accession influences national trade flows. For example, did accession bolster sales of traditional exports to existing markets or did it encourage entry into new markets?

Disaggregated product-line studies of Ecuador's and Bulgaria's exports to the industrialized Quad countries shed some light on whether the incentives created by WTO accession are working or not.[16] Kennett, Evenett, and Gage (2005) found that, once other determinants of market entry were controlled for, sales of long-standing exports to new markets were not helped by WTO accession. In contrast, sales of long-standing products to existing foreign markets were found to rise after WTO accession, suggesting that Bulgarian and Ecuadorian exporters responded positively to the incentives created by WTO accession.

Modest supply-side responses to WTO accession may be due to two potential factors. First, foreign barriers faced by some exporters in countries that joined the WTO may have changed little after accession. Second, exporters may have been unaware or unable to take advantage of improved market access abroad. This could be due to a lack of information, to expensive and inefficient infrastructure in the acceding country, or to a lack of experience in shipping goods abroad. In short, whether joining the WTO bolsters a nation's exports depends not only on the changes in market access that are supposed to follow from accession (in terms of greater predictability), but also on the steps taken by the government and firms in the applicant country.

To summarize, when comparing the grand objectives of nations that seek to join the WTO with the available empirical evidence on what happened to those countries after they joined, there is an evident mismatch. Although odd at first glance, this may not be surprising given the short-time elapsed since WTO accession occurred. The apparent mismatch certainly has not stopped many countries from applying for WTO membership. In addition, it is important to keep in mind that WTO accession can induce reforms that promote transparency and that strengthen domestic policies to cope with balance-of-payments crises and the like—important additional benefits for developing countries.[17] Over the past 12 months more information has come to light as to how nations can successfully make the most of WTO accession, a subject to which we now turn.

Making the most of the WTO accession

Developing countries need not see themselves as being at the mercy of existing WTO members during the accession process. Concrete steps have been taken by governments in developing countries before, during, and after accession to push the ratio of costs to benefits in a pro-development direction. Moreover, many donor agencies and international development institutions offer programs to build trade-related capacity and expertise. The overriding goal is to choose the mix of national and international initiatives that best meets the applicant's development objectives. The following remarks, based on developing country experiences, are offered with this goal in mind.[18]

As early as possible in the WTO accession process, it is desirable to identify precisely how binding commitments before the WTO can further reform and help attain national priorities. Cambodia, for example, identified textiles, clothing, and tourism as sectors that could benefit from reform and developed its negotiating priorities accordingly. Identification of goals, analysis of economic options, and formulation of negotiating priorities and fallback positions are required at this point. Binding commitments can influence the behavior of importers, foreign investors, and regulators, and knowing the likely economic and social impact of different legal commitments will help an acceding country to determine which legal commitments are priorities. Such reasoning will involve matters far beyond the typical reach of the ministry of trade, and ideally the national government should come to a collective view of the appropriate strategy with respect to WTO accession. Accession should not be treated as a technocratic negotiating exercise controlled by a small number of officials in the trade ministry.

Another important step is for applicant countries to form realistic expectations of what the WTO accession process involves. Applicants should expect the process to take at least five years. Given ministerial and staff turnover, a broad base of government, civil society, and private sector support for the accession initiative is required. This is possible only with broad consultation and a clear sense of the costs, benefits, and priorities of WTO accession.

On the basis of recent accession experience, current and future developing country applicants can expect to have their agricultural tariffs bound at an average rate well below 20 percent and nonagricultural goods below 10 percent. (Least developed countries appear to have been given more lenient treatment.) The implications of these market access commitments for import-competing sectors should be considered.

Applicants can also expect to sign around 25 rules-related commitments, some of which will have implications for sensitive policies such as protection of intellectual property rights. With respect to this class of commitments, applicants ought to develop the capacity to document and demonstrate why a proposal from an existing WTO member is against the applicant's development goals. Identifying national priorities is not enough. Being able to respond effectively to the negotiating proposals of other nations is important if flexibility is to be preserved. If pressed to accept expensive rules-related commitments, applicants should at a minimum insist on technical assistance to mitigate the implementation costs.[19]

Given the duration, complexity, and wide-ranging scope of the WTO accession process, accession countries should develop, in partnership with the providers of technical assistance, a road map that identifies the different types of assistance required at each stage of the accession process. The diagnostic tools associated with the Integrated Framework—successfully applied in Cambodia, for example, and currently being used in Ethiopia's accession—provide a comprehensive assessment of national needs. In this regard it is also important to avoid overlooking post-accession implementation needs, as deficits here can undermine the ability of the private sector to capitalize on any export opportunities created by joining the WTO.

Officials in developing countries have benefited from the experience of experts in other developing countries that have recently acceded to the WTO. Such so-called South–South learning can be very valuable. Jordan, for example, offers expertise to countries in the Middle East and North Africa that are seeking to join the WTO.

Shrewd officials from applicant countries have also sought to optimize the value of the technical assistance they receive by playing an active role in drafting the terms of reference for international consultants and participating in the process of selecting such consultants. It is also important to ensure that workshops and consultant visits are tailored to country-specific circumstances and involve follow-up. Picking the right officials to attend workshops and promoting the learning in official WTO languages contributes positively as well.

Concluding remarks

The first 20 completed WTO accessions have raised systemic concerns that ought to be of interest to existing WTO members as well as to applicants. The first is that the growing price of WTO accession is creating a multi-tiered world trading system in which recently acceded countries have more obligations and fewer rights. This, in turn, is manifesting itself in demands from some recent applicants to be treated differently in liberalization efforts under the Doha Development Agenda. Some observers have called for applicants to pay a price for accession that is both commensurate with their level of development and with the obligations of existing

WTO members at the same level of development.[20] The need to calibrate the process by level of development has been partially recognized by the WTO membership and was manifested in the WTO General Council's guidelines for the accession of least developed countries in December 2002.[21] To date, however, the call for parity, has been rejected by WTO members.

At a time when the world trading system is supposed to be taking the interests of developing countries more seriously, the lengthening of the time required to negotiate accession and the uncertainty created by the lack of a clear legal definition of the price of WTO accession are issues that merit attention. One has to ask whether it is reasonable to expect developing country's officials and civil society to sustain interest in a process that could take a decade and involve considerable complexity in return for uncertain and deferred rewards. Protracted negotiations give opponents of trade and investment reforms opportunities to exaggerate the negative and undermine support for the accession process. Leaders with anything but the longest time horizons are unlikely to support seriously an accession effort that may not begin to pay off for a decade. It is also worth noting that the WTO is probably the only international economic organization that asks nations to stick to a program of such length. Developmental needs and the necessity of sustaining initial support for joining the WTO should drive the design and operation of the WTO accession process and associated technical assistance. Failure to do so risks creating a growing group of disgruntled participants in the world trading system whose support for further trade reform is likely to be tepid.

Finally, it is important to recognize that the WTO accession process can play a useful role in the political economy of trade reform. Governments that are able to clearly identify their reform objectives *ex ante* are in a much better position to use the process to their own advantage, leveraging the multilateral process to advance domestic reform.

Notes

1. This paper was written by Simon J. Evenett, Professor of International Trade and Economic Development at the University of St. Gallen and a nonresident Senior Fellow of the Economic Studies Program at the Brookings Institution, and Carlos A. Primo Braga, Senior Adviser, International Trade Department, World Bank. Comments and assistance from U. Dadush, C. Fink, B. Hoekman, A. Hussain, P. Low, K. Lucenti, F. Maertens, W. Martin, P. Reichenmiller, P. Schuler, and C. Tully are gratefully acknowledged.

2. The working party on the accession of Vanuatu concluded its work in 2001. Vanuatu has not, however, completed its domestic ratification procedures. If one includes Vanuatu in the list of countries and custom territories pursuing accession to the WTO, the total number is 31.

3. Throughout this paper we define developing countries as encompassing low- and middle-income economies, according to World Bank definitions. Developing country status in the WTO, in turn, is determined by self-selection. Another country grouping used in the paper—and

recognized by the WTO—is the UN classification of least developed countries (LDCs).

4. See list of suggested readings and the references provided in this chapter.

5. These studies are part of a project entitled "Preparing For and Evaluating WTO Accessions" that was funded by the International Development Research Centre (IDRC) of Canada.

6. Iran's request to initiate accession procedures, first presented in 1996, was blocked 21 times by the United States for reasons unrelated to trade. It was finally accepted by the WTO General Council on May 26, 2005.

7. See WTO (1995, 2004a and 2004b) for details about the accession process.

8. Any current member of the WTO can join the Working Party established to consider the accession of a new member.

9. If one considers only the time taken from the submission of the Trade Memorandum until the completion of the process in the case of new WTO members, the time required falls to roughly five years.

10. The following figures provide useful comparators. According to Finger and others (1996) the average bound MFN tariff rate on imports of all merchandise goods by a group of 26 low- and middle-income countries was 25.2 percent. For industrial goods the comparable average bound MFN tariff rate was 20 percent. Anderson and Martin (2005) point out that by 2001, the average weighted agricultural import tariffs were 48 percent for developing countries (WTO taxonomy) and 78 for LDCs.

11. Nepal and Cambodia, the two LDCs that have joined the WTO since 1995, committed to 76 and 93 subsectors, respectively, in contrast to the average of 20 subsectors that LDCs had committed to during the Uruguay Round. For further details about services commitments in the GATS see Marchetti (2004).

12. Grynberg, Ognivtsev, and Razzaque (2002) came to a similar conclusion. They summarize their findings as follows: "At the most aggregate level, while WTO members have on average taken up some kind of commitment in six sectors out of a maximum of 12, the comparable figures for acceding countries is ten. At the 2-digit level, acceded countries took commitments in 36 sectors compared to only 17 taken by WTO members. Finally, at the most disaggregated level, acceding countries have commitments almost two and a half times bigger—103 as against 42. The accession negotiations have resulted in countries undertaking commitments that apparently bear no relationship to their level of economic development as reflected in per capita income" (page vii).

13. Another example of systemic change in the accession process from the GATT-era to the WTO years concerns the nonapplication provision, which allows a member not to apply the GATT as a whole or its schedule of concessions to an acceding member. In the GATT years, a contracting party could not invoke this provision after it had entered into bilateral negotiations with the acceding party. Under WTO rules, however, this provision can be invoked even after bilateral negotiations have started.

14. These determinants are the national incomes of the two trading partners and the geographical distance between them. Other determinants that are usually included in such analyses include proxy variables to pick up the effect of two nations sharing a common language and a common border and their respective memberships in regional trading agreements.

15. See, for example, Kennett, Evenett, and Gage (2005).

16. That is, to Canada, the members of the European Union, Japan, and the United States. Given the delays in the availability of international trade data, in 2004 Bulgaria and Ecuador were the only medium-sized nonlandlocked countries to join the WTO for which five years of post-accession trade data were available. The choice of these countries was, therefore, not arbitrary.

17. See, for example, Bacchetta and Drabek (2002).

18. The experiences of six developing countries in organizing for WTO accession can be found

in Evenett (2005a). Evenett (2005b) summarizes the interventions of several developing country participants on this subject at a joint World Bank-GTZ workshop held in November 2004. See Zarcone, Fink, and Primo Braga (2005).

19. It is said that certain developing countries have successfully used this approach in their WTO accession negotiations.

20. See, for example, Michalopoulos (2002) and Kennett, Evenett, and Gage (2005).

21. These Guidelines call on existing members to exercise restraint in seeking concessions on trade in goods and services from acceding LDCs. See WTO (2002).

References

Anderson, Kym, and W. Martin. 2005. "Agricultural Trade Reform and the Doha Development Agenda." Unpublished paper, World Bank, Washington, DC.

Bacchetta, Marc, and Zdenek Drabek. 2002 "Effects of WTO Accession on Policy-Making in Sovereign States: Preliminary lessons from the Recent Experience of Transition Countries." Staff Working Paper ERSD-2002-02, WTO, Geneva.

Evenett, Simon J. (ed.). 2005a. "Preparing for WTO Accession: Insights from Development Countries." Unpublished manuscript. Research project sponsored by the International Development Research Centre.

———. 2005b. "Summary of Participants' Remarks and Recommendations." Prepared after a Joint World Bank-GTZ workshop on WTO accession matters, Berlin, November 17-19, 2004. Unpublished manuscript. Deutsche Gesellschaft für Technische Zusammenarbeit (GTZ)

Finger, J. Michael, Melinda D. Ingco, and Ulrich Reincke. 1996. *The Uruguay Round: Statistics on Tariff Concessions Given and Received*. Washington, DC: World Bank.

Grynberg, Roman, Victor Ognivtsev, and Mohammad A. Razzaque. 2002. "Paying the Price for Joining the WTO: A Comparative Assessment of Service Sector Commitments by WTO Members and Acceding Countries." Economic Paper 54, Commonwealth Secretariat, London.

Kennett, Maxine, Simon J. Evenett, and Jonathan Gage. 2005. "Evaluating WTO Accessions: Legal and Economic Perspectives." Unpublished manuscript. Research project sponsored by the International Development Research Centre.

Marchetti, Juan A. 2004. "Developing Countries in the WTO Services Negotiations," Staff Working Paper ERSD-2004-06, WTO, Geneva.

Michalopoulos, Constantine. 2002. "WTO Accession." In *Development, Trade, and the WTO: A Handbook*, ed. Bernard M. Hoekman, Philip English, and Aaditya Mattoo. Washington, DC: World Bank.

Rose, Andrew. 2003. "Which International Institutions Promote International Trade?" CEPR Discussion Paper no. 3764. London, Centre for Economic Policy Research. http://www.cepr.org/pubs/dps/DP3764.asp.

Subramanian, Arvind, and Shang-Jin Wei. 2003. "The WTO Promote Trade, Strongly But Unevenly." IMF Working Paper WP/03/185, International Monetary Fund, Washington, DC.

WTO (World Trade Organization). 1995. "Accession to the World Trade Organization." WT/ACC/1. Geneva.

———. 2002. "Accession of Least Developed Countries." WT/COMTD/LDC/12. Geneva.

———. 2004a. "Technical Note on the Accession Process." WT/ACC/10/Rev. 2. Geneva.

———. 2004b. "Technical Note on the Accession Process: State of Play and Information on Current Accessions." WT/ACC/11/Rev. 4. Geneva.

———. 2004c. "Doha Work Programme." WT/L/579. Geneva.

Zarcone, Fabrizio, Carsten Fink, and Carlos A. Primo Braga. 2005. "Technical Assistance and WTO Accession: Lessons from Experience." Prepared after a Joint World Bank-GTZ workshop on WTO accession matters, Berlin, November 17-19, 2004. Draft manuscript.

Further Reading
Bhattasali, Deepak, William Martin, and Li Shantong (eds.). 2004. *China and the WTO: Accession, Policy Reform, and Poverty Reduction Strategy.* New York: World Bank and Oxford University Press.
Goldstein, Judith, Douglas Rivers, and Michael Tomz. 2003. "How Does the Trade Regime Affect International Trade?" Unpublished paper, Department of Political Science, Stanford University.
Hamada, Koichi. 2004. "China's Entry into the WTO and Its Impact on the Global Economic System." In *Doha and Beyond: The Future of the Multilateral Trading System*, ed. Mike Moore. Cambridge: Cambridge University Press.
Lissovolik, Bodgan, and Yaroslav Lissovolik. 2004. "Russia and the WTO: The 'Gravity' of Outsider Status." Working Paper WP/04/159, International Monetary Fund, Washington, DC.
Rose, Andrew. 2002b. "Do WTO Members Have More Liberal Trade Policy?" NBER Working Paper 9347. National Bureau of Economic Research, Cambridge, MA.
Rose, Andrew. 2004. "Do We Really Know That the WTO Increases Trade?" *American Economic Review* 94 (March): 98-114.

Annex 1. Countries currently seeking accession to the WTO (with application date)

Europe and Central Asia	Middle East and North Africa	East Asia and Pacific	Sub-Saharan Africa	South Asia	Latin America and the Caribbean
Russia (June 1993)	Algeria (Jun. 1987)	Vietnam (Jan. 1995)	Sudan* (Oct. 1994)	Bhutan* (Sep. 1999)	Bahamas (May 2001)
Belarus (Sep 1993)	Saudi Arabia (Jun. 1993)	Tonga (Jun. 1995)	Seychelles (May 1995)	Afghanistan* (Dec. 2004)	
Ukraine (Nov 1993)	Lebanon (Jan. 1999)	Vanuatu*⁽ᵃ⁾ (Jul. 1995)	Cape Verde* (Nov. 1999)		
Uzbekistan (Dec 1994)	Yemen* (Apr. 2000)	Lao PDR* (Jul. 1997)	Ethiopia* (Jan. 2003)		
Kazakhstan (Jan 1996)	Libya (Jun. 2004)	Samoa* (Apr. 1998)	Sao Tome and Principe* (May 2005)		
Azerbaijan (June 1997)	Iraq (Dec. 2004)				
Bosnia-Herzegovina (May 1999)	Iran (May 2005)				
Andorra (July 1999)					
Tajikistan (May 2001)					
Serbia ⁽ᵇ⁾ (Feb 2005)					
Montenegro (Feb 2005)					

Note: [a] The Working Party on the Accession of Vanuatu concluded its work on 29 October 2001. Vanuatu has not, however, followed up on its accession.
[b] Serbia and Montenegro made a joint application on January 2001. In February 2005 they withdrew that application and replaced it with two individual applications.
* = least developed country.
Source: Compiled by the authors on WTO data (2004a).

Annex 2. Chronological list of countries that have acceded to the WTO

No.	New member	Date of membership
1	Ecuador	Jan. 1996
2	Bulgaria	Dec. 1996
3	Mongolia	Jan. 1997
4	Panama	Sep. 1997
5	Kyrgyz Republic	Dec. 1998
6	Latvia	Feb. 1999
7	Estonia	Nov. 1999
8	Jordan	Apr. 2000
9	Georgia	Jun. 2000
10	Albania	Sep. 2000
11	Oman	Nov. 2000
12	Croatia	Nov. 2000
13	Lithuania	May. 2001
14	Moldova	Jul. 2001
15	China	Dec. 2001
16	Taiwan, China	Jan. 2002
17	Armenia	Feb. 2003
18	FYR Macedonia	Apr. 2003
19	Nepal	Apr. 2004
20	Cambodia	Oct. 2004

*Source:*Compiled by the authors on WTO data (2004a).

Regional Trade Agreements: Designs for Development

Richard Newfarmer

egional trade agreements (RTAs) are fundamentally altering the world trade landscape.[1] The number of agreements in force, now more than 200, has risen sixfold in just two decades (figure 1). Today, more than one-third of global trade takes place between countries that have some form of reciprocal RTA. The European Union and United States are playing a prominent role in this proliferation (figure 2). The Central American Free Trade Agreement is only the latest of more than a dozen U.S. RTAs.[2] The European Union, through its Economic Partnership Agreements, is using RTAs to restructure trading relations with the African, Caribbean, and Pacific countries that benefited from Cotonou preferences.

This chapter addresses two questions:

- What characteristics of RTAs strongly promote—or hinder—development for member countries?
- Does the proliferation of RTAs pose risks to the multilateral trading system? If so, how can those risks be managed?

Identifying what works: open regionalism

RTAs are often one component of a larger political effort to deepen economic relations with neighboring countries.[3] As such, they can create opportunities to expand trade through joint action to overcome barriers to trade, both institutional and policy-related. But the growth in RTAs also reflects the relative ease of making reciprocal reductions in border barriers when the participants are fewer and policymakers feel more in control of outcomes. RTAs also offer the flexibility to pursue trade-expanding policies not addressed well in global trading rules. RTAs therefore usually go beyond slashing tariffs to reduce trade impediments associated with standards, customs and border crossings, and regulations affecting trade in services—as well as broader rules that improve the overall investment climate.

Because RTAs often form cornerstones of larger economic and political efforts to increase regional cooperation, RTAs can help motivate and reinforce broader reforms in domestic policy; they can be designed to contribute to a political environment that is more conducive to stability, investment, and growth.

Not all RTAs create new trade and investment. Those with high external border protection may actually reduce members' trade overall even as trade within the group rises, a phenomenon known as trade diversion. When regional agreements consolidate high levels of external protection (figure 3), regional trade may expand, but at the expense of trade with lower cost suppliers. Figure 4 shows the effects of

Figure 1. South-South RTAs boom in number...

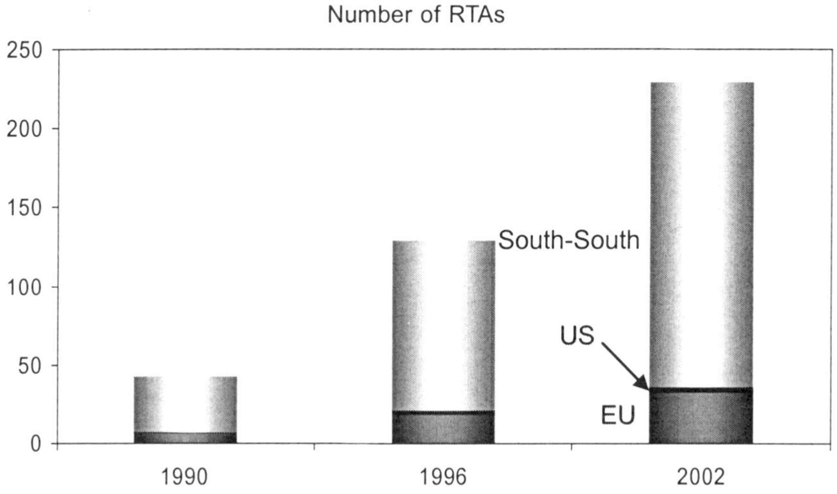

Number of RTAs

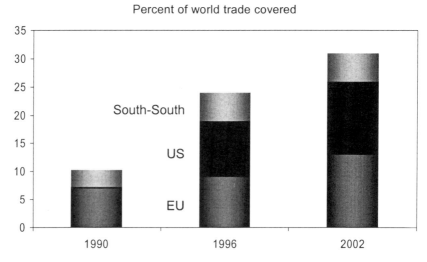

Source: WTO data and WTO staff.

Figure 2. ...but the EU and U.S. lead in trade coverage

Percent of world trade covered

Source: World Trade Organization.

various agreements, controlling for country size, income, proximity, and other factors, on trading patterns of member; agreements with relatively low external protection, such as those in the top half of figure 4 tend to increase all trade; those with higher levels of protection increased regional trade, but at the expense of more efficient trade with the world. A statistical analysis based on findings from econometric studies suggests that many agreements cost the economy more in lost trade revenues than they earn, because they discriminate against efficient, low-cost suppliers in nonmember countries. This finding does not take into account the potential dynamic gains, the positive effects associated with services liberalization, or any of the benefits from adopting new regulations. But it does underscore the point that regional agreements carry risks.

As agreements proliferate, a single country may become a member of several different agreements. The average African country, for example, belongs to four different agreements, and the average Latin America country belongs to seven. The result is a spaghetti bowl of overlapping arrangements (figure 5), each with differing rules of origin, tariff schedules, and periods of implementation. Those differences delay the passage through customs of goods covered by preferential arrangements, and longer processing times drive up the cost of trade.

Impact on trade

So what characteristics of RTAs lead to expanded trade and development? A prerequisite for the success of any trade policy is that it be part of a sound domestic policy framework. It is virtually impossible for entrepreneurs to take advantage of new opportunities—whether they originate in market access through an RTA, a multilateral agreement, or other sources—in the absence of macroeconomic stability, basic property rights, and adequate infrastructure regulation. Conversely, trade agreements can reinforce positive elements in the domestic reform program by anchoring policy to the agreement itself. But an RTA cannot substitute for sound domestic policies.

With prerequisites in place, the RTAs most likely to increase national incomes over time are those designed with:

* Low external most-favored-nation (MFN) tariffs
* Few sectoral and product exemptions
* Nonrestrictive rules-of-origin tests that build toward a framework common to many agreements
* Measures to facilitate trade
* Large ex-post markets
* Measures to promote new cross-border competition, particularly in services
* Rules governing investment and intellectual property that are appropriate to the development context
* Schedules of implementation that are put in effect on time.

Figure 3. Some agreements have much higher levels of external protection than others

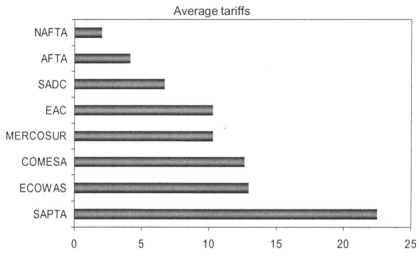

Note: Tariffs are import-weighted at the country level to arrive at PTA averages.
Source: UN TRAINS, accessed through WITS.

Figure 4. Intraregional trade may grow at the expense of extra regional trade

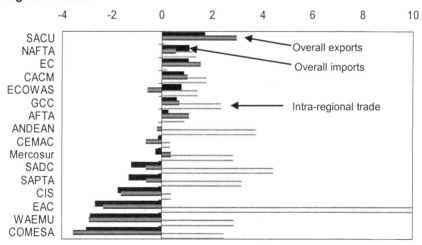

Note: In the chart above, the bars show the magnitude of the dummy variables, capturing respectively the extent to which intraregional trade, overall imports, and overall exports differ from the "normal" levels predicted by the gravity model on the basis of economic size, proximity, and relevant institutional and historical variables, such as a common language.
Source: World Bank, 2004.

Low external tariffs and wide coverage minimize the risks of trade diversion, while nonrestrictive rules of origin promote increased trade. The practice of excluding many agricultural products is common, but it can limit development payoffs. Trade facilitation measures, though worthwhile in and of themselves, receive more attention from policymakers when they are embedded in an RTA, and they often have positive trade-creating effects for all trade partners.

Well-designed agreements are of limited value if they are not implemented, and many RTAs have more life on paper than in reality. South–South agreements, in particular, are often poorly implemented. Monitoring mechanisms may be weak or not receive the sustained, high-level political attention necessary to drive institutional improvements related to tariff schedules, customs, and border crossings.

Against these benchmarks of success, it is difficult to give universally high marks to any single category of agreement. But in general, North–South agreements score better on implementation than South–South agreements.

Because North–South agreements can integrate economies with distinct technological capabilities and other differences in factor proportions, and because they usually result in larger post-agreement markets, their potential gains are usually greater. However, tighter rules of origin, more restrictive exclusions for particular sectors (such as agriculture), and a preoccupation with rules not calibrated to development priorities can undercut those benefits (figure 6).

North–South agreements, particularly those with the United States, have been more effective in locking in liberalization in services trade; they have pressed intellectual property rights beyond World Trade Organization (WTO) rules; and they have expanded the sphere of investment protections; but they contain few provisions to liberalize the temporary movement of labor.

South–South agreements sometimes outdo North–South deals at focusing on merchandise trade, minimizing exclusions, adopting less restrictive rules of origin, and lowering border costs. For example, the Caribbean Community (CARICOM) and the Common Market of Eastern and Southern Africa (COMESA) have reduced some border costs. But most South–South agreements have not adhered to implementation schedules, and they suffer from their small market size and economic similarity. And like the North–South agreements, South–South agreements rarely provide for the temporary movement of labor.

Consequences of RTAs for the multilateral system

The development consequences of RTAs are not limited to their effects on members; they also extend to the multilateral system. In one sense, RTAs are a step toward greater openness in the global trade system, in that they promote trade and generate new domestic constituencies with an interest in openness. Moreover, some regional trade policies—such as measures to improve customs, speed up transactions at ports or border crossings, and open services markets—can be

Figure 5. RTAs can complicate customs administration

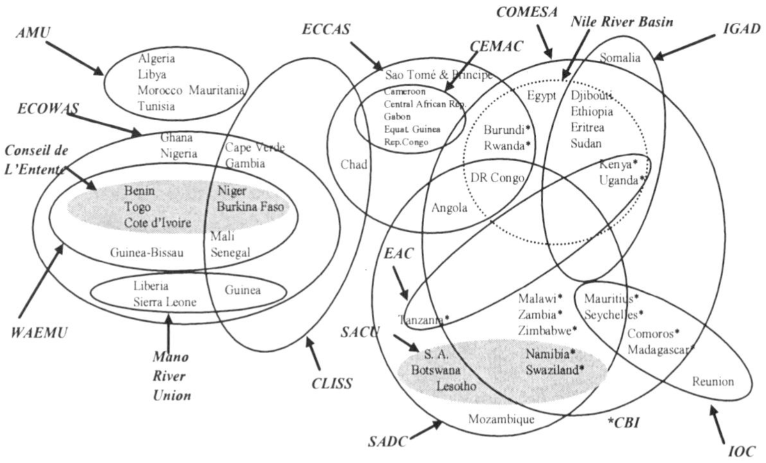

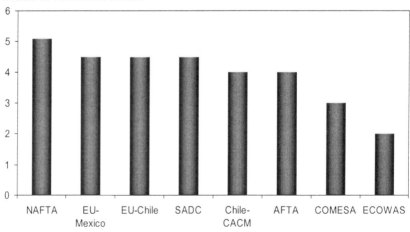

Source: Schiff and Winters (2003).

Figure 6. Rules of origin in North-South agreements are more restrictive than in South-South agreements

Index of restrictiveness

Note: Higher values of the index equals to more restrictive rules of origin.
Source: Derived from Estevadeordal and Suominen (2004).

beneficial in a nondiscriminatory way. Such measures can complement unilateral and multilateral policies.

However, this view overlooks the effects that RTAs can have on excluded countries. The fact is that preferences for some countries mean discrimination against others, whereas the General Agreement on Tariffs and Trade (GATT), born out of the sad experience of discrimination in the prewar years, is based on the principle of nondiscrimination.

Today, the adverse consequences for the excluded countries are much less severe than at GATT's inception, because tariffs and other barriers have come down sharply worldwide, mitigating the exclusionary effects of regional arrangements. (The exception—and it is not trivial—is agriculture.) Another mitigating factor is that many countries excluded by trade agreements between the United States and the European Union enjoy some degree of preferential access through voluntary preference schemes, such as the Generalized System of Preferences (GSP), the U.S. African Growth and Opportunity Act (AGOA), and the EU's Everything But Arms (EBA) program. To be sure, these programs lack the certainty of market access that MFN agreements and RTAs provide, because preferences are voluntary and subject to political whim, but they do mitigate the effects of exclusions for selected low-income countries. A third mitigating factor is that some developing countries—the spokes in the hub-and-spoke analogy—are signing bilateral agreements with each other and with other hubs.

Inevitably some countries get left out of trade agreements because they are not favored politically, because they cannot afford the costs of many separate negotiations, or because their region is less open. Countries as diverse as Bolivia, India, Mongolia, Pakistan, and Sri Lanka do not enjoy the same level of access to the United States or the EU as Chile, Jordan, and Mexico. When bilateral agreements are signed, they see their trade diminished.

RTAs can also undercut the incentives of governments to press for further multilateral trade liberalization. There is little evidence that major players in the current WTO negotiations have changed their negotiating positions or retreated from the multilateral process, even as they avail themselves of regional trade deals. However, as the discussions become politically difficult, the risk is ever present that they will abandon multilateralism in favor of regional agreements that are "good enough." The risk for smaller players, especially poor ones, is different. One consequence of the spread of regional agreements is that many poorer developing countries have diverted scarce negotiating resources to regional negotiations at the expense of more active participation in the Doha Round of global trade discussions. The average developing country belongs to five separate RTAs and is negotiating more. To protect hard-won market access under regional agreements, countries may choose to fight multilateral liberalization or even oppose further regional liberalization. A few small developing countries are indeed likely to lose advantages in preferential markets with further multilateral liberalization and may seek to scuttle global talks if their legitimate concerns are not addressed.

The importance of the Doha Round to "open regionalism"

The policy solution to these twin concerns—the need to design regional agreements that create trade and for regional agreements that have minimal exclusionary effects—comes together in the form of further reductions in MFN tariffs and other border barriers. An agreement that lowers border protection around the world promotes open regionalism by mitigating trade diversion. At the same time, it would diminish the exclusionary effects of discriminatory preferences built into regional agreements. The first order of business for the international community, therefore, is to accelerate progress on the Doha Agenda and to fill in the blanks of the July 2004 Framework Agreement with reductions in protection, especially for products produced by the world's poor.

For developing countries, a three-part strategy

Developing countries wishing to harness trade to their development strategy should see regional integration as one element in a three-pronged strategy that includes unilateral liberalization, multilateral liberalization, and regional liberalization.

Historically, unilateral liberalization, which is usually linked to a broader program of domestic reform, has accounted for most reductions in border protection. Most comprehensive trade reforms undertaken by large countries (Argentina, Brazil, and China in the early 1990s and, more recently, India) began as unilateral reforms designed to increase the productivity of the domestic economy. Many small countries, too, have adopted similar reforms. Of the 21 percentage point cut in average weighted tariffs of all developing countries between 1983 and 2003, unilateral reforms accounted for almost two-thirds. Tariff reductions associated with the multilateral commitments in the Uruguay Round accounted for about 25 percent, and the proliferation of regional agreements amounted to about 10 percent (figure 7).

Autonomous liberalization promotes global competitiveness by lowering costs of inputs, increasing competition from imports to drive productivity growth, and integrating the national economy into the global economy. In the presence of RTAs, autonomous trade reform loses none of its importance, because low border barriers minimize the risks of trade and investment diversion. They also promote trade in world markets, which is highly correlated with increases in intraregional trade, whether or not an RTA is in place.

Multilateral liberalization has the effect of translating domestic reforms into increased market access around the world. Collectively, developing countries stand to gain much more in the WTO arena than in any smaller regional market. Moreover, the multilateral forum is the only one in which developing countries, working together, can press for more open markets in agriculture and can seek disciplines on trade-distorting agricultural subsidies and contingent protection (i.e. anti-dumping measures and the like).

Some argue that RTAs are a good alternative to multilateral liberalization. They are not. Gains for all developing countries from RTAs, even under the most generous assumptions, are usually only a fraction of those from full multilateral liberalization. The appearance of benefits derives from the fact that countries signing early trade agreements with a high-income, large-market economy may benefit substantially, particularly if most other countries are excluded from preferential access. But those benefits wither as new countries sign additional agreements. In fact, developing countries would collectively lose if they were all to sign preferential agreements with the Quad (Canada, the European Union, Japan, and the United States) (figure 8) (see World Bank, 2004, Chapter 6). On balance, developing countries have a powerful collective interest in a successful Doha Round—even as they scramble to gain preferential market access to the Quad.

Forging policies on open regionalism is the third component of trade policy strategy. Desirable as multilateral liberalization is, the Doha Round is likely to realize only part of its development potential. For some types of policy, collective regional actions may be the first, best course and may result in effective nondiscriminatory benefits.[4] For example, RTAs can reduce regional political tensions, take advantage

Figure 7. Source of total tariff reduction, by type of liberalization, 1983–2003

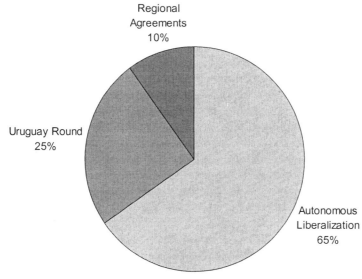

Regional
Agreements
10%

Uruguay Round
25%

Autonomous
Liberalization
65%

Source: World Bank (2004).

of scale economies in infrastructure provision, and lead to joint programs to improve border crossings related to liberalization in services.

But countries should sign on with their eyes wide open. The lessons of the study on which this note is based (and others before it)[5] are that—as with unilateral or multilateral policies—design and implementation determine the ultimate effects. It is important, therefore, to use trade policy to leverage domestic reforms that promote growth. It is essential that South–South agreements focus on some combination of full trade liberalization behind low external border protection, greater services deregulation and competition, and proactive trade facilitation measures that together benefit both intra- and extra-regional trade.

High-income countries and development

High-income countries, in order to realize their broad development objectives, must intensify their efforts to realize the development promise of the Doha Agenda. Doing so has the potential to open up trade, particularly in agriculture, in a way that would benefit low-income groups around the world. Because the high-income countries are the most powerful players in the system, they have a special interest in—and responsibility for—using effective multilateral reforms to discipline the discretionary aspects of the regional agreements. And if developing countries are to be convinced to concentrate scarce negotiating resources on the multilateral agenda the high-income countries may have to slow their efforts at expanding RTAs.

High-income countries should consider the following basic notions when designing agreements to promote development. First, the extensive exclusions for agriculture should be reversed. Doing so would bring income gains in rural areas of participating developing countries. Second, rules of origin should be more consistent and less restrictive across agreements to reduce the administrative barriers that increase the burden on customs administration and so often undermine agreements. Third, new regulations affecting investment and intellectual property should be appropriate to the level of development to reduce risks of undue enforcement costs.

Finally, trade-related technical assistance should be provided, not only in the implementation phase but also in the negotiating phase, to promote greater liberalization of services and lower MFN tariffs.

Acting collectively to mute the effects of discrimination

To minimize the discriminatory effects of RTAs at the multilateral level, all countries must assume greater responsibility for maintaining the multilateral system. The international community, working through the WTO, should revisit Article XXIV of its charter. If the stated disciplines cannot be enforced in the near term for collective political reasons, then increasing transparency and information should become a

Figure 8. Multilateral liberalization is far more beneficial than RTAs
Percent change in real income in 2015

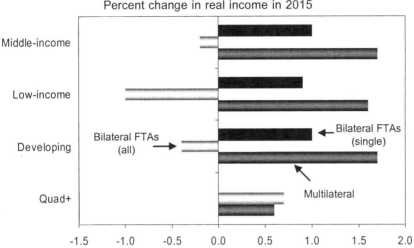

Note: Global refers to the global merchandise trade reform scenario, JBIL corresponds to the simulation where all developing countries sign bilateral agreements with the Quad-Plus, and BILAT corresponds to the simulation where the bilateral agreements are signed individually. Results un-weighted regional averages.
Source: World Bank reflect simulations with the Linkage model and GTAP release 6.04.

priority. At present, the WTO collects little or no information on the implementation of specific provisions—and on the trade consequences of those actions. It even fails to take advantage of extant public monitoring efforts in specific regions, which could inform its data collection effort. Collecting and publishing specific information on RTAs would allow members that find themselves excluded to challenge these agreements in the court of public opinion. Even the more modest goal of transparency will require building a new consensus and providing the staff of the WTO with more resources than are currently available. WTO members also should consider enhancing the existing rules to ensure that regional agreements have positive development and systemic outcomes. Enhancements (requiring only a modest tightening of current practice) might include setting quantitative indicators that define the term "substantially all trade." They might also include efforts to simplify and harmonize the rules of origin that are applied to both developed and developing countries. These items are on the Doha Agenda and may be ready for action.

Notes

1. This note draws from *Global Economic Prospects 2005*, Washington, DC: World Bank.

2. Negotiated as bilateral or multicountry treaties, regional trade agreements grant members assured preferential market access, usually at zero tariffs for eligible products. Following WTO convention, the term "regional trade agreement" includes both reciprocal bilateral free trade or customs areas and multicountry (plurilateral) agreements. These are distinct from nonreciprocal voluntary agreements, such as the generalized system of preferences (GSP). Also, for statistical purposes, unless otherwise noted, intra-EU trade is excluded from quantitative trade analysis. The EU is defined as including the 15 countries that belonged to the union before its enlargement in 2004.

3. See Devlin and Estevadeordal (2004) and Schiff and Winters (2003), among others.

4. See Robert Lawrence (1997), who develops the idea of subsidiarity as applied to regional agreements.

5. See Schiff and Winters (2003).

References

Devlin, Robert, and Antoni Estevadeordal. 2004. "Trade and Cooperation: A Regional Public Goods Approach." In *Regional Public Goods: From Theory to Practice*, ed. Antonio Estevadeordal, Brian Frantz, and Tam Robert Nguyen. Washington, DC: Inter-American Development Bank.

Lawrence, Robert. 1997. "Preferential Trading Arrangements: The Traditional and the New." In *Regional Partners in Global Markets: Limits and Possibilities of the Euro-Med Agreements*, ed. Ahmed Galal and Bernard Hoekman. London: CPER/ECES.

Schiff, Maurice, and L. Alan Winters. 2003. *Regional Integration and Development*. Washington, DC: World Bank.

World Bank. 2004. *Global Economic Prospects 2005: Trade, Regionalism, and Development*. Washington, DC: World Bank.

Further Reading

Hoekman, Bernard, and Maurice Schiff. 2002. "Benefiting from Regional Integration." In *Development, Trade and the WTO: A Handbook*, ed. Bernard Hoekman, Aaditya Mattoo, and Philip English. Washington, DC: World Bank.

Inter-American Development Bank. 2002. *Beyond Borders: The New Regionalism in Latin America, Economic and Social Progress in Latin America*. Washington, DC: World Bank

Krumm, Kathy, and Homi Kharas, 2004. *East Asia Integrates: A Trade Policy for Shared Growth*. Washington, DC: Oxford University Press and World Bank.

United Nations Economic Commission for Africa. 2004. *Assessing Regional Integration in Africa*. Addis Ababa: Economic Commission for Africa.

World Bank. 2003. *Trade, Investment, and Development in the Middle East and North Africa: Engaging with the World*. Washington. DC: World Bank.

NAFTA at 10 Years: Lessons for Development

Daniel Lederman, William F. Maloney and Luis Servén

The North American Free Trade Agreement (NAFTA) has raised Mexico's standard of living and helped bring the country closer to the levels of development of its NAFTA partners. Between 1994 and 2002, NAFTA made Mexico richer than it would have been without the agreement by about 4 percent of its gross domestic product (GDP) per capita (Lederman, Maloney, and Servén 2005). Statistical analyses suggest that the treaty resulted in a doubling of Mexico's global exports and an increase of 40 percent in foreign direct investment (FDI). As a result of the agreement, the amount of time required for Mexican manufacturers to adopt U.S. technological innovations was cut in half. Trade seems to be partially responsible for the moderate declines in poverty observed during the period and has likely had a positive effect on the number and quality of jobs. Nonetheless, NAFTA is not enough to ensure economic convergence among North American countries and regions because of limitations in its design and the need for crucial domestic reforms. These conclusions follow from careful empirical analysis of NAFTA's 10-year history.

Identifying NAFTA's effects is difficult for various reasons. First, only a relatively short time has elapsed since implementation of the agreement. Second, Mexico's post-NAFTA years started with the dramatic setback of the Tequila crisis in 1994–95, making it hard to disentangle the effects of the treaty on the Mexican economy. Third, care must be taken when extrapolating the NAFTA experience to the Central American Free Trade Agreement (CAFTA) or other FTAs in Latin America because of the considerable diversity of Latin American and Caribbean countries. The key priorities, necessary preparatory measures, and likely effects of accession thus differ considerably across countries.

The content of NAFTA

NAFTA eliminated most import tariffs and other restrictions to trade among Canada, Mexico, and the United States over its first 10 years. Mexico made the most substantial reforms, cutting average tariffs from about 12 percent in 1993 to 1.3 percent in 2001. U.S. tariffs on Mexican imports fell from 2.0 to 0.2 percent. In some instances, however, market access for Mexican exports remains inhibited by rules of origin, which set product- or sector-specific criteria for products to be considered as originating in a NAFTA country.

Like most trade agreements, NAFTA did not remove all trade distortions. While most agricultural imports from Canada and the United States have entered the

Mexican market duty free, Mexico's import-competing agriculture has benefited from income transfers and subsidies. Moreover, all member countries have continued to use anti-dumping and countervailing duties (AD/CVDs), and NAFTA allows the use of temporary safeguard duties when sudden import surges disrupt domestic production. For example, since 2003 Mexico has imposed temporary taxes on poultry imports from the United States. The agreement established various mechanisms to settle disputes related to the use of safeguards and AD/CVDs as well as other issues related to foreign investment and trade.

Beside trade-related measures, NAFTA includes a variety of provisions affecting investment flows, financial and other services, government procurement, and the protection of intellectual property rights. A full review of all these provisions was beyond the scope of the analysis upon which this note is based, but it is noteworthy that the agreement did not fully liberalize the financial system. In banking, the agreement allowed FDI to penetrate only up to a maximum of 25 percent of the banking system's aggregate capital. Although NAFTA did codify an open capital account for cross-border financial services, Mexico had already unilaterally liberalized its capital account prior to the implementation of the agreement in 1994.

The analytical challenge: identifying the impact of NAFTA
Mexican economic performance since 1980 has fluctuated widely, which partially explains the degree of controversy in the debate over NAFTA's impact on the Mexican economy. On the one hand, trade and FDI as shares of GDP were higher in the post-NAFTA period than in the previous years. But these rising trends also were evident during Mexico's unilateral trade reforms of the late 1980s. Moreover, trade grew quickly in the 1990s all over the world, and FDI rose in many other emerging markets. On the other hand, the growth of Mexican GDP per capita and real wages was unremarkable after NAFTA's implementation, and estimated poverty rates declined only after 1996. Of course, an important reason why growth and wages did not perform more favorably was the macroeconomic and financial crisis sparked by the devaluation of the peso in December 1994. Indeed, the evidence shows that trade and FDI cannot be blamed for the lackluster performance of wages, since wages in Mexico tended to be higher in sectors and regions that were and remain exposed to international competition and foreign investment.

Economic convergence in North America after NAFTA
Our research shows that trade liberalization has significantly benefited Mexico's economy, including the poor. NAFTA, along with the unilateral trade reforms of the 1980s, helped Mexico enter a process of economic convergence with respect to the United States, increasing trade, FDI, and growth. Real wages have recovered rapidly from the 1995 collapse, and the poverty rate has similarly improved. After 1995, the

gap in per capita GDP between Mexico and the United States has evolved more favorably than for other Latin American and Caribbean economies.

However, NAFTA is not enough to ensure economic convergence in North America. Mexico still suffers from important deficiencies in institutions and in education and innovation policies that constrain its long-run ability to catch up with its northern neighbors. In fact, econometric analysis indicates that the gap in the quality of public institutions is the biggest single factor behind the income gap between the two countries. Furthermore, the combined influences of all other factors that determine income in the long run—principally Mexico's status as an oil producer—actually suggest that Mexicans would be richer than their northern neighbors were it not for the institutional gap. The importance of institutions, which are not the primary focus of trade agreements, in determining income puts in perspective the economic benefits that should be expected from such treaties.

For the rest of Latin America and the Caribbean, the situation is very similar: institutional gaps are the biggest obstacle to income convergence with the United States. Institutional reforms, especially those intended to improve the rule of law and fight corruption, are therefore critical for the future economic development of the region.

While Mexico's institutions improved after NAFTA's implementation, improvements were observed throughout the region, and especially in Chile and Central America. This indicates that institutional improvements are not automatic by-products of North–South free trade agreements. Substantial unilateral efforts will be required to revamp Latin American and Caribbean institutions and quicken income convergence in the Americas.

Macroeconomic synchronization and policy coordination

In addition to long-run effects on per capita income and wages, trade agreements also have potentially major implications for macroeconomic fluctuations in member countries and, therefore, for the design of their macroeconomic policies. Through increased economic integration, the macroeconomic cycles of partner countries may become more closely synchronized—although this need not be the case, especially if the countries involved are very different. In the post-NAFTA years, fluctuations in the United States have accounted for an increasingly large fraction of the variation in Mexico's GDP growth.

Trade integration

Mexico's trade liberalization under NAFTA followed closely the unilateral reforms begun in 1986, after the country joined the General Agreement on Tariffs and Trade (GATT). Trade negotiations among Canada, Mexico, and the United States began informally in 1990, and more formally in 1991 after the United States administration obtained "fast track" authority from its legislature. It is therefore difficult to separate the effects of NAFTA on Mexico's volume and composition of trade from those of the unilateral reforms, especially given that the mere announcement of NAFTA talks could have had an impact on economic outcomes. Whatever the cause, in the 1990s Mexico's trade volume as a share of GDP became one of the highest in the region. Since catching up with Chile in this indicator of economic integration Mexico is fast approaching the high trade shares (around 100 percent of GDP) that are typically found among smaller economies, such as Costa Rica.

But the rapid expansion of Mexico's trade began just prior to NAFTA, around 1993. That expansion was accompanied by a marked change in the composition of trade, indicating that structural changes had occurred before the trade agreement. (For example, Mexico became a net exporter of machinery in 1992–93.) Those structural changes may have been delayed effects of the unilateral reforms of the mid-1980s; they may also reflect enhanced credibility and confidence resulting from the anticipated passage of NAFTA. In any case, econometric evidence suggests that NAFTA did not significantly (in the statistical sense) affect aggregate exports and imports between the United States and Mexico, while Mexico's global exports did increase significantly after NAFTA. Consequently, it seems that NAFTA helped consolidate ongoing trends by removing Mexico's longstanding policy biases against trade.

Agriculture

Contrary to some predictions, NAFTA has not had a devastating effect on Mexico's agriculture. In fact, both domestic production (measured in metric tons) and trade in agricultural goods rose during the post-NAFTA years. The expected negative consequences did not occur for at least three reasons. First, aggregate demand in Mexico and the United States grew in the latter half of the 1990s, thus allowing for simultaneous increases in Mexican production and imports. Second, some segments of Mexican agriculture experienced increases in land productivity. (This was the case for irrigated lands, but not for rain-fed lands.) Third, whereas the total amount of subsidies and income support for traditional agriculture did not rise during the NAFTA period, Mexico's unilateral reforms improved the efficiency of such subsidies. In particular, the *Programa para el Campo* (PROCAMPO), which became the main source of income support provided by the government for farmers who had historically produced import-competing crops such as maize and other grains, delinked the amount of public support from current and future production decisions.

Antidumping and countervailing duties

NAFTA's Chapter 19, which provides a panel-review mechanism for assessing whether AD/CVD decisions by the competent national agencies have been properly applied, has had no significant impact on U.S. AD/CVD activity against Canada or Mexico. U.S. AD/CVD actions against Canada and Mexico have been infrequent in the last ten years, as they were before NAFTA. On the other hand, the United States has traditionally been a major focus of Mexican antidumping cases; since the implementation of NAFTA, Mexico has significantly reduced its antidumping activity against both the United States and Canada. Nonetheless, all three countries should review their AD/CVD practices and move toward a system that relies more on the use of safeguard actions rather than AD/CVD investigations since NAFTA provisions themselves have not reduced the use of AD/CVD investigations by the United States.

Trade diversion resulting from NAFTA

When NAFTA was being negotiated in the early 1990s, many countries voiced concern that their exports to the United States (and, to a lesser extent, to Canada and Mexico) would be displaced by intra-NAFTA trade, even though many producers in those countries were more competitive than NAFTA producers. We find little evidence of trade diversion at the aggregate level, a conclusion that agrees with previous studies of NAFTA reviewed in the book (Lederman, Maloney and Servén 2005). The absence of trade diversion is also suggested by the fact that Mexico's export share in non-NAFTA markets rose as much as, or even more than, its share in NAFTA markets. Likewise, the U.S. market shares of exports from other Latin American and Caribbean economies were not systematically affected during the post-NAFTA period.

Although NAFTA may have reduced Asian imports of textiles and apparel into the U.S. market, trends in apparel trade provide no solid evidence that neighboring countries lost market share because of NAFTA preferences. Although all countries in Central America and the Caribbean faced the same change in U.S. preferences relative to those enjoyed by Mexico, their post-NAFTA performances showed considerable diversity. Most Central American countries managed to raise their export share in NAFTA apparel markets; Caribbean economies fared less well. This suggests that factors other than NAFTA preferences are responsible for much of this diverse post-NAFTA performance.

Among such factors, export incentives granted by several countries in export processing zones (EPZs) may have played an important role. It is thus possible—although hard to verify—that the upward trend in the region's apparel export shares might have been achieved at significant costs, such as forgone fiscal revenues and other potential distortions often associated with EPZs.

Capital

In addition to increasing trade, an FTA may deepen the degree of financial integration of member countries, prompting a substantial rise in foreign investment. Indeed, higher FDI is often one of the main benefits that prospective members expect from upcoming trade agreements with the United States. Mexico's experience with NAFTA appears to validate these expectations: aggregate FDI flows to Mexico did rise significantly after the agreement was signed, and econometric analysis suggests that the agreement played an instrumental role in the rise. On the whole, however, Mexico's FDI performance in the post-NAFTA period was not significantly above the Latin American norm, except in the years immediately following passage, thus suggesting that the impetus for FDI was positive but transitory. A separate statistical analysis, however, suggests that the accumulated effect of NAFTA on FDI into Mexico was such that overall FDI would have been about 40 percent lower by the year 2000 without NAFTA.

There is little evidence that increased investment in Mexico came at the expense of other countries in the region—that is, that NAFTA led to investment diversion. The neighboring countries of Central America and the Caribbean, which stood to lose the most from a redirection of FDI flows to Mexico, did not suffer generally as investment hosts after NAFTA.

Labor

The lessons on labor markets emerging from Mexico are necessarily tentative, but the overall evidence warrants cautious optimism. There is some evidence of convergence toward U.S. wage levels, but inference is made very difficult by the collapse of Mexican real wages following the Tequila crisis. Although manufacturing wages increased after unilateral liberalization and rose sharply in the years following NAFTA, there is no strong evidence that this was substantially affected by increased trade. On one hand, wages are higher and have grown faster in states with more trade, FDI, and *maquilas*. On the other hand, the apparently tighter integration of wages along the border, in traded and nontraded industries alike, suggests an important role for migration in driving the limited convergence seen so far. Chile provides a longer-run precedent: after its very similar version of the Tequila crisis following unilateral liberalization in the early 1980s, the country generated impressive real wage growth of 3.2 percent a year from 1986 to the present, with large declines in poverty rates.

Despite popular perception, there is little ground for concern that NAFTA, or FTAs in general, will have a detrimental effect on the availability or quality of jobs. In Mexico and throughout the region, there is little indication of higher unemployment, increased volatility of the labor market (after the initial adjustments), or increased informalization associated with trade liberalization. As is true of firms of the region generally, Mexican firms that are more exposed to trade tend to pay higher wages (adjusted for skills), are more formal, and invest more in training. The (probably temporary) widening of the wage gap between skilled and unskilled workers observed throughout the region can be seen as reflecting a welcome increase in the demand for skilled workers by new and upgrading firms.[1]

When NAFTA was signed, the Mexican labor market was characterized by fluctuations in real wages, which partly accounts for the low levels of unemployment during periods of sectoral reallocations and the 20-year low reached by 1999. Even during the Tequila crisis, Mexico kept unemployment low by allowing inflation to erode pact-guided wages. Arguably, this flexibility in real wages is the critical difference from countries such as Argentina and Colombia, where relatively rigid real wages contributed to high and sustained unemployment during macroeconomic crises in the 1990s. The experience of Mexico and other industrialized countries suggests that neither prolonged spells of unemployment nor degradation of job quality are necessary or even likely results of increased trade or an FTA, and adjustments to trade-related or other shocks can be facilitated by higher degrees of nominal wage flexibility.

This discussion raises two questions about side agreements on labor issues. First, given that Latin American labor legislation is generous by *industrialized country standards,* would it not be better for agreements to facilitate the transition to systems that both protect workers better and promote dynamic growth, rather than to insist on the enforcement of archaic structures? Second, and more fundamental given the increasing evidence that foreign and trade-oriented firms offer higher wages and better working conditions, should not the effort to improve labor standards focus on all sectors of the economy and be freestanding (perhaps coordinated by an organization like the International Labour Organization) rather than linked to particular trade agreements? In light of the potential for protectionist abuse of side agreements, both questions merit careful debate as other FTAs go forward.

Notes

1. The regionwide trends in the quality and availability of jobs, as well as the skill premium and its determinants, are amply documented in reports from the World Bank's Latin America and the Caribbean Region (World Bank 2001 and 2002).

References

Lederman, Daniel, William Maloney, and Luis Servén. 2005. *Lessons from NAFTA for Latin America and the Caribbean.* Palo Alto, CA: Stanford University Press.

U.S. International Trade Commission. 1997. *The Impact of the North American Free Trade Agreement on the U.S. Economy and Industries: A Three-Year Review.* Publication 3045. Washington, DC.

World Bank. 2001. *From Natural Resources to the Knowledge of Economy.* Latin American and Caribbean Studies, Washington, DC: World Bank.

———. 2002. *Closing the Gap in Education and Technology.* Latin American and Caribbean Studies, Washington, DC: World Bank.

Beyond Cotonou: Economic Partnership Agreements in Africa

Lawrence Hinkle, Mombert Hoppe, and Richard Newfarmer

n 2000, the Cotonou Agreement between the European Union and the former colonies that make up the Africa, Caribbean, and Pacific (ACP) countries laid out the framework for a new trade and development relationship, called Economic Partnership Agreements (Epas). The trade component of the 1975 Lomé convention, which offered ACP countries preferential access to EU markets, discriminated against other developing countries and thus was not WTO-compatible. (Lomé had been sustained only because other WTO members granted two waivers on the understanding that its preferences would be phased out.) Cotonou laid the basis for new, reciprocal, and WTO-consistent trading agreements between the European Union and six groupings of ACP states by 2008, the date of expiration of the waiver. The EPAs would replace the Lomé system of unilateral trade preferences with more comprehensive, modern, free trade agreements that would be legal under Article XXIV of the General Agreement on Tariffs and Trade (GATT).

The negotiations, proceeding fitfully but with increasing intensity for three years, have propelled to the surface serious concerns about the design of EPAs—among them loss of tariff revenues and diversion of trade and development resources, the latter because of commitments on the so-called Singapore issues.[1] Indeed, a poorly structured EPA could undermine development for all countries in the ACP group. At the same time, they also represent an opportunity for the ACP countries to harness the power of the trade negotiations to promote their internal regional development and gain additional access to European markets. To capitalize on that opportunity, however, both the ACP countries and the European Union will need to take steps to create a pro-development EPA. The ACP countries must develop negotiating strategies to harness the EPAs to their domestic reform program; the European Union must be willing to provide greater market access through nonrestrictive rules of origin, to expand "aid for trade," and to defer its own preferences in ACP markets until important MFN liberalization has occurred in the regions.

Recasting the EU-ACP trade and development relationship

The ACP countries have enjoyed a special relationship with the European Union for half a century. Since 1963, two Yaoundé and four Lomé conventions (I–IV) granted preferential access to the European market. The Yaoundé conventions dealt with development assistance through the European Development Fund (EDF), whereas the Lomé conventions introduced preferential trade access for ACP countries to the (expanding) European Union. The Cotonou Agreement broadened the relationship between the two groups of countries by strengthening the political and development dimensions.

The EPAs are intended to replace the European Union's present unilateral preferences with the ACP group with six reciprocal free trade agreements. Taken together those agreements will constitute a comprehensive approach to development (including aid for trade), covering trade in goods and services, investment, competition, trade facilitation (the four Singapore issues), and some aspects of intellectual property rights. They will allow for some differentiation between LDCs and non-LDCs, primarily during the phasing-in of reforms of external tariffs and other regulatory measures. To be consistent with WTO Article XXIV, the preferential free trade agreements are to be based on the principle of reciprocity in "substantially all trade," which, although nowhere defined, is widely understood to mean about 90 percent of the current bilateral EU–ACP trade flows.

The division of the 79 ACP countries into six negotiating groupings[2] was not based solely on negotiating convenience. The creators of the Cotonou Agreement saw the potential of forming larger regional units from states too small to produce many goods and services competitively. Larger units would also be able to provide the government regulatory services necessary to support growth. (The average population of the nations in the ACP group was about 9.4 million in 2002, with a GDP of about $5.6 billion.) The concept was to create "North–South–South" agreements linking the European Union, the world's largest customs union, with aspiring customs unions in the South. At the moment, all six groupings consist of partially overlapping free trade areas, customs unions, and nonaffiliated countries (table1).[3]

Negotiating issues and obstacles
The negotiations will have to deal soon with five related sets of problems, the resolution of which will determine the effectiveness of any EPA:
- Poorly integrated regional markets for products.
- Regional groupings with varying levels of MFN protection, and tariff peaks.
- Losses in tariff revenues associated with EPA agreements.
- Unintegrated—and in some cases unliberalized—services markets, and the Singapore issues.
- Infrastructure and aid for trade.

Regional integration of product markets
Within Sub-Saharan Africa, intraregional trade is limited. Only 15 percent of merchandise exports go to other countries in the region, and only 10 percent of merchandise imports originate in the region.[4] Even though regional agreements have proliferated, significant barriers to trade remain, mostly because of imperfect implementation of agreements, high border costs, restrictive rules of origin even

within customs unions, and poor infrastructure. None of the four free trade agreements involved in the EPA negotiations has unimpeded commerce among its members.[5] The existing customs unions are far from perfect; all, save the South African Customs Union (SACU), still collect tariffs on internal trade and maintain other barriers to intraregional trade. Moreover, agreements on the reduction of intraregional barriers—as well as on implementation of common external tariffs (CETs)—are rife with product exceptions and long "transition" periods.

Other internal barriers stem from the absence of common standards and systems of certification and from inconsistent (and inconsistently applied) tax policies. An important internal agenda includes reaching agreement on product standards, mechanisms to ensure compliance and resolve disputes, mutual recognition of trade policies, and adopting internally consistent rules of origin. All are prerequisites for effective regional integration.

Crucial role of MFN tariffs

The average tariffs of some countries of Sub-Saharan Africa are still two to three times higher than tariffs in the most competitive developing countries. Furthermore, because of (often prohibitive) peak tariff rates in many countries and the proclivity to apply these rates to *all* imports that compete with domestically produced goods, the protective effects of tariffs in the region are substantially greater than average tariff rates suggest. High levels of protection mean that the European Union retains market share despite higher costs—because of preferences.

Moving toward a CET is difficult in any political context—especially where large differences in applied tariffs exist among members of the group. In the Eastern and Southern African Region (ESA) group, average tariffs range from Madagascar's 4.6 percent to more than 20 percent for Burundi, the Seychelles, and Sudan (table 1). While tariffs are relatively similar for most of the ECOWAS countries, Nigeria's are nearly three times those of (Union Économique et Monétaire Ouest Africaine) UEMOA. Moreover, Nigeria applies several bans on imports.

Differences emerge even more starkly when one looks at the structure of the tariffs that protect different categories of goods. Nigeria's and Ghana's unweighted tariff averages in several categories are compared to those of the UEMOA countries in figure 1. On average Ghana's tariffs exceed UEMOA's by 1 percent, whereas Nigeria's tariffs exceed UEMOA's by 17.8 percent. Figure 1 also shows that relative protection (protection on a particular category relative to average protection) differs significantly between UEMOA, Nigeria, and Ghana, the three largest economies in ECOWAS. In the Caribbean, tariff rates in the Bahamas are usually much higher than in other countries (figure 2).

These patterns will complicate the introduction of a CET, for not only must average tariff levels converge, but the *structure* of tariffs must converge as well. Defining a common list of sensitive products to be excluded from the negotiations

Table 1. Tariffs in ACP countries by EPA constellations

Central African Group	Simple average	CARIFORUM Group	Simple average
CEMAC		OECS	
Cameroon , Central African	18.0	*Antigua and Barbuda*	9.6
Republic, Chad, Congo (Rep.),		*Dominica*	9.9
Gabon , Equ. Guinea		*Grenada*	10.5
Sao Tome and Principe [a]	n.a.	*St. Kitts and Nevis*	9.4
		St. Lucia	8.9
		St. Vincent and the Gren.	9.8
ECOWAS Group		*Bahamas, The*	30.6
UEMOA		*Barbados*	13.1
Benin, Burkina Faos, *Côte*	12.0	*Belize*	10.5
d'Ivoire , Guinea-Bissau, Mali,		*Guyana*	11.0
Niger, Senegal, Togo		Haiti	n.a.
Cape Verde	n.a.	*Jamaica*	7.2
The Gambia	12.7	*Suriname*	17.5
Ghana	13.1	*Trinidad and Tobago*	7.9
Guinea	6.5	*Dominican Republic*	8.5
Liberia	n.a.		
Nigeria	30.0	**Pacific Group**	
Sierra Leone	14.9	*Cook Islands*	n.a.
Mauritania [b]	10.9	East Timor	n.a.
		Fiji	7.3
		Kiribati	n.a.
ESA Group		*Marshall Islands*	n.a.
EAC		*Micronisia*	n.a.
Kenya, Uganda	12.3	*Nauru*	n.a.
Burundi	23.4	*Niue*	n.a.
Comoros	n.a.	*Palau*	n.a.
Djibouti *a)*	30.8	*Papua New Guinea*	6.0
Congo, Dem. Rep.	12.0	Samoa	n.a.
Eritrea	7.9	Solomon Islands	22.2
Ethiopia	18.8	*Tonga*	n.a.
Madagascar	4.6	Tuvalu	n.a.
Malawi	13.1	Vanuatu	13.8
Mauritius	18.4		
Rwanda	17.4	**SADC Group**	
Seychelles	28.3	SACU	
Sudan	24.5	*Botswana* , Lesotho,	11.4
Zambia	14.0	*Namibia, Swaziland, South*	
Zimbabwe	16.4	Angola	8.8
		Mozambique	12.1
		Tanzania (also EAC)	12.3

Note: Names of least developed countries are printed in roman type: non-LDCs are in italics.
a. Sao Tome is not a member of CEMAC.
b. Mauritania is not a member of ECOWAS.
Source: UNSD COMTRADE and UNCTAD TRAINS data for most recent years available, except as follows. Data for Djibouti, Fiji, Guinea, Rwanda, and the Solomon Islands are from WTO IDB. Data for The Gambia, Sierra Leone, and South Africa are from WTO Trade Policy Review. Data for Kenya, Tanzania, and Uganda are from EAC Secretariat.

with the European Union will involve complex negotiations because protection differs from country to country.[6]

Falling tariff revenue

Tariff revenues average 1 percent of GDP and 7–10 percent of government revenue in Sub-Saharan Africa, a heavy level of dependence. A few governments (including those of The Gambia and Cape Verde) count on tariffs for up to 20 percent of their revenue.

With EU products representing 40 percent of total imports in the region, eliminating all tariffs on EU imports would considerably lower tariff revenues—in some cases by as much as 15–20 percent of government revenue. The net effect on budgets depends on the change in import structure and some additional factors. Trade diversion from external to EU suppliers would further increase the loss of tariff revenues, as the share of EU imports is expected to rise by 9 percent in the median West African country (Busse and others 2004).[7] Revenue losses as a share of total government revenue in West Africa would be 5 percent or less in five countries, 5–10 percent in another five, and 10 percent or greater in four (Busse and others 2004). Expected revenue losses differ by region. In SADC they would be less than 2.5 percent of total government revenue; in East Africa, between 0.7 and 11.8 percent (table 2).

Figure1. Nigeria's tariffs are higher than Ghana's or UEMOA's

Percentage point difference in average tariff rates compared to UEMOA

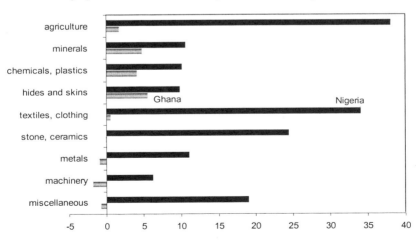

Source: UNCTAD TRAINS data base accessed through WITS; World Bank staff calculations.

Figure 2. Tariff peaks differ in CARIFORUM
Average tariff rates by category (percent)

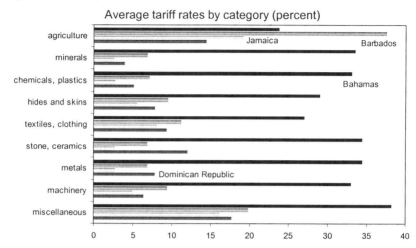

Source: UNCTAD TRAINS data base accessed through WITS; World Bank staff calculations.

Although significant for a few countries, the revenue loss problem is easily overstated. First, the granting of tariff exemptions is widespread in Sub-Saharan Africa. Eliminating those exemptions would limit revenues losses. Busse, Borrmann, and Grossmann (2004) find that on average tariff collections are 70 percent or less of potential tariff revenues for ECOWAS countries; collection efficiency was below 30 percent in Ghana and below 40 percent in Guinea-Bissau. These figures suggest that improvements in tariff administration could dampen the effect of reduced tariff rates. Second, the revenue effect of eliminating tariffs on imports from the European Union could be limited by excluding from preferential liberalization those imports for which the tariffs yield the most revenue. Third, to the extent that countries do not currently levy value-added tax (VAT) and excises on imports, they could impose them (or improve the administration of existing taxes or raise them). Fourth, the implementation period of the EPAs is likely to be 12 years or longer; with assistance in the form of aid for trade, there should be a reasonable amount of time for strengthening other components of the public revenue system to offset reductions in tariff revenues. Finally, the transition from a revenue system heavily dependent upon tariffs to one that is more broadly based and diversified is a necessary step for all countries integrating into the global economy. The aid for trade component of the EPAs could provide the opportunity to make the necessary transition with greater technical and financial assistance than is normally available.

Services and the Singapore issues

Trade-related services are less efficient in Sub-Saharan Africa than in other regions. Fifty-two percent of firms report unreliable electricity supply as a constraint, compared with 42 percent in South Asia and 24 percent in East Asia and Latin America (World Bank 2005). The Economic Report on Africa 2003 (UNECA 2003) comes to a similar conclusion: electricity and transport costs are seen by 65 percent of surveyed businesses as restrictively high. Charges for electricity, telecommunications, transport, and water are often higher in low-income countries than elsewhere, and access is limited. Prices are high and access low for other trade-related services, as well—including financial and transport services. In Botswana and Zimbabwe, for example, charges for both air and sea freight are 50–100 percent higher than in neighboring South Africa; telecommunications charges in Kenya and Botswana are 80 percent higher; and electricity charges in

Table 2: Revenue loss as a share of total government revenue as a result of EPAs

	UNECA (2005)	Nielsen (2005)	Busse et al. (2004) [a]	Karingi et al. (2005)		UNECA (2004)	Khandelwal (2004)
ECOWAS					**ESA**		
Benin	6.7	9.7	8.6		Burundi		6.9
Burkina Faso	6.1	4.2	5.6		Comoros		6.3
Cape Verde		21.2	19.8		Kenya		7.7
Cote d'Ivoire	5.6	8.1	4.6		Madagascar		1.9
Gambia		16.7	21.9		Malawi		3.3
Ghana	19.2	7.7	10.3		Mauritius		11.8
Guinea		6.2	4.9		Rwanda		10.2
Guinea-Bissau	19.4	4.1	5.6		Uganda		0.7
Mali	4.5	8.1	3.8		Zambia		4.0
Mauritania	7.1		6.3		**SADC**		
Niger	7.6	6.8	3.6		Angola	2.4	
Nigeria	2.3	3.3	2.5		Botswana	0.2	
Senegal	6.0	7.4	10.7		Lesotho	0.0	
Sierra Leone		8.5			Mozambique	1.5	
Togo	12.5	16.7	7.4		Namibia	0.5	
CEMAC [b]					Swaziland	0.4	
Cameroon				10.6	Tanzania	2.3	1.1
Congo				11.7			
Chad				13.6			

Notes: a. Estimations using medium scenario of Busse and others (2004).
b. Karingi and others (2005) report revenue shortfalls for all regions in monetary terms. Estimations provided here are expressed as a share of government revenue using most recent revenue figures from IMF International Financial Statistics.
Source: UNECA (2005), Nielsen (2005), Busse et al. (2004), Kaningi et al. (2005), UNECA (2004), Khandelwal (2004); IMF IFS.

Botswana are 300 percent higher than in South Africa. Access to telephone services remains low, with the number of mobile phone subscribers averaging 58 per 1,000 inhabitants in 2002 (and ranging from 0.2 in Niger to 447 on the Seychelles).

Regional integration can help overcome these problems. In some regions, markets are too small to realize full economies of scale in network services and their regulations. Already the ECOWAS countries, for example, are exploring a power pooling arrangement. Second, regions can establish a regulatory framework that allows for greater potential competition, with positive effects on prices and efficiency. But implementation of regional programs has been fitful. EPAs, properly designed, might help bring them to fruition.

Related to services, the Cotonou Agreement envisages that investment, competition, transparency in government procurement, and trade facilitation—the so-called Singapore issues—will be included in EPAs. Trade facilitation is broadly accepted, but there is little agreement yet between the European Union and the ACP countries on how to approach the other three in the EPA negotiations. Several governments in Africa have taken the position that because they have been dropped from the global agenda, they should also be left off the EPA agenda.

Infrastructure and institutions: aid for trade
A significant constraint to export expansion evident in all diagnostic studies of the ACP countries is the inadequacy of roads, railroads, ports, and trade-related institutions. These inadequacies saddle exporters with high costs of inputs, high transport costs, and costly delays in reaching global markets. Increased donor development assistance can alleviate these supply-side constraints.

The European Union has pledged an additional €300 million annually in aid for trade, bringing its annual giving to €1 billion. However, it has steadfastly insisted that additional assistance should not be discussed in the EPA negotiations for fear of turning a discussion of policies into a negotiation over money. While this concern is understandable, the tactic has left negotiators from the EPA groups with diminished incentives to engage in the process and without the certainty that an EPA agreement will contain provisions to address supply-side constraints.

Risks of a poorly structured EPA—and alternatives to an agreement
Because tariffs are relatively high and internal barriers within groupings still prevalent, enacting EPAs without prior action on these issues could result in a hub and spoke pattern of trade integration, trade diversion, and, in a worst-case scenario, net losses of income. Karingi and others (2005) estimate that the amount of trade diversion would be significant if undertaken without modifications to existing MFN tariff structures even though, on balance, more trade would be created. (The authors point out that their estimations are partial and exclude services, so the results must

be treated with caution). Without action on external and internal barriers, giving EU firms preferential access to ACP markets could well divert trade to EU producers from more efficient producers based, say, in Asia, nearby African countries, and even the United States. If there is insufficient competition among EU suppliers, liberalizing trade with the European Union might not lead to lower consumer prices but rather to a transfer of tariff revenue to EU producers. This risk is aggravated by the fact that many national markets in Africa are small and costly to reach. Competition for such markets, which are often dominated by a single external supplier, is not likely to increase after the implementation of the EPAs. Therefore, in cases where external tariffs are still high, ACP countries will need to reduce those tariffs on an MFN basis before implementing preferential reductions in tariffs on imports from the European Union.

Out of 46 African countries, 33 are least developed countries (LDCs) that qualify for preferences under the European Union's Everything But Arms (EBA) program. This initiative grants duty-free, quota-free access to the EU market, leaving the LDCs with little incentive to join the EPAs. For the non-LDCs, signing EPAs would *maintain* access to EU markets or increase it to include those products not covered by the Cotonou Agreement (a total of 919 tariff lines in sensitive sectors). Without an EPA, non-LDC countries would revert to GSP preferences, which generally have narrower product coverage and lower preference levels. The effect on economic growth when switching from Cotonou-type to the General System of Preferences (GSP), however, is not likely to be large for most non-LDCs. Hinkle and Newfarmer (2005) find that the value of the tariff savings under Cotonou as compared to GSP was substantial for only three non-LDC countries in 2002. Those values were 16 percent for the Seychelles (fish), 20 percent for Mauritius (sugar and knit garments), and 39 percent for Swaziland (meat). Moreover, because senior EU officials have indicated that no ACP country would see its market access reduced if the Cotonou preferences were to expire without an EPA being signed, the European Union may look for other ways to maintain open markets rather than revert to the GSP. Nonetheless, reversion to the GSP could inhibit diversification to the extent that new product exports did not automatically qualify for the GSP. If the alternative to concluding an EPA were simply a (temporary) return to GSP or EBA preferences, the ACP countries would lose relatively little in terms of market access.

However, if governments were to opt out of the EPA negotiation process, they would miss a potentially valuable opportunity to spur regional integration and to gain greater access to the EU.

A spur to regional integration—and integration with the world
An important contribution that EPAs could make to ACP development would be to spur adoption of policies that speed both regional integration and integration with the global economy. To achieve this objective, policy-makers in the various regional

groupings have to adopt a comprehensive strategy that harnesses the EPA process to domestic reforms needed to promote integration, improve competitiveness, and accelerate growth. This requires that the regional groupings work together in formulating programs of outward-oriented regional integration, and then forging this into a strategy that links these to the EPA timetable. This strategy would allow governments to lever domestic reforms to the cause of greater market access to the EU.

Epas and market access

EPas can offer ACP countries two important improvements in market access over the EBA-plus-GSP alternative: *more favorable rules of origin* and *certainty of access*. The European Union has long posited that the goal of the demanding rules of origin under both the Cotonou Agreement and the European Union's GSP (and hence EBA) is industrial development and integration in beneficiary countries. But two decades of restrictive rules of origin have not induced integrated industrial developments in ACP countries or contributed to more dynamic export performance. They have not led to the emergence of an efficient ACP-wide textile industry, despite the presence of cotton producers in the ACP group. Generally the penalty for using eligible inputs (lower quality, higher prices) often exceeds the benefits of EU preferences, while the small size of most ACP markets makes vertical integration uneconomic. Even when it is economically feasible to comply with the production requirements of the European Union's rules of origin, problems in proving origin due to weak customs controls and costly documentation requirements have stopped exporters from taking advantage of preferential access. As a result of this and other factors, exports of ACP countries have remained concentrated in few, mainly unprocessed products.

If EPA groups could obtain *more favorable rules of origin* under EPAs, they could markedly improve their access to the EU market. Moreover, even the prospect of change would encourage both LDCs and non-LDCs to pursue EPA negotiations, since less restrictive rules could, among other things, facilitate the export of clothing, as the U.S. African Growth and Opportunity Act (AGOA) has done. A uniform criterion of 10 percent value added—as proposed by the Blair Commission for Africa—or a simple change-of-tariff-heading rule could significantly increase export opportunities for ACP countries. Allowing global cumulation from all other developing countries, including ACP neighbors outside the EPA, would further spur exports.[8]

EPAs can also provide greater *certainty of market access* than can voluntary preferences. Enrollment of a product in the positive lists under the GSP is subject to periodic review and withdrawal, creating uncertainty that deters the private investment needed to diversify export production in the ACP countries. Although EBA preferences last for as long as a country remains an LDC, successful exporting countries can, as experience has shown, quickly graduate from LDC status and thus to the less favorable GSP.

Eight elements of a pro-development EPA strategy

To realize these twin objectives of accelerated integration and greater market access to the EU, a pro-development EPA could be structured around the following eight elements, all fundamental to the development strategies of the countries involved:

- *A 10 percent value-added rule as a nonrestrictive rule of origin.* If the value-added requirement is higher, cumulation rules should be global to allow ACP producers maximum access to the world's lowest-cost inputs and to avoid putting regional suppliers outside the EPA group at a disadvantage.
- *Additional aid for trade.* This should take the form of a program of technical and financial assistance for trade facilitation, sanitary and phytosanitary standards, and other supply-side measures (such as infrastructure). Putting additional aid for trade on the table as part of an EPA negotiation could increase the incentive of all countries to enter into an arrangement.
- *MFN reductions in external tariffs.* MFN reductions in external tariffs should be phased in, consistent with regional development programs.
  − Phases 1 and 2: Promote internal trade by progressively eliminating all internal barriers within customs unions and, for free trade agreements, adopt common nonrestrictive rules of origin.
  − Phases 1 and 2: Reduce MFN peak tariffs to the average levels to promote intra-African and other efficient trade with third parties.
  − Phases 2 and 3: Reduce to East Asian levels average levels of MFN tariffs within the EPA grouping.
  − Phase 3: Enact EU preferences. Making this the final step lessens the risks of trade diversion and hub-and-spokes development.
- *Reform of tax administration and intraregional tax policy.* A program to harmonize tax structures through gradual but purposeful reform of tax administration and intraregional tax policy would promote regional integration and replace lost tariff revenues. Such a program could complement tariff and customs reforms at the regional level, with support through new aid for trade.
- *Liberalized trade in services.* A phased, region-specific program of services liberalization could expand access to efficient trade-related services, such as telecommunications, electricity, and transport. To avoid entrenching monopolies, liberalization should be done on an MFN basis.
- *Trade facilitation.* A program of trade facilitation measures—for example, improvements in customs, ports, border posts—should be linked to intraregional programs to lower the costs of trading, with special attention to lowering the transit costs of landlocked countries. The program, a high priority for all regions,

should include specific benchmarks for implementation.

* *Temporary movement of persons.* The temporary movement of persons to supply services (mode 4 of the General Agreement on Trade in Services), although not part of the current EPA negotiations, may be easier to deal with in regional arrangements than in multilateral talks.

* *Rules on investment and intellectual property rights (IPR).* EPAs could include new IPR rules and rules on investment, but these should be calibrated in accordance with a region's capacity to implement them—and to benefit from them. Agreements could include competition policies consistent with national development strategies and in accordance with a region's implementation capacity.

Conclusion

The European Union and the ACP countries will have to work hard to achieve pro-development EPAs. Time is short, and much remains to be done. To succeed, the European Union must subordinate narrow commercial interests to its broader interests in supporting economic growth and regional integration in the ACP countries. It must be willing to provide greater market access through nonrestrictive rules of origin, to expand aid for trade, and defer its own preferences in ACP markets until important MFN liberalization has occurred there. Strong cooperation between trade negotiators and development experts of the EU would help to put development at the center of the EPAs and increase coherence of EU development policies. For their part, each EPA grouping must use the negotiating process to put forward internal reforms to promote their own competitiveness, regional integration, and growth, and to be willing to lock-in a program of implementation consistent with its own development priorities and pace of reform.

Notes

1. Investment, competition, transparency in government procurement, and trade facilitation have become known as the "Singapore issues."

2. Four of the ACP countries, Cuba, East Timor, Somalia, and South Africa, will not sign any EPA agreement.

3. There are some still unresolved issues concerning the EPA country groupings, especially among the two groupings in southern and eastern Africa. Several countries are members of both the Common Market of Eastern and Southern Africa (COMESA) and the Southern African Development Community (SADC). Tanzania withdrew from COMESA in 2000 and elected to join the SADC EPA group. However, it also entered into the East African Community (EAC), a customs union with Kenya and Uganda, both of which elected to join the ESA EPA group. Unless the key provisions of the SADC and ESA EPAs turn out to be identical, Tanzania will either have to withdraw from EAC or switch to the ESA EPA grouping. The latter step is apparently under consideration and is strongly encouraged by the European Commission and the EAC secretariat.

In addition, South Africa's existing free trade agreement with the European Union complicates EPA arrangements in southern Africa. Four (Botswana, Lesotho, Namibia, and Swaziland) of the seven member of the SADC EPA group also belong to the South African Customs Union (SACU) along with South Africa. South Africa is not eligible for an EPA under the Cotonou Agreement because its economy is larger and more advanced than those of the other countries of Sub-Saharan Africa. However, the EU–South Africa free trade agreement applies de facto to the four other members of SACU, which share the SACU common external tariff with South Africa. That agreement cannot be amended without the consent of South Africa. It appears that special, ad hoc EPA arrangements will need to be made for the SACU countries.

4. Aggregated COMTRADE data, available through WITS.

5. The four are COMESA, SADC, the Economic Community of West African States (ECOWAS), and Central African Economic and Monetary Union (CEMAC).

6. An analysis of MFN tariff rates for Nigeria and the UEMOA at the six-digit level indicates that while the correlation of tariff rates is high (0.61), correlation of tariffs for those tariff lines where either of the two countries has an above-average tariff is very close to zero (–0.01)—and only 0.10 for those tariff lines where UEMOA exceeds its average tariff rate. This indicates that the two schedules protect different goods. Correlation coefficients for the protected tariff lines in the ESA grouping are very low, ranging from 0.14 to 0.7, with most around 0.5. The Seychelles have a particularly low correlation coefficient with all other countries, at about 0.25. Analysis of the SADC region leads to similar results. Tariff data for all countries is available for 4,618 six-digit tariff lines; correlation coefficients are 0.47 (Angola/SADC), 0.59 (Mozambique/SADC), and 0.52 (Tanzania/SADC). For the Caribbean, they are generally higher, with the exception of the Bahamas, which shows negative coefficients with all other countries. There are only 46 tariff lines where all countries have tariff peaks, while in 90 percent of all tariff lines at least one country has a tariff peak. In the four African EPA groupings, there is little overlap in high-tariff products that member countries wish to exclude from liberalization (Stevens and Kennan 2005). These divergences indicate that negotiations for the common list of products to be excluded for each EPA grouping will be tough.

7. However, lower tariffs will translate into lower consumer prices only if EU suppliers operate in reasonably competitive markets, an assumption that cannot be taken for granted. If consumer prices of imports from the European Union do not fall, the demand for nonpreferential imports will remain unchanged. In that case, trade diversion will not occur, and there will be no additional loss of tariff revenues.

8. For more on rules of origin, see "Enhancing Trade Preferences for LDCs: Reducing the Restrictiveness of Rules of Origin" in this volume.

References

Brenton, P. 2003. "Integrating the Least Developed Countries Into the World Trading System—The Current Impact of EU Preferences Under Everything But Arms." *Journal of World Trade* 37(3): 623–46.

Busse, M., A. Borrmann, and H. Großmann. 2004. "The Impact of ACP/EU Economic Partnership Agreements on ECOWAS Countries: An Empirical Analysis of the Trade and Budget Effects." Institut für Wirtschaftsforschung, Hamburg.

Castro, L., Ch. Kraus, and M. de la Rocha. 2004. "Regional Trade Integration in East Africa: Trade and Revenue Impacts of the Planned East African Customs Unions." Africa Region Working Paper 72. World Bank, Washington, DC.

Hinkle, L. E., and R. Newfarmer. 2005. "Risks and Rewards of Regional Trading Arrangements in Africa: Economic Partnership Agreements (EPAs) Between the EU and SSA." Development Economics Department, World Bank, Washington, D.C.

Hinkle, L. E., and M. Schiff. 2004. "Economic Partnership Agreements Between Sub-Saharan

Africa and the EU: A Development Perspective." *World Economy* 27(9): 1321–33.

Karingi, S., R. Lang, N. Oulmane, R. Perez, M. Sadni Jallab, and Hakim Ben Hammouda. 2005. "Economic and Welfare Impacts of the EU-Africa Economic Partnership Agreements." ATPC Work in Progress 10, United Nations Development Program, New York.

Khandelwal, P. 2004. "COMESA and SADC: Prospects and Challenges for Regional Trade Integration." WP/04/227, International Monetary Fund, Washington, DC.

Munalulu, T., C. Cheelo, S. Kamocha, and Nkanga Shimwandwe. 2004. "Revenue Impacts of the Economic Partnership Agreement Between the European Union and Eastern and Southern African Countries." Second draft of unpublished paper. COMESA, Lusaka, Zambia.

Nielsen, L. 2005. "ECOWAS—Fiscal Revenue Implications of the Prospective Economic Partnership Agreement with the EU." Unpublished paper, International Monetary Fund, Washington, DC.

Stevens, C., and J. Kennan. 2005. "EU-ACP Economic Partnership Agreements: The Effect of Reciprocity." IDC Briefing Paper, Institute of Development Studies, University of Sussex.

UNECA. 2004. "The EU-SADC Economic Partnership Agreement: A Regional Perspective." Unpublished paper. Trade and Regional Integration Division, Addis Ababa.

————. 2005. "Assessment of the Impact of the Economic Partnership Agreement between the ECOWAS Countries and the European Union." ECA/TRID/EPAS/49/05, Addis Ababa.

World Bank. 2005. *World Development Report 2005—A Better Investment Climate For Everyone*. Washington, DC.

Enhancing Trade Preferences for LDCs: Reducing the Restrictiveness of Rules of Origin

Paul Brenton

The 2001 Doha ministerial declaration reaffirmed WTO's commitment to the least developed countries (LDCs) through trade preferences and trade-related technical assistance. The declaration lays down the objective of "duty-free, quota-free market access for products originating from LDCs" and pledges to "consider additional measures for progressive improvements in market access for LDCs" (paragraph 42). How the terms in the first objective are defined and enforced is crucial in determining how much market access preferences actually provide. The European Union's Everything But Arms agreement (EBA) provides an example. EBA offers duty- and quota-free access to LDCs.[1] But the rules that it imposes[2] to define whether a product in fact originates in an LDC and is therefore eligible for preferences are very restrictive. Other preference schemes have similarly restrictive rules of origin. A move to less restrictive rules would bring significant improvements in market access for LDCs.

Here we concentrate on the rules of origin for EU preferences, which are currently being reviewed. The review offers an opportunity for the European Union to enhance the preferences that it offers to developing countries, especially the least developed. However, there is plenty that other developed countries can do to improve their trade preference schemes. For example, the U.S. generalized system of preferences (GSP) excludes a wide range of products of relevance to LDCs. The African Growth and Opportunity Act (AGOA) includes some of these products, such as clothing, while excluding others—among them textiles and certain agricultural products—as well as all products from LDCs not covered by AGOA. Thus there is still much that the United States could do to achieve the objective set forth in the 2001 Doha ministerial declaration, starting with a review of the rules of origin applied in the GSP and AGOA.

The nature of the rules of origin

Rules of origin ensure that only products from beneficiary countries are granted trade preferences by preventing trade deflection, whereby products from nonbeneficiary countries are transshipped through the beneficiary (with minimal processing) so as to avoid the payment of tariffs. Avoiding trade deflection is in the interest of the country that grants the preference as well as the one that receives it. However, rules of origin for trade preferences are set by the preference-granting country, and are often manipulated to achieve other objectives, such as protecting domestic producers. When domestic interests are allowed to influence the scope and terms of rules of origin, the outcome tends to be far more restrictive than is necessary to prevent trade deflection. Too often, the result is that market access for the beneficiaries is limited, and the objective of promoting developing-country exports is undermined. In practice, products that are important for many developing countries—such as textiles, clothing, and processed agricultural products—are often excluded from preference schemes (pointing to the need for duty-free access for *all* products). When preferences are made available for sensitive products, they are usually accompanied by particularly restrictive rules of origin.

When a product is produced in a single stage or is wholly obtained in the beneficiary country then its origin is relatively easy to establish. In all other cases rules of origin must specify the methods to be used in ascertaining that the product has undergone *sufficient working* or processing or been subject to a *substantial transformation* in the beneficiary country. Such tests are designed to determine that products have not been transshipped from a nonqualifying country or been subject to only minimal processing. The higher the level of working that is required by the rules of origin, the more difficult they are to satisfy and the more they constrain market access (relative to what would be required simply to prevent trade deflection).

For many products, and for almost all sensitive products, the current EU rules of origin link the implied definition of "substantial transformation" to the sourcing of raw materials.[3] Thus, a clothing producer in Africa who imports fabrics from Asia may not receive preferences. A cannery may not use fish originating from outside the preferred jurisdiction. A producer of bakery products may not use imported flour. In effect, the rules of origin deny producers in developing countries freedom to choose the source of their inputs, which often means that production capacities that could have had a substantial economic and development impact are denied preferential access to the European Union. In some cases it may mean that investment in such capacities may not take place.

If needed inputs are competitively produced by local firms, exporters will always source locally to avoid transport and other trade-related costs. However, if the right inputs are not available locally at a competitive price, then producers must look to overseas suppliers. When rules of origin prohibit the use of imported inputs they may force exporters to use materials of higher cost, thus undermining their ability to compete in global markets. The aim of trade preferences, of course, is to stimulate exports and export diversification in beneficiary countries and so to provide a boost toward achieving global competitiveness and sustainable economic activity. That objective can be completely undermined by rules of origin that dictate the use of high-cost inputs.

The opportunity for reform in the European Union

The reform of rules of origin currently being considered by the European Union is a critical opportunity to support exporters in the LDCs. EU trade preferences would be considerably enhanced if producers in small developing countries were allowed to choose freely the source of the inputs they require, a freedom denied by the current rules. The opportunity to give meaning to existing preferences will be lost, however, if protectionist interests succeed in maintaining or even increasing the restrictiveness of the rules of origin

The current EU rules of origin are product-specific, sometimes complex, and often restrictive. Their restrictiveness is reflected (a) in low utilization rates of preferences and (b) the significant expansion of exports under other preference schemes that have more liberal rules. They are particularly restrictive with respect to products of comparative advantage for Africa and low-income countries, namely, processed agricultural products and clothing.

Restrictive rules of origin lead to underutilization of preferences

For those LDCs that are eligible for the EBA but for no other EU preference scheme,[4] less than 50 percent of the available EBA preferences are utilized. The principal export of Bangladesh to the European Union is clothing, yet exporters request preferences for only half of their clothing exports. Why? Because to be competitive they must use the cheapest and most appropriate fabrics. The best source of such fabrics may be China, but EU rules of origin disqualify from preferences clothing made from Chinese fabrics.

Utilization rates for certain ACP countries, which may choose between GSP/EBA and the Cotonou Agreement, can be higher. However, these data can be misleading. The EU's restrictive rules of origin for key products such as clothing can be prohibitive for small, low-income countries, keeping them out of the market altogether. Utilization rates show the share of *actual exports* that are eligible for preferences but do not request them. They do not capture the potential export capacities stifled by restrictive rules of origin. The differential supply responses in Africa to U.S. and EU preferences for clothing illustrate this principle. Liberal rules of origin have strongly stimulated U.S. imports of clothing from African LDCs, while EU imports have stagnated because of strict rules of origin (figure 1).

Restrictive rules of origin constrain export diversification

Clothing can be a key sector for export diversification, and thus for development. By manufacturing clothing, developing countries can exploit their comparative advantage in low-labor-cost operations. Advanced technology is not required, start-up costs are comparatively small, and scale economies are not important— all of which favor production in locations with low labor costs. Current EU rules for clothing, however, prohibit the use of imported fabric. To obtain preferences, clothing

279

Figure 1. With liberal rules of origin, US clothing imports surge
US $ million

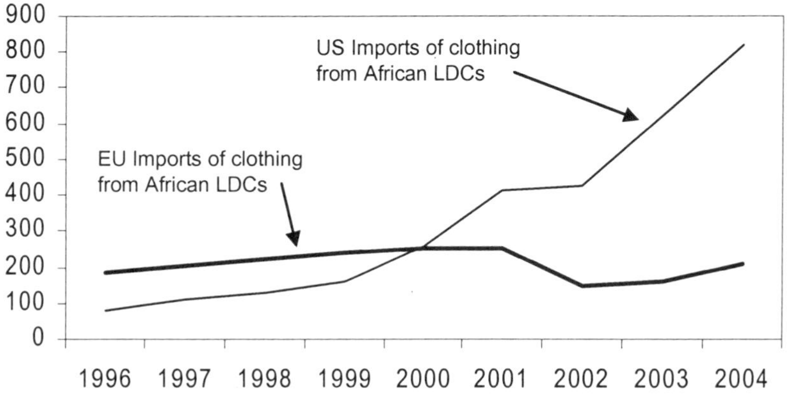

Source: USITC Dataweb and EUROSTAT.

producers must use local or EU fabrics (or fabrics from countries with which cumulation is permitted). They may not use fabrics from the main fabric-producing countries in Asia and still qualify for EU preferences—a binding restriction, since few countries in Africa have competitive fabric industries.

Since 2000, with the passage of AGOA, the United States has offered preferences on imports of clothing from African countries under much more liberal rules of origin: making up fabric into clothing is sufficient to confer origin. The U.S. rule allows African clothing manufacturers flexibility in sourcing fabrics.[5] In the face of restrictive rules of origin, EU imports of clothing from African LDCs are lower in 2004 than they were in 1996, while U.S. imports have flourished, increasing 10 fold since 1996 and are now almost four times greater than the value of EU imports of clothing from African LDCs (see figure 1).

The rapid increase in exports from African LDCs to the United States has had a negligible impact on the U.S. market, where African LDCs still account for little more than 1 percent of total U.S. imports of clothing and a much smaller proportion of total U.S. consumption of clothing products. Even so, the United States does not offer comparable access to all LDCs; those in Asia are still excluded. Further, the third-country fabric rule of AGOA is due to be removed in 2007, before many countries in Africa have had the opportunity to benefit and with detrimental impact on those that have been able to do so. The general rule of origin for the U.S. GSP and AGOA is a value-added requirement of 35 percent, which is likely to be very difficult for many small developing countries to meet in the absence of rules comparable to the AGOA third-country fabric rule, because the higher the value-added requirement, the more difficult it is for low labor cost countries to satisfy the rule relative to countries with higher labor costs.

If the full market-opening opportunities of EBA and the EU's GSP are to be realized, a significant relaxation of EU rules of origin will be required. Recognizing that rules of origin have constrained the developmental impact of the GSP, the European Commission has proposed a value-added rule to define origin for all products. A preferable alternative, would be to give developing countries, especially LDCs, the flexibility of satisfying *either* a value-added rule *or* a change-of-tariff-heading requirement. At what level should the value-added requirement be set and what degree of cumulation should be allowed? The Blair Commission proposed a value-added requirement on all products of no more than 10 percent, which would allow African exporters the flexibility to source inputs and to exploit their comparative advantage in labor-intensive products.

The issue of cumulation

Cumulation is an instrument that allows producers to import materials from a specific country or regional group of countries without undermining the origin of their product. In so doing, it offsets the restrictiveness of a particular set of rules of origin. However, as long as the most efficient producer of the required inputs is excluded from the area of cumulation then the offset will be partial and may well be worthless. We have no strong empirical evidence of the importance of cumulation provisions, but the information we do have does not suggest a strong impact.[6]

If the value-added requirement is low enough, there is no need for cumulation. If it is high, then the rules must allow for *global* cumulation if LDCs are to be able to exploit their comparative advantage. With global cumulation, inputs from any developing country, including China, would count as qualifying content. Current EU proposals for limited regional cumulation are likely to do little to mitigate the restrictiveness of high value-added requirements. Global cumulation, by contrast, would allow sourcing of inputs from regional partners and help promote regional integration; by not limiting cumulation to the region, it also would avoid excluding the lowest-cost source of inputs.

However, a low value-added requirement (10 percent) common across all products would be more transparent, simpler for firms to satisfy, and easier to administer by customs and other agencies. Setting a high value-added requirement (such as 40–50 percent) and allowing limited regional cumulation is most unlikely to provide for a substantial easing of the rules of origin. It could even make them *more* restrictive.

Fears that a low value-added requirement or global cumulation would benefit mainly China are overstated. In fact, the benefits to China probably would be very small. Many producers in developing countries already choose to use Chinese inputs, because the cost penalty of not using the least expensive inputs is often greater than the tariff preference. Restrictive rules of origin and limited cumulation will not induce these producers to use other sources of inputs. By contrast, a low value-added requirement (or global cumulation) will allow developing-country producers that have chosen for competitive reasons to use Chinese inputs to receive preferences and, in principle, realize higher returns for their exports. If competitive inputs are available locally they will always be used. Global cumulation will benefit China only in cases where producers previously sourced inputs domestically or from a country in an area of cumulation solely for the purpose of receiving preferences.

Conclusions

Reform of the rules of origin governing preferences offers the European Union a crucial opportunity to improve market access for LDCs and other developing countries and to enhance the value of their trade preferences.

Current EU rules of origin severely limit the ability of producers in small developing countries to source inputs on a global basis and still receive preferences. Trade preferences should be designed to help countries reach global competitiveness in industries in which they have a comparative advantage. In the globalized economy such competitiveness must be based on the freedom to source inputs from the most suitable and least expensive location. The global market exacts a high penalty on producers that use inappropriate or high-cost inputs.

The U.S. experience with AGOA shows that a bold approach to rules of origin can provoke substantial supply responses from developing countries and help them build a more diversified export base.

By reforming the rules of origin for LDCs to provide a value-added requirement of no more than 10 percent across all products in the EBA (with the alternative of satisfying either the value-added rule or a change-of-tariff-heading requirement), the European Union would widen access to its market in a manner consistent with the Doha process and with the ongoing adjustment to the expiration of quotas on textile and clothing products. If a beneficiary country feels that this is not commensurate with its development objectives they should be allowed to petition for a permanent derogation of more restrictive rules on their exports to the European Union.

Similar arguments apply to Japan and the United States, which could enhance the preferences they offer by broadening product and country coverage to provide duty- and quota-free access for all products produced by all LDCs, and also by reviewing the effectiveness of their rules of origin in stimulating the exports of LDCs.

Notes

1. The vast majority of products exported by LDCs to the European Union were already eligible for duty- and quota-free access under existing provisions of the GSP.

2. There are no multilateral rules or disciplines on preferential rules of origin. An attempt was made in the Uruguay Round to harmonize *nonpreferential* rules of origin, which define origin for purposes of basic trade-policy measures such as the application of tariffs, the marking of goods, and the collection of statistics, and for use in contingent protection (such as antidumping, countervailing, and safeguard measures). Some progress has been made on these rules, but the negotiations have bogged down, and several deadlines for the completion of the work program have been missed.

3. Block and Grynberg (2005) draw this out very clearly for processed fish.

4. Afghanistan, Bangladesh, Bhutan, Cambodia, Laos, Maldives, Nepal, Yemen.

5. Initially, South Africa and Mauritius were excluded from the more liberal rule of origin. They faced a far more restrictive NAFTA-type rule requiring production from fiber. Mattoo and others (2004) show how the more liberal rules for clothing could increase the gains to these excluded countries by as much as a factor of five. Mauritius subsequently lobbied hard to become eligible for the less-restrictive rule.

6. See, for example, UNCTAD and Commonwealth Secretariat (2001).

References

Block, L and R. Grynberg. 2005. "EU Rules of Origin for ACP Tuna Products" HS Chapter 16.04). mimeo. Commonwealth Secretariat, London.

Mattoo, A., D. Roy, and A. Subramanian. 2002. "The African Growth and Opportunity Act and Its Rules of Origin: Generosity Undermined?" *World Economy* 26: 829–51.

UNCTAD (U.N. Conference on Trade and Development) and Commonwealth Secretariat. 2001. "Duty and Quota Free Market Access for LDCs: An Analysis of Quad Initiatives." London and Geneva: UNCTAD and Commonwealth Secretariat. http:/192.91.247.38/tab/otherpubs.asp.

Tightening TRIPS: Intellectual Property Provisions of U.S. Free Trade Agreements

Carsten Fink and Patrick Reichenmiller

Over the past few years, the United States has pursued bilateral and regional free trade agreements (FTAs) in different parts of the world (table 1). This has marked a considerable shift in U.S. international trade diplomacy. While the U.S. Government entered into regional trade agreements in the past—notably in the case of the North American Free Trade Agreement (NAFTA)—it relied mostly on the multilateral trading system to advance the progressive opening of world markets and to create legally enforceable trading rules.[1]

Prominent in the recent set of bilateral FTAs are strong rules for the protection of intellectual property rights (IPRs), a key market access interest of the United States—supported by private sector constituents who derive significant revenues from exports of intangible assets. Indeed, the trade promotion authority, under which these agreements were negotiated aims explicitly to promote intellectual property rules that "reflect a standard of protection similar to that found in United States law."[2] U.S. trading partners generally have more defensive negotiating interests in intellectual property, but they are willing to commit to stronger intellectual property rules as a quid pro quo for concessions in other areas—notably preferential access to U.S. markets for agricultural and manufactured goods.

This note offers an overview of key elements of recent U.S. FTAs that go beyond multilateral standards on intellectual property as set forth in the Agreement

Table 1. Recent U.S. free trade agreements

Signed and approved by U.S. Congress	Signed but not yet approved by U.S.	Under negotiation
Vietnam (2001) [a]	Bahrain	Andean countries (Bolivia, Colombia, Ecuador, Peru)
Jordan (2001)		Thailand
Singapore (2003)		Panama
Chile (2003)		Southern African Customs Union
Morocco (2004)		Free Trade Area of the Americas
Australia (2004)		
DR-CAFTA (Dominican Republic, Costa Rica, El Salvador, Guatemala, Honduras, Nicaragua) (2005)		

a. The U.S. bilateral agreement with Vietnam is not a free trade agreement, but a bilateral agreement intended to establish normal trade relations under U.S. trade law. It is included in this note for purposes of comparison. The United States has signed similar agreements with other countries, such as Cambodia and Laos.

on Trade-Related Aspects Intellectual Property Rights (TRIPS). It also offers a perspective on the intellectual property bargain in trade agreements, outlines key economic and social implications from the adoption of new intellectual property standards, and discusses several lessons learned.

Where do U.S. FTAs go beyond the TRIPS standards?

The IPR chapters of recent U.S. FTAs include provisions that affect all types of intellectual property instruments and the mechanisms available to administer and enforce exclusive rights. Although the detailed provisions differ from agreement to agreement, there are certain common obligations which go beyond the TRIPS standards (table 2).

Protection of patents and pharmaceutical test data

As in TRIPS, all of the FTAs listed in table 1 provide for a patent term of 20 years. However, they also require that the patent term be extended in the event of delays caused by regulatory approval processes, such as obtaining approval for marketing a new drug. In addition some agreements call for extensions for delays in the granting of the patent itself.

Three agreements (U.S.–Australia, U.S.–Morocco, U.S.–Bahrain) extend the scope of patentability by mandating that patents must be available for new uses of known products. All bilateral agreements go beyond TRIPS in enhancing patent protection for plants and animals. The strongest agreement in this regard is U.S.–Morocco, which explicitly mandates patent protection for life forms. Others do not exempt plants and animals from patentability, an option provided under TRIPS. The weakest agreement is the one with the Dominican Republic and six Central American countries (U.S.–DR–CAFTA), which simply calls for "reasonable efforts" to provide for patentability of plants.[3]

In the area of medicines, the bilateral agreements contain provisions that limit the ability of governments to introduce competition from generic producers. First, to override the market exclusivity of patent holders, governments must grant so-called compulsory licenses to generic manufacturers. TRIPS allows the use of compulsory licenses without specifying the grounds for issuing them. Four of the bilateral agreements (with Australia, Jordan, Singapore, and Vietnam) limit the use of compulsory licensing to emergency situations, antitrust remedies, and cases of public noncommercial use.[4]

Second, to make effective use of compulsory licenses, generic drug manufacturers must be able to obtain regulatory permission to enter the market. Provisions in the bilateral agreements impose an obstacle in this respect. All but two agreements (those with Jordan and Vietnam) prohibit the signatories from approving the marketing of a generic drug during the patent term without the consent of the patent holder—an issue on which TRIPS imposes no obligation. In other words, compulsory licenses may become ineffective in introducing competition from generic drug makers.

Third, obtaining marketing approval for drugs requires the submission of test data on a drug's safety and efficacy to regulatory authorities. Such data is protected by separate legal instruments that differ from country to country. The TRIPS agreement requires only that test data be protected against "unfair commercial use." By contrast, most of the bilateral agreements mandate exclusivity of test data, as under U.S. law. Once a company has submitted original test data, no competing manufacturer may rely on those data for a period of five years to support a request for approval for its own drug.[5] The compilation of new test data by competing manufacturers may take several years and be prohibitively expensive. For that reason, test-data exclusivity may pose a second obstacle for governments to make effective use of compulsory licensing.

Several of the bilateral agreements go further on data exclusivity. When pharmaceutical companies seek marketing approval for previously unapproved uses of drugs already registered, regulatory authorities typically require the submission of "new" clinical information. The agreements with Morocco and Bahrain provide for an additional three years of data exclusivity whenever new clinical information is presented. Drugs benefiting from this type of marketing exclusivity include not only newly patented products, but also older generic products for which the patents have expired (though generic competition for previously approved uses of such drugs would remain unaffected).

Sometimes drug regulatory authorities recognize the marketing-approval decisions of foreign regulators in making decisions to approve the same product at home. The intellectual property chapter of the U.S.–Singapore Agreement mandates, in this regard, that foreign data exclusivity also applies at home. In other words, no competing manufacturer is allowed to rely on the test data submitted to a *foreign* regulator when seeking marketing approval at home.

The agreements with Australia, Bahrain, and the DR-CAFTA countries reach even farther. Even if regulatory authorities do not recognize foreign marketing approvals, competing manufacturers are prevented from using test data submitted to a drug regulatory agency in another territory. In other words, test-data exclusivity applies automatically in all FTA jurisdictions once a company submits test data to a drug regulator in one territory—even outside the FTA area.

A fourth aspect of intellectual property regulations affecting the supply of medicines is the permissibility of parallel importation of pharmaceutical products that have been placed on the market in foreign countries. Parallel importation can be a means of exerting downward pressure on prices of pharmaceuticals that are sold more cheaply abroad. The TRIPS agreement affords World Trade Organization (WTO) members flexibility in determining whether to permit parallel importation of patented drugs.[6] By contrast, the U.S. agreements with Australia, Morocco, and

Table 2. Intellectual property provisions of recent U.S. bilateral and FTAs that go beyond

	U.S.–Vietnam	U.S.–Jordan	U.S.–Singapore	U.S.–Chile	U.S.–Morocco	U.S.–Australia	U.S.–DR-CAFTA	U.S.–Bahrain
Protection of patents and pharmaceutical test data								
Patent term	Extension given for delays caused by regulatory approval process.	Extension given for delays caused by regulatory approval process.	Extension given for delays caused by regulatory approval process. In addition, extension given when a delay in the granting of the patent exceeds 4 years from the filing of the application (5 years for U.S.–Chile or 2 years after a request for examination (3 years for U.S.–Chile).					
Second-use patents	No specific provision				Obligation to provide patents for new uses of known products		No specific provision	Same as U.S.–Australia
Patenting of life forms	Certain plants and animals may not be excluded from patentability.[a]	No general exclusion of plants and animals from patentability.[b]			Explicit obligation to provide patent protection for plants and animals	Exclusions only allowed for moral, health and safety reasons	Reasonable efforts have to be undertaken to provide for patentability of plants.[c]	Explicit obligation to provide patent protection for plants, but animals can be excluded
Compulsory licenses		Compulsory licenses limited to national emergencies, as antitrust remedy, and for public non-commercial use		TRIPS standards apply		Same as U.S.–Singapore	TRIPS standards apply.	
Linkage between patent status and drug marketing approval	No specific provision	Patent owner must be notified when marketing approval is sought during the patent term.	Marketing approval of a generic drug is prohibited during the patent term, unless authorized by the patent owner. In addition, the patent holder must be notified of the identity of the generic company requesting marketing approval					
Test data protection for pharmaceutical products	Data exclusivity for a 'reasonable' period, normally not less than 5 years.	TRIPS standards apply. In addition, length of protection should be the same as in the originator's country.	Data exclusivity for 5 years. In addition, where drug regulators rely on foreign marketing approvals, data exclusivity applies automatically at home	Data exclusivity for 5 years.	Data exclusivity for 5 years. Additional 3 year data exclusivity triggered by 'new clinical information'	Data exclusivity for 5 years. In addition, data exclusivity applies in all FTA member countries, once first obtained in another territory. In the case of U.S.–Bahrain, additional 3 year data exclusivity triggered by 'new clinical information' (with equivalent provisions on cross-border application).	TRIPS standards apply.	
Parallel imports of patented products	No specific provision.[d]	TRIPS standards apply.	Patent holders may limit parallel imports of pharmaceutical products through licensing contracts	TRIPS standards apply	Patent holders may limit parallel imports through licensing contracts		TRIPS standards apply.	
Side letters on public health?	No	No	No	No	Yes	No	Yes	Yes

Table 2. Intellectual property provisions of recent U.S. bilateral and FTAs that go beyond TRIPS standards (continued)

	U.S.–Vietnam	U.S.–Jordan	U.S.–Singapore	U.S.–Chile	U.S.–Morocco	U.S.–Australia	U.S.–DR-CAFTA	U.S.–Bahrain
Copyright protection								
Term of copyright protection	Same as TRIPS if determined by life of author. 75–100 years	Same as TRIPS	Life of author plus 70 years. If decided on a basis other than the life of the author, the term is 70 years from the publication or creation of the work					
Technological protection measures	No specific provision	'Adequate' protection and 'effective' remedies against acts of circumvention. Ban on circumvention devices	'Adequate' protection against acts of circumvention. Ban on circumvention devices. Civil liability in case of willful infringement. Criminal liability in case of willful infringement for commercial purposes. Exempted are nonprofit libraries, archives, educations institutions, as well as acts related to reverse engineering, troubleshooting, protection of minors, computer or network security, and lawfully authorized government activities					
Liability of Internet service providers	No specific provision	No specific provision	Limited liability of Internet service providers on the condition that they block infringing content upon notification by the copyright holder.					
Burden of proof in case of copyright infringement	No specific provision	Burden of proof placed on the defending party to show that works are in the public domain. However, copyright owners still have to prove infringement						
Parallel importation of copyrighted works	No specific provision	Copyright holder has right to block parallel imports	TRIPS standards apply.		Copyright holder has right to block parallel imports	TRIPS standards apply.		
Enforcement of intellectual property rights								
Institutional flexibility in IPRs enforcement	No specific provision			Resource constraints cannot be invoked as an excuse for not complying with specific enforcement obligations e		No specific provision	Same as U.S.–Chile	Same as U.S.–Singapore
Border measures	Apply to imported and exported goods	Scope of border measures not specifically defined		Apply to imported, exported, and transiting goods.		Apply only to imported goods (similar to TRIPS).	Same as U.S.–Chile	
Civil and administrative procedures	Obligation to fine infringers of copyright and trademark rights irrespective of the injury suffered by rights holders							
Criminal procedures and remedies	Similar to TRIPS.	Scope of criminal procedures and remedies not specifically defined		Similar to TRIPS. In addition, criminal procedures apply in case of willful infringements, not only for a financial gain.	Similar to TRIPS. In addition, criminal procedures apply in cases of willful infringements, not only for a financial gain, and specifically for knowing trafficking in counterfeit labels affixed to certain copyrighted works (e.g., CDs, software).			

Table 2. Intellectual property provisions of recent U.S. bilateral and FTAs that go beyond TRIPS standards

(Continued)

Source: This overview table is based on the texts of the FTAs, available at http://www.ustr.gov, and legal analyses by Abbott (2004) on the U.S.–DR-CAFTA and U.S.–Morocco agreements and Roffe (2004) on the U.S.–Chile Agreement.

Notes: a. Specifically, the agreement foresees that "[t]he exclusions for plant and animal varieties (as defined in Article 1 of UPOV Convention 1991) shall not apply to plant or animal inventions that could encompass more than one variety."

b. In the case of U.S.–Chile, the agreement does not explicitly oblige protection of life forms under the patent system, but mandates "reasonable efforts" to develop legislation related to patent protection for plants within four years from entry into force of the agreement.

c. In addition, member countries are required to accede to the International Convention for the Protection of New Varieties of Plants (1991) (UPOV Convention 1991) by 2006 (2007 for Costa Rica; 2010 for Nicaragua). However, if a member country already provides patent protection for plants, accession to UPOV 1991 is not a requirement.

d. The question of intellectual property rights exhaustion, which determines the permissibility of parallel importation, is not addressed in the U.S.–Vietnam agreement.

e. In the case of U.S.-Morocco, a side letter specifies the form in which notifications in case of alleged copyright infringement must be made.

Singapore allow patent holders to prevent parallel importation through contractual means.

Are the provisions on marketing approval during the patent term, test-data exclusivity, and parallel importation at odds with the Doha Declaration on TRIPS and Public Health? That declaration—issued at the WTO ministerial meeting in Doha, Qatar, in 2001—recognized the gravity of the public health problems besetting many developing and least developing countries. Among other things, it reaffirmed the right of WTO members to use the flexibilities of TRIPS in the realm of compulsory licensing and parallel importation to "promote access to medicines for all."[6] Moreover, in August 2003, WTO members created a special mechanism under the TRIPS agreement that allows countries with insufficient manufacturing capacity to make effective use of compulsory licenses by importing generic drugs (Fink 2005). Technically, the Doha Declaration and the August 2003 decision do not address test-data exclusivity or marketing approval during the patent term. However, the relevant provisions of the FTAs appear to be at odds with the spirit of these multilateral accords, to the extent that they preclude the effective use of compulsory licenses.

In side letters to the agreements involving Bahrain, Morocco, and the DR-CAFTA countries, the respective governments shared understandings that the intellectual property chapters did not affect their ability to "take necessary measures to protect public health by promoting medicines for all."[8] In a recent letter to a member of the U.S. Congress on the U.S.–Morocco FTA, the general counsel of the United States Trade Representative (USTR) provided further clarification:

> " "If circumstances ever arise in which a drug is produced under a compulsory license, and it is necessary to approve that drug to protect public health or effectively utilize the TRIPS/health solution, the data protection provision in the FTA would not stand in the way....
>
> As stated in the side letter, the letter constitutes a formal agreement between the Parties. It is, thus, a significant part of the interpretive context for this agreement and not merely rhetorical. According to Article 31 of the Vienna Convention on the Law of Treaties, which reflects customary rules of treaty interpretation in international law, the terms of a treaty must be interpreted "in their context," and that "context" includes "any agreement relating to the treaty which was made between all the parties in connection with the conclusion of the treaty." "[9]

At the same time, the U.S. government does not view the side letters as creating an exemption that would allow parties to the FTAs to ignore obligations in the agreements' intellectual property chapters.[10] The side letters merely signal the belief of the signing governments that the intellectual property rules of the FTAs will not interfere with the protection of public health.[11]

Copyright protection

TRIPS requires that copyright be protected for the life of the author plus 50 years. Except for the agreements with Jordan and Vietnam, the bilateral FTAs of the United States extend this term by an additional 20 years.

Most bilateral FTAs include obligations against circumventing so-called technological protection measures—devices and software developed to prevent unauthorized copying of digital works. This issue is not covered under TRIPS. It came to prominence only with advances in information and communication technologies that greatly facilitated the copying of literary or artistic works in digital form. The U.S. Digital Millennium Copyright Act of 1998 strengthened standards on circumventing technologies designed to prevent unauthorized copying of digital content. Those standards found their way to varying degrees into seven of the bilateral agreements. Related provisions in six of the FTAs define the liability of internet service providers when infringing content is distributed through their servers and networks. Again, these provisions are based on standards found in the U.S. Digital Millennium Copyright Act.

In copyright infringement cases, all of the bilateral agreements—except for the one with Vietnam—place the burden of proof on the defending party to show that works are in the public domain. TRIPS does not impose any such obligation. The FTAs thus strengthen the position of copyright holders, as artistic and literary works should generally be considered protected—unless they obviously belong in the public domain.

As in the case of pharmaceutical products, TRIPS does not mandate any rule on the permissibility of parallel imports of copyrighted works—such as books or musical Compact Disks (CDs)—that have been lawfully sold in foreign markets. Some countries, such as New Zealand, have permitted parallel importation of certain copyrighted products as a way to stimulate price competition. By contrast, the U.S. bilateral agreements with Jordan and Morocco give copyright holders the right to block parallel importation.

Enforcement of intellectual property rights

The TRIPS agreement—for the first time in an international agreement on intellectual property—introduced detailed obligations on the enforcement of IPRs. Certainly, without judicial enforcement of intellectual property laws, rules on patents, copyright, and other forms of protection could be seriously undermined. However, recognizing the institutional limitations of the institutions in many developing countries, TRIPS does not create any obligation "with respect to the distribution of resources as between enforcement of intellectual property rights and the enforcement of law in general."[12]

The agreements with Australia, Jordan, and Vietnam do not explicitly allow for the same institutional flexibility. In these cases, it may therefore be difficult to defend derogations from the specific enforcement provisions of the agreements' IPR chapters with inherent institutional constraints, such as limited budgetary or human resources. The agreements with Bahrain, Chile, Morocco, Singapore, and the DR-CAFTA countries go further, spelling out that resource constraints cannot be invoked as an excuse for not complying with the agreements' specific enforcement obligations.[13] Indeed, some of the specific enforcement requirements of the FTAs seem to create additional institutional obligations. For example, as in the case of TRIPS, the FTAs require customs authorities to stop trade in counterfeit and pirated goods. But TRIPS requires such measures only for imported goods, whereas most FTAs mandate border measures for imported and exported goods and, in some cases, even transiting goods.

Finally, the enforcement rules of the bilateral agreements mandate a stronger deterrent against IPR infringement. For example, TRIPS requires only the imposition of fines adequate to compensate IPR holders for the monetary damages they suffered. In the case of copyright piracy and trademark counterfeiting, all of the FTAs require the imposition of fines irrespective of the injury suffered by IPR holders. TRIPS mandates criminal procedures only in cases of willful trademark counterfeiting or copyright piracy on a commercial scale. Many FTAs go beyond this broad standard and define more explicitly the scope of acts of infringement subject to criminal procedures—including, for example, copyright piracy with a significant aggregate monetary value, but not necessarily for financial gain. Thus, certain forms of end-user piracy may be considered a criminal offense.

Intellectual property rights and investment rules

In addition to the rules contained in the intellectual property chapters of the FTAs, IPRs are subject to separate investment disciplines. Six of the bilateral agreements have separate chapters on investment (table 2). The U.S.–Bahrain and U.S.–Jordan FTAs do not have one, but the respective governments have negotiated bilateral investment treaties (BITs) with similar provisions.[14] As no multilateral agreement on investment exists at the WTO or elsewhere, these bilateral investment rules break new ground.

A common element of the investment chapters and BITs is that intellectual property rights are explicitly listed in the definition of what is considered an investment. Thus, the agreements' specific investment disciplines apply, in principle, to government measures affecting the intellectual property portfolios of foreign investors. This, for example, raises the question of whether granting a compulsory license could be considered an act of expropriation. Five of the FTA investment chapters explicitly remove compulsory licenses from the scope of expropriation, as long as such licenses comply with the obligations of the TRIPS agreement and the intellectual property chapter of the respective FTA. But the U.S.–Vietnam FTA and the two BITs with Bahrain and Jordan lack a comparable safeguard. Thus, if Vietnam, for example were to issue a compulsory license in case of a national emergency, could the patent holder challenge such a decision as an act of investment expropriation?

Questions like this may be important, as these investment agreements provide for direct dispute settlement between investor and state, going beyond the more

Table 3. Intellectual property rights and investment disciplines

	U.S.–Jordan, U.S.–Bahrain	U.S.–Vietnam	U.S.–Singapore, U.S.–Chile,	U.S.–Australia
FTA chapter or previous BIT?	Previous BIT	Separate FTA chapter on investment		
Expropriation	No explicit exemption.	Compulsory license and revocation/limitation of intellectual property right not considered expropriation, if in compliance with multilateral and bilateral trade rules.		
Investor-state dispute settlement	Investors have recourse to investor-state arbitration procedures.			No recourse to investor-state arbitration

Source: This overview table is based on the text of the relevant investment chapters and BITs, available at http://www.ustr.gov and http://www.tcc.mac.doc.gov.

traditional state-to-state dispute settlement procedures in most trade agreements. An exception is the investment chapter of the U.S.–Australia FTA, which allows only for the possibility that investor-to-state dispute settlement procedures might be negotiated in future. Investor-to-state dispute settlement may be more attractive to foreign investors, who can seek arbitration awards for uncompensated expropriation. By contrast, state-to-state dispute settlement can typically authorize only the imposition of punitive trade sanctions.

Notwithstanding these considerations, the reach of investment agreements into the intellectual property domain is still untested and remains in many ways legally uncertain (Correa 2004).

A good bargain?

Whether an FTA's package of commitments produces net welfare gains to all parties is an empirical question. However, FTAs with stronger rules on intellectual property complicate an assessment of economic benefits and costs—for three reasons.

First, the traditional logic that economists apply to mercantilist trade bargaining does not extend straightforwardly to intellectual property. While reduced import protection is seen as a concession by trade negotiators, it is generally regarded as a welfare-enhancing policy change by trade economists. Nonetheless, economists have supported mercantilist bargaining, as it helps governments make a stronger case for import liberalization: exporters that gain from improved access to foreign markets can become a political counterweight to firms that would lose out from more intense import competition.

From an economic perspective, IPRs are different. Put simply, they imply a trade-off between incentives for innovation and competitive access to new technologies.[15] To balance these trade-offs, governments limit the length and scope of the market exclusivity conferred by IPRs, according to national policy objectives. In particular, there is no assurance that stronger intellectual property rules will always be welfare-enhancing, and the direction and size of the welfare effect will depend on a country's level of economic development. While there is undoubtedly a market-access dimension to IPRs, subjecting standards of protection to mercantilist bargaining cannot be viewed in the same light as subjecting import barriers to such bargaining.

Second, improved access to U.S. markets for agricultural and manufactured goods is of a preferential nature. Preferences are time-bound, because they will be eroded once the United States reduces remaining tariffs and quotas on a nondiscriminatory basis in the current or future multilateral trading rounds (or once it signs additional FTAs). By contrast, a commitment to stronger IPR rules is permanent and likely to be implemented on a nonpreferential basis. Even if preferential treatment in the area of IPRs were technically feasible, it would likely be inconsistent with the TRIPS agreement, which mandates most-favored-nation (MFN) treatment of IPRs holders.[16] In contrast to the WTO's agreements on trade in goods and trade in services, the TRIPS agreement does not provide for an exception to the MFN principle for FTAs.

Third, it is inherently difficult to quantify the implications of changing intellectual property standards, let alone to compare them in monetary values to the gains derived from improved market access abroad. As will be explained further below, certain effects of stronger IPRs are conceptually not well-understood. But even where they are, the direction and size of net welfare changes depend on future developments that are difficult to predict—such as the nature of future innovations and their relevance to the country concerned.

Economic and social implications

As just pointed out, evaluating the social and economic implications of the U.S. FTAs in the area of intellectual property is a difficult task. First of all, it requires an understanding of the changes in laws and regulations required by obligations in the FTAs that do not reflect current legal practice in the countries concerned. For example, both Morocco and the United States had legislation in place prohibiting parallel imports of pharmaceutical products before they signed the FTA. To be sure, trade agreements are still relevant even if they do not require changes in laws, because they make it difficult for countries to change their minds and amend laws. Indeed, in the specific case of parallel importation many countries—including the United States—reexamine from time to time existing policies, sometimes deciding to change course.[17] Certainly, if policy changes were inconceivable, there would be no need to lock policy into trade agreements.

A full economic assessment of the new intellectual property obligations in the FTAs would require in-depth study in each of the affected countries, an effort that far exceeds the scope of this note. Still, we may ask, what are some of the general benefits and costs that may come with the new intellectual property standards outlined above?

A commitment to stronger intellectual property protection may send a welcoming signal to foreign investors, contributing to a country's increased participation in international commerce. The empirical evidence on this question is mixed, however. Fink and Maskus (2004) review studies undertaken to gauge the link between the strength of intellectual property protection and the attraction of foreign direct investment flows. They conclude that countries that strengthen their IPR regime are unlikely to experience a sudden boost in inflows of foreign investment. Other factors account for most of the variation across countries in the activity of multinational enterprises. At the same time, the empirical evidence does point to a positive role of IPRs in stimulating cross-border licensing activity, which affects formal technology transfers.

Moving on to sector-specific implications, the role of patent protection in the pharmaceutical industry is conceptually well-understood. Patents create an incentive to invest in pharmaceutical research and development (R&D), but the market exclusivity they confer leads to prices above marginal production costs—as illustrated by sharp price drops when patents expire and generic competition emerges. The benefits and costs associated with protecting pharmaceutical patents differ from country to country. Among other things, they depend on the relevance of drug discoveries to national disease patterns, the purchasing power of patients, and the availability of health insurance programs that cover drug expenses. As already pointed out, insufficient flexibility in overriding drug patents can have a detrimental impact on the protection of public health. The need for such flexibility has not been widespread so far, as generic sources for most medicines have still been available. However, it is likely to become more important in the future, as the implementation of TRIPS obligations will lead newly invented drugs to be protected by patents in most developing countries that host generic pharmaceutical industries.[18]

The benefits and costs of stronger and new copyright protection standards are less clear cut. Most countries have industries that rely on copyright protection and that may benefit from strengthened protection. And new technologies that greatly facilitate the copying of digital works pose challenges that policymakers need to address. At the same time, copyright laws have historically sought to strike a balance between the interests of copyright producers and the interests of the general public. So-called fair-use exemptions allow the copying of protected works for educational and research purposes. There are concerns that new rules on the term of protection, technological protection measures, the liability of Internet services providers, and the burden of proof in cases of copyright infringement could diminish the rights of consumers and the general public (CIPR 2002).

Such concerns have been voiced from within the United States, not only by consumer rights advocates and academic institutions, but also by computer manufacturers and communications service providers that distribute copyrighted works. For example, proposed amendments to the Digital Millennium Copyright Act would permit the circumvention of technological protection measures if it did not result in an infringement of a copyrighted work.[19] Ensuring fair use of copyrighted material seems particularly important for accessing educational material. The opportunities and gains from the use of digital libraries, Internet-based distance-learning programs, and online databases would be limited if access to such tools were unaffordable or otherwise restricted by copyright law.

Finally, strengthening the enforcement of intellectual property rights can be a costly exercise—both in terms of budgetary outlays and the employment of skilled personnel. For developing countries that face many institutional deficiencies, a critical question is whether stronger enforcement of IPRs would draw financial and human resources from other development priorities.

Lessons learned

The United States continues to negotiate FTAs, mostly with developing countries (see table 2), and still other negotiations are likely to be launched. Given the importance of intellectual property to the United States, it will be difficult for U.S. trading partners to avoid negotiating new IPR rules. What lessons can they learn from the recently signed agreements?

First, while there are common elements in the eight intellectual property chapters discussed here, there are also important differences (see table 2). With varying degrees of success, U.S. trading partners were able to advance their own, generally defensive interests. Of particular importance is the preservation of flexibilities to protect public health. Indeed, the United States is obligated by its own trade promotion authority "to respect the Declaration on the TRIPS Agreement and Public Health, adopted by the World Trade Organization at the Fourth Ministerial Conference at Doha."[20]

Second, the intellectual property chapters of the eight FTAs discussed here mostly reflect proposals put forward by the United States. It may be possible to change the negotiating dynamics in future FTAs, if U.S. trading partners put forward their own proposals on new intellectual property rules and related incentive mechanisms. These may pertain to policy areas in which developing countries have offensive interests, such as the protection of biodiversity and traditional knowledge. But they may also consist of alternative mechanisms of addressing the problems that new intellectual property rules are intended to fix.[21]

Finally, countries need to carefully assess the economic and social effects of tightened IPR standards, ideally before new agreements are negotiated. As pointed out above, these effects are multifaceted and depend on country-specific circumstances. An assessment should therefore involve consultations with relevant ministries, the private sector, consumer groups, and other stakeholders.

Notes

1. Comments by Federick Abbott, Carlos Braga, Jean-Christophe Maur, Richard Newfarmer, Lorenzo Pupillo, Pedro Roffe, Philip Schuler, Rudolf Van Puymbroek, as well as James Medenhall and other staff from the Office of the USTR are gratefully acknowledged.

2. See the Bipartisan Trade Promotion Authority Act of 2002, available at http://www.tpa.gov.

3. At the same time, the U.S.–DR–CAFTA Agreement requires countries that already provide patent protection for plants to maintain such protection.

4. The TRIPS provisions on compulsory licensing require a government first to make efforts to obtain a voluntary license from the patent holder, although this requirement may be waived in emergency situations or for public noncommercial use. The obligations of bilateral agreements are similar or identical in this respect.

5. In the case of agrochemical products, most of the bilateral agreements require data exclusivity for 10 years.

6. The permissibility of parallel importation is governed by rules on the exhaustion of patents. A system of international exhaustion is associated with free parallel trade, while patent holders can restrict parallel importation if patent rights exhaust only nationally. TRIPS Article 6 does not mandate a particular exhaustion regime, as long as its application is nondiscriminatory.

7. See paragraph 4 of the Doha Declaration on TRIPS and Public Health, available at http://www.wto.org.

8. The side letters also clarify that the intellectual property chapters of the FTAs do not prevent the effective utilization of the August 2003 decision by WTO members described in the text.

9. See the letter from USTR General Counsel John K. Veroneau to Congressman Levin dated July 19, 2004, available at Inside U.S. Trade.

10. As clarified by USTR staff in correspondence with World Bank staff.

11. The agreements with DR–CAFTA, Chile, Australia, and Jordan contain provisions affirming the rights and obligations of member countries under the TRIPS agreement. To some extent, these provisions may be interpreted as preserving the flexibilities of the TRIPS agreement. However, the value of these non-derogation clauses in bilateral disputes is legally uncertain (Abbott 2004).

12. See Article 41.5 of the TRIPS Agreement, available at http://www.wto.org.

13. The U.S.–Chile and U.S.–DR–CAFTA agreements have language similar to that of the TRIPS agreement, acknowledging that no obligation is created regarding the distribution of law enforcement resources. But the fact that resource constraints may not be invoked as an excuse for not meeting the agreements' specific enforcement obligations appears to significantly weaken this flexibility.

14. These bilateral investment treaties entered into force in 2001 (U.S.–Bahrain) and 2003 (U.S.–Jordan).

15. From an economic perspective, trademarks and geographical indications are different intellectual property instruments. They primarily seek to remedy asymmetries of information between buyers and sellers of goods and do not entail a trade-off between innovation and competitive access. See Fink and Maskus (2004).

16. It is worth noting that Vietnam is not a member of the WTO and therefore not bound by the TRIPS disciplines. However, Vietnam is in the process of acceding to the WTO and must therefore bring its intellectual property system into compliance with the TRIPS Agreement.

17. For example, Australia removed parallel import restrictions for CDs in 1998. The European Union considered in 1999 to free parallel importation of trademarked goods from countries outside the Union, but in the end decided to maintain its existing regime. Legislation to allow parallel importation of prescription drugs into the United States has been extensively debated in the U.S. Congress, but no decision has been taken as of October 2005.

18. Least developed countries are not required to protect pharmaceutical patents until 2016, with a possibility of a further extension (see Fink 2005).

19. See the proposed Digital Media Consumers' Rights Act, introduced in the U.S. House of Representatives (http://www.house.gov/boucher/internet.htm). Companies supporting the proposed legislation include computer manufacturers such as Gateway and Sun Microsystems; component manufacturers such as Intel; and telecommunications companies such as Verizon, Qwest, and BellSouth. For a full list, see http://www.house.gov/boucher/docs/107supporters.htm.

20. See the Bipartisan Trade Promotion Authority Act of 2002, available at http://www.tpa.gov.

21. For example, in the area of data protection, instruments other than data exclusivity exist to protect test data against unfair commercial use (CIPR 2002).

References

Abbott, Frederick. 2004. "The Doha Declaration on the TRIPS Agreement and Public Health and the Contradictory Trend in Bilateral and Regional Free Trade Agreements." Occasional Paper 14, Quaker United Nations Office.

CIPR (Commission on Intellectual Property Rights). 2002. "Integrating Intellectual Property Rights and Development Policy." Report of the Commission on Intellectual Property Rights established by the U.K. Secretary of State for International Development.

Correa, Carlos M. 2004. "Bilateral Investment Agreements: Agents of a New Global Standard for the Protection of Intellectual Property Rights?" Available at http://www.grain.org/briefings/?id=186.

Fink, Carsten. 2005. "Intellectual Property and Public Health: Putting the WTO's August 2003 Decision into Perspective." Reprinted in this volume. World Bank, Washington, DC.

Fink, Carsten, and Keith Maskus. 2004. "Intellectual Property and Development: Lessons from Recent Economic Research." New York and Washington, DC: Oxford University Press and World Bank.

Roffe, Pedro. 2004. "Bilateral Agreements and a TRIPS-plus World: the Chile-USA Free Trade Agreement." TRIPS Issue Paper 4. Quaker International Affairs Programme, Ottawa.

Compensating Lost Revenue in Regional Trade Agreements

Peter Walkenhorst

The proliferation of free trade agreements and customs unions since the early 1990s has been remarkable. Today most countries are party to one or more regional trade initiatives (World Bank 2004). Economic integration at the regional level allows the members to reap benefits from specialization while accommodating the particular needs and adjustment capacities of the countries involved. Structural and fiscal adjustment cannot be avoided entirely, however, and in some cases special provisions to contain adverse impacts on countries and foster coherence among members have been devised. One type of provision compensates for losses of government revenue from intraregional tariff reductions.[1]

Multilateral or regional trade liberalization does not necessarily lead to revenue losses. If tariff reductions (to levels above zero) trigger a more-than-proportional increase in trade flows, government revenues from trade taxes may in fact rise. Moreover, revenues from taxes on value-added (sales) and income taxes are likely to grow because of higher domestic consumption arising from lower prices of tradables, as well as higher growth resulting from the improved allocation of resources in the economy. If revenue shortfalls occur, however, countries with sound administrative capacity will often be able to recover the losses by strengthening domestic indirect taxes, broadening the tax base, and increasing the efficiency of raising funds for the government (Keen and Ligthart 2001).

However, low-income countries, and particularly the least developed countries (LDCs), frequently lack adequate administrative capacity and a well functioning domestic tax system. They tend to rely heavily on trade taxes as sources of government revenue. Lowering or eliminating tariffs on trade with regional partners, therefore, can constitute a significant risk to a country's fiscal position (Baunsgaard and Keen 2005). For example, estimates of the prospective impact of the Economic Partnership Agreement between the European Union and the Economic Community of West African States (ECOWAS) indicate that some of the participating African countries could lose more than 20 percent of their government revenues as a result of preferential tariff reductions (Busse and Grossmann 2004).

To alleviate such potentially important fiscal effects, revenue loss compensation arrangements (RLCAs) have been introduced into some regional integration initiatives (RIIs). Most RLCAs involve the establishment of a compensation fund from which payouts for tariff revenue losses are made. Several examples can be found in RIIs in Africa (table 1). However, lack of progress in the underlying schemes has often hampered implementation. For example, in ECOWAS a minority of members

Table 1. Characteristics of revenue sharing and compensation arrangements in regional integration

Agreement	Stage of integration	No. of members (of which LDCs)	Financing mechanism	Allocation criteria	Period of operation	Remarks
Caribbean Community (CARICOM)	Common market	14 (0)	Imposition of intra-regional tariffs.	Retention of revenues from intraregional tariffs.	Temporary, according to decision by Council for Trade and Economic Development.	Upon application by less-developed members to Council for Trade and Economic Development.
Common Market for Eastern and Southern Africa (COMESA)	Preferential/free trade agreement	19 (12)	To be determined in protocol.	To be determined in protocol.		RSA protocol in development.
Economic Community of Central African States (ECCAS)	Cooperation agreement	11 (8)	Saved tariff expenditure on intraregional exports.	Lost tariff revenue on intraregional imports.		RSA not implemented.
Economic Community of West African States (ECOWAS)	Preferential trade agreement	15 (11)	Community levy of 0.5 percent on imports from third countries.	Lost tariff revenue from intraregional imports, according to customs declaration.	Four years (from January 2002), degressive compensation.	RSA not operational.
Southern African Customs Union (SACU)	Customs union	5 (1)	Common revenue pool of all customs and excise duties.	Combination of projected intraregional import shares and gross domestic product.	Not determined.	Portion of funds raised is used for other purposes.
West African Economic and Monetary Union (WAEMU)	Economic and Monetary union	8 (7)	Community solidarity surcharge of 1 percent on imports from third countries.	Lost tariff revenue from intraregional imports, according to customs declaration.	Six years (from January 2000), degressive compensation.	Portion of funds raised is used for other purposes than revenue loss compensation.

Source: World Bank staff.

have yet to implement their trade liberalization commitments or pay their contributions to the compensation fund. The RLCAs in the Common Market of Eastern and Southern Africa (COMESA) and the Economic Community of Central African States (ECCAS) appear even further away from effective implementation. By contrast, the revenue sharing funds in the Southern African Customs Union (SACU) and the West African Economic and Monetary Union (WAEMU) have been operational for several years.

RLCAs differ in their design and implementation characteristics, particularly with respect to their duration and their handling of resource mobilization and payout criteria. We will discuss each of these features in turn before describing an operational RLCA, SACU's revised Common Revenue Pool.

Resource mobilization

There are many ways to raise resources to compensate for revenue losses. The resource mobilization schemes in existing RLCAs can be classified according to whether they rely on existing or new revenue sources, and again according to whether they are based on domestic or trade taxes.

- *Existing (or new) domestic and trade taxes.* Contributions are paid from general government revenues. A (nonoperational) example is ECCAS, where the contributions of members to the compensation fund are determined according to the saved tariff expenditures on intraregional exports.

- *Existing trade taxes.* Customs duty revenues are allocated to a compensation or revenue sharing fund. An example is the customs component in SACU's Common Revenue Pool.
- *New trade taxes.* Tariffs on imports are increased to raise revenues for use as compensation. For example, ECOWAS and WAEMU apply surcharges to third country imports, while the Caribbean Community and Common Market (CARICOM) allows its less developed members to apply for the temporary (re)introduction of intra-RII tariffs in order to overcome tariff revenue shortfalls.

All existing RLCAs are based at least partly on trade taxes, and many on newly introduced ones. Import duties have the advantage of being relatively easy to administer. They represent, however, one of the most economically costly forms of taxation (Clarete and Whalley 1987). Moreover, in order to minimize distortions in the economy, it is generally desirable to first try to enhance revenue collection by broadening the tax base, e.g. by curtailing tax or import duty exemptions, before increasing tax rates.

Designated taxes are used in all existing RLCAs, except ECCAS, as the instruments to raise funds for compensation. This earmarking of revenue sources protects the compensation fund largely from annual budget discussions in member countries. On the other hand, it tends to expose the fund to volatility in the underlying revenue source, to which other funding arrangements, such as those based on the relative economic size of partner countries, would not be subject.

Payout criteria

RLCAs also differ in how payments from compensation funds are allocated. The criteria used in existing RLCAs to determine the payouts to beneficiary countries are based on intraregional trade shares or incurred revenue losses.

- *Trade shares.* The funds available for compensation or revenue sharing are distributed among member countries in proportion to their shares in total intraregional imports. SACU's customs component payout is an example of a trade share–based compensation scheme.
- *Incurred revenue loss.* Compensation is paid on the basis of submitted customs declarations on intra-RII trade for the period under consideration and the loss in revenue associated with the nonapplication of most-favored-nation (MFN) tariffs to partner country trade. Such a scheme is operated, for example, by WAEMU (and envisaged by ECCAS and ECOWAS). The compensation payments are determined by multiplying MFN tariff rates by intraregional trade flows after removal of intra-RII tariffs. This method overestimates the loss of tariff revenue, as the liberalization of intraregional trade will trigger an increase in the exchange of goods among partner countries. A scheme based on historical intraregional

trade flows (that is, flows before establishment of the RII) would avoid this estimation bias, but it would not take into account changes in intraregional trade flows that might occur for reasons other than regional integration. The administration and monitoring of a payout scheme becomes more demanding depending on the degree of precision the partner countries require in the calculating and tracking the tariff revenue losses. Schemes based on historical trade patterns or aggregate intraregional trade shares are much less cumbersome to handle than those centered on shipment-specific customs declarations, for example. Although customs operations in many countries are intensifying their use of computers and, hence, becoming more capable of treating large amounts of data quickly and reliably, considerable scope for error in handling RLCA-relevant information remains.

The establishment of RLCAs has often been propelled by concerns that the benefits from regional integration might be unequally distributed and accentuate disparities in development levels within the region, with the stronger, larger economies gaining at the expense of weaker, smaller countries. In addition to being instruments of compensation for lost tariff revenues, therefore, RLCAs may be seen as vehicles of economic solidarity weighted in favor of the poorer countries in the group. For that reason many compensation funds also have a role in supporting development and cohesion. For example, the development component of SACU's Common Revenue Pool is distributed among member countries in inverse proportion to their per capita income, thus favoring less-developed members.

Duration of arrangements

As intraregional liberalization leads to expanded trade, revenues from domestic value-added, excise, and income taxes can be expected to increase, reducing the necessity for revenue redistribution over time. Many RLCAs, though not all, are therefore of a temporary nature.

- *Fixed duration.* The period of operation for the RLCA may be limited to a certain number of years. For example, for ECOWAS the duration of the arrangement is four years; for WAEMU, six years.
- *Duration determined by administrative decision.* The period of operation of the RLCA may be decided case by case. Such an arrangement exists in CARICOM, where the Council for Trade and Economic Development accepts applications for the revenue safeguard fund from less-developed members.
- *Duration not determined.* The duration of the RLCA may be open-ended. Such an arrangement exists in SACU.

The compensation payments in ECOWAS and WAEMU are scheduled to be scaled down over time before the RLCA expires. A similar development might occur in SACU, as further bilateral or multilateral trade liberalization reduces customs revenues and hence the funds available to compensate for revenue losses. The scaling down of RLCA payouts over time gives countries an incentive to pursue their fiscal reform processes and strengthen nontrade sources of government revenue.

The example of SACU's Common Revenue Pool

In October 2002, the members of SACU (Botswana, Lesotho, Namibia, South Africa, and Swaziland) signed a new agreement that revised the union's revenue sharing arrangements, the purpose of which is to increase members' fiscal stability. The arrangement stipulates that all customs, excise, and additional duties collected in the common customs area are to be paid into a Common Revenue Pool. The pooled revenues are then categorized into components for distribution purposes. SACU members agreed that their respective shares during any financial year would be calculated from each of three distinct components, net of the budgeted costs of financing the administration of the arrangement.

- *The customs component*, consisting of all customs duties actually collected, is distributed on the basis of each country's percentage share of total intra-SACU imports, excluding reexports. As South Africa currently has a large trade surplus with its SACU partner countries, its share in total intra-SACU imports is relatively small, and its payout from the customs component is less than proportional to the country's relative economic size. Conversely, the four less-developed SACU members receive a share of total customs revenues that exceeds their relative size.

- *The excise component*, consisting of all excise duties actually collected on goods produced in the common customs area (net of the development component), is allocated on the basis of each country's share in total SACU gross domestic product (GDP). The inclusion of excise duties in the common pool was motivated by the difficulty of administering separate excise regimes in a region with porous borders. Payouts from the excise component currently do not have a marked redistributional effect.

- *The development component* is funded initially from 15 percent of the total excise component and distributed on the basis of each country's GDP per capita, with lower income countries receiving a larger than proportional share of the payouts.

The revenue shares of each component was supposed to be calculated from audited data on trade, GDP, and GDP per capita, as well as agreed customs and excise forecasts, with possible adjustments in the ensuing two years to reflect actual collections (Kirk and Stern 2003). The distribution of revenues is approximate and implicit, thereby avoiding a cumbersome handling of customs declarations in the compensation process. The flexible and symmetric setup also facilitates the possible expansion of customs union membership to other countries in the region. However, in practice the revenue sharing formula has provided countries with incentives to overstate their intra-SACU imports in order to obtain larger payouts, so that it has been very difficult –if not impossible– to reach agreement on the base for revenue distribution.

Policy implications

For countries that have weak domestic tax administrations and rely heavily on trade taxes for government finances, lowering or eliminating tariffs on trade with regional partners can pose a significant fiscal risk. To pursue regional integration despite that risk, provisions on revenue sharing have been added to several RIIs, although not all are operational. Analysis of existing arrangements suggests several desirable design features for RLCAs—among them the use of domestic tax revenues instead of economically more costly trade taxes as the preferred means of raising revenues for compensation. Moreover, simple payout criteria, possibly historically based, facilitate the monitoring and administration of the mechanism. And finally, limited periods of duration and a reduction of compensation payments over time are consistent with the revenue-enhancing effect of trade-induced growth and preserve the incentive for governments to pursue fiscal reforms.

As our survey of RLCAs showed, there are very few examples of operational arrangements; even these are generally of a temporary nature. This means that most regional trade agreements do not foresee or implement provisions for revenue sharing or revenue loss compensation. Hence, countries that are confronted with markedly adverse impacts on their fiscal balance as a result of preferential liberalization can not rely on designated resources from regional partners but must cope with the revenue shortfalls domestically through complementary policy reforms. In some cases, improvements in customs collection through better compliance with existing regulations may be sufficient to offset the revenue losses. In others, more comprehensive reform measures to broaden the tax base and shift revenue generation away from trade taxes will be required. Such fiscal reforms are not easy to design and implement, but they are often necessary to complement trade reforms and reap the full benefits of economic integration.

Notes
1. This chapter was prepared by Peter Walkenhorst, Senior Economist, International Trade Department, World Bank.

References
Baunsgaard, T., and M. Keen, 2005. *Tax Revenue and (or?) Trade Liberalization.* Working Paper WP/05/112. International Monetary Fund, Washington, DC.
Busse, M., and H. Grossmann. 2004. *Assessing the Impact of ACP/EU Economic Partnership Agreement on West African Countries.* HWWA Discussion Paper 294. Hamburgisches Welt-

Wirtschafts-Archiv, Hamburg.

Clarete, R., and J. Whalley. 1987. "Comparing the Marginal Welfare Costs of Commodity and Trade Taxes." *Journal of Public Economics* 33: 357–62.

Keen, M., and J. Ligthart. 2001. "Coordinating Tariff Reductions and Domestic Tax Reform." *Journal of International Economics* 56: 407–25.

Kirk, R., and M. Stern. 2003. *The New Southern African Customs Union Agreement.* Africa Region Working Paper Series 57. World Bank, Washington, DC.

World Bank. 2004. *Global Economic Prospects 2005: Trade, Regionalism, and Development.* Washington, DC: World Bank.

Regionalism vs. Multilateralism?

Dominique van der Mensbrugghe, Richard Newfarmer and
Martha Denisse Pierola

Though few would argue that regionalism is an alternative to multilateralism, the rapid proliferation of regional trade arrangements (RTAs)[1] contrasts vividly with the slow pace of multilateral liberalization. It is worthwhile, therefore, to assess the projected benefits of both approaches to get a sense of what would happen if the Doha Round should whither on the vine. And, as developing countries pursue RTAs, it is worth exploring what types of arrangements—and under what circumstances—produce the greatest benefits.[2]

The major conclusion of the simulations reported here is that developing countries would be worse off under a complex system of overlapping bilateral and regional agreements: they would suffer losses averaging 0.4 percent in real income (and 1 percent for low-income countries alone). When the simulations are applied to selected North–South and South–South agreements, the gains obtained are significantly lower than those that could be obtained from a multilateral arrangement. All in all, multilateralism produces the most development friendly outcomes.

The prospect of obtaining first-mover advantages by signing bilateral trade agreements with major trading partners before others can do so has been one of the main reasons for preferring regionalism over multilateralism. But the days of first-mover advantages are probably over. The proliferation of RTAs around the world has already eliminated the possibility of obtaining the quick gains countries sought from regional deals. In addition, the profusion of RTAs is leading to the formation of trading blocs, a scenario in which weak economies can easily be marginalized.

The landscape of national policy strategies: current trends

Since the early 1990s there has been a significant acceleration in the number of RTAs signed around the world. As of January 2005, 312 RTAs had been notified to the GATT/WTO, 170 of which are currently in force (Crawford and Fiorentino 2005). The increase in the number of RTAs was pronounced after 1993 (figure 1).

Crawford and Fiorentino (2005) identified the following trends in the formation of RTAs:

- The formation of RTAs is a phenomenon observed across countries. In fact, regionalism is, for an increasing number of countries, the main element of their trade policy.

Figure 1. The number of RTAs has strongly increased

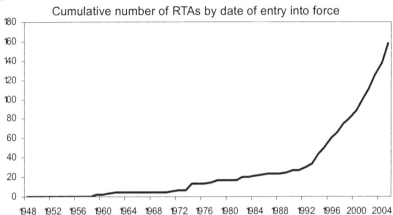

Cumulative number of RTAs by date of entry into force

Note: We use the term RTA to refer to agreements signed either by pairs of trading partners or by a group of countries.
Source: World Trade Organization (WTO) (http://www.wto.org/english/tratop_e//region_e/ eif_e.xls).

- Today's RTAs are broader in coverage than in the past. In that sense, they are becoming more complex. They contain provisions applicable to subjects that go beyond those negotiated at the level of the WTO—among them investment, competition, environment, and labor, among other topics.

- Reciprocal preferential North–South agreements are increasing in number. There is also a significant emergence of South–South partnerships.

- RTAs are expanding and consolidating across regions and within continents. Most countries today belong to at least one RTA. Indeed, a "spaghetti bowl" of multiple and overlapping RTAs around the globe has emerged.[3]

As far as typology of RTAs is concerned, Free Trade Agreements (FTAs) are the most common type (84 percent at all RTAs in force vs. 8 percent for Custom Unions and 8 percent for Partial Scope Agreements). As for the configuration of RTAs, bilateral agreements account for more than 75 percent of all RTAs notified and in force, and for almost 90 percent of those under negotiation.

Most RTAs are between transition economies (29 percent), followed by North–South agreements (26 percent) and South–South agreements (21 percent) (figure 2). Among the North–South agreements, those involving the states of the European Union and those of the European Free Trade Association (EFTA) together account

Figure 2. RTAs: Everybody is doing it

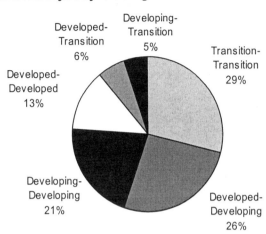

Note: Notified RTAs in goods by type of partner (as of February 2005).
Source: Crawford and Fiorentino (2005).

for more than half. The number of South–South agreements has increased significantly in recent years. Trade within RTAs covered a third of world trade in 2002; however, if MFN rates of zero are excluded, the RTA share declines to 20 percent (World Bank 2005).

Why have countries favored bilateral or regional trade strategies over multilateralism? There are three major reasons. First, countries may hope to maximize their benefits through so-called first-mover advantages. That is, they focus on the gains they could obtain from signing an agreement with a large trading partner before competing countries do so. Or they may seek to preempt other countries, by denying them first-mover advantages. The validity of this argument will be analyzed in the next section. Second, countries may seek to guarantee permanent access to particular markets. Signing an agreement bilaterally or regionally may be the quickest and easiest way of achieving that goal. Third, a bilateral agreement may be used as leverage to facilitate domestic reforms, particularly in areas that are not dealt with multilaterally, such as investment, competition, and environmental and labor standards.

Is regionalism better than multilateralism? Results from simulations

In this section we evaluate the gains and losses that a country might expect to realize by pursuing a bilateral or regional trade strategy instead of multilateralism. The methodology used in our simulations is based on the database of the Global

Trade Analysis Project (GTAP), headquartered at Purdue University. The GTAP database is widely used to assess the global, regional, and country implications of alternative trade liberalization scenarios. The database used to obtain the results has 2001 as its base year and takes preferential trade access into account. To assess the relative impacts of various RTAs, we performed a benchmark simulation on a global reform scenario in which all merchandise trade distortions, domestic distortions in agriculture,[4] and import quotas in the textile and clothing sectors are removed. Services reform is left out for lack of sufficient data. Under this scenario, the ultimate outcome of successful multilateralism, global gains in 2015 amount to $263 billion, or an increase of 0.8 percent in baseline income.[5]

In addition to the benchmark, three scenarios were simulated:

•   All developing countries sign a bilateral agreement with Quad-plus countries: Canada, European Union, Japan, and the United States, plus Australia and New Zealand.

•   Developing countries minus large countries—Brazil, China, and India—sign a bilateral agreement with Quad-plus countries.

•   Individual developing countries or regions sign an a bilateral agreement with the Quad-plus countries, while other developing countries do not.[6]

The results from the first simulation show that, as a group, developing countries are substantially worse off than with a multilateral agreement.[7] Instead of gaining $109 billion from global reform, they lose $22 billion relative to a baseline scenario, with no change in protection (Table 1).[8] Looking at countries separately, the results are similar. Only a handful of developing countries—for example, Brazil and China—would gain more from a system of bilateral agreements. High-income countries, too, would generally lose from this set of bilateral agreements compared with global reform, yet the impact is not uniform.[9] Both, the United States and the European Union (the most aggressive advocates of bilateral deals) would appear to benefit more from pursuing bilateral agreements with all developing countries than from global reform ($7 and $27 billion respectively). Although they would have to open up their agricultural markets to some extent (assuming exemptions were disallowed), they would not have to dismantle domestic support programs. In agriculture, the Quad-plus agricultural exporters—Australia, Canada, and New Zealand—would prefer multilateralism, because the gains from access to European, Japanese, and American markets and from the dismantling of distortionary agricultural support programs would be highly beneficial for their farmers.

In the second simulation, many developing regions still lose in absolute terms compared with the baseline scenario. They also lose relative to the benchmark global reform scenario, although in some cases (Indonesia, rest of Latin America and Caribbean, and rest of world), the gains from bilateral agreements approach those in the global reform scenario. The gains for the high-income countries are

Table 1. Comparison of bilateral scenarios to global trade reform

Change in real income in 2015 compared to baseline

	Global merchandise trade reform	All developing sign bilateral with Quad-plus	All developing (minus large countries) sign bilateral with Quad-plus
	(1)	(2)	(3)
		US$ billions	
High-income countries	154.4	133.6	46.9
Low-income countries	16.6	–19.0	–1.9
Middle-income countries	92.2	–2.6	–4.7
All developing countries	108.8	–21.5	–6.6
World total	263.2	112.0	40.3
		Percent	
High-income countries	0.6	0.5	0.2
Low-income countries	0.9	–1.0	–0.1
Middle-income countries	1.2	0.0	–0.1
All developing countries	1.2	–0.2	–0.1
World total	0.8	0.3	0.1

Source: World Bank simulations.

significantly lower when the large developing countries are excluded—not surprising given their weight in global trade with the Quad countries. Finally, the impact on the excluded countries is mixed: Brazil and China, which would gain according to the results obtained from the first simulation, lose when excluded. The other excluded regions—India, Mexico, Russian Federation, rest of East Asia, and rest of South Asia—would see a dampening of their losses.

With the results from the third simulation, in which each developing country or region signs an agreement with the Quad-plus countries while no other country or region does so, we address the question of first-mover advantages, one of the chief reasons for preferring a bilateral or regional strategy over a multilateral one. The results from the simulation support the notion of first-mover gains: about half of the developing regions would be better off with a bilateral agreement than with a global agreement (Appendix 1).[10] In some cases, however, this conclusion does not hold: the rest of the Sub-Saharan Africa region could suffer losses from a bilateral agreement with the Quad because this region already has relatively free access to the Quad markets. Permitting greater imports from the Quad would worsen their terms of trade and negate gains from the bilateral agreement. The Russian Federation and the Middle East are dependent on energy exports, which face low tariffs in industrial countries (even if energy is heavily taxed), so these regions have little to gain from additional market access.

The chief reservation about the third simulation, of course, is that it is starkly counterfactual. The idea that a single developing country or region would be able to sign an exclusive agreement with the Quad countries without competition from other developing countries is unrealistic. The increase in the number of agreements over the last decade means that a sizable portion of any first-mover advantage already has been eroded.

Conclusions

Developing countries could gain an (unweighted) average of 1.7 percent in real income from a global agreement. However, if all developing countries signed bilateral agreements with the Quad, creating a complex system of bilateral and regional agreements, developing countries would suffer losses averaging 0.4 percent (1 percent for the low-income countries). Virtually all developing countries would be worse off than at present,

While some individual developing countries might have gained from entering exclusive agreements with Quad countries, the proliferation of RTAs probably has already eliminated that first-mover advantage.

In general terms, multilateralism is the most development friendly outcome.

This conclusion is highlighted if we extend the simulation to several hypothetical North–South and South–South regional trading blocks (figures 3 and 4).[11] Several of these (a broad free trade region in East Asia, for example) offer significant gains, but not as great as the gains from global merchandise trade reform. The difference can be much more pronounced in the case of South–South agreements, where the multilateral alternative clearly dominates the regional one. Forming North–South regional blocks individually always produces higher gains than forming them simultaneously.

The potential benefits of RTAs are now well understood. They can be easier to negotiate because they involve fewer partners; they can help consolidate a domestic reform agenda; they usually extend beyond the reduction of tariffs to include other cross-border issues; and they can confer political benefits, such as strengthening regional relations.

Also well understood are the characteristics of the most successful and sustainable RTAs:

- Low external MFN tariffs
- Few sectoral and product exemptions
- Nonrestrictive rules-of-origin tests that build toward a framework common to many agreements
- Measures to facilitate trade
- Large ex post markets
- Measures to promote new cross-border competition, particularly in services

Figure 3. Global reform dominates North–South

Change in real income in 2015 relative to the baseline in percent

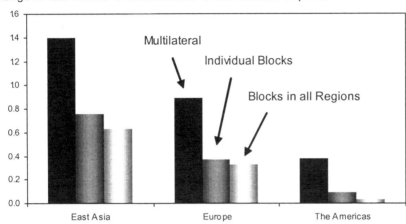

Note: *Multilatera* refers to the global merchandise trade reform scenario, *Individual Blocks* is when the North/South regional blocks are formed individually and *Block in all Regions* is when the North/South regional blocks are implemented simultaneously.
Source: World Bank simulations

Figure 4. ...and South–South agreements

Change in real income in 2015 relative to the baseline in percent

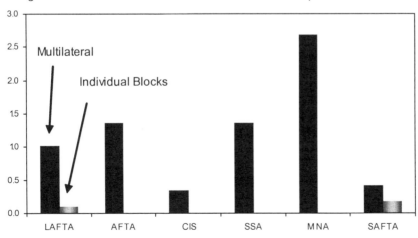

Note: *Multilateral* refers to the global merchandise trade reform scenario, and *Individual Blocks* is when the South/South regional blocks are formed in isolation.
Source: World Bank simulations.

315

* Rules governing investment and intellectual property that are appropriate to the development context.

The simulations reported here confirm the contention that to create trade and exert the fewest possible exclusionary effects, regional agreements must have low MFN tariffs and mild border barriers, so their impact gets closer to that of a global reform scenario. The best way to ensure that regional agreements have these characteristics is to accelerate progress on the Doha Round and to fill in the blanks of the July 2004 Framework Agreement with multilateral reductions in protection, especially for products produced by the world's poor.

Notes

1. We use the term RTA to refer to agreements signed eiether by pairs of trading partners or by a group of countries.

2. Note based on chapter 6 in Global Economic Prospects 2005.

3. Of all the WTO member countries, only Mongolia is not engaged in an RTA. Eleven nonmembers of WTO are not party to an RTA.

4. The distortions included are input and output subsidies, direct payments, and export subsidies.

5. The results described herein were produced using the GTAP V6.01 database. Using the most recent version of the database, the gains from global merchandise trade reform amount to $287 billion, but these minor differences in outcomes have little bearing on the overall findings.

6. Under the bilateral agreements, domestic distortions are not removed because they are not specific to any individual trading partner.

7. All scenarios overstate bilateral and multilateral effects because they assume that no sectors are exempt and that rules of origin are not restrictive.

8. A detailed table of effects is provided as Appendix 1.

9. Note that some of the high-income Asian countries—for example Republic of Korea and Singapore—are excluded from the bilateral agreements and therefore tend to lose, in part, because of trade diversion.

10. According to this scenario, the winners (relative to global liberalization) are: China, Indonesia, Mexico, Southern African Customs Union, rest of South Asia, and EU accession countries. Among the losers: Brazil, India, Russian Federation, Vietnam, rest of East Asia, rest of Europe and Central Asia, Middle East and North Africa, rest of Sub-Saharan Africa, and rest of Latin America and the Caribbean.

11. The three North–South agreements include a broad East Asia region that encompasses both the high-income and developing countries, the FTAA in the Western Hemisphere, and a broad free trade area centered on the European Union, including the new accession countries and extending to the Middle East and North Africa and Sub-Saharan Africa. The South–South agreements include a Latin American–wide RTA (LAFTA), a developing East Asian RTA (AFTA), a Europe and Central Asia RTA that excludes the EU accession countries (CIS), a Sub-Saharan African RTA (SSA), the Middle East and North Africa (MNA), and a South Asian RTA (SAFTA).

Further reading

Crawford, Jo-Ann, and Roberto V. Fiorentino. 2005. "The Changing Landscape of Regional Trade Agreements." WTO Discussion Paper 8. World Trade Organization, Geneva.
World Bank. 2005. *Global Economic Prospects: Trade Regionalism, and Development* 2005. Washington, DC: World Bank.

Appendix 1. Comparison of bilateral agreements with global trade reform

Change in real income in 2015 compared to baseline

| | Billions of dollars | | | | Percent | | | |
| | Global merchandise trade reform | Bilateral agreements between Quad-plus and all developing countries | Bilateral agreements between Quad-plus and developing countries excluding large countries | Bilateral agreements between Quad-plus and each developing country | Global merchandise trade reform | Bilateral agreements between Quad-plus and all developing countries | Bilateral agreements between Quad-plus and developing countries excluding large countries | Bilateral agreements between Quad-plus and each developing country |
	(1)	(2)	(3)	(4)	(5)	(6)	(7)	(8)
Australia, Canada, and New Zealand	8.4	6.0	0.5		0.7	0.5	0.0	
United States	24.9	32.3	10.7		0.2	0.3	0.1	
European Union with EFTA	55.0	82.4	33.6		0.7	1.1	0.4	
Japan	29.7	25.0	4.8		0.9	0.8	0.1	
Korea and Taiwan (China)	26.4	-9.8	-2.3		2.6	-1.0	-0.2	
Hong Kong (China) and Singapore	9.8	-2.4	-0.3		2.8	-0.7	-0.1	
Brazil	8.0	1.5	-1.7	7.3	1.4	0.3	-0.3	1.3
China	14.1	9.7	-7.2	21.8	0.6	0.4	-0.3	1.0
India	4.3	-10.0	-3.1	2.1	0.5	-1.2	-0.4	0.2
Indonesia	3.6	-2.3	3.0	5.1	1.4	-0.9	1.2	2.1
Mexico	0.3	-1.5	-1.3	2.6	0.0	-0.2	-0.2	0.3
Russian Federation	2.9	-1.7	-1.3	0.8	0.8	-0.5	-0.3	0.2
South African Customs Union	2.5	-0.3	0.8	3.7	1.8	-0.2	0.5	2.6
Vietnam	2.4	-0.2	0.6	0.9	5.0	-0.5	1.3	1.9
Rest of East Asia	19.6	-5.0	-2.8	7.4	4.7	-1.2	-0.7	1.8
Rest of South Asia	0.4	-3.2	-1.1	1.2	0.2	-1.3	-0.4	0.5
EU accession countries	0.8	-2.0	-0.5	0.9	0.2	-0.4	-0.1	0.2
Rest of Europe and Central Asia	2.3	-3.3	-1.3	0.4	0.5	-0.7	-0.3	0.1
Middle East	6.1	-2.7	-0.1	1.3	0.9	-0.4	0.0	0.2
North Africa	19.1	1.9	4.3	5.7	6.7	0.6	1.5	2.0
Rest of Sub-Saharan Africa	2.9	-3.0	-2.5	-0.2	1.1	-1.2	-1.0	-0.1
Rest of Latin America and Caribbean	16.3	0.9	6.4	9.6	1.6	0.1	0.6	0.9
Rest of world	3.0	-0.3	1.2	4.0	1.3	-0.1	0.6	1.8
High-income countries	154.4	133.6	46.9		0.6	0.5	0.2	
Low-income countries	16.6	-19.0	-1.9		0.9	-1.0	-0.1	
Middle-income countries	92.2	-2.6	-4.7		1.2	0.0	-0.1	
All developing countries	108.8	-21.5	-6.6		1.2	-0.2	-0.1	
World total	263.2	112.0	40.3		0.8	0.3	0.1	

Source: World Bank Simulations

Aid for Trade

Julia Nielson

Many poor countries have been unable to use trade as an engine for growth. Some lack the necessary infrastructure—roads, ports, telecommunications—to link their producers to global markets. Others have inefficient institutions—for customs, tax, and product standards—that drive up the costs of trading. Or producers may lack knowledge about market opportunities and how to access them. For countries that have such problems, market access is not the major challenge; many are unable to use their existing—and often preferential—access to large markets for lack of transport facilities or the ability to meet high standards in export markets.

A second set of constraints is rooted in the political economy of domestic policy. Some poor countries are reluctant to undertake trade-policy reforms that may be in their long-term interest because of concerns about short-term adjustment costs. They may be reluctant to cut tariffs, for example, for fear of losing government revenue. Trade reforms typically create winners and losers, and many poor countries face considerable challenges in providing safety nets, retraining, and other means of adjustment for affected groups.

More recently, the potential costs of adjusting to liberalization by *other* countries have raised similar concerns. Some countries fear the erosion of their preferential market access as trading partners reduce their tariffs on a nondiscriminatory basis. Some net food importers are concerned about the impact of rising food prices following reform of agricultural subsidies in rich countries.

Against this background, many poor countries see more threats than opportunities in the current trade talks. With little confidence that they will be able to benefit from further market opening, and amid concerns about the potential adjustment costs of their own and others' liberalization, many of the poorest countries have adopted a defensive position across the board in the Doha Round, thereby threatening the success of the talks.

There is thus a compelling case, from the perspectives of development and trade, for helping countries overcome the constraints that prevent or discourage them from taking advantage of new market openings. The development case is the most important: countries that are unable to integrate into global markets miss out on important sources of sustainable growth and poverty reduction. But the trade case is important, too: additional assistance is essential to encourage the poorest countries to support an ambitious outcome from the Doha Round, and thus to maintain a strong and effective multilateral trading system—both very much in the interests of poor countries. Additional assistance is thus a key complement to, but not a substitute for, ambitious trade liberalization under the Doha Round. This is the reasoning behind the current push to increase "aid for trade."

What is "aid for trade"?

In practical terms, aid for trade encompasses five main activities:

- *Technical assistance*: the provision of technical assistance, advice, and expertise to assist countries confronted with the complexities of modern trade.
- *Capacity building*: building the capacity of developing countries to deal with trade issues, for example, through the training of government officials.
- *Institutional reform*: helping to create a framework of sound and well-functioning institutions for trade—in customs, quality assurance, and other areas.
- *Infrastructure*: improving roads and ports to link the poor and the goods they produce to markets through investment in infrastructure.
- *Assistance with adjustment costs*: fiscal support and policy advice to help countries cope with any transitional adjustment costs from liberalization.

Successful aid-for-trade projects generally combine most of these elements. For example, the World Bank is working with Vietnam on a project for comprehensive customs reform, encompassing capacity building, simplification of clearance procedures, modernization of the legal framework, and improved information and communication technology. Likewise, the Standards and Trade Development Facility, initiated by the World Bank and the World Trade Organization (WTO), uses a mixture of financing, technical assistance, and donor coordination to build the capacity of developing countries to meet international standards in food and agricultural exports.

In this sense, aid for trade is not new—mechanisms aimed at increasing the supply-side capacity of developing countries and easing adjustment concerns have been part of development programs for some time (box 1).

The purpose of the current push on aid for trade is to significantly scale up this aid and to make it more effective. This is timely for a number of reasons:

- First, annual development aid is expected to increase by $50 billion by 2010, if recent promises are kept. The increase will bring greater scrutiny of the extent to which aid contributes to sustained growth. Important new agreements have also been reached on increasing aid effectiveness through a greater focus on country ownership, donor coordination, and harmonization of aid policies.
- Dealing with the real currency appreciation from increased aid will require greater attention to trade liberalization, facilitation, and international competitiveness.
- Recent international initiatives on debt relief should be complemented by action to increase the trade capacity of the poorest countries if they are to avoid future unsustainable debt.

Box 1. Rwandan coffee: challenges, opportunities, and the role of aid for trade

Coffee is a key export crop in Rwanda. In 2003, an aggressive strategy was developed to increase total exports of coffee and move the industry into the high-quality, specialty end of the market. The strategy will require an estimated investment of $69 million: $24.75 million from donors and NGOs, $23 million from the private sector, and $21.25 million from the Rwandan government.

Major efforts are needed to achieve a reputation for Rwanda as a quality producer through international exhibitions, demonstrations, and contests—and strict quality control. Two long-term, donor-funded projects have been assisting producers in developing buyer–seller relationships and helping growers raise quality. Aid projects have also helped farmers to form cooperatives to meet the requirements of "fair trade" coffee and to experiment with organic and shade-grown coffees, all of which command a substantial premium over ordinary coffee.

Increased access to washing stations has increased farmers' incomes by up to 55 percent. Washing and grading the coffee cherries has made it possible to obtain higher prices for products of higher quality, giving farmers an incentive to increase quality. At one aid-for-trade project, washing stations track the output from individual farmers so that if a particular batch is sold at an exceptional price, part of the revenue flows back to the individual farmer. Regulatory reform has also allowed individual Rwandan cooperatives and private owners to negotiate directly with specialty roasters in the United States and Europe, enabling them to sell to specialty markets at more than twice the market rate.

The quality and the image of Rwandan coffee have improved markedly as a result of these efforts. However, the industry still faces challenges, for which further aid for trade is needed. Those challenges include: *access to finance* (donors are already providing some help in steamlining rural finance among producers' organizations); *access to low-cost transport* (the cost of transporting coffee from the farm gate to the port is 80 percent of the amount received by the coffee farmer, and major upgrading of transport infrastructure is needed); *access to training* (half a million Rwandan farmers need extensive training in all aspects of coffee production, but there are few agronomists); and *developing associations and cooperatives* (technical assistance is needed to strengthen coffee farmers' cooperatives and to form an overall industry association, along with reform of unclear government regulations).

Source: World Bank-IF 2005.

Figure 1. Trade assistance is expanding...

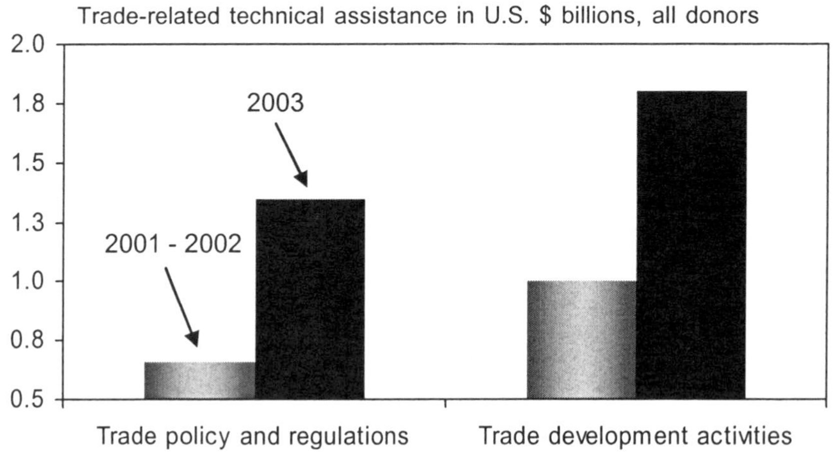

Trade-related technical assistance in U.S. $ billions, all donors

Source: OECD-DAC/WTO database.

- Finally, the critical juncture of the Doha Round provides a political focus for aid for trade. Global, nondiscriminatory trade liberalization under the WTO has some of the characteristics of a global public good—that is, a good from which everyone benefits but to which not everyone has sufficient incentive to contribute. All countries benefit from one country's trade reforms and trade-related investments, and benefits are increased when undertaken by several countries concurrently. However, the full benefits of reform are not necessarily captured by the country itself, which may lead to underinvestment in reform. Aid for trade is one way to ensure the provision of this global public good.

Steadily increasing aid for trade

Recent trends form a strong basis on which to build. Data compiled jointly by WTO and the Organization for Economic Cooperation and Development/Development Assistance Committee (OECD/DAC) indicate that resources devoted to trade-related capacity building and technical assistance increased significantly in 2003, after being static between 2001 and 2002 (figure 1).

Commitments for *trade policy and regulations* increased from about $660 million per year in 2001–02 to almost $1 billion in 2003. These sums support effective participation in multilateral trade negotiations, analysis and implementation of multilateral trade agreements, trade-policy mainstreaming, development of technical standards, trade facilitiation (including tariff structures and customs regimes), regional trade agreements, and human-resource development in trade.

Commitments for *trade development activities* increased from $1.35 billion per year in 2001–02 to $1.8 billion in 2003. This covers business development and activities aimed at improving the business climate, access to trade finance, and trade promotion in the productive sectors (agriculture, forestry, fishing, industry, mining, tourism, services) including at the institutional and enterprise level. The OECD/DAC database does not include *activities to enhance infrastructure* necessary for trade (roads, storage, communications, energy) due to difficulties in assessing the extent to which they are related to international trade, as opposed to the general economic climate of the country.

The World Bank has been rapidly expanding its support for trade through enhanced investments in infrastructure and support for trade facilitation. (Details of the Bank's activities, projects and lending related to trade are outlined in chapter 5.) Additionally, the Bank has a major program of trade research and a growing program of trade capacity building. It also is committed to incorporating trade-expanding projects into its country programs as a crucial step toward higher long-term growth. To that end, the Bank has been deeply involved in the Integrated Framework for Trade-Related Technical Assistance (box 2).

But despite these and other initiatives by donors and international organizations, demand for aid for trade continues to outstrip supply, and many poor countries have the capacity to absorb significantly more assistance. More needs to be done, and there is presently a window of opportunity to move forward.

What more can be done?

In February 2005, the G-7 Finance Ministers called on the World Bank and International Monetary Fund to develop proposals for additional assistance to countries to ease adjustment to trade liberalization and to increase their capacity to take advantage of more open markets. The call was reinforced by the Bank's 184 shareholders in April and again by the G-8 in July. Following extensive consultation, the Bank and Fund put forward a package of three proposals that received strong endorsement from ministers at the joint Bank-Fund annual meetings in September 2005. Work is now under way on their implementation.

Consultations held by the Bank and Fund revealed a sharp difference over the best way forward. For some, aid-for-trade needs would be best met by the establishment of a dedicated multilateral fund, as the only way to ensure that sufficient, *additional* resources were made available. Trade, they argue, is never likely to rank high enough among a country's priorities to receive funding via regular channels—particularly for poor countries with pressing demands in basic services such as health, and education. Countries should not have to choose between meeting basic needs now and investing in future growth; the "market failure" on trade should be addressed by a separate fund.

Box 2. The Integrated Framework and the least developed countries

The Integrated Framework for Trade-Related Technical Assistance (IF) brings together multilateral agencies (the International Monetary Fund, International Trade Centre, U.N. Conference on Trade and Development, U.N. Development Programme, World Bank, and WTO) and bilateral donors to assist least developed countries (LDCs). It has two objectives: (i) to integrate trade into national development plans such as poverty reduction strategies; and (ii) to assist in the coordinated delivery of trade-related technical assistance in response to needs identified by the LDC. The IF is built on the principles of country ownership and partnership.

The first step in the application of the IF to a given country is preparation on a diagnostic trade integration study (DTIS). The DTIS specifies the main elements of a policy framework for national trade integration and an action matrix that maps out the delivery of trade-related technical assistance while identifying trade-related investment needs. A special facility created in May 2003 finances small, priority technical assistance and capacity building projects of up to $1 million per country.

By the end 2005, DTISs will have been completed in 21 countries; seven more LDCs have started the process and nine more have applied to join the IF. At the end of May 2005, 22 projects had been approved in 12 countries, amounting to $8 million, covering many areas—among them building capacity for trade negotiation (Cambodia, Ethiopia, Madagascar), export-related information gathering and dissemination (Yemen), and sector-specific institutional and technical support (Burundi, Ethiopia, Senegal). Some 17 donors had pledged $30.2 million to the trust fund that finances the IF.

Notwithstanding the mismatch between its highly ambitious objectives and very modest resources, the IF has produced some good results. It has provided concrete capacity building projects (with just $8 million); made solid progress in the difficult task of coordinating donors and international agencies; contributed to greatly increased understanding of the constraints facing poor countries; and brought IF governments to the table on trade.

For others, such dedicated funds interfere with countries' ability to set their own priorities for donor financing; an ability that is a cornerstone of internationally agreed principles of aid effectiveness. Dedicated funds, it is argued, risk skewing priorities toward areas where external funding is available. Programs determined simply by the availability of funding tend to be insufficiently owned, and thus less likely to succeed. And, in any case, it is very difficult to know when funding is truly additional; creation of a new multilateral fund is no guarantee that funds have not been reallocated from other areas. The debate will continue.

So what's on the agenda for aid for trade?

Enhancing the Integrated Framework (IF)

The key initiative is enhancing the IF. Built on sound principles—country ownership, donor coordination, and mainstreaming of trade into national development strategies—the IF already has shown achievements to date, but it has lacked the scale to bring about real transformations at the national level. Challenges have included weak in-country capacity, lack of systematic follow-up at the country level, insufficient and uncertain financing, and variable donor response to priorities identified in the diagnostic trade integration study that provides the road map for national action under the IF.

Recent enhancements to the IF address those issues. They include a significant, multiyear expansion of resources for technical assistance and capacity building, and for strengthened governance and increased ownership at the country level. The main objective is still to mainstream trade into national development strategies to ensure policy coherence, increase donor coordination, and maximize financing of trade-related projects through bilateral and multilateral channels. Key features of the enhanced IF are:

- *Increased resources*: predictable, multiyear financing on the order of $200–$400 million, to be disbursed to participating LDCs over an initial five-year period, and taking the form of grants, not loans. Additional resources are also required for more effective governance at both the country and global levels.
- *Strengthened in-country structures*: increased up-front resources to help countries implement the IF at the national level—for example, by establishing implementation units within or closely linked to key economic ministries and developing coherent trade strategies. Involvement of the private sector and civil society in consultative bodies and project delivery has increased. Ongoing funding allocations are subject to performance.
- *Strengthened governance*: a lean and effective governance structure to ensure rapid and accountable disbursement of funds, with a professional, fully funded secretariat.
- *Improved links to donor processes*: stronger links between identified large-

scale needs (such as trade-related infrastructure) and donor funding through project-preparation studies in areas of priority. An essential corollary to the increased resources of the IF is increased donor willingness to fund aid for trade in the poverty reduction strategy (PRS) process. Several bilateral donors have already indicated their intention to devote more resources to aid for trade.

- *Multiyear programs of technical assistance and capacity building*: related to, for example, trade policy and strategy, strengthening of core trade-related institutions and functions, administrative and regulatory reforms, intragovernmental coordination, and private sector capacities and initiatives.[1]
- *Possibility of extended coverage*: while the IF has traditionally been a program for LDCs, consideration could be given to extending it to other low-income countries on the understanding that benefits for LDCs should not be diminished.

With thorough and meaningful implementation, the enhanced IF should address most aid-for-trade needs through countries' increased capacity to build trade needs into the PRS process, and through donors' increased willingness to make funds available for aid for trade in that context. This approach provides greater certainty that funds will be available to meet key needs, while preserving the centrality of country priorities determined in the PRS process, in line with agreed principles of aid effectiveness.

Regional and cross-country issues

While country priorities should be taken into account by the enhanced IF, some trade-related issues may not be sufficiently addressed in the PRS process—for example, regional issues. Cross-country issues may be particularly important for small, very poor, or landlocked countries that are dependent on action by neighbors for whom the issue may not be a high priority. For example, the roads that Rwanda requires to reach the ports of Mombasa and Dar es Salaam require the cooperation of Kenya, Tanzania and Uganda, but for those countries, roads in the hinterland may be a low priority. With 20 landlocked countries in the low-income group, there is a need to ensure that these issues do not fall through the gaps.

Small, very poor, or landlocked countries are also likely to face competing demands for existing resources. It may make sense for them to consider cost-effective regional machinery for trade, such as regional laboratories for standards testing or even regional infrastructure or regulatory frameworks to support liberalization in services such as electricity or telecommunications.

In the coming months, the Bank and Fund will examine the extent to which regional and cross-country needs are being met by existing mechanisms and whether there is a need for new ones. Possible new mechanisms to be explored include the opportunities offered by the enhanced IF, the scope for extending existing World Bank instruments, and a dedicated multilateral fund to provide grant cofinancing for regional projects in close coordination with other multilateral development banks and relevant agencies. Rather than cutting across country priorities, a fund in this instance could fill the gap left by the country-focused PRS process, addressing public goods among countries where all stand to gain.

Smoothing adjustments to trade liberalization

Trade liberalization creates adjustment problems for some countries; in some cases, the adjustment can be considerable. Countries suffering adjustment shocks from trade liberalization, including the Doha Round, need to be assured of transitional support from the international community.

A first step is identifying the countries affected. The Bank and Fund plan to assess the nature and magnitude of adjustment needs of countries that present a *prima facie* case of significant adjustment shocks. That group is likely to include, for example, countries negatively affected by the end of textile quotas and by preference erosion, net food importing countries, and countries undertaking major programs of trade reform.

Assessing the impact of adjustment shocks requires consideration of a wide range of factors, including: the possibility of offsetting lost tariff revenue through customs reform and more efficient collection of tariffs; the likely time frame for adjustment; the extent to which existing preferences were used (theoretical access does not always translate into actual exports because of strict rules of origin); the extent of liberalization undertaken by trading partners on products subject to preferences; and the characteristics of affected industries and groups.

On the basis of these assessments, the international agencies will work with countries to design policies to help manage adjustment impact. They also will identify opportunities to provide assistance through instruments such as structural adjustment loans from the World Bank and the IMF's Trade Integration Mechanism.[2] Where a country is suffering particularly severe adjustment costs, they will coordinate with other donors to marshal additional assistance.

An investment in the future

Implementation of these initiatives, coupled with increased aid-for-trade resources in bilateral assistance programs, form a sound basis for exploiting the development potential of trade. The investments required now may seem large, but aid for trade is an investment in the future—one that promises a high rate of return by supporting higher growth in poor countries. Aid for trade should thus be seen as another component of stepped-up international efforts—greater overall aid, debt relief, and trade liberalization under the Doha Round—to help the poorest countries achieve the Millennium Development Goals.

Notes
1. Projects depend on country needs and priorities but may include: trade policy capacity, customs (computerization, risk management), standards (training, surveillance, and accreditation), development of export and investment promotion agencies, sectoral support (product development, supply chain upgrading), and development of regulatory frameworks to support services liberalization.
2. The Trade Integration Mechanism is designed to assist member countries to meet balance-of-payments difficulties that might result from trade liberalization by other countries. Two countries have taken advantage of it to date—Bangladesh ($78.03 million) and the Dominican Republic ($32.03 million).

References
World Bank-IF. 2005. *Rwanda: Diagnostic Trade Integration Study.* Washington, DC: World Bank.

Further Reading
Bhagwati, J. 2004. *In Defense of Globalization.* Oxford University Press.
Finance and Development, March 2005. Volume 42, Number 1. IMF.
Prowse, S. and B. Hoekman. 2005. *Economic Policy Responses to Preference Erosion: From Trade as Aid to Aid for Trade*, World Bank Working Paper 3721 available at http://econ.worldbank.org.
World Bank and IMF. 2005. *The Doha Development Agenda and Aid for Trade*, paper for the Development Committee DC 2005 - 00016, available at www.worldbank.org.
Zedillo, E., P. Messerlin and J. Nielson. 2005. *Trade for Development: Report of the Task Force on Trade to the Millennium Project*, available at http:// www.ycsg.yale.edu/focus/index.html.

Preference Erosion: The Terms of the Debate

Bernard Hoekman, Will Martin, Carlos A. Primo Braga

ondiscrimination is the cornerstone of the multilateral trade system. As expressed in the most-favored-nation (MFN) clause embodied in Article I of the General Agreement on Tariffs and Trade (GATT), it was the defining principle of the trading system that emerged in the post–World War II era—largely as a reaction to the folly of protectionism and preferential trading arrangements that had contributed to the global economic depression of the 1930s. However, GATT allowed for exemptions to the MFN rule: reciprocal preferential agreements and unilateral preferences granted to developing countries.[1]

The rationale for grants of preferential access to the markets of industrialized countries emerged from arguments in favor of special and differential treatment (SDT) for developing countries under GATT. The underlying justification for SDT, in turn, reflected development thinking in the early 1960s, notably the theory of import-substitution industrialization. That theory was premised on the argument that developing countries needed to foster industrial capacity both to reduce import dependence and to diversify away from traditional commodities that were subject to declining terms of trade over the long term (and often also affected by short-term price volatility). The practical expression of that argument was the policy of erecting trade barriers to protect infant industries. At the same time it was recognized that exports were important as a source of foreign exchange and that the local market might be too small for local industry to be able to capture economies of scale. The second plank of the SDT agenda, therefore, was preferential access—a general system of preferences that would give developing countries better treatment in the major markets of the world. The Generalized System of Preferences (GSP), the framework for providing such preferences, was established in 1968 under the auspices of the United Nations Conference on Trade and Development (UNCTAD).

Trade preferences are a central issue in ongoing efforts to negotiate further multilateral trade liberalization in the Doha Round. Middle-income countries are increasingly concerned about the discrimination they confront in OECD markets as a result of the better access granted to preferred countries, whether developing or other industrialized countries covered under regional free trade agreements. Conversely, the least developed countries (LDCs) and non-LDC countries in the Africa, Caribbean, and Pacific (ACP) group worry that general, MFN-based liberalization of trade will erode the value of the preferential access they presently enjoy. Matters are compounded by the fact that for many of the poorest countries preference programs have become more valuable at the margin as OECD countries have granted duty- and quota-free access for a larger number of products (and sometimes all products). Preference-receiving countries are also concerned that multilateral liberalization may affect their terms of trade and raise the price of imports that currently are subsidized in OECD markets.

The value of preferences

But how valuable are the preferences available to developing countries? OECD preference programs explicitly differentiate between developing countries (by region, level of development, and export capacity) and impose significant "conditionality" in the determination of eligibility and product coverage, including rules of origin and nontrade requirements. In addition to the GSP, high-income countries maintain a variety of schemes. The European Union has preferences for ACP members as well as a separate program for the LDCs (Everything But Arms). The United States has maintains several regional schemes (for example, for the Caribbean and Africa). This plethora of preferences makes empirical assessments of their effects difficult, a task further complicated by the difficulty of identifying the specific impact of preferences as opposed to other factors. The observed growth rate of exports from recipients to the countries granting trade preferences, for example, is not informative without controlling for other factors.

The policy literature has tended to rely on descriptive indicators to assess the impact of preferences. Four indicators are particularly common:

- *Preference margins:* the difference between MFN and preferential tariffs for products
- *Potential coverage:* the ratio between products covered by a scheme and the dutiable imports originating in beneficiary countries
- *Utilization:* the ratio between imports that actually receive preferential treatment and those that are in principle covered
- *Utility:* the ratio of the value of imports that get preferences to all dutiable imports from that exporter (the lower this number, the less generous the preference scheme).

Such indicators provide at best a partial perspective of the economic value of preferences. To get a more precise estimate of the value of preferences one has to take into account: (i) the cost of compliance with documentary requirements; (ii) the economic costs of rules of origin insofar as these require sourcing inputs from more expensive sources; (iii) other limitations and constraints embodied in preferential schemes; and (iv) the distribution of any rents that are created (part of these rents may be captured by importers).

The average estimate in the recent empirical literature is that documentary requirements imply costs of some 3–5 percent of the value of processed goods. This means that MFN tariffs must be about 4 percent higher than preferred rates, on average, for preferential access to be meaningful. Given that the average MFN tariff in the OECD is close to 4 percent, preferences can only matter where there are tariff peaks or quotas.

The simplest measure of the transfers generated by a preferential regime is to calculate the difference between the applied tariffs facing a country and the MFN tariffs that would otherwise have applied. This measure is an upper bound on the value of the transfers, since many countries receive preferences. Thus, the true preference margins for a country should be adjusted for the preferences being received by other countries. Unfortunately, the literature does not currently provide a number of estimates of these "true" preference margins. We therefore focus on the simpler, traditional, margin of preference as an indication of the overall per unit value of preferences (table 1).

There are some important conceptual differences among the various measures presented in table 1. Those calculated by Brenton and Ikezuki (2005) give the margin relative to the overall value of exports from the country to the granting market. By contrast, Low, Piermartini, and Richtering (2005) refer to the margin only on those exports for which there is a nonzero duty and a positive apparent preference. Despite these methodological differences, table 1 suggests substantial consistency across alternative measures. The average margins tend to be higher in Eu-

Table 1. Nonreciprocal preference margins for developing country exporters

(percent)

Beneficiary countries	Granting Countries					
	EU	U.S.	Japan	Canada	Australia	Quad + Australia
	6.6^a	3.2^a	2.6^a			
LDCs	4.1^d	2.6^d	10.9^d	4.2^d	3.6^d	4.6^d
Sub-Saharan Africa	4.0^b	1.3^b	0.1^b	—	—	—
African LDCs	2.3^b	2.1^b	0.4^b	—	—	—
LIX	3.8^c	0.5^c	—	—	—	—
	3.8^a	2.6^a	2.0^a			
All	3.4^d	2.6^d	3.4^d	1.6^d	1.5^d	3.4^d

— No data.

Note: LDCs = United Nations' list of least developed countries. LIX = World Bank low-income countries excluding India. GSP = all potential recipients of GSP. Quad = Canada, European Union, Japan, United States.

Sources: a. IMF (2003: 8); b. Brenton and Ikezuki (2005: 27); c. van der Mensbrugghe (2005).; d. Low, Piermartini, and Richtering (2005).

rope relative to the other markets, while average preference margins are lower in Japan than in the European Union or the United States. There are surprisingly small gaps between the preference margins granted to LDCs and to developing countries as a whole under the GSP in the European Union, the United States, and Japan. In contrast, Canada and Australia appear to give substantially higher margins of preference to the LDCs. A similar result was found in World Bank and IMF (2005) using a measure of the overall tariff equivalent of trade policies. The latter measure includes nontariff measures such as health and safety standards (sanitary and phytosanitary measures) applied by the OECD countries—policies that are not affected by preference programs.[2]

A measure of the overall value of preferences corresponding with the preference margin numbers in table 1 can be obtained by multiplying the margins by the value of imports to which they apply. Table 2 reports such figures, using the margins and associated trade numbers of Low, Piermartini, and Richtering (2005), because that study uses disaggregated and up-to-date estimates of the imports subject to preferential treatment. Of the total of $587 million in estimated potential value of preferences to LDCs, $287 million, or almost half, is provided by the European Union. The United States is the next largest provider, at $131 million per year. Japanese preferences amount to almost $50 million per year, while Canada and Australia are much smaller at $14 million and $0.4 million per year. The comparison of the preferences received by LDCs and other developing countries shows that the bulk of preferences accrue to non-LDCs, reflecting the small share of LDCs is total developing-country exports.

Independent of their estimated aggregate value, preferences have been an important factor in stimulating diversification into manufactures for certain developing countries, as illustrated by the case of apparel. For example, the U.S. African Growth and Opportunity Act (AGOA) has led to substantial increases in

Table 2. Estimates of the value of preferences to LDCs and all developing countries
(US$ million)

	EU	U.S.	Japan	Canada	Australia	Quad+
LDCs	287	131	49	14	0.4	587
All	4,945	3,953	743	215	46	11,565

Note: Quad = Canada, EU, Japan and U.S. Quad + = Quad + Australia
Source: Authors' compilations based on data from Low, Piermartini, and Richtering (2005).

imports from a number of Sub-Saharan Africa countries. However, the scope for preferences to facilitate diversification into the apparel sector is limited by the lack of consistency across the different preference schemes. Manufactured products from a country that can enter under one preference scheme often will not be able enter under another due to differences in rules of origin. Harmonization of preferential schemes around liberal rules of origin—in effect moving back to the idea of one umbrella framework for preferences as originally envisaged by the GSP—would help enhance the value of preference programs.[3]

The magnitude of potential preference erosion

Preference erosion is not a new concern. Until recently, however, it was not a particularly strong constraint on MFN-based reforms because GSP programs typically offered a *preference,* and not duty- or quota-free access. Thus, even if MFN rates were lowered, it was possible to maintain a given preference margin by lowering the preferential tariff or expanding the coverage of the scheme. But new programs such as EBA and AGOA feature duty- and quota-free access for virtually all products; therefore *any* reductions in MFN tariffs lower the preference margin.

Using a partial equilibrium framework, IMF (2003) examined the potential overall impact on the exports of LDCs of preference erosion arising from a 40 percent cut in protection by the Quad. Assuming that LDCs have free access to these markets (a strong assumption given the evidence on rules of origin and other constraints), the study concludes that the potential loss at the aggregate level amounts to 1.7 percent of total LDC exports. Individual LDCs may suffer a more significant loss from preference erosion if their exports consist chiefly of products that enjoy deep preferences. By this measure, Malawi, Mauritania, Haiti, Cape Verde, and São Tomé and Príncipe are the most vulnerable to preference erosion. Malawi would experience a loss of 11.5 percent of total exports from the hypothetical cut in Quad protection. The next four countries would suffer a loss of between 5 and 10 percent. Another 10 countries would lose between 3 percent to 5 percent. The total (aggregate) value of lost export revenue would be around $530 million (two-fifths accounted for by Bangladesh alone). Note that these are small numbers from a macro perspective—equivalent to only 1 percent of annual official development assistance—but they may mean substantial adjustment for some of the economies involved.

Alexandraki and Lankes (2004) complement this analysis by focusing on middle-income economies, including in their analysis of sugar, textiles, and bananas. Their study, as well as that of Stevens and Kennan (2004), suggests that the potential erosion problem is heavily concentrated in small island economies that are dependent on quota-type preferences and the associated rents in these sectors (sugar, beef, and bananas). The problem is therefore also commodity-specific—concentrated in areas where OECD protection and preference margins are the highest—including bananas and sugar. As the sugar and banana regimes are reformed in the European Union, such countries will have to adjust.

Grynberg and Silva (2004) report that the losses in income transfers for producers of sugar, beef, bananas, and textiles and clothing in economies dependent on trade preferences would come to $1.7 billion per year. These estimates are heavily influenced by the weight of disappearing quota rents associated with the phaseout of the Agreement on Textiles and Clothing which account for $1.1 billion of the loss estimate and was a consequence of the Uruguay Round, rather than of potential future negotiation outcomes.

Computable general equilibrium (CGE) estimates of the value of preference erosion provide additional insights. CGE techniques make it possible to account for

Table 3. Estimates of losses from tariff preference erosion

Authors	Affected countries	Granting countries	Reform	Change, US$ millions Exports	Change, US$ millions Real income	How measured?
Hoekman, Ng, and Olarreaga (2002)	Developing countries	Quad	Tariff peak elimination	−71	—	Partial equilibrium
IMF (2003)	LDCs	Quad	40% cut in tariffs	−530	−265[a]	Partial equilibrium
Alexandraki and Lankes (2004)	Middle-income	Quad	40% cut in preference	−914	−457	Partial equilibrium
Grynberg and Silva (2004)	Developing countries	Quad	Elimination of preferences	—	−570	Partial equilibrium
Francois, Hoekman and Manchin (2005)	African LDCs	EU liberalization	Full MFN liberalization	—	−458	General equilibrium
Ibid.	African LDCs	OECD	Full MFN liberalization	—	−110	General equilibrium
Ibid.	African, Asian LDCs	OECD	Full MFN liberalization	—	−198	General equilibrium
van der Mensbrugghe (2005)	East Asia	All	Full MFN liberalization	—	12,000	General equilibrium
Ibid.	South Asia	All	Full MFN liberalization	—	500	General equilibrium
Ibid.	Middle East and N.Africa	All	Full MFN liberalization	—	4,800	General equilibrium
Ibid.	Sub-Saharan Africa	All	Full MFN liberalization	—	2,200	General equilibrium
Ibid.	Latin America	All	Full MFN liberalization	—	8,200	General equilibrium

—No data.

Note: a. Because the elasticity of supply of exports is 1.0, the real income effect is exactly half the change in the value of exports.

Source: Hoekman, Ng, and Olarreaga (2002); Alexandraki and Lankes (2004); Grynberg and Silva (2004); Francois, Hoekman and Manchin (2005); van der Mensbrugghe (2005).

terms-of-trade effects, better market-access for nonpreferential trade following MFN liberalization, and the asymmetrical effects of preference erosion in different markets (reflecting different hierarchies of preference in OECD markets, not only because of different rules of nonreciprocal programs, but also the impact of free trade agreements). In general, CGE analyses tend to provide lower estimates of the preference-erosion effect. Francois, Hoekman, and Manchin (2005), for example, estimate that EU liberalization would translate into income losses of $460 million for African LDCs. That figure drops to $110 million when the experiment is extended to include OECD-wide liberalization.

Key results from a number of recent studies of preference erosion are summarized in table 3. The initial results associated with the nonreciprocal schemes alone generally produce results that are less than the full potential value of preference estimates presented in table 2. The major exception is van der Mensbrugghe (2005), a study that includes the effects of reciprocal, as well as nonreciprocal, preferences. He adopts a counterfactual MFN-only scenario to estimate that current preferences generate an additional $1.6 billion for low-income countries (excluding India). His results suggest that the effects of reciprocal preferences are much larger than the nonreciprocal preferences. Another important result shown in the table is that these preferences reduce the benefits to be attained from further liberalization, but do not change the sign of such a movement. Liberalization still generates substantial gains for all regions.

These estimates are not strictly comparable, not only because of the different methodologies used (partial equilibrium versus CGE) and the differences in focus (welfare effects versus trade effects), but also because they tend to operate with distinct liberalization scenarios to estimate the potential for preference erosion (Doha-related forecasts, full liberalization before the ATC phaseout, or full liberalization after the ATC phaseout, and so on). It is also important to underscore that these figures tend to overestimate the value of existing preferential regimes because they typically do not take into account the costs of compliance with preferential regimes (an exception is Francois and others 2005).

These estimates do make clear, however, that preferences are very small, in aggregate, as a means of transferring revenues from industrial to developing countries. Relative to the potentially enormous gains to developing countries from comprehensive trade reform—estimated at $86 billion per year in Anderson, Martin and van der Mensbrugghe (2005)—the transfers in the order of $500 million from nonreciprocal transfers estimated above pale into insignificance. The net benefits to developing countries of these transfers are, of course, even smaller since a major share of these benefits comes at the expense of trade diversion from other developing countries. However, as has been emphasized by many authors, including IMF (2003) and Alexandraki and Lankes (2004), the benefits of preferences remain important for particular developing countries and products.

Dealing with preference erosion: potential policy responses

Two major approaches can be taken to address preference erosion losses—one within the World Trade Organization (WTO) (a "trade solution") and the other outside the WTO (an "aid solution"). Potential trade-based solutions include the following:

- Enhancing existing preference programs by widening access (for example, by harmonizing preferential regimes around liberal rules of origin and reducing compliance costs) or extending of their coverage, leveraging utilization rates, and increasing their effectiveness. Such enhancements could partially counterbalance the economic impact of preference erosion.
- Implementation of new preferential trade regimes by non-OECD importers.
- Multilateral trade concessions designed to shield preference-dependent countries (by delaying the liberalization schedules for "sensitive" products, for example) or to address negotiating priorities in other areas of the round (whether market access or rules).

Solutions undertaken from within the trading system may impose a significant opportunity cost from the perspective of global efficiency if they result in additional discrimination and have the effect of substantially reducing the overall level of ambition of MFN reforms in the Doha Round. A trading system that continues to rely on extensive discrimination in trade policy is not desirable. That said, there is a case for granting low-income countries preferential access to all OECD and large middle-income markets and pursuing an immediate and substantial simplification and liberalization of rules of origin. Doing so would attenuate short-term losses from preference erosion created by the Doha Round by maintaining for some period *effective* preference margins. However, as countries around the world continue to reduce levels of trade protection and conclude reciprocal trade agreements, it is unavoidable that the value of preferential access will be eroded. This suggests the need to concentrate on improving productivity and lowering transaction costs in beneficiary countries so as to enhance the competitiveness of their firms and farm sector. Here, much can and should be done through additional aid for trade.

Possible aid-based solutions for preference erosion include:

- Relying on existing financial mechanisms for adjustment financing such as the IMF's Trade Integration Mechanism (IMF 2004); and
- Establishing new stand-alone, grant-based compensation funds; and
- Addressing preference erosion as part of a broader aid-for-trade effort.

The limited number and small size of most of the economies that could be significantly affected by preference erosion suggest that measures to help mitigate the problem should be targeted closely on the countries at risk. An appropriate response might be for the OECD countries to convert the implicit "preference transfers" (the value of current preferences) into equivalent development assistance. Aid transfers have the advantages of not distorting trade flows and being able to target the countries concerned.

The specific vehicle for any such compensating transfers must be negotiated. Each has advantages and disadvantages. The advantage of existing financial mechanisms is that the assistance will be placed in the context of a country's overall macroeconomic and development policy framework. This may be beneficial as there are many other sources of shocks and adjustment pressures (in addition to preference erosion) that confront countries. However, the instrument used will generally be (concessional) loans as opposed to grants.

A specific compensation fund, as proposed by Grynberg and Silva (2004) and Page (2005), has the advantage of directly addressing the matter at hand but raises questions, notably ensuring that financing commitments are credible, that the associated aid is additional to existing flows, and that it is used effectively to address the adjustment burden in recipient economies. In the case of farmers in beneficiary countries who stand to lose from reforms in specific product areas (such as sugar and bananas), an option might to integrate them into OECD farm policies by extending decoupled income support to them as well as to national farmers.

Adjustment to MFN liberalization will affect many countries, not just those that have benefited from preferences. They, too, will require assistance to adjust. But in most cases the shocks that regularly confront countries can be expected to exceed those associated with preference erosion. The need to diversify is not unique to economies that have benefited from preferences but is common to many countries. This suggests that funding for adjustment and to enhance competitiveness should be provided within the context of an overall country development program. Doing so is particularly important for countries—including many of the poorest—that have proved unable to benefit much from preference programs. The trade-related assistance these countries need is clearly much greater than any estimate of the value of current preferences.

Concluding remarks

The debate about how best to address preference erosion in the context of multilateral negotiations will continue to be an important component of the negotiations on the development dimension of the Doha Round. While the overall benefits of nonreciprocal preferences to developing countries are clearly small relative to the potential gains from trade reform, they are important for a number of countries whose interests must be considered. Although the jury is still out on the overall developmental impact of trade preferences, support is growing for delinking development assistance from trade policy by shifting from "trade as aid" to "aid for trade" (Hoekman and Prowse 2005; IMF and World Bank 2005).

This growing consensus, however, is challenged by parallel efforts to deepen existing preferential regimes and to introduce new ones. Multilateral trade negotiations add additional ferment to the debate to the extent that they foster alliances between protectionist interests in OECD countries and preference-dependent industries in developing economies.

Notes

1.Bernard Hoekman is Senior Advisor, Development Research Group and International Trade Department, William J. Martin is Lead Economist, Development Research Group and International Trade Department, Carlos A. Primo Braga is Senior Adviser, International Trade Department, The World Bank. This chapter relies extensively on papers prepared for the International Symposium on "Preference Erosion: Impacts and Policy Responses" organized by the World Bank with the support of CIDA and DFID in Geneva, June 13-14. Comments and assistance from C. Tully are gratefully acknowledged.

2. Indeed, the analysis of overall OECD trade restrictiveness concludes that nontariff measures account for more than half of total trade restrictiveness (World Bank and IMF, 2005), suggesting that they should receive greater policy attention.

3. For details see Brenton and Ozden (2005).

References

Alexandraki, Katerina, and Hans Peter Lankes. 2004. "Estimating the Impact of Preference Erosion on Middle-Income Countries." IMF Working Paper, International Monetary Fund, Washington, DC.

Anderson, Kym, William Martin and Dominique van der Mensbrugghe. 2006. "Market and Welfare Implications of Doha Reform Scenarios." In Anderson, K. and W. Martin eds. *Agricultural Trade Reform and the Doha Development Agenda.* Palgrave Macmillan and the World Bank, Washington, D.C.

Brenton, P., and T. Ikezuki. 2005 "The Impact of Agricultural Trade Preferences, with Particular Attention to the LDCs." In *Global Agricultural Trade and the Developing Countries*, eds. Ataman Aksoy and John Beghin, Washington DC: World Bank.

Brenton, Paul and Caglar Ozden (2005) "Trade Preferences for Apparel and the Role of Rules of Origin - The Case of Africa," paper prepared for the International Symposim on "Preference Erosion: Impacts and Policy Responses," Geneva, June 13-14, processed.

Francois, J., Bernard Hoekman, and M. Manchin. 2005. "Quantifying the Magnitude of Preference Erosion Due to Multilateral Trade Liberalization." CEPR Discussion Paper 5153, Center for Economic and Policy Research, Washington, DC.

Grynberg, Roman, and Sacha Silva. 2004. "Preference-Dependent Economies and Multilateral Liberalization: Impacts and Options." Unpublished paper, Commonwealth Secretariat, London.

Hoekman, Bernard, Francis Ng and Marcelo Olarreaga. 2002. "Eliminating Excessive Tariffs on Exports of Least Developed Countries," *World Bank Economic Review 16(1),* pp. 1-22.

Hoekman, Bernard, and Susan Prowse. 2005. "Policy Responses to Preference Erosion: From Trade as Aid to Aid for Trade." Policy Research Working Paper 3721, World Bank, Washington, DC.

IMF (International Monetary Fund). 2003. "Financing of Losses from Preference Erosion, Note on Issues raised by Developing Countries in the Doha Round." Communication to the WTO from the International Monetary Fund, WT/TF/COH/14. 14 February.

———. 2004. "Fund Support for Trade-Related Balance of Payments Adjustments." http://www.imf.org/external/np/pdr/tim/2004/eng/022704.pdf

IMF and the World Bank. 2005. "Doha Development Agenda and Aid for Trade." Paper presented to the Development Committee, September 25, Washington, DC.

Low, Patrick, Roberta Piermartini, and Jürgen Richtering. 2005. "Multilateral Solutions to Preference Erosion." Paper prepared for the International Symposium on Preference Erosion: Impacts and Policy Responses. Geneva, June 13–14.

Page, Sheila. 2005. "A Preference Erosion Compensation Fund: A New Proposal to Protect Countries from the Negative Effects of Trade Liberalization." Overseas Development Institute (ODI) Opinions 35.

Stevens, Chris, and Jane Kennan. 2004. "Making Preferences More Effective." Briefing paper, Institute of Development Studies, University of Sussex.

Van der Mensbrugghe, Dominique. 2005. "The Doha Development Agenda and Preference Erosion: Modeling the Impacts." Paper prepared for the International Symposium on Preference Erosion: Impacts and Policy Responses. Geneva, June 13–14.

World Bank and IMF. 2005. *Global Monitoring Report 2005*, Washington DC: The World Bank and IMF.

From Marrakesh to Doha: Effects of Removing Food Subsidies on the Poor

Donald Mitchell and Mombert Hoppe

I f successful, the Doha Round may cut global subsidies to food production. The vast majority of developing countries should benefit, but some will lose through a deterioration of their terms of trade. How great is their loss likely to be? What will happen to poor consumers in those countries? What is the appropriate policy response?

In examining these questions, we find that:

- The collective magnitude of the likely losses of net food importers is between $300 million and $1.2 billion per year depending on the final agreement, an amount that could readily be financed by donors. This is less than 0.7 percent of total merchandise imports of these countries and even those losses will phase-in over a long period. The food price increases will be about half as large as the annual year-to-year variations in food prices.

- Only 7 countries would see their net food import bills increase by more than 5 percent of total export earnings. This number is relatively small, because the projected increases in food prices are small and because many developing countries would also benefit from increases in the prices of their exports.

- The international community has several instruments to help countries faced with a terms-of-trade loss. The International Monetary Fund (IMF) can use its Compensatory Financing Facility or its new Trade Integration Mechanism (TIM). The World Bank and bilateral donors can provide transitional adjustment assistance for affected countries. The current discussions of "aid for trade" to assist countries overcome constraints to exports may result in additional resources. On the other hand, certain approaches are not likely to work. Commodity stabilization funds, for example, have generally been ineffective in staving off long-term secular declines in prices, and hedging efforts have proven costly and difficult to manage.

- The effects on poor people—as opposed to countries—also merit analysis. Many of the poor will gain because they are subsistence farmers, but some may be net buyers of food. While each case must be managed on its own terms, one relatively easy response to help the poor is to lower tariffs that may keep domestic prices above the international price. Lowering such tariffs will also improve overall efficiency, although at some cost to government revenues. If this is not possible, development assistance may have to provide some transitional finance.

341

Background

The Marrakesh Ministerial conference that concluded the Uruguay Round in 1994 adopted a decision on "Measures Concerning the Possible Negative Effects of the Reform Program on Least Developed and Net Food Importing Developing Countries." That decision, which has become known as the Marrakesh Decision, was adopted in response to fears that subsidy cuts imposed on food exporting countries by the Uruguay Round Agreement on Agriculture (URAA) would have the effect of raising prices of imported foods. The Marrakesh Decision requires regular reviews of food-aid commitments and flows, the adoption of guidelines to ensure that food aid is given in grant form or on concessional terms, and technical assistance. But many food-importing countries remain concerned that food prices could rise with the reduction or elimination of subsidies in exporting countries. That concern has hampered an agreement on agriculture during the Doha Round. This is unfortunate, because the benefits of such an agreement for developing countries would greatly outweigh the negative impact of increases in the prices of food imports.

The Marrakesh Decision has become a catch-all for concerns about increases in food import prices, whether or not those increases can be traced to multilateral policy reforms. For example, the rise in wheat prices in 1995–1996[1] led to a proposal by 16 countries, including some net-food-importing developing countries (NFIDCs), to establish a revolving fund to help meet the short-term needs of financing normal levels of commercial imports. The proposed countercyclical subsidy mechanism would have triggered food and financial aid upon commodity price increases stemming from agricultural trade liberalization agreed to under the URAA. The proposal was motivated by the increases in wheat prices, despite the fact that little reform had been agreed under the URAA and almost none implemented by 1995–96 (Ingco 1995). Volatility is not unusual in world food prices, and a range of financial instruments are available to mitigate its effects.

This note examines the historical food imports and trade balances of the least developed countries (LDCs) and NFIDCs, examines the impact of price increases that might result from policy reforms under the Doha Round, and discusses measures that could be taken to address the problems of variability in food prices, some of which could be negotiated during the round. Of special note is the occasional ban on food exports to which some countries have resorted during periods of price increases. These export restrictions are potentially more important to national food security than the increases in food prices that result from policy reform, because they limit access to exports at the time when they are most needed. The note begins with a review of globally traded food prices.

Figure 1. Productivity gains have made food cheaper

Real food prices, 1970-2004 (index in 1990 constant dollars)

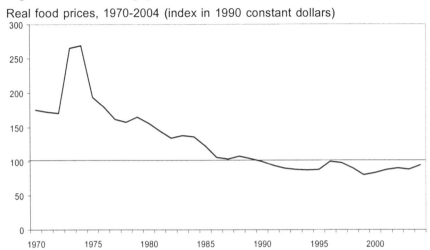

Note: This is the World Bank's index for internationally traded food commodities weighted by world export shares and deflated by the manufactures unit-value index in dollar terms of the G-5 countries.
Source: Development Prospects Group, the World Bank.

World food prices—lower and less volatile than during the 1970s

Part of the concern over prices is based on the experience of the 1970s, when internationally traded food prices rose sharply, causing shortages in some countries. At that time, real food prices showed high variability associated with specific events such as the emergence of OPEC and resulting higher oil prices, large grain purchases by the former Soviet Union, crop failures, and significant structural changes in the world economy. Since the mid-1970s, however, real food prices have trended lower relative to the index of manufactures and have generally exhibited lower year-to-year variability (figure 1). The relative price stability of the past two decades occurred despite some equally dramatic changes, such as the collapse of the Soviet Union in the late 1980s, the increasing importance of China in the global economy, and the Asian financial crisis of the late 1990s.

Which developing countries are net food importers?

The NFIDCs that are covered by the Marrakesh Decision include 73 countries—the 50 LDCs plus an additional 23 developing countries: Barbados, Botswana, Cuba, Côte d'Ivoire, Dominica, Dominican Republic, Egypt, Honduras, Jamaica, Jordan, Kenya, Mauritius, Morocco, Namibia, Pakistan, Peru, Saint Kitts and Nevis, Saint Lucia, Saint Vincent and the Grenadines, Sri Lanka, Trinidad and Tobago, Tunisia, and Venezuela (FAO 2005). Of 72 countries examined (data was

Table 1. Estimates of world price increases in percent for key food

Source	Scenario	Wheat	Coarse grains	Meat	Sugar	Rice	Oil-seeds	Dairy
Full liberalization scenarios								
BBDJ	3 tiers [a] (100% export subsidy reduction)	2.3	3.1	1.6	2.8	9.4	9.7	2.7
RST	3 tiers [b] (45% export subsidy reduction)	4.0–6.3	4.3–7.0	2.0–4.3		1.2–1.4	2.8–4.5	3.9–4.3
FAPRI [c]	Elimination of domestic farm programs and border measures	4.8	5.7	3.7–10.3		10.3	3.1	22.0–39.0
USDA	3 tiers with full domestic subsidy removal [d]	18.1	15.2	22.3 [e]	16.4	10.1	11.2	
Partial liberalization								
BBDJ	100% reduction in export support	0.1	0.1	0.1–1.5	5.6	0.1	0.0	2.3
USDA	Global export subsidy removal	2.0	0.6		3.3	1.5	0.1	
DHK	50% reduction in domestic support (OECD)	4.9	5.5	2.2	–0.6	0.3	3.5	–0.2
DHK	50% market price support reduction, re-instrumentalization [g]	0.8	1.0	–0.7	0.2	0.7	0.4	–0.2

a. "Three tiers" relates to reductions or elimination in export subsidies, a reduction in domestic support, and global tariff reduction.

b. The presented figures summarize three scenarios with the following parameters. An Amber Box reduction of 55 percent; a 60 percent Amber Box and 50 percent Blue Box reduction; and a 100 percent Amber Box and 50 percent Blue Box reduction.

c. Policy changes that result in the reported price increases were supposed to take place in 2002. The values differ widely for beef, pork, and poultry.

d. This scenario assumes full OECD domestic subsidy removal and worldwide export subsidy removals.

e. Price increase for livestock and products.

f. Scenario assumes a 100 percent reduction in export subsidies and a 55 percent reduction in domestic support linked to inputs and outputs, estimated effects on "world prices of developing countries trade."

g. Scenario assumes 50 percent cut in tariffs and export subsidy rates but allows for compensatory increase in domestic support.

Source: BBDJ = Bouet and others (2004). USDA = USDA (2001). RST = Rae and Strutt (2003). FAPRI = Beghin and Fabiosa (2002). DHK = Dimaranan et al (2004).

Source: World Bank calculations and summary of results from Table 1. Table 2. Comparison of commodity price changes and simulated impacts of reforms (percent)

not available for East Timor), 46 had a food-trade deficit and 38 had a trade deficit in primary agricultural materials during 1998–2002.[2] Of the countries with a food-trade deficit 34 were LDCs. Among the countries with a deficit in agriculture trade, only 22 were LDCs, leaving non-LDCs overrepresented (17 out of 23 had a deficit in this category). Using COMTRADE data for the 72 countries, we found that countries with the highest net food imports per capita in this group were island economies and countries in conflict or just emerging from conflict.

The most important food imports for LDCs and other NFIDCs in 2001 were wheat and wheat flour (21 percent), fruit and vegetables (11 percent), maize (10 percent), dairy products and eggs (9 percent), sugar (8 percent), rice (6 percent), soybeans and oil (6 percent), meat and preparations (4 percent), and palm oil (4 percent) according to the FAO.

Effects of a Doha Round Agreement

With slow progress in the Doha Round on an agreement to reduce agricultural subsidies and support, it is difficult to estimate how large the food price changes resulting from an agreement might be. However, quantitative estimates made in preparation for the negotiations (table 1) can be used as estimates of such changes. The various estimates are not readily comparable, however, since agricultural trade liberalization scenarios differ widely in their assumptions about (a) full or partial reduction of export subsidies in industrialized countries, (b) the reduction or elimination of schemes of domestic support, and (c) global tariff reductions. The estimates also vary with regard to the time frame of analysis, however, price increases generally assume full adjustment. The largest increases in food prices correspond to full liberalization which does not appear to be a likely outcome of the Doha Round at this time.

Table 2. Comparison of commodity price changes and simulated impacts of reforms (percent)

	Range of estimated price increases from reforms	Average of estimated price increases from reforms	Coefficient of variation of prices 1990–2004	Average year-to-year percentage change of prices 1990–2004
Commodity				
Wheat	0.1 - 18.1	5.1	16.9	11.8
Maize	0.1 - 15.2	4.6	17.2	10.1
Beef	0.8 - 22.3	5.1	15.4	8.6
Sugar	1.1 - 16.4	5.8	23.9	14.1
Rice	0.1 - 10.6	5.5	19.6	11.8

Source: World Bank calculations and summary of results from Table 1.

The results of the various studies are summarized in table 2 and compared with historical variations in prices. The comparison shows that the average increase in prices of major food items under the various scenarios of reform are generally less than the coefficient of variation or average year-to-year percent price change of these foods (table 2). For example, the average increase in wheat prices from the various studies is 5.1 percent while the coefficient of variation for wheat prices was 16.9 percent during 1990-2004 and the average year-to-year percent change was 11.8 percent. The impact on net-food-importing developing countries' import bills ranges from about $300 million to $1.2 billion in the individual scenarios (table 3), and the actual increases in food import costs are likely to be toward the lower end of this range.

The average net food imports of NFIDCs totaled $3.85 billion per year for the five year period from 1998–2002, with LDCs' net imports averaging $2.63 billion and other NFIDCs net imports averaging $1.22 billion. These imports were 6.3 percent of total merchandise imports for LDCs and 1.2 percent of total merchandise imports for other NFIDCs. However, these aggregates do not reflect the situation in individual countries who may need assistance to cope with higher food import costs. For example, the net food imports were 34 percent of total imports in the case of Haiti and 25 percent for Yemen. Net food imports exceeded 100 percent of export earnings in Eritrea, Haiti, Djibouti, Cape Verde, and Tuvalu, with the deficit financed by aid assistance. In some countries, higher food import costs may be offset by higher prices for their agricultural exports. For example, in Benin the share of net food imports of total imports is 22.3 percent, while the net export balance in agricultural products is 11.6 percent. Similar offsetting effects can be expected for Burkina Faso (22.6 percent and 26.4 percent), Chad (20.2 percent and 33.7 percent), the Lao Democratic Republic (21.7 percent and 26.1 percent), Mozambique (6.8 percent and 9.9 percent), and others. Some countries may also receive large food-aid imports and may not be as directly affected by food price increases. For example, Bangladesh is a large food importer with relatively small food exports. However, it is also a large recipient of food aid.

To determine which countries are most at risk from higher food import costs, we consider changes in the costs of imports net of changes in exports with a partial equilibrium analysis of different scenarios for price increases following elimination of export subsidies and domestic support. Using COMTRADE data as the values for food imports and exports, we calculate the dollar increases in the net-food-import bills for all LDCs and NFIDCs under different assumptions for world price changes after the Doha Round.[3] The effects of price increases for five main food commodities (rice, cereals, meat and meat products, oilseeds, and dairy products) are considered and then the analysis is repeated including a subset of other food commodities (vegetables and fruit, fish, live animals, beverages, animal and vegetable fats, animal feeds, sugar, and miscellaneous food products) to capture the broader impact on foods which would not be directly affected by reduced subsidies. This effectively takes some net export commodities into account. Tropical export commodities such as coffee, tobacco, cotton, tea, and cocoa are excluded from the analysis, but including them would improve the balance of payments for most countries—substantially for the group as a whole. Prices for these commodities would likely rise with food prices because agricultural commodity prices are highly correlated due to substitution possibilities in both production and consumption. The increases in food import costs (table 3) are small for LDCs and NFIDCs compared with the total expected gains from trade liberalization.[4]

Under a scenario that uses average predicted price increases, only 16 countries would see their net food import costs for the five main commodities increase by more than 5 percent. A few countries would see larger increases, but the additional financial burden still represents a small share of total imports. Summarizing the results of our simulations, net food import costs as a share of the total food import bill are likely to rise by more than 5 percent for 13 countries (Benin, Chad, Comoros, Congo DR, Cote d'Ivoire, Cuba, Haiti, Jordan, Liberia, Senegal, St. Lucia, Tuvalu, and Yemen). The expected rise in food costs is not homogenous across simulations for all countries. Some of these countries and some other countries could see their food import costs rise more strongly. The increase in the cost of food imports as a share of the total food bill exceeds 7.5 percent in at least one scenario for: Benin, Burkina Faso, Burundi, Central African Republic, Chad, Comoros, Congo DR, Cuba, Egypt, Eritrea, Ethiopia, Jordan, Liberia, Kiribati, Maldives, Senegal, St. Lucia, Tuvalu, Uganda, and Yemen. When looking at the wider set of food commodities and the average of the price increases in the simulations, only 8 countries experience an increase in food import costs of 5 percent or more of their total food imports (Burundi, Central African Republic, Chad, Comoros, Congo DR, Eritrea, Jordan, and Tuvalu).

Higher world prices will lead to a supply response
Fifty-five of the LDCs and other NFIDCs examined are net importers of goods in general. It therefore does not suffice to analyze the static effect of price changes, as Cline (2004) points out. Increased world-market prices for food can be expected to induce an increase in food production in developing countries that enjoy a comparative advantage in food production (43 of the 72 analyzed) or agriculture (38 out of the 72 analyzed) according to Cline.[5] Over the long term, NFIDCs with a comparative advantage might become less dependent on food imports.

Price increases are likely to induce other changes, such as the distribution of income in developing countries. In parallel with rising world market prices, domestic prices will increase, though probably less than proportionally. Where the rural population is self-sufficient in food production, it will therefore not be adversely affected by higher food prices. To the degree that rural producers also supply the local market, they will gain from increasing food prices. With urban dwellers adversely

Table 3. Estimates of increased net food import costs for NFIDCs based on various scenarios for reforms

	Total extra cost of five main commodities [a] (millions of dollars)	As percentage of total imports	Percentage increase in net food import bill for five main commodities	Extra cost for wider set of commodities [b] (millions of dollars)
Simulations				
Full liberalization scenarios				
BBDJ, 3 tiers (100% export subsidy removal)	251	0.15	2.70	266 [c]
RST, 3 tiers (55% Amber box reduction and 45% export subsidy reduction)	329	0.20	3.60	327 [d]
FAPRI, Elimination of domestic farm programs and border measures (max/min)	1125 / 774	0.68 / 0.47	12.3 / 8.50	n.a.
USDA, 3 tiers, with full domestic subsidy removal	1236 [e]	0.75	13.50	1096 [f]
Partial liberalization scenarios				
BBDJ, 100% reduction in export support	52	0.03	0.60	69 [c]
USDA, Global export subsidy removal	110 [e]	0.07	1.20	31 [f]
DRK, 50% reduction in OECD domestic support	610	0.19	3.40	342 [g]
DRK, 50% market price support reduction, re-instrumentalization	47	0.03	0.50	42 [g]

Note: Net imports calculated by country and commodity using 2003 mirror data from COMTRADE for Afghanistan, Angola, Bangladesh, Barbados, Benin, Bhutan, Botswana, Burkina Faso, Burundi, Cambodia, Cape Verde, Central African Republic, Chad, Comoros, Dem. Rep. Congo, Cote d'Ivoire, Cuba, Djibouti, Dominica, Dominican Republic, Egypt, Equatorial Guinea, Eritrea, Ethiopia, The Gambia, Guinea, Guinea-Bissau, Haiti, Honduras, Jamaica, Jordan, Kenya, Kiribati, Lao PDR, Lesotho, Liberia, Madagascar, Malawi, Maldives, Mali, Mauritania, Mauritius, Morocco, Mozambique, Myanmar, Namibia, Nepal, Niger, Pakistan, Peru, Rwanda, Samoa, Sao Tome and Principe, Senegal, Sierra Leone, Solomon Islands, Somalia, Saint Lucia, Saint Kitts and Nevis, and Saint Vincent and the Grenadines, Sri Lanka, Sudan, Tanzania, Togo, Trinidad and Tobago, Tunisia, Tuvalu, Uganda, Vanuatu, Venezuela, Yemen, and Zambia.

Extra import costs calculated by multiplying the net trade balance of these countries by the estimated price changes. Results do not take forgone preferential market access into account.

Key: BBDJ = Bouet and others (2004). USDA = USDA (2001). RST = Rae and Strutt (2003). FAPRI = Beghin and Fabiosa (2002). DHK = Dimaranan et al (2004).

a. Definitions for the five main commodities are according to SITC1: rice (042), other cereals (04-042), meat and meat products (01), oilseeds (22), and dairy products (02).

b. Adds vegetables and fruit, fish, life animals, beverages, animal and vegetable fats, animal feeds, sugar, and miscellaneous food products

c. Does not add fish, animal and vegetable fats, and animal feed

d. Adds only miscellaneous food products

e. Excluding dairy products

f. Adds only sugar, live animals, vegetables and fruit, and miscellaneous food products

g. Does not add vegetables and fruit, fish, beverages, and animal feed

Source: World Bank Staff estimates.

affected, income will be transferred from urban centers to rural areas, reducing poverty rates in these areas. Cline (2004) comes to the conclusion that liberalization in agricultural trade will lower rural poverty in most of the countries he analyzed.[6] With price increases trickling down from world to national to rural markets, returns to rural factors of production will increase, strengthening incentives for rural production and leading to a better integration of rural and urban markets. This would allow an increase in allocative efficiency in the long run.

These conclusions are supported by Anderson, Martin, and van der Mensbrugghe (2005) who estimate that full trade liberalization would lead to an increase in the volume of Sub-Saharan African net exports of agricultural and processed food products from $6 billion in 2001 to $27 billion in 2015. Net exports would be $8 billion higher than under their baseline scenario with no further policy changes. Net export volumes increase despite an offsetting movement in the terms of trade. Assuming no supply capacity constraints, annual farm output growth between 2004 and 2015 would be 4.9 percent following full liberalization compared to 4.5 percent in the baseline scenario. Output growth under the full liberalization scenario exceeds the estimated growth rate resulting from trade liberalization with Special and Differential Treatment for non-agricultural goods for developing countries (4.7 percent).

Freer trade can help feed the poor

Countries can take unilateral actions to reduce the impact of higher food import prices on the poor such as lowering tariffs. Such tariffs are often used to protect high-costs domestic producers, but hurt poor consumers most because they spend a higher share of their income on food. Such tariffs often provide little support to rural poor because they leave out two large groups among the rural poor: those who own no farmland, but pay higher prices as consumers, and those who own farmland, but do not produce commercially. Even commercial farmers may not benefit, because protectionism encourages them to continue planting low-value food crops instead of diversifying into nontraditional exports of higher value, a better way of raising income and escaping poverty. In turn, the lack of export production reduces the country's ability to earn foreign exchange and undermines the structural capacity to import food and other products.

Legitimate concern over temporary disruptions in food supplies caused by man-made or natural disasters is sometimes used to justify protectionist measures to stimulate domestic food production. However, the impact of such disruptions could be mitigated through other measures, such as reserves in cash or kind, better distribution channels, and reformed food-aid policies, all of which would be more effective and less costly than stimulating inefficient domestic food production. To the extent that disruptions are caused by export cutbacks or bans in times of high world prices (figure 2), developing countries should act through the WTO to seek

Figure 2. Export restrictions during times of greatest need: Wheat prices and export restrictions

U.S. fob price in $/ton

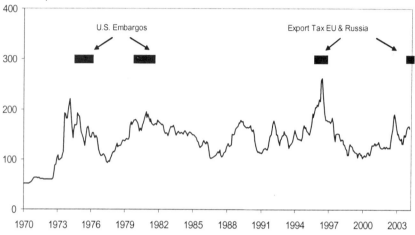

Sources: United States Department of Agriculture and World Bank.

to constrain such behavior in the Doha agreement.

Measures to deal with food-price shocks

Several mechanisms are available to help developing countries deal with short-term food-price shocks (Ingco, Mitchell, and Nash 2004). The IMF's Compensatory Financing Facility (CFF) is specifically designed to help alleviate adverse effects of certain commodity-price movements that result in balance-of-payments problems. Commercial risk management instruments are also available to protect against short-term price movement. For example, options can be used to lock in a specific price or to ensure that prices will not be greater (or lower) than a specified level. These could be used by large importers of food—in the public and private sectors—to protect against a sharp increase in food import prices. They could also be used by governments to insulate safety nets from budgetary crises arising from food price increases. The World Bank offers commodity swaps to link debt-servicing costs to movements in the price of a specific commodity or a basket of commodities. Food aid is available from the international community and unilateral donors to deal with food emergencies and disruptions in domestic supplies. In addition, there are new approaches to dealing with short-term price movements and food security concerns that could be developed and implemented. One proposal made in response to the Marrakesh Decision is to establish a system to distribute food vouchers to the needy when food prices rise. These could be redeemed through normal commercial market channels, thereby increasing the demand for food imports without distorting domestic food markets. Another proposal involves an ex ante fund for trade finance.

Conclusion

Agricultural liberalization will stimulate growth and help raise the incomes of the poor. It also may hurt a relatively few countries. The hurt should not be overstated: the predicted rise in prices will occur over several years and be considerably less than annual fluctuations associated with the business cycle and year-to-year yield variations. Still, both the international community and national governments should take actions to mitigate the costs of adjustment. The international community should provide aid for trade using the IMF's Trade Integration Mechanism (TIM) and CFF, as well as resources to support reform programs. For national governments, the first order of business should be to lower trade barriers to keep prices from rising in the local market. If that instrument is not available, governments should allow the exchange rate to depreciate to avoid passing on the full effect of price adjustments to the poor.

Notes

1. Average annual wheat prices rose by 38 percent from 1994 to 1996 primarily in response to low stocks caused by a poor harvest in the United States.

2. Food is defined as the UN's Standard International Trade classification codes SITC1 0-071-074+1-12+22+4; agriculture as SITC1 0+1+2-27-28+4.

3. We assume that the underlying trade quantities remain unchanged as the magnitude of trade elasticities is debated and varies most probably strongly between countries, by category and even within categories.

4. Nearly two-thirds of the potential gains from multilateral trade reforms stand to come in agriculture. However, achieving such gains will require WTO members to make very substantial cuts to their bound tariff rates and domestic farm subsidy commitments. If that is done, the global welfare gains from completely freeing merchandise trade over 2005–10 will be $287 billion per year by 2015. Of that, $85.7 billion would go to the developing countries (Anderson, Martin, and van der Mensbrugghe 2005: table 12.4). Although the largest gains go to developed countries, the developing countries gain twice as much as a percentage of their incomes.

5. A country is considered having a comparative advantage in food or agricultural production, if the ratio of food (agricultural) exports to food (agricultural) imports exceeds the same ratio for non-food (non-agricultural) exports and imports.

6. Under the most likely scenario, rural worldwide poverty will decline by 255 million, while urban poverty will increase by 54 million people.

References

Anderson, Kym, Will Martin, and Dominique van der Mensbrugghe. 2005. "Market and Welfare Implications of Doha Reform Scenarios." Development Prospects Group, World Bank, Washington, DC.

Anderson, Kym, Will Martin, and Dominique van der Mensbrugghe. 2005. "Would Multilateral Trade Reform Benefit Sub-Saharan Africans?" World Bank Policy Research Working Paper 3616, World Bank, Washington, DC.

Beghin, John C., and Jacinto F. Fabiosa. 2002. "The Doha Round of the WTO: Appraising Further Liberalization of Agricultural Markets." FAPRI Working Paper 02-WP-317. University of Missouri, Columbia.

A Bouet, J. C. Bureau, Y. Decreux, and S. Jean. 2004. "Multilateral Agricultural Trade Liberalization: The Contrasting Fortunes of Developing Countries in the Doha Round." IIIS Discussion Paper 60. Institute for International Integration Studies, Trinity College, Dublin.

Cline, William R. 2004. *Trade Policy and Global Poverty*. Washington, DC: Institute for International Economics.

Dimaranan, Betina, Thomas Hertel, and Roman Keeney. 2004. "OECD Domestic Support and Developing Countries." In *The WTO, Developing Countries and the Doha Development Agenda*, ed. Basudeb Guha-Khasnobis. United Nations University.

Ingco, Merlinda, Donald Mitchell, and John Nash. 2004. "Food Security and Agricultural Trade Policy Reform." In *Agriculture and the WTO: Creating a Trading System for Development*, ed. Merlinda D. Ingco and John D. Nash (chapter 9). Washington, DC: World Bank.

Ingco, M. 1995. "Agricultural Trade Liberalization in the Uruguay Round: One Step Forward, One Step Back?" World Bank Conference on the Uruguay Round and the Developing Countries, January 26–27, 1995, Washington, DC.

Nash, John, and Donald Mitchell. 2005. "How Freer Trade Can Help Feed the Poor: An Agenda for Easing Hunger Worldwide by Reducing Trade Protectionism." *Finance and Development*, March.

Rae, A. N., and A. Strutt. 2003. Doha Proposals for Domestic Support: Assessing the Priorities, Draft paper presented at the Conference of the International Agricultural Trade Research Consortium, Capri, 24–26 June.

USDA. 2001. "The Road Ahead: Agricultural Policy Reform in the WTO—Summary Report." *Agricultural Economic Report* 797, January.

Further reading:

Aksoy, M. Ataman, and John C. Beghin (eds.). 2005. *Global Agricultural Trade and Developing Countries*. World Bank. Washington, DC.

Ingco, Merlinda D., and John D. Nash. 2005. *Agriculture and the WTO: Creating a Trading System for Development*. World Bank. Washington, DC.

Sanitary and Phytosanitary Regulation: Overcoming Constraints

Steve Jaffee

Increasingly stringent food safety and agricultural health standards in industrialized countries pose major challenges for continued developing country suc-cess in international markets for high-value food products, such as fruit, vegetables, fish, meat, nuts, and spices. Much of the literature casts sanitary and phytosanitary (SPS) standards as a barrier to trade, because some appear to be thinly disguised protectionist measures or discriminate against certain suppliers, or because of the high cost of compliance. Yet, in many cases, such standards have played a positive role, providing the catalyst and incentives for the modernization of export supply and regulatory systems and the adoption of safer and more sustainable production practices.

Much of the policy discussion pertaining to SPS standards and developing country trade centers on finding ways to increase the participation of developing countries in international standard-setting bodies, or otherwise influencing the level and nature of the standards themselves. If the standards were the problem, it would be logical to emphasize renegotiation of the rules of the game. But new findings from the World Bank's research program on SPS standards (appendix 1 and World Bank 2005) suggest that adjustment of standards represents at best a partial solution, and that the challenges and opportunities posed by standards can be better addressed by strengthening public and private capacities to manage food safety and agricultural health risks.[1]

According to the findings, developing countries faced with rising SPS standards in their export markets can maintain and improve market access, position industries for long-term competitiveness, mitigate potential adverse effects on vulnerable groups, and improve domestic food safety and agricultural productivity by adopting a strategic approach to food safety, agricultural health, and trade. For well-prepared countries and suppliers, rising standards represent an opportunity; for those that are poorly prepared, they pose risks related to safety and market access. Rather than adopt differential standards or procedures for suppliers from different countries, high-income countries should increase development flows to help developing countries build their capacities to plan and execute the necessary strategies.

Growing trade in high-value food products
International trade in high-value food products has expanded enormously over the last decades, fueled by changing consumer tastes and advances in production, transport, and other supply-chain technologies. Developing countries have

successfully participated in this growing trade (figure 1). Fresh and processed fruits and vegetables, fish, meat, nuts, and spices now account for more than 50 percent of the total agro-food exports of developing countries, while the share of traditional commodities—such as coffee, tea, cocoa, sugar, cotton, and tobacco—continues to decline. Growing demand for differentiated products from increasingly sophisticated consumers, along with the growth of integrated international supply chains, will provide continuing opportunities for competitive suppliers of high-value foods by allowing them to target a market segment that suits their competitive profile.

Underpinning the growth in demand for high-value foods is the steady growth in the world's population. Demand for food of all types will increase dramatically in the next 20–30 years, as the world's population grows by two billion people—mostly in developing countries. Growing populations, increased wealth, and reduction of traditional trade barriers (through the Doha Round and thereafter) will promote rapid expansion in trade in high-value products worldwide and among developing countries—so-called South–South trade.

SPS standards have been important to the expansion of world trade in high-value perishable products because they have helped manage risks associated with the spread of plant and animal pests and diseases and the incidence of microbial pathogens or contaminants in food. In recent years standards have been tightened or extended into new areas in the wake of a spate of food scares in industrialized countries (table 1) and in the face of increased scientific knowledge, official concerns

Figure 1. Developing countries move into high value foods
Exports, 1980 - 2003

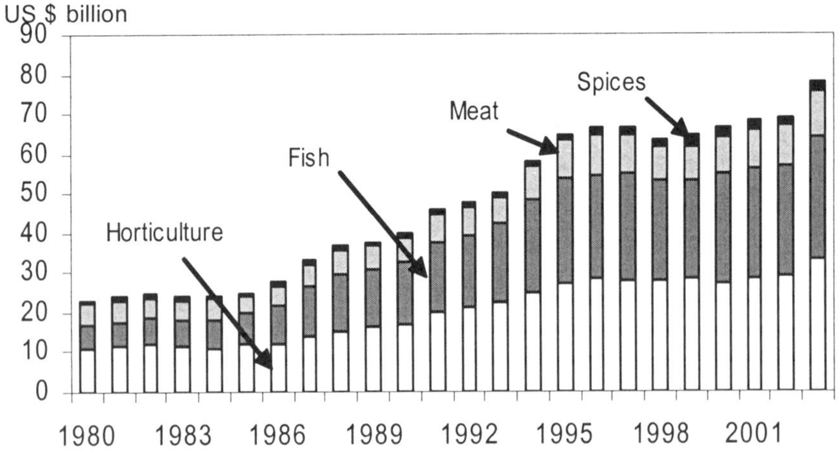

Source: FAOSTAT.

Table 1. Recent food safety events in industrialized countries

Year	Event	Country
1987-1988	Beef hormone scare	Italy/European Union
1988	Poultry salmonella outbreak/scandal	United Kingdom
1989	Growth regulator scare for apples	United States
1993	E.Coli outbreak in fast-food hamburgers	United States
1996	Brain-wasting disease linked to BSE (mad cow disease)	United Kingdom
1996-1197	Microbiological contamination—berries	United States, Canada
1995-1997	Avian flu spreads to humans	Hong Kong, Taiwan (China)
1999	Dioxin in animal feed	Belgium
2000	Large-scale food poisoning (dairy)	Japan
2001	Contaminated olive oil	Spain
2002-2004	Isolated but repeated incidents of BSE	United States, Canada

Source: World Bank (2005).

over bioterrorism, and public concerns about the environment. The private sector has reacted to consumer concerns and official requirements by developing codes of practice and altering its product sourcing practices to emphasize limited sets of "preferred" or company-affiliated suppliers. While some efforts have been made to harmonize standards—at industry, regional, or international levels—the overall trend is toward a proliferation of standards and an increasingly complex commercial and regulatory environment. In this rapidly changing context, developing countries strive to keep up.

Impact of standards on trade in high-value agro-food products

While there is general agreement that food safety and agricultural health measures strongly affect international agro-food trade, there is no consensus on the relative importance of individual measures in relation to other trade-distorting measures, or on the aggregate net effect of those measures. The absence of consensus is not surprising, for testing the impact of such standards on trade presents enormous empirical difficulties. Consider these variables:

• What assumptions are made about how the broad array of measures is *actually enforced* and how enforcement deters or encourages potential export suppliers? Depending on the enforcement regime, the adjustments required of different suppliers may be significant or modest. This variable cannot be aggregated because it differs from country to country and among different industries.

• Food safety and agricultural health requirements may have many secondary and tertiary effects by provoking shifts in sourcing, affecting complementary and competitive goods, and inducing changes in the measures taken by other countries, to name just a few possibilities.

- Specific measures are frequently not a dominant determinant of observed trade flows. There is a risk in ascribing to agro-food standards shifts in trade that are driven by more fundamental economic or technical factors.
- Defining the counterfactual situation presents obvious problems. What would have happened in the absence of the measure? Would trade have continued unimpeded or might distributors and consumers have shifted to other suppliers? Might overall demand have declined for a product for which certain problems were identified?
- Many food safety and agricultural health measures will affect domestic suppliers as well, producing shifts in the relative competitiveness and market share of the different players.

Different methodologies have been used to estimate the impact of rising standards on developing country trade. Several studies based on gravity or other econometric models have tended to estimate very large losses in trade. In contrast, most industry case studies identify an array of competitive factors affecting trade (of which standards are one) and typically point to both winners and losers, rather than to an absolute decline in trade. For example, when Argentina encountered international market-access problems in the wake of outbreaks of food-and-mouth disease in its cattle herd in 2000 and 2001, the beef industry in Brazil stepped in with aggressive marketing and substantially increased its exports. When the Guatemalan raspberry industry faced official and private market-access problems in the late 1990s after an outbreak of food-borne illnesses in North America was attributed to its products, many leading operators shifted their production base across the border into Mexico. That country's raspberry exports have since blossomed. When U.S. beef is kept out of the Japanese market due to concerns about BSE, other countries expand their beef trade with Japan, and Japan increases its imports of nonbeef sources of protein.

Trade in high-value foods can be inhibited by interceptions of products at border points or by outright restrictions on trade due to the presence of certain animal diseases or plant pests or diseases in potential exporting countries. We consider these two possibilities in turn.

Some countries make available data on interceptions of food consignments for safety reasons, but the data do not include the volume or value of the products intercepted. Drawing on official data and consultations with private traders, Jaffee and Henson (2004) provide an order-of-magnitude estimate of the impact of rejections at the border: in 2000–01, some $3.8 billion in world agro-food trade was affected, about 1 percent of all trade. Reflecting their dominant market share in certain product groups for which the incidence of border detentions is relatively high (for example, meat and dairy products; processed fruit and vegetables), high-income countries are estimated to account for 53 percent of rejected exports (and for some 63 percent of world agricultural and food product exports). The estimated value of developing country agro-food border rejections is $1.8 billion, three-fourths of which is accounted for by middle-income countries.[2]

The proportion of agro-food trade that encounters official rejections is, for most food categories, probably substantially lower than the proportion of sales subjected to price discounts by private buyers because of quality defects, lack of timeliness, and poor presentation. Further, only a small proportion of rejected consignments is actually destroyed at the point of import, while some (perhaps significant) proportion of the product is reshipped, reconditioned, or otherwise managed for sale in the domestic market of the exporter or some other international market. And the products with the highest estimated proportion of rejections are also among those that have seen the highest rates of growth in international agricultural trade.[3]

Based on these and other estimates, border rejections on grounds of food safety or related technical issues have probably had only a modest impact on overall trade in agricultural and food products, notably that of developing countries. But border rejections probably represent only a small part of the constraint on international trade in agricultural and food products associated with food safety and agricultural health measures. Far more inhibiting is the broad array of measures that render large numbers of countries ineligible to supply many livestock products and food crops to other countries. Meat and dairy products are subject to the highest level of rejections in global trade. Decades of traditional trade protections and trade-distorting subsidies in industrialized countries have kept these categories insignificant for low-income countries and probably of secondary importance for most middle-income countries. But animal disease controls act to exclude many developing countries from world markets for these products altogether.[4] In part this reflects the prevalence of endemic infectious animal diseases in many low and middle-income countries. The costs of establishing and maintaining disease-free areas can be considerable and may be beyond the means of many of the poorest countries. But even where there is no evidence that such diseases are present, many developing countries lack the capacity for surveillance and risk assessment required to demonstrate that they do in fact have areas that are disease-free and to have those areas recognized as such by the World Organisation for Animal Health, known by its French acronym OIE (Office International des Epizooties).[5]

Even where developing countries have established disease-free areas, they face the risk that trade will be disrupted should outbreaks of disease occur. Restrictions applied to exports of poultry from Thailand and Vietnam after an outbreak of avian flu are just one example. In such cases exporters may be forced to divert products to domestic markets, causing a collapse of local prices. The overall impact of animal disease issues, therefore, is to enhance the risks associated with trade in livestock products, placing a great onus on public authorities not only to invest in the establishment of disease controls, but also to ensure their continued efficacy over time.

Most low-income countries engaged in livestock trade have been unable to meet importers' food safety and agricultural health requirements pertaining to livestock disease and hygiene. Most are restricted to trade in live animals rather than livestock products, for which hygienic slaughter in an abattoir, meat inspection, and refrigerated transport must be provided.[6] Examples of the export of live animals include intraregional trade in West Africa and supplies from East Africa to the countries of the Persian Gulf. However, even if their capacity in the area of animal disease and hygiene capacity could be enhanced, these countries would need to compete with well-established livestock product exporters—notably Argentina and Australia, reliable producers with fewer animal health problems and standardized production (Upton 2001).

Similar issues arise with plant pests and diseases, which arguably have the greatest impact on many developing countries, given the importance of trade in fresh fruit and vegetables, grains, and nuts. For example, many Caribbean countries face restrictions on the fresh fruits and vegetables that they can export to the United States because of the presence of various species of fruit fly. Jamaica, for example, is unable to export mangos to the United States because of the presence of West Indian and Caribbean fruit fly. In some cases exports are prohibited altogether, whereas in others prescribed treatments are required. These treatments can involve fumigation or use of hot water to kill pests. Such treatments impose costs on the exporter and reduce shelf-life and lower product quality. Further, the costs of establishing such facilities can be considerable. In some cases the impact of plant disease controls on trade in agricultural and food products can be mitigated through cooperation between governments, for example, through the sharing of plant pest surveillance data or the establishment of preclearance programs.

Rethinking the impact of stringent SPS standards—costs and benefits, winners and losers

The cost of complying with food safety and agricultural health standards has been a major source of concern in the international development community and among developing countries. Many worry that SPS standards will work increasingly to the disadvantage of developing countries that lack the administrative, technical, and other capacities to comply with new or more stringent requirements. However, the available evidence indicates that, in many instances, these challenges are manageable and the compliance costs a worthwhile investment, especially relative to the value of exports and associated benefits.

Developing country suppliers rarely face all-or-nothing choices when determining the changes and investments needed to conform to emerging standards. Only occasionally do SPS standards pose an absolute barrier to international market

Box 1: Discrimination in the Application of SPS Standards?

An Agreement on the Application of Sanitary and Phytosanitary Measures (the SPS Agreement) was annexed to the 1994 Marrakech Agreement that created the World Trade Organization. While the SPS Agreement sets out broad ground rules for the legitimate application of SPS measures, it has not eradicated the differential application of standards—and it is unrealistic to expect it to do so. Differentiation in the application of SPS measures is a necessary part of any risk-based food safety and agricultural health control system. At the country, industry, and enterprise levels, the hazards to be monitored and the control measures implemented must be prioritized to make the best use of limited resources. An effective risk management system will go further, to differentiate explicitly between alternative sources of supply based on differences in production conditions, past experience, and assessments of risk management capabilities in the supply chain. Many countries automatically detain imported products from countries with a history of noncompliance with food safety or agricultural health requirements.

In circumstances in which regulators and others have wide discretion and where various forms of differentiation are required for cost-effective management of food safety and agricultural health, there remains ample scope for anticompetitive mischief. Yet separating legitimate differentiation from illegitimate discrimination is problematic. It is even more difficult to prove that a given standard is wholly protectionist in intent. For example, in two widely cited cases where protectionism was assumed to have been an important motivating factor (involving restrictions on exports of Mexican avocadoes and Argentine citrus fruits to the United States), scientific justification was produced for the application of measures to prevent the spread of plant diseases, although less restrictive measures could have been applied (Roberts and Orden 1997). In other cases, trading partners have differing perspectives on the state of scientific knowledge or the need to make allowance for uncertainty. Perhaps the most prominent case is the dispute between the European Union (EU) and United States over restrictions on exports of beef produced with the use of hormones (Bureau and others 1998).

Among the many questions that remain about the use of food safety and agricultural health controls to discourage imports is whether foreign suppliers must comply with higher requirements than domestic suppliers. No systematic research has been done on this subject. On the basis of general impressions and anecdotes, it would appear that many countries, both industrialized and developing, do have a lower tolerance for certain animal and plant health risks in imports than in domestic products. Some countries have restricted supplies from countries where a plant pest or animal disease

Box 1. *(continued)*

occurs, even though the pest or disease in question is prevalent domestically. Similar observations can be made for some food safety controls. For example, the United States has long argued in trade forums that a broad array of countries have a near zero tolerance for salmonella in imported poultry products, yet this pathogen is widely present in their domestic supply chains. Other cases of discriminatory practices have been brought to the attention of the SPS Committee and addressed through bilateral or multilateral discussions (Josling and others 2004).

A second question relates to whether the enforcement of food safety and agricultural health measures is more stringent for imports than for domestic supplies. In discussions with high-value food exporters in developing countries one frequently hears the accusation that the controls they face are more rigorous than those imposed on domestic suppliers in certain industrialized countries. Frequently, however, this perception springs from the intensive oversight and monitoring performed by private entities, especially supermarkets and their buying agents, rather than from official systems of surveillance and product monitoring. In other cases, the methods of control they face are more visible than are domestic controls, in that compliance is assessed at the border, and on this basis entry can be denied. Domestic suppliers, by contrast, are regulated through inspection of their processing facilities, with a focus on system-based controls or market surveillance. Conversely, anecdotal evidence suggests that oversight for certain products and markets is more stringent on domestic rather than imported supplies. For example, over a typical three-year period the U.S. Food and Drug Administration (FDA) will undertake inspections of all the domestic firms that produce low-acid canned foods, yet the same inspections are conducted on just 3 percent of foreign facilities exporting such products to the United States. Even after substantially increasing resources for the inspection of food imports, the FDA still only inspects between 1 and 2 percent of the more than six million consignments of food and cosmetic products imported each year.

access—and then usually in relation to animal diseases and plant pests. Barriers created by food safety standards are usually relative—that is, they favor suppliers that can comply with the standards and tax those that cannot. Suppliers therefore need to weigh the costs and advantages associated with participating in different market segments. In some cases, they may have large and profitable opportunities to service the domestic market, the regional market, or market segments in industrialized countries that impose less stringent standards or allow more time to implement certain measures.

Even when targeting markets with relatively stringent standards, the level and relative significance of compliance costs varies greatly from industry to industry, between different countries, and among different firms and farms within the same industry. Several factors contribute to this variability:

- Typically there are several ways to meet a standard. Countries and firms that have chosen to be proactive—that is, to prepare in advance to meet anticipated standards—are better able to weigh and compare various options and to adopt those that are cost-effective. Entities that elect to delay compliance until after a crisis has occurred are likely to have less flexibility and may need to adopt costly measures simply to restore market access.
- Firms, industries, and countries operate from different starting points and with varying assets obtained from past investments. For a relatively modern and mature industry, a change in standards may require only incremental changes by producers or exporters and perhaps some modest adjustment in public sector oversight. However, for an underdeveloped supply chain, or where there is a lack of clarity on institutional roles, the new standard may require major investments in infrastructure and significant legal or organizational change.
- Market factors often affect the level and distribution of certain benefits. In some industries, price premiums are paid for products that can be labeled as "safe" or "sustainable," or that bear other evidence of desirable attributes. In other industries, competitive pressures have made such attributes the minimal norm or driven down the value of such price premiums.

Many of the potential benefits of complying with stringent SPS standards and of improved SPS management by producers are long-term, intangible, or accrue to stakeholders that do not incur the associated costs (appendix 2). Benefits such as productivity gains, reduced wastage, worker safety, environmental benefits, and even the value of continued market access may be underestimated. This is unfortunate, because the perception that SPS compliance costs exceed the related benefits discourages needed investments and deters proactive approaches, thus increasing the likelihood of severe trade-related problems arising from adverse food safety or agricultural health events.

Many aspects of standards compliance do not require large investments or sophisticated technical or administrative capacities. The most significant challenge often is building broad awareness about the need for proper SPS measures and facilitating the broad adoption of good agricultural and manufacturing practices. A coherent regulatory framework and a system to assess compliance and conformity are also needed. Even in very poor countries, these systems and capacities can be developed if a proactive approach is adopted. Compared with the present and future volume of trade and other benefits, the costs of compliance usually are relatively low.

Although the overall trade of developing countries as a group has not been adversely affected by the tightening of SPS standards, the different approaches to this challenge and differences in underlying technical and administrative capacities have resulted in some relative winners and losers. Larger, incumbent suppliers tend to have an incremental advantage, because they can realize economies of scale, have better access to information, and benefit from well-established reputations (for example, with overseas inspectors). Small, poor countries and industries tend to be disadvantaged. Still, effective action can make a difference. There are examples of well-organized industries and well-managed firms and supply chains in low-income countries that have maintained or even enhanced their competitiveness and market share during this period of more stringent standards.

Although compliance (and noncompliance) can bring about changes that have a negative impact on the poor, those who are able to participate in evolving supply chains may benefit. This can certainly apply to small farmers operating in suitable locations with adequate infrastructure, including effective producer organizations and long-term relationships with buyers. Also, the tightening of standards has sometimes increased off-farm employment opportunities, especially in product cleaning, handling, processing, and packing, and in a broad array of process controls.

Presently, among low- and (to a lesser extent) middle-income countries, weaknesses in food safety and agricultural health management, both in the private and public sectors, constrain productivity and competitiveness. Such constraints almost certainly will take on greater importance in the coming years, given trends in consumer attitudes and preferences, changes in supply-chain governance and market structures, and continued advances in science and technology. Interventions to strengthen SPS management capacities can contribute to growth and poverty reduction by removing those constraints.

Using one's room for maneuver—toward a proactive approach to SPS management

As the demand for high-value food products grows rapidly over the coming decades, countries and individual producers that approach standards compliance as part of an overall competitive strategy are likely to thrive. Certain developing country industries—Kenya's horticulture sector, for example (box 2)—have succeeded in meeting standards by adopting a proactive approach to compliance—staying abreast of shifting technical and commercial requirements in their chosen markets and anticipating future changes. These firms have pursued and used higher standards to reposition themselves in remunerative market segments, sometimes by adding value to commodities.

More generally, a forward-looking approach requires certain national and industry capacities, including those for channeling information and interpreting international regulatory and commercial trends, conducting risk analysis, undertaking hazard surveillance and monitoring, and applying contingency planning in SPS management (appendix 3). A successful proactive campaign also requires that policymakers, firms, and industry organizations adopt the perspective that effective SPS management is a core element of overall competitiveness. Failure to address

Box 2. Kenyan horticulture: high costs and high gains at the top of the market

Kenya's experience with fresh vegetable exports demonstrates that a well-organized industry in a low-income country can use standards for competitive gain. The leading firms in Kenya's fresh produce industry chose in the early 1990s to "ride the tail" of British supermarkets, investing in products, internal systems, and supply chains to service the premium-quality end of the market, including the growing demand for salads and other semi-prepared vegetable products. These firms and their farmer suppliers bore most of the costs of compliance—and reaped most of the benefits.

The costs of the tail-ridingstrategy have included the construction of high-care processing facilities, investment in private laboratories, and the development of full supply-chain traceability. Leading companies have upgraded and expanded their facilities, installing new lighting and water sanitation systems, advanced cold treatment and storage systems, facilities for worker hygiene and quality management (such as hazard analysis and critical control point systems).

Yet the benefits from these investments and of general compliance with the requirements of upscale supermarkets also seem to have been significant. The net profit margins of large Kenyan exporters can be as high as 14 percent for "high-care" packaged goods, compared to 2 percent for bulk vegetables packed loose in cartons. Other benefits perceived by the exporters include regularity of demand, advance information from supermarket clients on market trends, certainty with respect to quality and hygiene specifications, and enhanced reputation.

The payoff on Kenya's proactive investment has been great. Over the past decade, as EU imports from nonmember countries were flat, Kenya was able to increase the value of its fresh vegetable exports significantly, in large part by shifting the product composition of its trade, meeting the highest standards in EU markets, and achieving an upward shift in the unit value of its exports. From 1991 to 2003, the value and volume of Kenya's exports of fresh vegetables increased five fold.

SPS problems or concerns may undermine an industry's access to remunerative international markets. But where fundamental supply-side problems persist, the resolution of SPS constraints will not yield sustained export success.

The foregoing observations imply that many developing countries can profit by viewing strict standards as a stimulus for investments in supply-chain modernization, providing incentives for the adoption of better safety and quality control practices in agriculture and food manufacturing, and clarifying the appropriate and necessary roles of government in food safety and agricultural health management. Rather than degrading the comparative advantage of developing countries, the compliance process can result in new forms of competitive advantage and contribute to more sustainable and profitable trade over the long term.

Moving ahead: a capacity-building agenda for developing countries

Improved SPS capacity is the key to a successful proactive approach to compliance. The proactive approach to standards compliance is most likely to succeed when supported by adequate capacity in food safety and agricultural health control, and when policymakers have the confidence to voice their concerns about the standards imposed by trading partners and buyers. Every new SPS standard, public or private, favors those market players that are able to anticipate it. Private producers must have the capacity to target the right markets and to be ready to comply or make other adjustments before standards are imposed and trade is disrupted. Policymakers must draft sensible regulations; regulators must have the capacity to enforce those measures. Standards can represent both an opportunity and a catalyst, but for those poorly prepared or disinclined to take active steps, they will almost certain prove a barrier to trade. To make further progress in this domain:

*   Rich countries and pertinent technical agencies should increase and reorient their assistance to developing countries for SPS capacity building, providing it before crises occur. Many past interventions have been triggered by emergency situations, such as trade disruptions or disputes, rather than by the prospect of forging a strategic approach to SPS management and investment. Future capacity-building efforts should be geared toward maximizing the strategic options available to both government and the private sector in developing countries faced with new or more stringent SPS standards.
*   Industrial country governments should harmonize SPS product and process requirements with those of other countries (and with established international norms), where there is an identified benefit of doing so. Through memoranda of understanding, twinning arrangements, and other programs, they should work closely with developing country trading partners to achieve mutual recognition of SPS management systems and to ensure that the impact on developing countries of proposed SPS measures is understood in advance.
*   To reduce costs and ensure sources of supply, the private sector in industrial

countries should harmonize or mutually benchmark the growing array of overlapping and competing private protocols on good agricultural and manufacturing practices, and other process standards. It should consult developing country suppliers when developing or revising standards so as to make their implementation more user-friendly and cost-effective. Supply chain leaders should consider joining with governments and donor agencies to provide technical assistance to suppliers to enable them to meet emerging requirements.

• Developing country governments should move beyond control functions to build awareness about SPS management and to facilitate individual and collective action by private companies, farmers, and others. Adopting a long-term, strategic approach to managing SPS standards and international market access obliges policymakers and technical administrators to work closely with the private sector to identify emerging challenges and opportunities, make appropriate regulatory changes, and choose suitable strategies and needed investments. Clear distinctions should be made between food safety and agricultural health challenges. Many of the former can be addressed by individual company actions, whereas many of the latter require systemic approaches or controls that extend beyond the sphere of individual firms or supply chains.

• The private sector in developing countries should incorporate current and expected requirements related to SPS and other standards into business plans, including considerations of product-market combinations, customer and supply relationships, production technology, logistics, and investments in processing and marketing facilities. It should work through industry organizations to advocate for effective public sector support and to implement programs to build awareness, encourage adoption of good practices and codes of practice, and otherwise strengthen food quality and SPS management within their industries.

Appendix 1. The World Bank's research program on sanitary and phytosanitary (SPS) measures

The World Bank's research program on sanitary and phytosanitary (SPS) measures was designed to improve understanding of an emerging set of policy and commercial issues in the area of food safety and agricultural health. It does not cover other standards, such as labor, environmental or animal welfare requirements. The program has involved a series of case studies covering selected commodity supply chains in nine low- and middle-income countries—Ethiopia, India, Jamaica, Kenya, Morocco, Nicaragua, Senegal, Thailand, and the countries of Latin America's Southern Cone. The commodity chains are those related to fish, horticulture, livestock products, nuts, and spices. They were chosen because the products involved have posed SPS compliance challenges for a significant number of developing countries and have been the subject of many recent food safety events or crises in industrialized countries. Countries were selected to capture regional diversity, varied market orientations, and a range of experiences, from emerging to long-standing industries. Complementary "buyer studies" were also carried out, involving representative importers and retailers of shrimp and selected fruits and vegetables in the European Union, Japan, and the Untied States.

The major themes and questions addressed in the research program have been:

- *Overall context and prominence.* How difficult are the challenges posed by rising private and public SPS standards for developing country suppliers? What is the relative significance of these challenges, compared with other factors affecting competitiveness?
- *Dynamics and differences in standards.* What are the similarities and distinctive features of the evolving standards for different product groups and in relation to different industrial country destination markets? What are the main driving forces behind the newer standards? What can be expected in the future?
- *Strategies to comply with or influence standards.* What strategies have been used and have worked to meet the emerging requirements or influence their application? What are some key factors influencing the viability and sustainability of different approaches?
- *Costs and benefits of compliance.* What is the nature, magnitude, and overall significance of costs and benefits associated with supplier (and country) compliance with external market standards?
- *Structural and distributional implications.* What are the implications of standards-related barriers and compliance for market structures and for the participation of small-scale farmers and firms in export-oriented supply chains?
- *Lessons from donor-supported programs.* What have been the patterns of capacity-building assistance in this field in recent years? What lessons can be drawn about the timing, institutional features, effectiveness, and sustainability of capacity-building programs?

Table A1. Country and commodity case studies in the World Bank's research program

Fish, shrimp, and fish products	India, Jamaica, Kenya, Nicaragua, Senegal, Thailand
Fruits and vegetables	Jamaica, Kenya, Morocco, Thailand
Animals/animal products	Ethiopia (live animals), Latin America's Southern Cone (beef and Foot-and-mouth Disease (FMD) control)
Nuts and spices	India (spices), Senegal (groundnuts)

Source: World Bank (2005).

Table A2. Costs and benefits of complying with SPS standards

Costs—Investment: 0.5–5 percent of the multiyear value of trade; Recurrent: 1–3 percent of annual sales	Benefits—Often hard to compute
• Upgrade of laboratory infrastructure	• Crisis containment, as when traceability system prevents an alert from becoming a crisis
• Upgrade of processing facilities	• Increased attention to overall efficacy of controls
• Investments in farm-level facilities to comply with GAP requirements	• Access to more remunerative markets and supply chains
• Reduced investment in new product development	• Greater efficiency, thus lower costs
• Reduced investment in domestic food safety controls	• Less waste in production processes
• Collection and analysis of laboratory tests	• Reduced incidence of product inspection and detention abroad
• Additional costs for 'certified' raw materials	• Enhancement of product quality
• Additional costs for implementing hazard analysis and critical control point system	• Higher morale of inspection and production staffs
• Reduced flexibility in production processes	• Improved reputation of firm and/or country
• Reduced domestic food safety enforcement	• Improved worker safety and reduced environmental degradation

Source: World Bank (2005).

Table A3. Common food safety and agricultural health management deficiencies in selected sectors

Fish products	Horticultural products	Animal health
▪ Inadequate legislation relating to hygiene controls in fish processing	▪ Weak regulatory systems relating to the import, production, and sale of pesticides.	▪ Weak systems to monitor emerging regulatory changes related to animal disease controls on imports in existing or potential export markets
▪ Poorly defined administrative responsibilities for approval and inspection of processing facilities and certification of exports	▪ Lack of capacity to undertake pest-risk analyses	▪ Inadequate legislation and undocumented procedures relating to animal health controls
▪ Weak inspection systems for processing facilities, including lack of documented procedures, insufficient inspection staff, limited skills and weak reporting	▪ Weak controls relating to plant pests and diseases at borders	▪ Weak controls relating to animal diseases at borders
▪ Weak laboratory testing capacity for microbiological and chemical contaminants and for residues of antibiotics	▪ Low capacity to implement quarantine measures and enforce pest-free areas	▪ Weak capacity to implement quarantine or control/eradication measures in the event of a disease outbreak
▪ HACCP systems not widely implemented in fish-processing plants and not extending to fishery capture and production	▪ Limited farmer knowledge of alternative pest-management approaches and appropriate use of pesticides	▪ Weak capacity to undertake disease surveillance and risk assessments
	▪ Limited application of HACCP principles by fresh vegetable packers/exporters (especially SMEs)	▪ Weak laboratory testing capacity related to the diagnosis of animal diseases and monitoring programs
	▪ Limited systems for fresh-produce traceability	▪ No incentive to divulge or publicize outbreaks of animal diseases

HACCP = Hazard analysis and critical control point
Source: World Bank (2005).

Notes

1 This note is based primarily on the report "Food Safety and Agricultural Health Standards: Challenges and Opportunities for Developing Country Exports" (Washington, DC: World Bank, 2005), http://www.worldbank.org/trade/standards.

2 Jaffee and Henson (2004) estimate the value of agro-food exports from low-income countries rejected at the border of importing countries at $275 million, slightly less than 1 percent of the agro-food exports of those countries. Fish and fishery products probably account for more than one-half of this affected trade.

3 Although the overall impact of border rejections on trade may not be very significant, the costs may be considerable for individual suppliers (or countries), both in terms of the value of lost products and adverse effects on the supplier's reputation.

4 For example, the United States currently permits imports of beef from only 33 countries and imports of chicken from only four countries.

5 Currently, the OIE recognizes only 57 countries as being totally free of foot-and-mouth disease without vaccination, of which 26 are developing countries and only 3 are low-income countries.

6 Indeed, widespread cases of both new and well-established animal diseases have led to heightened concerns about the role of international trade in the spread of such diseases. In the case of BSE, widespread restrictions have been applied to trade in live animals, meat, animal feed, and an array of by-products used in cosmetics, pharmaceuticals, and other industries.

References

Bureau, J., S. Marette, and A. Schiavina. 1998. "Non-Tariff Trade Barriers and Consumers' Information: The Case of the EU-US Trade Dispute over Beef." European Review of Agricultural Economics 25: 437–462.

Jaffee, S. 2003. "From Challenge to Opportunity: Transforming Kenya's Fresh Vegetable Trade in the Context of Emerging Food Safety and Other Standards in Europe." Agriculture and Rural Development Discussion Paper 2. World Bank, Washington, DC.

Jaffee, S., and S. Henson. 2004. "Standards and Agri-Food Exports from Developing Countries: Rebalancing the Debate." Policy Research Working Paper 3348. World Bank, Washington, DC.

Josling, T., D. Roberts, and D. Orden. 2004. Food Regulation and Trade: Toward a Safe and Open Global System. Washington, DC: Institute for International Economics.

Orden, D., and D. Roberts. 1997. "Determinants of Technical Barriers to Trade: The Case of U.S. Phytosanitary Restrictions on Mexican Avocadoes." In Understanding Technical Barriers to Agricultural Trade, ed. D. Orden and D. Roberts. International Agricultural Trade Research Consortium, University of Minnesota.

Upton, M. 2001. Trade in Livestock and Livestock Products: International Regulations and Role for Economic Development. Rome: Food and Agricultural Organization.

World Bank. 2005. Food Safety and Agricultural Health Standards: Challenges and Opportunities for Developing Country Exports. Washington, DC: World Bank.

Further Reading

Buzby, J., ed. 2003. "International Trade and Food Safety: Economic Theory and Case Studies." Agricultural Economic Report 828. U.S. Department of Agriculture, Washington, DC.

ITC (International Trade Centre). 2003. Influencing and Meeting International Standards: Challenges for Developing Countries. Geneva.

OECD. 2003. "Trade Effects of the SPS Agreement." Directorate for Food, Agriculture, and Fisheries, Paris.

Unnevehr, L., ed. 2003. *Food Safety in Food Security and Food Trade*. Washington, DC: International Food Policy Research Institute.

World Trade Organization. 2005. *World Trade Report 2005, Exploring the Links Between Trade, Standards, and the WTO*. Geneva.

The World Bank in Trade: The New Trade Agenda

Richard Newfarmer and Dorota Nowak

The World Bank's engagement on trade has intensified in recent years. After high levels of trade-related lending during the 1980s, the Bank turned its attention away from trade during most of the 1990s.[1] However, by 2001, as it became clear that developing countries' participation in the globalization process was uneven and as the debate on globalization began to intensify, the Bank began to ramp up its trade work once again in 2001.[2]

But the agenda was different in 2001 than in earlier periods. No longer were Bank activities primarily focused on tariffs and other border barriers to trade (many of which had come down significantly), but rather on the "complementary policies" necessary to ignite growth and ensure participation of the poor in globalization. The "New Trade Agenda" of the World Bank has three goals. The first is to make the world trading system more supportive of development at the global level, particularly in the products the poor produce—namely agriculture and labor-intensive products. The second is to improve the trade-creating aspects of preferential trade agreements at the regional level. The third is to help developing countries incorporate trade into national development strategies to promote growth. The Bank's country work is focused on overcoming the supply-side constraints that prevent developing countries, particularly low-income countries, from taking advantage of the opportunities inherent in globalization.

This chapter charts the evolution of the World Bank's activities in trade, provides an overview of the Bank's current program, and concludes with a look at the challenges that lie ahead.

Two decades of trade work at the World Bank: a natural evolution

The Bank's assistance to developing countries in support of trade, while varying in intensity, has been substantial over the last 25 years. More than 500 lending operations were dedicated fully or partially to trade in 117 countries. Total lending amounted to $38 billion, or some 8.1 percent of total Bank commitments during this period. Lending activities continued to be supported by a great deal of economic and sector work, research, and, more recently, an increasing volume of capacity building and training activities.[3]

In the 1980s, many developing countries began eliminating quantitative restrictions on imports and reducing tariffs. The Bank supported those efforts with structural and sectoral adjustment loans. Its aim was to help countries reduce the disincentives to exporting implicit in high border barriers and to reduce the

Figure 1. Number of trade-related lending has decreased overall

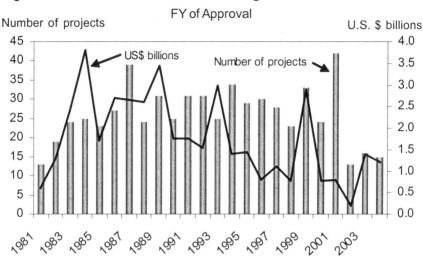

Source: World Bank, TAE Project Database.

distortions and monopoly rents that often accompanied the barriers. The Bank also supported macroeconomic reforms that eliminated multiple exchange rates and discretionary allocation of foreign-exchange subsidies. Lending remained relatively high throughout the 1980s, reaching its apex in fiscal year 1987 with approximately 40 trade projects approved (figure 1).

By the 1990s, most countries had enacted major trade reforms. Led by East Asia (and with South Asia trailing behind), average unweighted tariffs in developing countries declined sharply from their high levels of the late 1980s (figure 2). With these developments, the Bank turned its attention to other impediments to growth. Fiscal year 1993 marked the start of a decline in trade-related lending that lasted until 2002, with a spike in lending to the crisis-affected countries of East Asia in 1999.

Throughout this period, the Bank's core trade research team remained intact. Its steady stream of timely policy-oriented studies included work on trade and poverty, agricultural trade, services, trade facilitation, regionalism, and foreign direct investment. The team's work formed the basis for the Bank's eventual reengagement on trade issues at the global, regional and country levels.

Figure 2. Average tariffs have decreased accross all regions

Average tariffs, percent

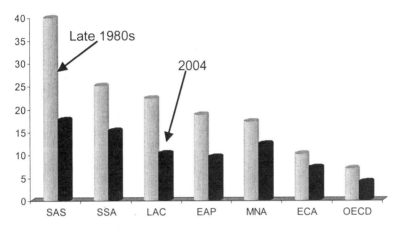

Source: WITS database.

The New Trade Agenda: a resurgence of trade activity at the Bank

The steady expansion of the global marketplace proved to be an important driver of growth in developed and developing countries alike. Global merchandise trade grew at an annual average of more than 6 percent in the 1980s and 1990s. As a group, developing countries benefited from the expansion, increasing their share of the non-oil market from 21.1 percent in 1980 to 37.4 percent in 2003.

But beneath this process lurked uneven country performances. Low-income developing countries have had far less success in penetrating global markets than middle-income countries, and their average growth has lagged behind that of developing countries as a group. While middle-income countries increased their share of the global market for non-oil trade by some 14 percentage points between 1990 and 2003, low-income countries managed an increase of just 0.5 percentage point. The least developed countries (LDCs) barely maintained their market share. Correspondingly, growth rates of the low-income countries were substantially lower as well, although they accelerated with the rise of commodity prices after 2001. During the 1990s, growth of the low-income countries was 0.4 percent slower than for middle-income countries, and 1.1 percent lower in per capita terms.

The slower growth of low-income countries can be traced in part to trade problems—among them over reliance on volatile commodities, lack of diversification, and inability to take advantage of profitable opportunities in global markets. The lowering of tariffs exposed "behind-the border" constraints to trade related to the investment climate (e.g., poor macroeconomic policy, weak governance, and lack of enforcement of property rights), institutions (customs), and infrastructure (ports and telecommunications). Without progress on these problems, the price incentives of lower border barriers by themselves could not induce growth.

Another obstacle to growth in developing countries' exports was the high level of protection of agriculture in the developed countries. As manufacturing tariffs came down, agricultural tariffs stayed high, while domestic support programs in the advanced economies depressed world prices for the agricultural commodities so important to developing countries' trade.

Two other factors called for a new trade agenda at the Bank. The first was the opportunity presented by the emergence of a new round of multilateral trade talks, dubbed the Doha Development Agenda. The second was the explosion of "competitive liberalization" at the regional level, as the United States, in particular, accelerated its pursuit of regional trade agreements (RTAs), thereby opening a second front along which developing countries could expand their markets.

In April 2001 a report to the World Bank's Executive Board of Directors (World Bank 2001) outlined a new trade strategy with three mutually reinforcing goals:

- at the global level, to help make the world trading system more conducive to development.
- at the regional level, to help shape the growing agenda on regionalism and bilateral agreements in such a way that trade is created and integration deepened; and
- at the country level, to help developing countries integrate trade into growth strategies.

The report also laid the groundwork for the subsequent creation of a new International Trade Department in 2002.

The program today

To achieve these objectives, the Bank's trade program consists of operational activities, research, analysis, advocacy, training, and capacity building at the global, regional, and country levels.

Toward a development-friendly multilateral system

The Bank's participation in global discussions of trade policy has intensified significantly since 2001, with a focus on the Doha Round. To help make the world trading system more conducive to development, the Bank has undertaken new research and channeled existing research more directly into policy dialogue. For example, the Bank devoted its *Global Economic Prospects* reports from 2001 to 2004 to trade-related policy analysis and recommendations (World Bank 2001a, 2002, 2003a, 2004a).

Box 1. A new initiative in trade facilitation

In the growing area of trade facilitation, the Bank is complementing its operational activities with an ambitious outreach program to support the Doha negotiations. The main goal is to help developing countries approach the negotiations with tools they need to make informed decisions. Better knowledge of the cost and benefits of reforms will help developing countries undertake stronger commitments—to their own benefit. Of particular importance is LDC participation in the commitment process. If they are left out of the reform process, LDCs will be further marginalized in the world trading system.

The main aspects of the World Bank program, which is being implemented in coordination with the Negotiating Committee at the WTO and the WTO Secretariat, are: (a) publication and dissemination of the *Customs Modernization Handbook* (de Wulf and Sokol 2005); (b) preparation of a self-assessment tool that will allow countries to quickly analyze proposals put forward at the negotiations; (c) participation of LDCs in all relevant forums, with a special focus on Africa in coordination with the Africa Union. Working together with the World Customs Organization and with support from Britain's Department for International Development, the Bank will also pilot a self-assessment tool in four countries.

Source: World Bank.

Making RTAs work for developing countries

In the last 15 years the number of regional and bilateral reciprocal trade agreements in force around the world increased from about 50 to more than 200. These agreements can have a positive or negative effect on trade and incomes, depending on their design, and can also affect the multilateral trading system (see Richard Newfarmer's chapter in this volume). The Bank has analyzed these issues in research papers and studies such as Schiff and Winters (2003) and World Bank (2004a).

The Bank has produced trade reports for five of its six regions, focusing on competitiveness, trade reforms, services, and other behind-the-border trade questions.[4] It also has an ambitious program in support of Eastern Europe's accession to the European Union (the program links regional initiatives to domestic reforms).

In the last two years, the Bank has begun to respond to client requests for technical assistance in regional trade negotiations, particularly those involving the European Union and United States. In addition, the Bank is investing an increasing amount in trade-facilitation projects and regional transport corridors, notably in Africa. As part of a recently released Africa Action Plan, the Bank's Africa region will conduct surveys of transport costs in export corridors and work with donors on new projects to promote regional integration.

Country work: increasing investment in trade

As tariffs have come down, governments have sought the Bank's advice on overcoming supply-side constraints to trade. For LDCs, the Bank has spearheaded work on the Integrated Framework (IF) for Trade-Related Technical Assistance—a multidonor trust fund managed by the United Nations Development Programme with participation from the International Monetary Fund, World Trade Organization, International Trade Center and the United Nations Conference on Trade and Development (see Julia Nielson's article in this volume).[5] The cornerstone of the IF are country-specific diagnostic trade integration studies (DTIS), which analyze internal and external obstacles to the country's integration into the world economy and identify areas in which technical assistance and policy actions can help overcome those obstacles. Of 50 LDCs eligible to receive assistance through the IF, 37 (including 29 in Africa) are participating. By the end of 2005, 21 DTISs will have been completed and 7 more will start. Nine studies are planned in 2006.

For non-LDCs, work on trade diagnostics has continued to expand. Whereas in 2002 almost all of the Bank's trade diagnostic work focused on IF countries, by 2005 that work encompassed more than 35 non-LDC countries. Virtually all of this work has started with a comprehensive approach to trade integration, simultaneously focusing on trade policy, infrastructure, customs and trade facilitation, and sometimes other aspects of the business environment.[6]

Meanwhile, the Bank's lending activities (in dollar terms and in the number of lending operations) have rebounded from a record low of approximately $200 million in FY2001[6] to $1.2 billion in 2004. And they continue to grow. Today, approved and projected commitments for new trade operations for the three-year period FY2004–2006 are significantly larger than the total commitments of operations active in FY03, which had been approved over a period of eight years (figure 3).

From conditionality to collaboration

Implementing the New Trade Agenda requires improving institutions, making productive infrastructure investments, and fine-tuning policies over time, tasks that do not lend themselves well to 1980s-style adjustment lending in support of "stroke of the pen" policy changes. Because of the new requirements and the move away from balance-of-payments support characteristic of the turbulent 1980s, adjustment lending as a share of total trade lending has fallen. The content of the Bank's lending program has shifted to investment lending in trade-related, infrastructure and institutional reform.[7] Today, loans for trade facilitation alone accounts for one-fourth of all new lending (figure 4). Approved and projected

Figure 3. Trade lending has increased since late 1990s

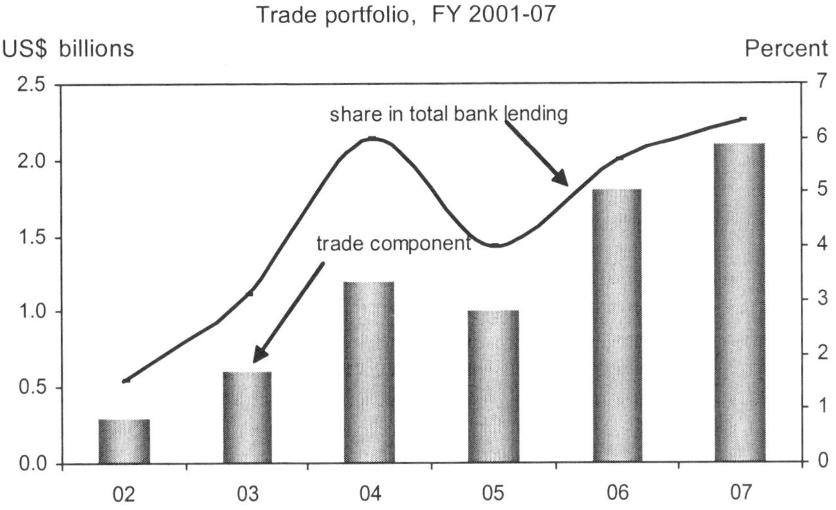

Trade portfolio, FY 2001-07

US$ billions   Percent

Note: Data for FY06-07 are projected in the Bank's lending program

Figure 4. Bank activities, FY 1996 - 2006

U.S. $ billion

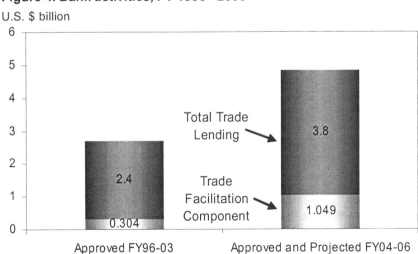

Note: Data for FY06–07 are projected in the Bank's lending program.

Box 2. Conditionality in World Bank lending for trade has decreased

Conditionality directed at reducing trade barriers has fallen systematically since the 1980s. The reasons for the decline mirror larger developments in the Bank's program: the greater openness of developing country economies since trade reforms in the 1980s, and the Bank's shift toward long-term reforms of institutional and supply-side policies. Not only has Bank adjustment lending in support of reductions in border barriers fallen, but the number of overall conditions in Bank adjustment loans has also fallen.

The graph below shows the shift away from conditionality related to trade and economic management in adjustment lending in favor of public sector governance. Within the economic management sphere it is probable that the number of trade conditions focused on tariff reductions has also fallen.

Figure 5. Trends in the share of conditions by thematic area

Percent

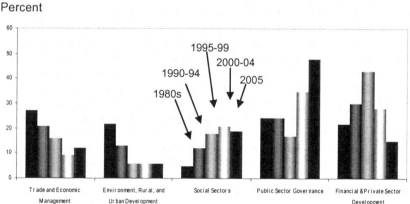

Source: ALCID, World Bank.

commitments for FY2004–06, at more than $1 billion, are triple the commitments for trade facilitation in active operations during FY1996–2003. A striking feature of Bank trade lending has been the significant decrease in the use of conditionality (Box 2).

Often projects support several integrated aspects of trade-related projects. For example, the Bank has supported restructuring efforts, policy changes, and new investments designed to increase the productivity of West African countries in cotton production–even as the Bank has advocated reducing subsidies in rich countries that undercut global prices (see Box 3).

As with trade facilitation, the demand for work on standards compliance in agriculture has grown exponentially. Many developing countries have succeeded in diversifying their agricultural exports into perishable products of higher value, especially horticultural and fish products. Yet the sustainability of this success is uncertain because of increasingly stringent official and private standards in industrialized countries. Demand for technical assistance and capacity-building

Box 3. Easing the vulnerability of the "Cotton 4"

Benin, Burkina Faso, Chad, and Mali—known as the "Cotton 4"—depend heavily on cotton exports, leaving them vulnerable to the price-depressing subsidies of rich countries and volatility in world cotton markets. While advocating reductions in those subsidies, the Bank (with partners) has tried to reduce countries' vulnerability to fluctuations in cotton prices by increasing their competitiveness, strengthening their research capacity, and reinforcing producer associations. The Bank also is helping countries consider diversification to other crops, including traditional cereals and cash crops, and exploring the potential for protecting producers from risks through a combination of crop insurance and instruments to manage price risks.

In close coordination with other donors and international agencies, the Bank is supporting additional reforms of the cotton sector to lower costs and increase productivity. To support restructuring in *Benin*, the World Bank has an ongoing Cotton Sector Reform Project ($18 million). In *Burkina Faso*, the World Bank and the government are preparing a new Agricultural Diversification Project ($35 million) to strengthen producer organizations. In *Chad*, progress on cotton reforms has been somewhat limited because of the fiscal difficulties of Cotonchad, the parastatal cotton processing company, and the slow pace of reforms by the government. The Bank is considering a Cotton Sector Reform Project (proposed at $15 million) if and when the government launches a reform program. In *Mali,* the government has decided to postpone the privatization of the parastatal cotton company. The Bank has recently approved an Agricultural Competitiveness and Diversification Project ($46.4 million) that focuses on cotton and diversification of crops. The French development agency is working with producers' organizations to build their capacity.

Source: World Bank staff.

support in this field has grown rapidly, outpacing the response by the development community.

Research and capacity building

As the Bank's trade program has grown, research has provided a solid foundation. Trade staff at the Bank have published in refereed journals and written 125 research papers in the World Bank Policy Research Working Papers series. Launched in 2004, a new World Bank Trade and Development Series now includes a dozen books on issues relevant to the ongoing multilateral trade negotiations. Four new works in the series will be released in late 2005 or early 2006.[8]

Thematically, the Bank's research agenda continues to evolve to meet the changing demand from operational units and client countries, with the overarching aim of understanding the large differences in growth performance across countries and the role of trade policies and agreements in encouraging reform.[9] Today, research work falls into three areas: national trade policies and related behind-the-border policies and how these affect growth and poverty reduction; the global agenda, in particular the ongoing Doha Round of WTO negotiations; and the design and impact of regional integration and preferential trade agreements. Bank researchers continue to refine their analysis of the impact of alternative agricultural reforms on development and poverty.[10] One study examines specific proposals for agricultural trade reform that are consistent with the WTO's July 2004 Framework Agreement (Martin and Anderson 2005). Another examines the implications of these reforms on poverty in key developing countries and globally (Hertel and Winters 2005).

The World Bank Institute (WBI) is directing its operational priorities and projects to support countries preparing to join WTO and those that have recently joined. WBI also is devoting resources to help member countries in the global negotiations and in regional negotiations in agriculture, services, and trade facilitation. With 28 countries in the WTO accession process, WBI support can be an important catalyst for reforms. The Bank's strategy for engagement includes activities to leverage its support and reach as many clients as possible. For example, the Bank has convened negotiators of regional agreements from developing countries to share experiences and learn from one another. To leverage impact, WBI continues to work with many external partners.

The challenges ahead

Trade ministers and their governments will soon determine the fate of the Doha Round. Regardless of events in the short-run, the Bank through seminars, research, and dialogue with policymakers will continue to stress the need for changes in the global system to widen access of poor countries to markets in rich countries and to put them on a footing of equal trade opportunity with richer countries.

At the regional level, the proliferation of regional trade agreements risks wasting reform momentum in poorly designed arrangements. In the hope that ongoing research, training, and capacity building work on RTAs may help to mitigate these risks, the Bank will continue to expand its dialogue with the countries involved and to provide analysis and technical assistance to see that regional programs are linked adequately to the domestic reform agenda.

The great bulk of the Bank's work will continue to be at the country level. Here, despite substantial progress, needs remain great indeed. The challenge is to help countries better integrate trade-policy reforms that promote growth into national development strategies, and to help finance the infrastructure and institutions necessary to overcome supply-side constraints. The anticipated rise in "aid for trade" should help countries in this task.

Notes

1. The authors thank Denisse Pierola for her research, and acknowledge the helpful comments of Jean Francois Arvis, Paul Brenton, and Carlos Braga, and inputs from Yvonne Tsikata.

2. An important turning point was the staff paper presented to the Bank's Board in April 2001, "Leveraging Trade for Development" (World Bank 2001b). After tracing trade patterns and describing the trade problems of developing countries, the paper outlined a Bank strategy for moving forward.

3. For a more detailed discussion on the World Bank's training and capacity building activities in trade, see World Bank (2003b). For more information on trade-related research at the World Bank, see World Bank (2004b) and Hoekman (2004).

4. For Europe and Central Asia, see Broadman (2005). For East Asia and the Pacific, see Krumm and Kharas (2004). For the Middle East and North Africa, see Dasgupta and Nabli (2003). For Latin America and the Caribbean, see De Ferranti and others (2001). For South Asia see World Bank (2004c).

5. The Integrated Framework (IF) is the central mechanism for interagency cooperation on aid for trade, brings together bilateral and multilateral donors and multilateral agencies to help LDCs integrate trade into their national development plans and to coordinate delivery of trade-related technical assistance in response to needs identified by LDCs. Seventeen donors, including the World Bank, have contributed $28.1 million to the IF to date. A further $10.5 million is required for 2005 to adequately meet the needs of LDCs.

6. See, for example, de Wulf and Sokol (2005) and World Bank (2005a).

7. For example, on May 31, 2005 the World Bank Board of Executive Directors approved credits from the International Development Association of $7.5 million for the Republic of Burundi and $5 million for the African Trade Insurance Agency to provide additional funds for the ongoing Regional Trade Facilitation Project. The original project was approved in 2001 and covered Burundi, Kenya, Malawi, Rwanda, Uganda, and Zambia. Another example of lending in trade facilitation is the ECA Trade and Transport Facilitation project in Southeast Europe, which aims to strengthen and modernize customs administration and other border control agencies in Albania, Bosnia and Herzegovina, Bulgaria, Croatia, Macedonia, Moldova, Romania, and the Federal Republic of Yugoslavia.

8. For a list of World Bank trade publications visit: www.worldbank.org/trade.org

9. For a detailed discussion of the Bank's trade research program, see Hoekman (2004).

10. Current work takes into account existing preferences, the reforms that took place between 1997 and 2001, and the critical distinction between bound and applied tariffs.

References

Anderson, K., and W. Martin (eds.). 2005. *Agricultural Trade Reform and the Doha Development Agenda*. New York: Palgrave Macmillan and Washington D.C.: World Bank.

Broadman, H. 2005. *From Disintegration to Reintegration: Eastern Europe and the Former Soviet Union in International Trade*. Washington DC: World Bank

Dasgupta, D., and M. Nabli (eds.). 2003. *Trade, Investment and Development in the Middle East and North Africa: Engaging with the World*. Washington DC: World Bank.

de Ferranti, D., G. E. Perry, D. Lederman, and W. F. Maloney. 2001. *Natural Resources to the Knowledge Economy: Trade and Job Quality*. Washington, DC: World Bank.

de Wulf, L., and J. Sokol (eds.). 2005. *Customs Modernization Handbook*. Washington DC: World Bank.

Hertel, T., and A. Winters (eds.). 2005. *Poverty and the WTO: Impacts of the Doha Development Agenda*. New York: Palgrave Macmillan and Washington D.C.: World Bank.

Hoekman, Bernard. 2004. "The World Bank Trade Research Program: Summary and Synthesis." Development Research Group, World Bank, Washington, DC. Mimeo.

Krumm, K., and H. Kharas. 2004. *East Asia Integrates: A Trade Policy Agenda for Shared Growth*. Washington DC: World Bank.

Nielson, J. 2005. "Aid for Trade." In *Trade, Doha and Development: A Window into the Issues*. World Bank: Washington, DC.

Schiff, M., and A. Winters. 2003. *Regional Integration and Development*, Washington, DC: World Bank.

Tsikata. 2005. "Trade Conditionality in World bank Adjustment Lending" background paper prepared for forthcoming Trade Assistance Evaluation.

World Bank. 2001a. *Global Economic Prospects 2002: Making Trade Work for the Poor.*. Washington, DC.

———. 2001b. "Leveraging Trade for Development." A report presented to the World Bank's Board of Executive Directors. April.

———. 2002. *Global Economic Prospects 2003: Investing to Unlock Global Opportunities*. Washington, DC.

———. 2003a. *Global Economic Prospects 2004: Realizing the Development Promise of the Doha Agenda*. Washington, DC.

———. 2003b. "Leveraging Trade for Development: The World Bank Agenda," A report to the World Bank's Board of Executive Directors. September.

———. 2004a. *Global Economic Prospects 2005: Trade, Regionalism, and Development*. Washington, DC.

———. 2004b. "Leveraging Trade for Development: The World Bank Research Agenda." A report presented to the World Bank's Board of Executive Directors, March.

———. 2004c. *Trade Policies in South Asia*. Report No. 29949. Washington, D.C.

———. 2005a. *Food Safety and Agricultural Health Standards: Challenges and Opportunities in Developing Country Exports*. Washington, DC.

———. 2005b. *Review of World Bank Conditionality*. Washington, DC.

World Bank and International Monetary Fund. 2005. "Trade Progress Report: Doha Development Agenda and Aid for Trade. A report presented to the World Bank Board of Executive Directors. August 18.

Eco-Audit

Environmental Benefits Statement

The World Bank is committed to preserving Endangered Forests and natural resources. W‹ print this book on 30 percent postconsumer recycled paper, processed chlorine free. Th‹ World Bank has formally agreed to follow the recommended standards for paper usage s‹ by Green Press Initiative—a nonprofit program supporting publishers in using fiber that i not sourced from Endangered Forests. For more information, visit www.greenpressinitia‹ tive.org.

The printing of this books on recycled paper saved the following:

Trees*	Solid Waste	Water	Net Greenhouse Gases	Electricity
16	759	6,882	1,490	2,768
'40' in height and 6-8" in diameter	Pounds	Gallons	Pounds	KWH